The Complete Idiot's Reference Card

The Playing Field

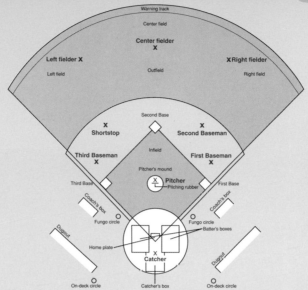

The Positions in the Field

Position	Abbrv.	No.*	All-Time Great	Current Great
Pitcher	P	1	Cy Young	Greg Maddux
Catcher	C	2	Johnny Bench	Ivan Rodriguez
First base	1B	3	Lou Gehrig	Mark McGwire
Second base	2B	4	Joe Morgan	Roberto Alomar
Third base	3B	5	Mike Schmidt	Chipper Jones
Shortstop	SS	6	Ernie Banks	Alex Rodriguez
Left field	LF	7	Ted Williams	Barry Bonds
Center field	CF	8	Mickey Mantle	Ken Griffey Jr.
Right field	RF	9	Babe Ruth	Sammy Sosa

* For those who are scoring the game

Major League Baseball by the Numbers

30	Teams (16 National League, 14 American League)
27	Outs needed to win a regulation game
25	Players on each team's active roster
9	Batters in the batting order
9	Defensive players in the field
9	Innings in a regulation game
7	Ways to get on base (see other side)
4	Bases on the playing field
4	Balls needed to reach first base with a walk
4	Umpires in a regular-season game
3	Outs per team in an inning
3	Strikes a pitcher needs to strike a batter out
1	Major league (American) that uses the designated hitter
0	Times a player can reenter a game once taken out

alpha books

Ways to get on base (see other side)

How a Batter Gets on Base

- ➤ **base hit** He hits a single, double, triple, or home run.
- ➤ **base on balls** He takes four balls before the pitcher can throw three strikes.
- ➤ **error** The defense misplays a ball that he hits.
- ➤ **fielder's choice** He hits a ground ball and the defense opts to force out another runner instead of throwing the batter out at first base.
- ➤ **hit by a pitch** He's awarded first base because a pitch hits him.
- ➤ **catcher's interference** He's awarded first base because the umpire rules that the catcher has inhibited him (almost always by reaching forward and nicking the batter's swing with the glove).
- ➤ **muffed third strike** A third strike gets past the catcher, who can't throw the batter out before he reaches first.

How a Batter Makes an Out

- ➤ He hits a fly ball (fair or foul) that a fielder catches before it touches the ground (or the infield fly rule is called).
- ➤ He hits a ball on the ground that a fielder picks up and throws to first base before the batter touches that base.
- ➤ He strikes out, by accumulating three strikes in his time at bat, or by bunting foul on a third strike, or if the catcher catches a foul tip on the strike.
- ➤ He hits a fair ball that touches him before a fielder touches it.
- ➤ After hitting the ball, his bat touches the ball a second time in fair territory, or he throws his bat and it interferes with a defensive player in fair territory.
- ➤ He runs outside the baseline and is ruled to have interfered with a fielder's throw.
- ➤ He steps out of the batter's box to hit the ball, or steps from one batter's box to the other while the pitcher is in position to pitch.
- ➤ He interferes with the catcher's fielding or throwing.
- ➤ He uses an illegal bat, or bats out of order.

How a Baserunner Makes an Out

- ➤ A fielder tags him with the ball while the runner is not touching a base.
- ➤ In a force situation, he fails to reach the next base before a fielder tags him or that base.
- ➤ In the umpire's judgment, he runs out of the baseline to avoid being tagged.
- ➤ A ball that's hit in the air is caught and thrown to the base that he left before he can get back.
- ➤ He's hit by a fair ball in fair territory before the ball has touched or passed an infielder.
- ➤ He intentionally interferes with a thrown ball, or with a defensive player trying to field a batted ball.
- ➤ He passes a runner ahead of him on the basepaths.
- ➤ In the umpire's judgment, one of the base coaches physically assists him in returning to or leaving a base.
- ➤ He misses a base, or leaves a base early when tagging up, and the defense successfully appeals the play.
- ➤ He runs the bases in reverse order.

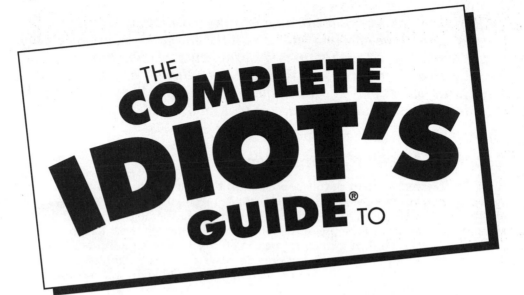

THE COMPLETE IDIOT'S GUIDE® TO

Baseball

by Johnny Bench
with Larry Burke

alpha books

A Division of Macmillan General Reference
A Pearson Education Macmillan Company
1633 Broadway, New York, NY 10019-6785

To Dad, who told me that catching was the quickest way to the big leagues, started me out, and gave me all the encouragement and the opportunity to play. And to William and Teddy, my two older brothers, who let me play even when I was four years old (even though my outs didn't count). If I hadn't played against older competition, then I probably wouldn't have seen the rapid success that I did.—J.B.

To Mom and Dad. Thanks for everything.—L.B.

Copyright © 1999 by Johnny Bench

Macmillan General Reference books may be purchased for business or sales promotional use. For information please write: Special Markets Department, Macmillan Publishing USA, 1633 Broadway, New York, NY 10019.

International Standard Book Number: 0-02862951-5
Library of Congress Catalog Card Number: 99-60666

02 01 00 99   4 3 2 1

Interpretation of the printing code: the rightmost number of the first series of numbers is the year of the book's printing; the rightmost number of the second series of numbers is the number of the book's printing. For example, a printing code of 99-1 shows that the first printing occurred in 1999.

Printed in the United States of America

Alpha Development Team

Publisher
Kathy Nebenhaus

Editorial Director
Gary M. Krebs

Managing Editor
Bob Shuman

Marketing Brand Manager
Felice Primeau

Acquisitions Editor
Jessica Faust

Development Editors
Phil Kitchel
Amy Zavatto

Assistant Editor
Georgette Blau

Production Team

Development Editor
Phil Kitchel

Production Editor
Michael Thomas

Copy Editor
Amy Borelli

Cover Designer
Mike Freeland

Illustrator
Jody Schaeffer

Book Designers
Scott Cook and Amy Adams of DesignLab

Indexer
Greg Pearson

Layout/Proofreading
Angela Calvert
Mary Hunt
Julie Trippetti

Contents at a Glance

Part 1: The Grand Old Game   **1**

1   It's America's Game   3
Why our national pastime is as American as mom, apple pie, and calling in sick the day after Thanksgiving.

2   A Brief History Lesson   13
Get ready for a crash course in baseball history—and don't worry, you don't have to take notes.

3   A Salute to Tradition   31
A look at the rites and rituals that make this game so special.

4   Baseball's Best: Outstanding in the Field   45
These players and teams were the best of the best.

Part 2: Get Ready to Take the Field   **71**

5   The Playing Field: This Diamond Is a Gem   73
Understand what all those lines are for, and learn to say "fungo" without giggling.

6   Tools of the Trade   85
A look at all that gear baseball players wear—and what it's all for.

7   Uniforms: Clothes Make the Man   97
How major leaguers look the part, from head to toe.

8   Baseball 101   107
You've gotta crawl before you can walk: Breaking down the basic rules of the game.

9   Men in Blue (and Gray): The Umpires   121
Don't shout, "Kill the umps!" until you understand their job.

10   Hitting It Big: The Major Leagues   135
A look at the ins and outs at the top of the baseball world.

Part 3: The Name of the Game Is Pitching and Defense   **147**

11   Pitchers: Armed and Dangerous   149
Those magnificent men and their 95-mile-an-hour fastballs.

12   Pitching Strategy: Throwing with Your Head   165
There's a lot more to success on the mound than just rearing back and throwing.

13 Catchers: The Men Behind the Mask   177
Their equipment is called the "tools of ignorance," but that doesn't mean catchers are stupid.

14 The Other Defensive Positions: Who Does What   189
A trip around the horn to look at the traits that make for good glove men.

15 The Thinker's Guide to Defense   201
Sure, you've gotta be able to catch the ball—but that's only the beginning.

Part 4: You Still Have to Score Runs to Win   215

16 The Science of Hitting   217
Whoever said hitting a baseball is the toughest feat in sports knew what they were talking about.

17 Batting Around the Order   231
There's a lot more to making out a lineup than meets the eye.

18 Offensive Strategy: Baseball's Chess Game   241
How to scratch out a run or two in baseball's game-within-the-game.

19 The Brains in the Dugout   255
A trip inside the world—and the mind—of a major league manager.

20 Johnny's Greatest Hits (of Yesterday and Today)   267
The all-time greatest offensive players: hitters, baserunners, and base stealers.

Part 5: Take Me Out to the Ballgame: A Fan's Guide   279

21 Baseball Means Business   281
Everything you need to know about the fiscal side of the game.

22 Bringing Baseball Home   297
On TV or the radio, it's the next best thing to being at the ballpark—except there's no hot dog vendor.

23 Everybody Grab a Bat   313
Baseball for the rest of us—men and women, boys and girls.

24 Be a Superfan   327
How to pick a team to root for, and how to follow it in good times and in bad.

25 Baseball's Future: Gazing into the Crystal Ball 345
*The 1998 season was spectacular, but what will baseball
do for an encore?*

Appendices

A Johnny's Glossary of Diamond Dialogue 355
*The low-down on baseball lingo, from backdoor to back-
stop, Triple Crown to triple play, whiff to whiffle ball.*

B Johnny's Baseball Who's Who: The Names You
Need to Know 383
*Bios of the game's best-known names of yesterday and
today, both on and off the field.*

C Baseball in Print, at the Movies, and on the Web 399
*Your guide to the game in the major media, including
suggestions for your movie list and your library.*

D The Major League Honor Roll 405
*Complete lists of MVP, Cy Young, and Rookie of the Year
award winners, plus Hall of Famers, retired numbers, and
more.*

E The Major League Record Book 425
*All-time career and single-season leaders in hitting and
pitching.*

Index 433

Contents

Part 1: The Grand Old Game   **1**

1 It's America's Game   **3**

Our National Pastime 4
   Boyhood Games 4
   Handing It Down 6
Baseball Is a Game of Clichés 6
   "Baseball is a game of inches." 6
   "It ain't over till it's over." 7
   "Keep your head in the game." 7
   "Take it one day at a time." 8
   "Stay within yourself." 8
   "Good pitching beats good hitting." 9
   "He didn't have his best stuff." 9
Size Doesn't Matter... 10
...But Brains and Heart Do 10
Why You've Gotta Love This Game 11

2 A Brief History Lesson   **13**

The Myth of Abner Doubleday 13
The 1900s: The Game Is a Hit 15
The 1910s: Growing Pains 17
The 1920s: The Babe Saves the Day 18
The 1930s: Outslugging the Depression 19
The 1940s: Breaking Down Barriers 22
The 1950s: Baseball's Golden Age 23
The 1960s: A Time for Change 24
The 1970s: The Floodgates Are Opened 25
The 1980s: Some Bumps in the Road 27
The 1990s: Modern Problems 28
The Good Old Days? 29

3 A Salute to Tradition   **31**

A Game for Fathers and Sons...31
"Casey at the Bat" 32
Team Nicknames: Official and Unofficial 33
Johnny's Favorite Player Nicknames 35
Pennants, Monuments, and Retired Numbers 38
Throwing Out the First Ball—and the Presidential Connection ...40
The National Anthem 41
The Seventh-Inning Stretch and "Take Me Out
   to the Ballgame" 41
The New York Yankees: Baseball's Most Storied Team 41
Teams That Just Can't Win...42

4 Baseball's Best: Outstanding in the Field   **45**

The Greatest of All Time 45
The Greatest of My Time 48
The Best Teams of All Time 50
And the Winner Is… 52
The Hall of Fame 53
Perfect Games 54
No-Hitters 56
Triple Crowns 57
Triple Plays 58
The Game's Most Unbreakable Records 59
The Best Pennant Races of All Time 62
The Best Games of All Time 63
The Best World Series 65
Other Memorable Moments 66
Johnny's Most Memorable Moments from His Career 68

Part 2: Get Ready to Take the Field   **71**

5 The Playing Field: This Diamond Is a Gem   **73**

The Lay of the Land 73
Who Plays Where? 75
  The Pitcher's Mound *76*
  The Outfield *77*
  The Coaches' Boxes *78*
  The On-Deck Circles *79*
  The Fungo Circles *79*
The Dugout 80
The Bullpen 80
The Clubhouse 81
The Friendly Confines 81
  Outdoors or Indoors? *81*
  Real Grass vs. Artificial Turf *81*
  Groundskeepers: Baseball's Unsung Heroes *82*
Rain Delays and Other Weather Hazards 82

6 Tools of the Trade   **85**

How Far We've Come: The Evolution of Equipment 85
The Baseball 86
The Bat 88
A Glove for Every Position 90
The Hitters' Hardhat 92
Other Gadgets 93
Catcher's Gear 93
In the On-Deck Circle 95
On the Pitcher's Mound 95

7 Uniforms: Clothes Make the Man   97

Fashion Statement: The Evolution of Uniforms 97
Home Whites and Road Grays 100
The Cap 100
The Jersey 101
The Pants 102
Socks and Stirrups 102
The Spikes 103
Stability vs. Change 104
Johnny's Best and Worst Uniforms 105

8 Baseball 101   107

Twenty-Five on a Side (But Only Nine—or 10—at a Time) 108
The Object of the Game 108
It (Usually) Takes 27 Outs to Win 110
Terminology of a Run Scored 111
Substitutions 115
The Balk Rule 115
The Appeal Play 116
The Infield Fly Rule 117
Pitching Deliveries 117
Quick Pitch 117
Interference and Obstruction 118

9 Men in Blue (and Gray): The Umpires   121

The Role of Umpires 121
The Problem with Umpires 122
The Golden Rules for Umpires 124
Training Umpires 125
The Umpiring Crew 126
Umpire Signals 128
The Most Difficult Calls 129
Calling Balls and Strikes 130
The Post-Season Controversy 131
When the Men in Blue Make You See Red 131
Memorable Arguments in My Career 133
The Official Scorer 133

10 Hitting It Big: The Major Leagues   135

The Leagues and Divisions 135
You Call This Organized? 136
The National League 137
The American League 138
Stability and Expansion 139
The Schedule: A Mere 2,430 games 140
Interleague Play 141
Spring Training: Working the Kinks Out 142

Opening Day: The Pageantry 142
The All-Star Game: A Midsummer Night's Dream 143
The Playoffs: Who Gets In—and How You Win 144
The World Series: Truly a Fall Classic 145

Part 3: The Name of the Game Is Pitching and Defense   147

11   Pitchers: Armed and Dangerous   149

Baseball's Most Valuable Players 149
Mixing It Up: Different Types of Pitches 150
    Four-Seam Fastball (or Basic Fastball) 152
    Two-Seam Fastball (or Sinker) 152
    Curveball 153
    Slider 154
    Split-Fingered Fastball and Forkball 154
    Change-up 155
    Knuckleball 155
    Screwball 156
    Palmball 156
The Toughest Pitches to Hit 156
Different Types of Pitchers 157
    Starters 160
    Long and Middle Relievers 160
    Setup Men 160
    Closers 161
The Benchmarks of Excellence 161
Power and Finesse: Johnny's Picks 163
    The Best Pitchers Johnny Faced 163
    The Best Today 163

12   Pitching Strategy: Throwing with Your Head   165

Pitch Selection: Reading the Signs 165
Setting Up Hitters 167
Changing Speeds 168
The Importance of Control 169
The Right Pitch at the Right Time 169
Righty vs. Righty and Lefty vs. Lefty 171
The Intentional Walk 171
The Pitchout 172
Brushbacks and Inside Pitches 172
The Windup and the Stretch 173
On the Defensive: Get Ready for Some Rockets 174
The Call to the Bullpen: Making a Pitching Change 175

13 Catchers: The Men Behind the Mask   **177**

Get Ready to Take a Beating 178
I Can Do This with One Hand Behind My Back! 179
Stayin' Alive 180
Baseball's Iron Men 181
A Full Plate 182
Calling the Shots 182
The Catcher's Couch 185
The Recipe for the Ideal Catcher 186
Johnny's Best Behind the Plate 186

14 The Other Defensive Positions: Who Does What   **189**

First Base: Footwork Is Important 190
Second Base: The Acrobats of Baseball 191
Shortstop: The Ballerinas of Baseball 193
Third Base: They Call It the Hot Corner 194
Left Field: Bring Your Glove 196
Center Field: You Gotta Have Wheels 197
Right Field: It Helps to Carry a Gun 198
Defense off the Bench 198

15 The Thinker's Guide to Defense   **201**

Getting in Position 201
Cutoffs and Relays 202
Single to left, no runners on 203
Single to left, runner on second 203
Drive down the left-field line, runner on first, less than two outs 204
Bringing the Infield In 205
Guarding the Lines 206
The Shift 207
Defending the Bunt 208
Pickoff Plays 209
Gunning Down a Would-Be Basestealer 210
Blocking the Plate 211

Part 4: You Still Have to Score Runs to Win   **215**

16 The Science of Hitting   **217**

Slumps and Soft Beds 217
Coping with Failure 219
The Mind-Body Connection 219
Different Types of Hitters 220
The Mechanics of Hitting 221
The Bat 221
The Grip 221
The Position 222

The Stance 222
The Look 223
The Stride 223
The Swing 224
Pulling the Ball vs. Going to the Opposite Field 226
Why Pitchers Can't Hit 227
The Quest for 70 Home Runs 228
The Quest for .400 229
The Benchmarks of Excellence 230

17 Batting Around the Order   231

Putting Together the Lineup 232
Tailoring the Lineup to the Ballpark 232
The Leadoff Hitter 233
The Second Spot 233
The Third Spot 234
The Cleanup Hitter 234
The Fifth Spot 235
Protection 235
The Bottom of the Order 236
The Designated Hitter 237
The Greatest Lineup of All Time 237

18 Offensive Strategy: Baseball's Chess Game   241

The Seven Ways to Get on Base 242
Bunting: Drags, Sacrifices, and Squeezes 242
The Sacrifice Fly 245
Hitting Behind the Runner 245
The Hit-and-Run (and the Run-and-Hit) 245
Coming Through in a Pinch 246
Who Pinch Hits? 246
Speed in Reserve 247
Base Coaches: Can't You Read the Signs? 248
Life on the Basepaths 249
The Cardinal Rule 249
Taking a Lead 249
Sliding 250
The Art of the Steal 251
The Double-Steal 251
Stealing Home 252
Breaking Up the Double Play 253

19 The Brains in the Dugout   255

The Manager 255
The Book 256
Baseball Is a Numbers Game 257
Does a Manager Really Matter? 257

A Matter of Style 258
Why Bad Players Make Good Managers—and Vice Versa 258
Why Catchers Make Good Managers 261
The Coaches: Increasing Specialization 261
The Scouting Report 261
Using the Bench and the Bullpen 262
Dealing with Players 263
Dealing with the Media 264
Johnny's Best Managers 265

20 Johnny's Greatest Hits (of Yesterday and Today) 267

Johnny's All-Time Lineup 268
The Best Pure Hitters 272
The Best Clutch Hitters 274
The Best Basestealers 276
The Smartest Baserunners 277

Part 5: Take Me Out to the Ballgame: A Fan's Guide 279

21 Baseball Means Business 281

Want to Buy a Team? 282
The General Manager and the Front Office 283
Let's Make a Deal 284
Free Agency: Anything but Free 285
The Amateur Draft 287
Other Ways to Acquire Players 288
Growing Talent: The Importance of a Farm System 288
Small Markets vs. Big Markets 289
Why Those Outlandish Player Salaries Aren't So Outlandish 292
The Perils of Salary Arbitration 293
The Post-Season Payoff 294
Strikes, Lockouts, and Other Public Relations Nightmares 294

22 Bringing Baseball Home 297

Baseball Writers: The Media's First Bridge to the Fans 297
Radio Days: Baseball, B.T. (Before Television) 299
The Clever Art of Re-Creations 301
A Brief History of Televised Baseball, 1939–99 302
Where the Games Are 305
Worthwhile Baseball Shows on TV 306
How TV Coverage Has Improved 306
The Job of a Broadcaster 307
Johnny's Picks: The Best Behind the Mike 308

23 Everybody Grab a Bat   **313**

The Minor Leagues 313
College Baseball 315
The Road to the Big Leagues: College vs. the Minors 316
Independent Leagues 316
The World's Game: International Competition 317
Finding the Right Level 319
Youth Leagues 320
Adult and Semipro Leagues 321
Women's Baseball 322
A League of Your Own 323

24 Be a Superfan   **327**

How to Read a Box Score 327
How to Score a Game 332
How to Read the Standings 336
    The Magic Number *336*
A Guide to Some Basic Stats 337
The Best on the Internet 338
Peerless Periodicals 339
At the Old Ballyard 340
Old Stadiums vs. New Stadiums 340
Where to Sit at a Game 342
What to Watch—and When 343

25 Baseball's Future: Gazing into the Crystal Ball   **345**

A Homer-Happy '98: Increasing the Fan Base 345
Looking Ahead 348
Improving the Game off the Field 348
Improving the Game on the Field 349
Improving the Players 350
Tomorrow's Stars: Coming Soon to a Ballpark Near You 351
Today's Brightest Young Stars 352

Appendices

A Johnny's Glossary of Diamond Dialogue   **355**

**B Johnny's Baseball Who's Who: The Names
You Need to Know**   **383**

C Baseball in Print, at the Movies, and on the Web   **399**

Johnny's Baseball Library 399
    Selected Bibliography *401*
Johnny's Favorite Baseball Movies 401

Periodicals 403
Johnny's Favorite Baseball Web Sites 403
  News Organization Web Sites 404

D The Major League Honor Roll   **405**

Hall of Fame Members 405
Most Valuable Player Award Winners 411
  National League 411
  American League 412
Cy Young Award Winners 413
  National League 413
  American League 414
  Major Leagues 414
Rookie of the Year Award Winners 414
  National League 414
  American League 415
  Major Leagues 415
All-Star Game Results 415
All-Star Game MVPs 417
Division Champions and Wild Cards 418
  National League 418
  American League 419
League Championship Series Results and MVPs 420
  National League Championship Series Results and MVPs 420
  American League Championship Series Results and MVPs 421
World Series Results and MVPs 422

E The Major League Record Book   **425**

Career Batting Leaders 425
Career Pitching Leaders 427
Single-Season Batting Leaders 429
Single-Season Pitching Leaders 431

Index   **433**

Foreword

The 1998 baseball season was one for the books—the record books, that is. Mark McGwire and Sammy Sosa spent the summer swinging away in pursuit of Roger Maris' single-season home run record, and the chase was unforgettable not only for its daily drama but for the sportsmanship and class that the two great sluggers displayed.

When it was over, McGwire had an unfathomable 70 home runs; a slugging percentage of .752, the seventh-highest of all-time and the best in 71 years; a National League-record 162 walks; and a league-leading on-base percentage of .470. Sosa had 66 homers to go with a .308 batting average and major league-leading totals in RBIs (158), runs (134), and total bases (416); he also had the National League MVP Award and his team, the Chicago Cubs, in the playoffs for the first time since 1989. Meanwhile, baseball fans around the country had countless memorable moments, the most indelible of which occurred on the night of September 8, when McGwire lined his record-breaking 62nd homer of the year over the left field wall of St. Louis' Busch Stadium. That was truly one of those "Where were you when...?" events.

Yes, Big Mac and Sammy made '98 a season to savor, but they weren't the only ones. The Yankees won an American League-record 114 regular-season games en route to a world championship, and on May 17 against the Minnesota Twins, New York's David Wells pitched the 15th perfect game in major league history. That same month, Chicago Cubs' Rookie of the Year Kerry Wood turned in one of the most dominant pitching performances ever, a 20-strikeout, no-walk, one-hitter against the Houston Astros. And on September 20, Baltimore's Cal Ripken Jr. ended his eye-popping "Iron Man" streak of 2,632 consecutive games played when he opted to sit out the Orioles' final home game of the year.

All these great memories show why this game is truly our country's national pastime, and why there's no better time to be a baseball fan—or to become one. Now I know that to a new fan, baseball may seem difficult to learn. But take it from me, a Hall of Fame pitcher who won 311 games in the big leagues: For the guys on the field, baseball is extremely complicated. But a fan doesn't have to master all the intricacies to enjoy the game. Hey, if you want to, all the better—but baseball can be enjoyed on many levels, from the simple to the complex. That's one of the inherent beauties of the game.

And that's where this book will prove invaluable, helping you quickly master the fundamentals and gain an appreciation for the beauty and symmetry of baseball, and then build on that until you're ready to trade your box seat for a seat in the dugout. And whether you're looking for a refresher course, a crash course, or a full tutorial on the game, I can't think of anyone more qualified to do the teaching than Johnny Bench, the greatest catcher in baseball history and one of the game's most intelligent players.

Johnny and I were teammates with the Cincinnati Reds for six years in the late '70s and early '80s, and I've always had the utmost admiration for his knowledge and passion for the game. Early in a ballgame not too long after I was traded from the New York Mets to the Reds, I was struggling. The first three or four hitters had just pounded the ball. So Johnny calls for time, and comes sauntering out to the mound in that big,

Oklahoma way of his, and gets right in my face—doesn't even take his mask off. And he says, "Are you *trying?*" It just cracked me up, and settled me right down. That's Johnny. He always knew the right thing to say.

When I pitched my no-hitter in Cincinnati on June 16, 1978, against the St. Louis Cardinals—the only no-hitter I ever pitched in my 20-year major league career—Johnny was in the hospital with a back injury. So Don Werner, a rookie, caught the game. After we got the last hitter out, the celebration spilled into the clubhouse, and Johnny called me from the hospital. Well, I think he was as excited as anyone—including Werner!

I have no doubt that as you read through the pages that follow, you'll come to share Johnny's wisdom—and love—for this great game. Enjoy the book, and I look forward to seeing you in the stands.

—Tom Seaver

George Thomas Seaver stands as one of the greatest pitchers in major league history. The flamethrowing right-hander joined the New York Mets in 1967, whereupon he won National League Rookie of the Year honors, appeared in his first All-Star Game, and posted a 16–13 record with a 2.76 ERA and 170 strikeouts. "Tom Terrific," as he became known, led the formerly last-place Mets to their first-ever World Series victory over the Baltimore Orioles in 1969. That year he won 25 games, had a 2.21 ERA, and struck out 208 batters; he went on to win both the NL Cy Young Award and The Sporting News National League Pitcher of the Year Award.

Seaver's illustrious career included a record nine consecutive seasons with 200 or more strikeouts (1968–76), most consecutive strikeouts in a game (10, April 22, 1970), and most opening day starts (16). He led the league in strikeouts five times (1970, '71, '73, '75, and '76); wins three times ('69, '75, and '81); shutouts twice ('77 and '79); and ERA twice ('70 and '71). Seaver also won the NL Cy Young Award twice more ('73 and '75) and was named to the National League All-Star Team 12 times. On June 16, 1978, he pitched his first and only no-hitter, for the Cincinnati Reds.

Seaver played his final seasons with the Chicago White Sox and the Boston Red Sox. In 1987, he signed a free-agent contract with the New York Mets, but never joined the major league roster; he officially announced his retirement on June 22, 1987, after 20 magnificent seasons. Seaver's career totals included 311 wins, 3,640 strikeouts, a 2.86 ERA, and 61 shutouts. Perhaps the greatest tribute to Tom Terrific—"the master of the art of pitching"—came in 1992, when he was elected into the National Baseball Hall of Fame in Cooperstown, New York, by the highest percentage in history (he was named on 98.84 percent of the ballots).

Introduction

As a catcher, I've spent countless hours of my life crouched down, inviting very strong men to throw a very small, very hard object in the general direction of my face. Sure, I wore some equipment to protect myself, but even the most understanding psychologist would probably consider such behavior a little "self-destructive," or at least slightly "abnormal."

Maybe so. But if I had it all to do over again, I wouldn't change a thing. Sure, I took foul balls off of every part of my body, and I strained muscles I didn't even know I had, but I did it all so I could play baseball, and every cut, every bruise, and every welt was worth it.

Baseball is the greatest game ever invented. For 20 years it was my full-time occupation—and basically my life. Baseball gave me some of my greatest memories, some of my best friends, and taught me some valuable lessons. This book is all about baseball, and all the things that make the game great. I hope that after you read it, you'll have a better understanding of why I would choose to spend two decades of my life sitting in the path of a hard ball traveling 90 miles per hour. Simply put, I did it because I love the game, and I want to share my love and knowledge of the game with you.

How to Use This Book

This book is divided into six parts, each dealing with a different aspect of baseball. It's arranged sort of like a textbook, but there won't be any pop quizzes or a final exam, and you won't need a No. 2 pencil. We're going to keep things fun, because that's what baseball is all about.

Part 1, "The Grand Old Game," deals with the history of baseball and why it has achieved such a lofty status in the nation's collective heart. We'll look at how the game was invented, check out highlights from each decade, examine the traditions of the game, and look at some of the best—and most colorful—players to ever take the field.

Part 2, "Get Ready to Take the Field," deals with the basics of the game. We'll examine the field on which baseball is played, as well as the equipment and uniforms used to play it. We'll also cover the basic rules and talk about the guys who enforce them—the umpires. Finally, we'll look at how the game's ultimate showcase, the major leagues, are set up.

Part 3, "The Name of the Game Is Pitching and Defense," deals with the defensive team in the field. We'll talk about what pitches pitchers throw, and how they select them. We'll also talk about catchers (a position that I know a thing or two about) as well as the other players in the field. Once we finish covering the defense, we'll be ready to move on to the hitters.

Part 4, "You Still Have to Score Runs to Win," talks about the mechanics of hitting, as well as the various strategies employed by managers when their team is up to bat. We'll also touch on baserunning, and then take a look at some of my all-time favorite hitters—the guys who make up my dream lineup.

Part 5, "Take Me Out to the Ballgame: A Fan's Guide," deals with baseball and you. We'll look at how you can get the most out of being a fan—at the ballpark, on TV, and through various other media. We'll also talk about the various levels of baseball in which you can get involved, from Little League on up to college ball and the minor leagues. Finally, we'll take a peek at baseball's future.

You'll Need to Know the Signs

Like a baseball team, we'll have our own set of "signs" in this book. These boxes will highlight helpful bits of information:

Talkin' Baseball

Here various baseball luminaries will offer words of wisdom—sometimes insightful, sometimes humorous—on the topic at hand.

Catching On

Here you'll find definitions of some common (and some not-so-common) baseball terms.

From the Bench

These boxes provide expert tips on how to watch and enjoy the game, and how to be a better fan.

Warning Track

In this space we'll provide some words of caution—tipping you off to the mistakes you'll want to avoid.

Extra Innings

These boxes contain additional information of interest, such as records and anecdotes.

Acknowledgments

Good baseball starts with good teaching. And I got a lot of that through my managers in both the minor leagues and the major leagues. Much of the philosophy and the teaching reflected in these pages comes from the likes of Jack Cassini, Pinky May, Don Zimmer, Dave Bristol, Hal Smith, and Sparky Anderson. I wouldn't have been a success without all the great members of the Cincinnati Reds.

Every baseball player should pay tribute to Babe Ruth, who made the game of baseball what it is and gave us all a chance to play.

Thanks also to my co-author, Larry Burke, a terrific writer, for the effort and dedication he put into this project from start to finish.

—J.B.

This book simply wouldn't have gotten done without the contribution of Steve Hubbard, who lent his considerable talents and energies in a critical long-relief role. Valuable innings were also turned in by seasoned pros Lars Anderson, Mark Bechtel, and David Sabino. Pat Kelly of the National Baseball Hall of Fame and Museum provided invaluable research assistance. Scott Waxman also deserves thanks for his ongoing support. And Beth Burke continually astounds with her patience and perseverance.

—L.B.

Trademarks

All items mentioned in this book that are known to be or are suspected of being trademarks or service marks have been appropriately capitalized. Alpha Books and Macmillan General Reference cannot attest of the accuracy of this information. Use of a term in this book should not be regarded as affecting the validity of any trademark or service mark.

Photo Credits

AP/Wide World Photos: Pages 64, 193, 254, 318, 347.

Steve Schwab: Page 346, lower.

Brian Spurlock: Page 346, upper.

Tony Triolo/Sports Illustrated: Page 67.

UPI/Corbis: Page 65.

National Baseball Hall of Fame Library, Cooperstown, NY: Remainder.

Part 1
The Grand Old Game

For six months a year, baseball captivates millions of fans around the country. Some of the best athletes in the world compete on lush fields of green, reminding all of us of the game we played as kids. As the season rolls on, teams experience the highest of highs and the lowest of lows—often the very next day. Baseball, you see, is a lot like life.

The first part of this book looks at what makes baseball our national pastime. We'll see how the game was invented, and how it has grown over the past 100 years. Since baseball is such a tradition-rich sport, we'll talk about some of the better-known rites of the game. Then I'll give you my picks for the best teams and best players of all time. This will give you a good foundation of knowledge for when we move to the on-field aspects of the game.

Chapter 1

It's America's Game

In This Chapter

➤ The best things about baseball

➤ Why this sport and this country go together

➤ Those old sayings are really saying something

➤ Anyone can play this game

What do I like about baseball? The first thing that comes to mind is the smell. The grass. The leather of the gloves. The hot dogs and popcorn in the stands. The summer breezes. Just the whole feeling and atmosphere and presentation of what the game is all about. But it's much more than that, of course.

Baseball is a game of standards. It's white chalk lines and dugouts and on-deck circles. It's the green field, the brown basepaths, and the white bases. It's the bat boy putting the resin and the pine tar and the lead bat out in the batting circle.

It's the strategy. It's the manager trying to be patient with his pitcher: *"I've gotta get him three innings, I can't take him out right now."* Then it's the seventh inning and he has to think about matchups and get a relief pitcher ready: *"Who's their left-handed hitter and if they bring up so-and-so to pinch hit, do I make the change then?"*

It's the footwork of a first baseman digging out a throw in the dirt. It's a catcher throwing out a basestealer at second. It's the transfer of the ball from the glove to the hand for a throw, from a second baseman like Bill Mazeroski turning the double play, or a little guy at shortstop, like Pee Wee Reese or Phil Rizzuto.

It's Willie Mays, rounding second base with his hat flying off, and it's Willie McCovey, so intimidating at home plate. It's the grace of Mickey Mantle, whether hitting a home run or swinging at a third strike and wincing in pain. It's the joy of Yogi Berra jumping into Don Larsen's arms after Larsen's perfect World Series game. It's Roberto Clemente fielding a line drive in the corner, then whirling and throwing to third base for the out.

It's the confrontation in the ninth inning that puts your best hitter up against their top reliever—and the tremendous thrill when the hitter beats the pitcher—unless you're rooting for the team in the field.

It's the coaches who hit 500 ground balls in infield practice, who throw batting practice, who make sure that the balls are all picked up and ready to go for the next day and that the lineup card is out, and who tell a guy making $12 million a year to watch out for the double play or the line drive.

It's the radio and TV voices—Harry Caray, Vin Scully, Red Barber, Mel Allen, Marty Brennaman—and the P.A. announcers who introduce the lineups, who call out the players' names as they take the field.

It's the exhilaration of leaving the ballpark laughing and happy that your team won, appreciating those moments that you may have shared with your child. It's that little six-year-old boy who wants the star's autograph because he's his hero, not because it's worth something. It's the kid who goes to the ballpark and learns how to be a fan—not someone who screams at the players, but someone who rises with their good fortune and suffers with them in their loss.

Talkin' Baseball

"Baseball, my son, is the cornerstone of civilization."

—Dagwood Bumstead in the comic strip *Blondie*

Catching On

Many kids play variations on the game centering on the pitcher-hitter confrontation, without a large field or a lot of players. The two most common are **stickball**, in which players hit a rubber ball with a broomstick, and **whiffle ball**, in which a plastic ball and bat are used.

Our National Pastime

You've probably heard people refer to baseball as "America's game" or our "national pastime." There's a simple reason for that: More than any other sport, baseball and the United States grew up together. The first organized baseball game was played in 1846, more than 16 years before President Lincoln freed the slaves by signing the Emancipation Proclamation. It was 30 more years before basketball or football were born. It's part of our nation's history, and it's part of almost everyone's personal story. (We'll take a closer look at the game's origins in Chapter 2.)

Boyhood Games

Just about everybody I know grew up playing baseball in one form or another. When I was a kid in Binger, Oklahoma, a town of 660 people, we played all the time. When you live in a town that size, there aren't a lot of other things to do. My brothers and the neighbors down the street always had a game going, and we played everything: Whiffle Ball, Tin Can, and other games we invented. I knocked every piece of gravel out of my driveway—twice.

To play Tin Can, we'd take an empty evaporated milk can with a couple of holes punched in it and use that as a ball—throw it and hit it with a bat. If it went so far on the fly, you'd get a base hit; a little farther, a double; and so on for a triple or a home run. And if you hit it into that little door in the shed, you'd get a grand slam.

By the time that old milk can got beat up a little bit, we were starting to throw curveballs, screwballs, and sliders, and by the end of the game that thing was a wicked, sharp-edged projectile. And we weren't always playing with gloves; if you go to Binger today you'll see a bunch of those "kids" (who are now in their 50s) with scars all over their hands from playing Tin Can.

Home Run Derby, based on the TV program of the same name, was also a popular game. I think I became a home run hitter because I played that game so much and because I always used a big bat. My buddies David Gunter, Danny Lopez, Spud Domebo, and I would take turns pitching, and whoever was the batter would get a certain number of pitches to hit as many home runs as he could. That's how I learned the importance of throwing strikes, and how I developed a home run swing.

Talkin' Baseball

"Whoever wants to know the heart and mind of America had better learn baseball, the rules and realities of the game."

—Jacques Barzun, Columbia University philosophy professor, in the book *God's Country and Mine*

From Binger all the way to the big leagues: That's me swinging for the seats with the Reds.

5

Handing It Down

Baseball has always been a game that has been linked to a great family tradition. It was definitely that way in my family—my dad loved the game and played semipro ball himself, and he passed on that love to his four children.

Talkin' Baseball

"Baseball's inherent rhythm, minutes and minutes of passivity erupting into seconds of frenzied action, matches an attribute of the American character. But no existential proclamation, or any tortured neo-Freudianism, or any outburst of popular sociology, not even—or least of all—my own, explains baseball's lock on the American heart. You learn to let some mysteries alone, and when you do, you find they sing themselves."

—Donald Hall, Fathers Playing Catch With Sons

These days you can watch five games on TV in the same night, but when I was a kid you were lucky if you got to see the *Game of the Week* on Saturday afternoon. My dad and I would go down to Helms' Grocery on Saturdays and buy a half-gallon of Neapolitan ice cream. Then we'd come home and sit on the couch and eat all the ice cream while we watched the New York Yankees and the Cleveland Indians, the Brooklyn Dodgers and the New York Giants, or whichever teams were on that day, on our black-and-white TV. And I'd listen to my dad, who had played semipro ball, say, "I could hit that guy." Or he'd point out how the catcher did this or the pitcher did that. It was always something.

The first time I faced Bob Gibson, the Hall of Fame pitcher for the St. Louis Cardinals, my parents drove up from Oklahoma to St. Louis to see the game. I struck out my first three times up. After the third time I was walking back to the dugout and I sort of smiled. My manager, Dave Bristol, said, "What the hell are you smiling about?" And I said, "I was just thinking, I don't think Dad could hit this guy."

Baseball Is a Game of Clichés

Talkin' Baseball

"Baseball? It's just a game—as simple as a ball and a bat. Yet, as complex as the American spirit it symbolizes. It's a sport, business—and sometimes even religion."

—Ernie Harwell in The Sporting News

There are probably more sayings about the game of baseball than any other sport, and I guess most of them more or less hold water. There's no question that knowing the more popular ones will help you better understand the game. That's the beauty of a lot of these sayings: They're simple thoughts, but they provide a window into the complexities of the game. Here's a compendium of some of the most common clichés, and what they mean (you may find that you understand some of them even better once you peruse the glossary and the chapters that follow).

"Baseball is a game of inches."

Sure, it's true. Many games are won or lost by inches, or fractions thereof: A baserunner gets thrown out by a step. A batter hits a long fly ball that falls just inside the foul pole—or hits it. Another hitter lays down a bunt that stops on the chalk line. A fielder is in the wrong position by a hair. A pitch is two inches off the plate. The batter misses a pitch by an inch.

But by the same token, any sport is a game of inches: barely getting a first and 10 in football or having a shot hit the back of the rim and bounce away in basketball. I think baseball is more a game of skill and timing than it is of inches.

"It ain't over till it's over."

I believe legendary Yankee catcher Yogi Berra said this. You might also hear this variation: "It takes 27 outs to win." It's true: A baseball game, unlike other sports, isn't required to end in a certain number of minutes, so the team that's ahead can't simply run out the clock. Your team can be trailing by two or three runs, and down to its last pitch, and still have plenty of time to come back and win. That's one reason why baseball, at its best, is so exciting.

In the decisive fifth game of the 1972 National League Championship Series, the Pittsburgh Pirates were leading my Cincinnati Reds, 3–2, when I led off the bottom of the ninth inning with a home run off Dave Giusti, a relief pitcher who had always been tough on us. You can still hear the echoes throughout the Reds' home ballpark, Riverfront Stadium, because it took the fans from the depths of despair to the heights of elation. First it's, *"We're gonna lose. This thing's over."* Then, all of a sudden, *"It's outta here!"* And—boom!—*"We're back! We're tied! We've got a chance!"* And we went on to score again and win that game.

"Keep your head in the game."

Speaking as a former catcher, I know catchers certainly can't be thinking about anything other than the game. They've got another pitch coming. They have to know where every baserunner is. That's what sets the greats apart from the not-so-greats: They know what they're doing, and they know, peripherally, what everybody *else* is doing.

Talkin' Baseball

"Close don't count in baseball. Close only counts in horseshoes and grenades."

—Hall of Fame outfielder Frank Robinson

Warning Track

It's one thing to walk out on a football or basketball game when the outcome appears all but decided, but I wouldn't do that at a baseball game, unless you want to risk missing something spectacular. The annals of baseball are filled with tales of dramatic, come-from-behind wins, many of which were missed by fair-weather fans who were trying to beat the traffic.

Every player has to be aware. You have to anticipate. If you make a mistake, you have to be able to avoid making it again. You must know where you are on the field at all times, and what the situation calls for: where your cutoff man is if you're an outfielder, or where the outfielder's cutoff man is if you're approaching third and looking to score. Certainly, if you don't have your head in the game, you either don't care about the game, or you don't plan on being there very long. Or both.

From the Bench

Just as the players in the field are anticipating where the ball might be hit and thinking about what will happen next, so is the knowledge-able fan. As you learn more about baseball's complexities, you'll find that thinking like a player and anticipating the action—and eventually thinking strategically like a manager—enhances your enjoy-ment when watching a game. Oh, and watch out for foul balls.

"Take it one day at a time."

At the major league level, the baseball season is 162 games long—that takes about half a year, not including the playoffs. So even though you're trying your best to win every time out, you can't beat yourself up over one game. You have to keep things in perspective; you might have another game tomorrow.

That way of thinking is important for baseball players and fans at every level. My dad started a Little League team, the Binger Bobcats, when I was six. We had 10 or 11 kids and we rode to the games in the back of a pickup truck. When we'd lose, Dad would say, "That's all right, we'll get 'em tomorrow." And we'd go have a cheeseburger. So I learned early on not to get too upset over losing a baseball game.

In the big leagues I always felt that if there was an easy pitcher out there, then I was going to try to take him that night. And if I was facing a tough pitcher, I couldn't look past him or he was going to make me go 0-for-4. So I definitely took it one game at a time.

"Stay within yourself."

It sounds funny, but all it means is that a player shouldn't try to do more than he's capable of. A line drive hitter shouldn't swing for the fences; a finesse pitcher shouldn't try to blow the ball by people.

Anyone who has played this game has learned that if you don't overswing or over-throw, if you just trust your natural ability, things will work out. Muscle, skill, and coordination work much better than trying to force something to happen.

As a player, you have to be relaxed to play well. Not too relaxed, of course; you still have to be on your toes at all times, anticipating what might happen and being ready to react when something does. But if you get too uptight and let the pressure get to you—and believe me, there's plenty of it in the major leagues—you're in trouble.

"Good pitching beats good hitting."

I think this is true, although it should probably be "great pitching" or "smart pitching" instead of just "good pitching." There are just those exceptional guys—Sandy Koufax, Bob Gibson, Juan Marichal, Randy Johnson, and Greg Maddux—who simply get hitters out.

Tom Seaver, a former teammate of mine with the Reds, is another. But like all the great ones, Tom would also sometimes pitch around a tough hitter to get to the next guy, who he *knew* he could get out. That was always our philosophy. There were guys who pitched for me with the Reds—and I say "for me" because I was calling the pitches—who I wouldn't let throw strikes to certain hitters. I knew we could get the next guy out, or we at least had a better chance, and I didn't want my pitcher to beat himself. Sometimes you'll see a pitcher walk a guy and you'll wonder why he can't throw strikes. Well, he probably has good reason.

"He didn't have his best stuff."

Nobody will ever figure out why a team can score 15 runs one day and get no-hit the next day. That's what's so puzzling—and also what's so beautiful—about baseball.

It's a mystery that the pitchers, the guys trying to get the hitters out, are continually trying to solve. A pitcher has to pitch with as much finesse and control as speed. The *movement* of the ball, both inside and outside of the strike zone, is very important. It's not easy, and no pitcher has his best stuff—speed, control, location—every time he starts. That's when the great pitchers pitch with their heads, outsmarting hitters even without their best stuff. You'll read more about the pitching game in Chapters 11 and 12.

Extra Innings

One of the most amazing things about baseball is that a pitcher can be on top of the world one day—no one can get a hit off the guy—and look like a bum the next day. Consider the story of Bobo Holloman of the St. Louis Browns, who on May 6, 1953, became the first pitcher in history to throw a no-hitter in his first major-league start. But Holloman lost seven of his next nine decisions, allowing more than five runs a game, and was back in the minor leagues by July. He never pitched in the big leagues again.

Size Doesn't Matter...

I think the most amazing thing about the game of baseball is that everybody can play it. It doesn't matter how big or small you are. You can be 5'5" like Freddie Patek, the shortstop who was the Kansas City Royals' spark plug in the 1970s, or you can be 6'10" like Randy Johnson, the Seattle Mariners' overpowering lefty. Everybody can swing a bat and catch a ball and throw it.

Freddie Patek (left, holding bat) wasn't much bigger than the bat boys, but he played in the major leagues for 14 years. Randy Johnson is 17 inches taller, but that alone isn't what makes him so dominant—it's that he can throw hard and he knows how to pitch.

But if you want to play basketball, you have to outjump Michael Jordan, stop Wilt Chamberlain, and get your shot past Bill Russell. If you're not that big or that fast, you probably can't play football, because Barry Sanders is going to run for his yards and the 320-pound guys on the line are going to run right over you.

...But Brains and Heart Do

On the other hand, baseball isn't a sport where you can get by on physical attributes alone. Anyone who's seven feet tall might make a halfway decent basketball center, and if you tip the scales at 250 pounds, you might be a decent offensive lineman, but baseball takes more. No particular advantage in size or strength will make you a decent baseball player without talent and a lot of hard work.

Conditioning in baseball was always different than in other sports. Being in great physical shape was never as important. We're specialists. I always say, the only thing we have to do is hit a round ball with a round bat—and hit it square.

For example, hand-eye coordination is very important in baseball. The eyes are always taking in information. Strong hands are also important. Every great hitter and great pitcher has had strong hands and strong fingers—a pitcher uses those fingers to get more rotation and spin on the baseball. But the necessary coordination—the knowledge of what to do with the information your eyes give you, and how and where to spin and direct a pitch—comes from hours and hours of *practice*. Yes, some people are naturals, but you can work at it and become even better through patience and discipline.

Extra Innings

Big, strong hands are a great asset in baseball, and I've always had them. Calisthenics were never my thing, but I could palm a basketball before I was in high school, and I've always been a tremendous arm wrestler. During my playing days my favorite trick for photographers was to hold seven baseballs in one hand. Size and strength alone aren't enough, though. You need reflexes, agility, and coordination to go along with them.

Some baseball players possess natural talent. Then there's the guy who has to really work at it, who loves it so much that he's willing, like I was, to stay out in the backyard for hours throwing a ball against the wall, or the steps, or, in my case, a propane tank (my father had a propane business) and fielding it as it bounces back. Or standing out in the driveway hitting rocks with a bat for hours. It's a commitment you have to make.

Why You've Gotta Love This Game

I'd advise anyone who thinks baseball is boring to read this book and learn to appreciate the subtleties of the game, then sit down and *watch*. Sure, baseball follows a leisurely pace. We all need to sit back and take a breath every now and then, and baseball provides an opportunity for that—then somebody lines a single through the hole, the runner beats the throw to the plate in a cloud of dust, and the crowd goes wild!

But it's more than that. Baseball isn't just a guy throwing a ball. It's a pitcher applying pressure to different parts of the ball, changing the angle of his release, putting the ball farther back in his hand to deliver a pitch at a certain speed. It's the batter trying to guess what the pitcher's going to throw, and the pitcher trying to guess what the batter's guess is. He tries to throw a pitch that the batter doesn't expect and can't hit—

or throw a pitch in a certain spot over the plate so that if it *is* hit, it will be hit on the ground and the infielders can turn a double play.

So then what? It's just a ground ball—6–4–3, as they say, a double play. But consider the grace of the shortstop as he scoops up the ball on the run, transfers it from the glove hand to the throwing hand, quickly positions himself to throw—underhanded, off-balance—at chest level to the second baseman, who tags the bag, takes a step—or maybe leaps over the sliding runner—and throws to first base with enough speed and accuracy to get a runner who's racing down the basepath in track shoes on artificial turf. Consider the grace of all of that.

Baseball is knowing what to watch for. In the 1997 World Series, both catchers, Charles Johnson of the Florida Marlins and Sandy Alomar Jr. of the Cleveland Indians, put on an exhibition of how to block balls in the dirt.

Or you can watch Mark McGwire carefully get his hands in the right position, perfect the timing of his swing, wait for a pitch to hit, and hit that ball squarely.

Or sometimes there are pitchers with such great skills, like Greg Maddux of the Atlanta Braves, that we sit in the stands and say, "Why can't they hit this guy? He's not throwing hard, he's putting it right there. He wears glasses—he looks like a professor! Why can't they hit him?"

Talkin' Baseball

"Baseball is the only thing besides the paper clip that hasn't changed."

—Bill Veeck, legendary baseball owner

To understand that, you have to understand the subtleties of the game. Once you do, you'll enjoy the game even more. And you'll agree with me that there's nothing more exciting than a winning homer in the ninth inning. There could be 50,000 people at a ballgame. Walking out of the ballpark, 25,000 are jubilant and 25,000 are sad, but they've all seen the same thing. It can bring you up and it can bring you down. There's nothing like it.

The Least You Need to Know

➤ Baseball was born in the United States and has been around for more than 150 years, a lot longer than football or basketball.

➤ The game has a unique place in American culture and lore, which is why there are so many baseball clichés flying around.

➤ Strong hands, reflexes, coordination, and agility are much more valuable in baseball than height or size, so everyone with the patience to learn the basics can play the game at some level.

➤ There's a lot more to baseball than meets the eye, and an appreciation of the game's subtleties will add greatly to your enjoyment.

Chapter 2

A Brief History Lesson

In This Chapter

➤ Why you should learn your baseball history

➤ Separating fact from fiction regarding the game's roots

➤ The top stories of each decade, 1900 to the present

➤ The top players of each decade—and of the 19th century

I know a thing or two about baseball history. When you spend a good part of your childhood checking out books on Lou Gehrig from the library, I guess that makes you a student of the game. These days, I have books in my library at home that cover the history of the game from old times to modern times.

The sport is so steeped in tradition and lore that to be a serious fan—and to have a proper level of respect for the game—it's important to know at least the high points of baseball's first century and a half. I admit it's tougher today than it used to be; players come and go so quickly, it's like, "Who's on first?" It's hard enough keeping track of the guys on your team this week, much less 50 years ago.

The Myth of Abner Doubleday

There are two main versions of the birth of baseball: One is a popular legend made up almost entirely by one person, and the other is a much more plausible story with considerably more evidence to support it.

According to the legend, as reported by Adam Graves to the Mills Commission (a group of experts impaneled in 1905 to determine the origins of baseball), Abner Doubleday was the game's founder. Doubleday was Graves' friend and an Army captain who served in the Mexican and Civil wars and fired the first shot for the Union at Fort Sumter. Based on Graves' account, the Mills Commission issued a report stating that in 1839 in Cooperstown, New York. Doubleday drew the first diagram of a baseball field and outlined the basic rules of play.

There were two problems: No copy of the diagram or the rules could be found, and no one in or around Cooperstown, other than Graves, knew anything about it. But Doubleday's name, the year 1839, and the city of Cooperstown—where baseball's Hall of Fame was subsequently built—all nonetheless became fixtures in the game's history.

Talkin' Baseball

"It is a game which is peculiarly suited to the American temperament and disposition.... In short, the pastime suits the people, and the people suit the pastime."

—Charles Peverelly in *The Book of American Pastimes*, 1866

Here's the more plausible version, which most historians believe:

Baseball's roots date back to the early 1800s, and although the game is uniquely American, it evolved as a loose variation of English games such as cricket and rounders. The first "Base Ball Diagram," a sketch of a playing field that included positions for 12 players (instead of the nine used in today's game) and asymmetrical distances between the bases (rather than the constant 90 feet used today), was drawn in New York in 1842.

The Knickerbocker Base Ball Club of New York, formed in 1845, appointed a committee headed by surveyor Alexander Cartwright to put together a standardized list of baseball rules. Cartwright designed a field that is, for the most part, the same baseball diamond used today.

Extra Innings

Baseball in the 1870s bore many similarities to today's game, but there also were some notable differences. For example, most fielders played bare-handed, the catcher stood directly behind the plate only when there was a runner on base, and batters were allowed to request a high or a low pitch. There were notable differences off the field, too: Tickets usually cost 50 cents, there was no alcohol sold, and no games were played on Sundays.

Cartwright's committee submitted its field diagram and a list of rules to the Knickerbocker Club in 1846, and, upon approval, the club made arrangements for the first organized baseball game, which took place on June 19 on the Elysian Fields in Hoboken, New Jersey. That day, the New York Nine, a cricket club, beat the Knickerbockers at their own game, 23–1, in four innings.

The game soon became quite popular at the club level and in 1871 the first professional league, the National Association of Professional Base Ball Players, was formed. That league fell on hard times and was replaced in 1876 by the National League of Professional Base Ball Clubs—the same National League that exists today. The league, the brainchild of Chicago White Stockings owner William Hulbert, had eight teams: Boston, Chicago, Cincinnati, Hartford, Louisville, New York, Philadelphia, and St. Louis, and each club played about 65 games in the first season.

Top Players, Pre-1900s

Cap Anson, first base	Tim Keefe, pitcher
Dan Brouthers, first base	King Kelly, right field
Ed Delahanty, left field	Bid McPhee, second base
Hugh Duffy, center field	Kid Nichols, pitcher
Buck Ewing, catcher	Amos Rusie, pitcher
Clark Griffith, pitcher	Sam Thompson, right field
Billy Hamilton, center field	Monte Ward, shortstop
Old Hoss Radbourn, pitcher	Mickey Welch, pitcher

The 1900s: The Game Is a Hit

1901 The American League becomes baseball's second major league and declares war on the established National League, using higher salaries to lure away about 30 everyday NL players and going head-to-head with the NL in Boston, Chicago, and Philadelphia.

1903 The National Agreement, the result of a settlement between the NL and AL, is signed, establishing a geographic setup of 16 teams that will remain intact for the next 50 years (see the following table).

1903 The Boston Pilgrims (who later became the Red Sox) defeat the Pittsburgh Pirates, five games to three, to win the first World Series.

The Major Leagues, 1903–53

National League (NL)	American League (AL)
Boston Braves	Boston Red Sox
Brooklyn Dodgers	Chicago White Sox
Chicago Cubs	Cleveland Indians
Cincinnati Reds	Detroit Tigers
New York Giants	New York Yankees
Philadelphia Phillies	Philadelphia Athletics
Pittsburgh Pirates	St. Louis Browns
St. Louis Cardinals	Washington Senators

Team nicknames in the early 1900s were not as standardized as they are today, when a team has one nickname (such as Dodgers) and sticks with it. Many clubs around the turn of the century were known by several nicknames, and those names sometimes changed every few years. Also, teams in the National League were sometimes referred to as Nationals (for example, the Braves were once known as the Boston Nationals), and likewise some AL clubs were called Americans. (The one exception was the Washington team, which, despite being American League, called itself the Washington Nationals for a time.) Got all that?

The following table lists some of the most common "pseudonyms" used by some major league teams in this period (most predate the more well-known nickname):

Most Common "Other" Nicknames of the Early 1900s

Best-Known Name	Other Nicknames
Boston Braves	Doves, Nationals
Brooklyn Dodgers	Superbas
Chicago Cubs	Colts, Orphans
Boston Red Sox	Americans, Pilgrims, Puritans, Plymouth Rocks, Somersets
Chicago White Sox	White Stockings
Cleveland Indians	Blues, Bronchos, Naps
New York Yankees	Highlanders (formerly the Baltimore Orioles)
St. Louis Browns	Ravens (formerly the Milwaukee Brewers)
Washington Senators	Nationals

Top Players of the 1900s

Mordecai "Three Finger" Brown, pitcher, Chicago Cubs
Johnny Evers, second base, Chicago Cubs
Willie Keeler, right field, Brooklyn Superbas, New York Highlanders
Napoleon Lajoie, second base, Cleveland Naps
Christy Mathewson, pitcher, New York Giants
Joe McGinnity, pitcher, New York Giants
Eddie Plank, pitcher, Philadelphia Athletics
Honus Wagner, shortstop, Pittsburgh Pirates
Ed Walsh, pitcher, Chicago White Sox
Cy Young, pitcher, Boston Pilgrims

The 1910s: Growing Pains

1914   The Federal League declares itself a major league and throws down the gauntlet in front of the NL and AL, placing teams in Brooklyn, Chicago, Pittsburgh, and St. Louis, and stealing numerous star players by offering them better salaries. The FL will disband after two seasons.

1918   With World War I in full swing and baseball deemed a "non-essential" business, the season is ended prematurely on September 2 and many players are drafted or enlisted into the armed forces or go to work in war-related industries.

1919   Something seems suspicious about the Cincinnati Reds' five-games-to-three World Series upset of the powerful Chicago White Sox. The following September, the truth emerges—eight White Sox players (known as the "Black Sox"), disgruntled with their paychecks and with club owner Charles Comiskey, conspired with gamblers to throw the Series.

The Black Sox scandal was vivid proof of what money will do. A disenchanted group of players, who didn't give a damn about their owner, found a way—the wrong way—to get back at him, or so they thought. Instead, they tainted the game, hurt themselves, and damaged the game's credibility for the next few years. Until a man by the name of Babe Ruth came along and changed everything.

Talkin' Baseball

"Regardless of the verdict of juries, no player that throws a ball game, no player that entertains proposals or promises to throw a game, no player that sits in a conference with a bunch of crooked players and gamblers where the ways and means of throwing games are discussed, and does not promptly tell his club about it, will ever again play professional baseball."

—Kenesaw Mountain Landis on the Black Sox

Talkin' Baseball

"Say it ain't so, Joe."

—A young boy who met "Shoeless" Joe Jackson on the street after word of the Black Sox scandal had gotten out

Top Players of the 1910s

Grover Cleveland Alexander, pitcher, Philadelphia Phillies, Cubs
Frank "Home Run" Baker, third base, A's, New York Yankees
Ty Cobb, center field, Detroit Tigers
Eddie Collins, second base, A's, White Sox
"Shoeless" Joe Jackson, left field, Cleveland Naps, White Sox
Walter Johnson, pitcher, Washington Senators
John Henry Lloyd, shortstop*
George Sisler, first base, St. Louis Browns
Tris Speaker, center field, Boston Red Sox, Cleveland Indians
Zack Wheat, left field, Brooklyn Dodgers

* Indicates Negro league players

The 1920s: The Babe Saves the Day

1920 With black players banned from the major leagues—and a proposal to add two all-black teams to the major leagues having been rejected—Chicago American Giants manager Rube Foster brings together the owners of prominent black teams from across the country for a meeting at the Paseo YMCA in Kansas City to form the Negro National League, the first such major league of its kind. The original teams are the Chicago American Giants, Chicago Giants, Cuban Stars (based in Cincinnati), Detroit Stars, Kansas City Monarchs, St. Louis Giants, Dayton Marcos, and Indianapolis ABCs. The Atlantic City Bacharachs and a Hilldale club, based in the Philadelphia suburb of Darby, are added as associate members. The Negro league concept soon catches on: Three years later a group of white businessmen form a competing six-team league, called the Eastern Colored League, and in 1937 the eight-team Negro American League is formed. But the major leagues' move to accept black players in the 1940s spells the beginning of the end of the Negro leagues; they'll all be out of business by 1960.

1920 Strapped for cash, Boston Red Sox owner Harry Frazee sells his biggest star, pitcher-turned-outfielder George Herman "Babe" Ruth, to the New York Yankees for $125,000 and a $300,000 loan. The trade will haunt Boston for decades. Ruth puts up unprecedented numbers, including a record-shattering 54 home runs in 1920, and becomes the game's biggest drawing card, while the Red Sox, World Series champs in 1918, haven't won one since.

1921 Kenesaw Mountain Landis, in one of his initial moves as the game's first commissioner, bans for life the eight Black Sox involved in the 1919 World Series fix, even though the players were acquitted in their trial in Illinois.

Talkin' Baseball

"Given the proper physical equipment—which consists solely in the strength to knock a ball 40 feet farther than the average man can do it—anybody can play big league ball today. In other words, science is out the window."

—Ty Cobb's thoughts on the home run

Every so often in baseball there's one person who the media gravitates to, who's great with quotes, great on the field and off, a real character. Babe Ruth (a.k.a. the Sultan of Swat or the Bambino) was the right man at the right time for baseball. The Babe was no myth, he was real, but he was like Paul Bunyan, bigger than life. He became one of the first one-name stars: He wasn't "George Herman Ruth," he was simply "the Babe." And he hit home runs three, four, five times more often than anyone had ever hit them before. They were called "Ruthian clouts." Before Ruth, players tried to hit the ball to the open area where a defensive player wasn't standing. The Babe just hit the ball over the fence.

An imposing sight for a pitcher: Babe Ruth preparing to hit in 1924, coming off a season in which he led the league in home runs (with 46) for the fifth time in six years, and in which he won his only batting title, with a .378 average.

Top Players of the 1920s

Cool Papa Bell, center field*
Oscar Charleston, center field*
Frankie Frisch, second base, Giants, St. Louis Cardinals
Rogers Hornsby, second base, Cardinals
Rabbit Maranville, shortstop, Boston Braves
Sam Rice, right field, Senators
Edd Roush, center field, Cincinnati Reds, Giants
Babe Ruth, right field, New York Yankees
Pie Traynor, third base, Pirates
Hack Wilson, center field, Giants, Cubs

* Indicates Negro league players

The 1930s: Outslugging the Depression

1930   Concerned that attendance will decline because of the Depression, the National League tries to liven things up by wrapping its baseballs tighter and lowering the

Talkin' Baseball

"Today, I consider myself the luckiest man on the face of the earth."

—Lou Gehrig in his farewell speech at Yankee Stadium, 1939

Talkin' Baseball

"Age is a question of mind over matter. If you don't mind, it doesn't matter."

—The ageless Satchel Paige

height of the stitching. The results are some off-the-charts offensive numbers and a record total major league attendance of 10.1 million.

1935   In major league baseball's first night game, the Cincinnati Reds beat the Philadelphia Phillies, 2–1, in Crosley Field.

1939   Major league baseball, which has been broadcast on radio since 1921, plays its first televised game. The Cincinnati Reds beat the Brooklyn Dodgers, 5–2, in Ebbets Field.

The 1930s were a decade of lasts—New York Yankee greats Babe Ruth and Lou Gehrig played their final games and New York Giants manager John McGraw retired after 30 years and three world championships. But it was also a decade of firsts, in terms of honoring baseball's best: The Baseball Writers Association of America handed out its first Most Valuable Player Awards in 1931, the first All-Star Game was played in Chicago in 1933, and in 1936 the writers association named the first Hall of Famers (Ty Cobb, Walter Johnson, Christy Mathewson, Babe Ruth, and Honus Wagner).

Extra Innings

How much offense was there in the 1930 National League? The Philadelphia Phillies had eight .300 hitters that year (a pretty rare feat), but finished in last place with a 52–102 record, thanks to their pitching staff's record-breaking 6.71 earned run average.

Top Players of the 1930s

Dizzy Dean, pitcher, Cardinals	**Hank Greenberg**, first base, Tigers
Bill Dickey, catcher, Yankees	**Lefty Grove**, pitcher, A's, Red Sox
Jimmie Foxx, first base, A's, Red Sox	**Carl Hubbell**, pitcher, Giants
Lou Gehrig, first base, Yankees	**Mel Ott**, right field, Giants
Josh Gibson, catcher*	**Satchel Paige**, pitcher*

* Indicates Negro league players

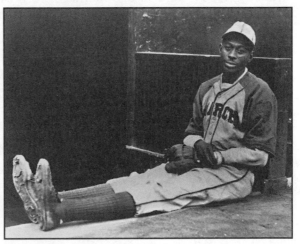

Barred from the major leagues until 1947, baseball's greatest black players of the early 1900s displayed their talents in the Negro leagues. The greatest Negro leaguers included (from left): John Henry Lloyd, Cool Papa Bell, Oscar Charleston, Josh Gibson, and Satchel Paige.

The 1940s: Breaking Down Barriers

1941   The increased U.S. involvement in World War II claims its first major league players, including Cleveland Indians ace pitcher Bob Feller and Detroit Tigers slugger Hank Greenberg. Within four years, 384 major leaguers will be lost to military service.

1943   The All-American Girls Professional Baseball League begins play with four teams and underhand pitching. It will survive until 1954.

1947   Jackie Robinson debuts with the Brooklyn Dodgers, becoming the first black player in the major leagues in the 20th century.

Jackie Robinson showed what the true meaning of sacrifice is. When he became the first black man to play major league baseball, the threats, abuse, and harassment he endured were appalling. For his first two or three seasons, it was always there, a constant. Jackie played with an intensity and a desire that you'd love to see everybody play with, and he played a big part in making the game what it is today.

Dodgers general manager Branch Rickey knew he needed a special player to pull off his "great experiment." After studying and interviewing Jackie, he determined that the Kansas City Monarchs' star shortstop was the right man for the job. It was the right choice. Jackie handled himself with class and dignity, even when those around him did not.

He was also a heck of a ballplayer. Playing for the Montreal Royals, the Dodgers' farm team, in 1946, the year before he joined the Dodgers, he led the International League in hitting. Then, in his first major league season, even though he had to tolerate abuse from opposing fans and players and adjust to his new position at first base, he hit .297 and led the league in stolen bases with 29, winning the inaugural Rookie of the Year Award. Jackie's instant success spurred other big-league clubs to follow suit; by 1949, there were four black players in the All-Star Game.

There were many people who did not want Jackie Robinson in the big leagues, but Jackie showed everyone that he belonged. In his first three seasons he twice led the National League in stolen bases, scored more than 100 runs each year, and was pretty handy with the glove, too—despite playing a new position, first base, as a Dodger rookie.

Extra Innings

Jackie Robinson broke major league baseball's color barrier in 1947, but he wasn't the first black player in the history of the major leagues. That was Fleet Walker, a college star at Oberlin who in 1884 hit .263 in 42 games as a catcher with Toledo of the American Association. Pressure from other players forced Walker out of the league after that season.

Top Players of the 1940s

Luke Appling, shortstop, White Sox	**Johnny Mize**, first base, Cardinals, Giants
Joe DiMaggio, center field, Yankees	**Hal Newhouser**, pitcher, Tigers
Bob Feller, pitcher, Indians	**Jackie Robinson**, second base*, Dodgers
Monte Irvin, left field*, Giants	**Enos Slaughter**, right field, Cardinals
Buck Leonard, first base*	**Ted Williams**, left field, Red Sox

* Indicates Negro league players

The 1950s: Baseball's Golden Age

1951   With a home run dubbed "the shot heard 'round the world," Bobby Thomson lifts the New York Giants past the Brooklyn Dodgers in the National League pennant playoff.

1953   The Boston Braves move to Milwaukee. Before the decade is out four other teams will move: the St. Louis Browns become the Baltimore Orioles in 1954, the Philadelphia Athletics shift to Kansas City in 1955, and—in a pair of moves that will change the face of New York City forever—the Brooklyn Dodgers (Los Angeles) and New York Giants (San Francisco) head to California in 1958.

1956   Don Larsen of the New York Yankees throws a perfect game—not allowing a single baserunner—in Game 5 of the World Series. It remains the only perfect game in World Series history.

Talkin' Baseball

"Hating the Yankees is as American as pizza pie, unwed mothers, and cheating on your income tax."

—Chicago newspaper columnist Mike Royko

I'm not sure I would have wanted to play in the 1950s—it seemed like the only two teams winning were the Brooklyn Dodgers and the New York Yankees. Those teams were covered by the large New York press corps and they were on national TV so often that they were thought to be the only teams that existed. With the advent of cable television and satellites, we can watch teams from all over the country, so we have a different perspective.

Top Players of the 1950s

Richie Ashburn, center field, Phillies

Yogi Berra, catcher, Yankees

Whitey Ford, pitcher, Yankees

Ralph Kiner, left field, Pirates

Mickey Mantle, center field, Yankees

Eddie Mathews, third base, Milwaukee Braves

Willie Mays, center field, New York/San Francisco Giants

Stan Musial, left field, Cardinals

Duke Snider, center field, Brooklyn/Los Angeles Dodgers

Warren Spahn, pitcher, Boston/Milwaukee Braves

The 1960s: A Time for Change

1961   The American League adds two teams: the Los Angeles Angels (who will become the California Angels in 1965) and the new Washington Senators (the old Washington Senators move to Minnesota and become the Twins). It's only the beginning of the expansion boom. The National League gets in the act in '62, adding the Houston Colt .45s (who will become the Astros in '65) and the New York Mets. In 1969 four more teams are added: the Montreal Expos and San Diego Padres in the NL and the Kansas City Royals (who replace the departed Athletics) and the Seattle Pilots (who last just one season before moving to Milwaukee to replace the Braves) in the AL. So by 1969 there are a total of 24 major league teams, 12 in each league, and both leagues split their teams into two six-team divisions, East and West.

1961   On the season's final day, New York Yankees slugger Roger Maris hits his 61st home run of the year to break Babe Ruth's single-season record.

1966   On the move again: The Milwaukee Braves move to Atlanta. Two years later, the Kansas City Athletics move to Oakland.

My first full season in the major leagues was 1968, a pretty tough year for a hitter to break in. The major league earned run average that season was a mere 2.99 and the overall batting average in the majors was just .237; only six hitters broke the .300 mark. It was no picnic facing guys like the St. Louis Cardinals' ace Bob Gibson (who had 15 straight wins at one point that year and finished with a 1.12 ERA) and Don Drysdale (who set a record with $58^{2}/_{3}$ consecutive scoreless innings).

Top Players of the 1960s

Hank Aaron, right field, Milwaukee/Atlanta Braves

Ernie Banks, shortstop, Cubs

Roberto Clemente, right field, Pirates

Bob Gibson, pitcher, Cardinals

Harmon Killebrew, first base, Senators

Sandy Koufax, pitcher, Dodgers

Juan Marichal, pitcher, Giants

Willie McCovey, first base, Giants

Brooks Robinson, third base, Baltimore Orioles

Frank Robinson, right field, Reds, Orioles

The 1970s: The Floodgates Are Opened

1970   More changes in the American League: The Seattle Pilots move to Milwaukee and become the Brewers. The next year the Washington Senators pull up stakes and become the Texas Rangers. Six years later the AL expands to Seattle (Mariners) and Toronto (Blue Jays).

1974   Hank Aaron of the Atlanta Braves hits his 715th home run to break Babe Ruth's career record. The AL's designated hitter rule, instituted the season before, helps Aaron play for two more years in Milwaukee and extend his career total to 755 homers.

1975   Three years after the players staged their first general strike, and six years after St. Louis Cardinals outfielder Curt Flood began his challenge against baseball's *reserve clause* (which bound a player to his team for life unless he retired or was traded), an arbitrator opens the door to free agency by ruling that the reserve clause ties a player to his team for just one year after his contract expires. A year later, 24 players comprise the major leagues' first free-agent class; half of them sign seven-figure contracts.

Curt Flood's saga began in 1969, when the Cardinals traded him to the Philadelphia Phillies. As far as Curt was concerned, he should have been allowed to

Warning Track

It's easy to get confused when you trace the history of some baseball teams, especially when there have been two different franchises that have used the same name. A note-worthy example is the Washington Senators, who have had two incarnations. The first, which was in Washington from 1901 to '60, is now the Minnesota Twins. The second, in Washington from 1961 to '71, is now the Texas Rangers.

make a deal for himself and not be traded at the club's discretion. He sat out the 1970 season and began a long battle against the reserve clause that went all the way to the Supreme Court. He lost his case, and he never played major league baseball again, but his suit nonetheless set a precedent for other players and helped pave the way for free agency in the major leagues.

Catching On

The **reserve clause** was the means by which a team used to automatically retain a player's rights in perpetuity, even after his contract ran out. On December 23, 1975, arbitrator Peter Seitz ruled that the reserve clause bound a player to his team for only one year after his contract expired. That ruling led to the institution of the free agency system that exists today.

Talkin' Baseball

"Blind people come to the park just to hear him pitch."

—Reggie Jackson on Tom Seaver

It took a lot of conviction on Curt's part to do what he did. I think all us players at some point felt very frustrated when trying to negotiate a contract. In 1970, I hit 45 home runs and drove in 148 runs, but after talking to the Reds' general manager, I was convinced I'd had a bad year. One year, around 1950, Ralph Kiner of the Pittsburgh Pirates hit about 50 home runs and went in for a raise at the end of the season, and the general manager said, "There's not going to be any raise." Ralph started to say, "Well, I hit…." And the general manager said, "Look, we finished last this year with you hitting all those home runs. We can finish last again next year without you." One year the great Joe DiMaggio of the Yankees held out for more money and endured the wrath of the fans in New York.

Management's attitude was that if you didn't like it, you could go somewhere else—but, thanks to the reserve clause, which bound you to a contract that all other major league teams had to honor, you *couldn't* go anywhere else in major league baseball. So, basically, you were free to either quit baseball or take what they gave you.

Many guys sat out, or held out, but they didn't take it to the next level. They may not have had the right person to stand behind them and say, "If you're willing to do this, we'll take them to court, and we'll win." Finally, Curt Flood stood up and said, "I'm willing." And he made a difference.

Top Players of the 1970s

Lou Brock, left field, Cardinals
Rod Carew, second base, Minnesota Twins, California Angels
Steve Carlton, pitcher, Cardinals, Phillies
Reggie Jackson, right field, Oakland A's, Yankees
Joe Morgan, second base, Houston Astros, Reds
Jim Palmer, pitcher, Orioles

Pete Rose, left field, Reds
Mike Schmidt, third base, Phillies
Tom Seaver, pitcher, New York Mets, Reds
Willie Stargell, left field, Pirates

* In the interest of modesty, I'm not including myself.

The 1980s: Some Bumps in the Road

1981   At odds with the owners over the issue of free agent compensation, the players' first in-season strike lasts seven weeks.

1983   Nolan Ryan of the Houston Astros strikes out his 3,509th batter to break Walter Johnson's career record.

1989   Pete Rose, who less than four years before had become baseball's all-time leader in hits, is suspended for life by commissioner Bart Giamatti for betting on baseball. The suspension makes Rose, a Hall of Fame shoo-in, ineligible for induction.

The Pete Rose story was a very damning thing for baseball. I think we'd all like to know everything that really happened. Will we ever know? Probably not. But it hurt all of us who had any kind of association with Pete. It's been probably the most disturbing thing in the game of baseball for me. I'm often asked if I think Pete should be in the Hall of Fame. Not until he's reinstated, I say. There's one all-important rule in the game of baseball: You can't gamble on baseball. Everybody knows the rule, everybody has to live by the rule, and everybody knows the penalties. People say to me, "I think Pete Rose should be in the Hall of Fame." And I say, "Well, he was a Hall of Fame *player*. But, unfortunately, there's more to it than that."

Should Pete be reinstated? Well, I don't have that vote. But the rule says "for life." "Shoeless" Joe Jackson of the Black Sox had to endure it. No player who has ever been on that list has ever entered the Hall of Fame. As Mrs. Tate, my eighth-grade teacher, said, "You make your own bed, you've gotta sleep in it."

Top Players of the 1980s

Wade Boggs, third base, Red Sox
George Brett, third base, Kansas City Royals
Gary Carter, catcher, Montreal Expos, Mets
Rickey Henderson, left field, Oakland A's, Yankees
Dale Murphy, center field, Braves
Cal Ripken Jr., shortstop, Orioles
Ryne Sandberg, second base, Cubs
Ozzie Smith, shortstop, Cardinals
Dave Winfield, right field, Yankees
Robin Yount, shortstop, Milwaukee Brewers

The 1990s: Modern Problems

1993 More teams, more divisions. First, the Colorado Rockies and Florida Marlins join the NL. The following year both leagues realign into three divisions: East, Central, and West. In 1998, the Arizona Diamondbacks join the NL, the Tampa Bay Devil Rays join the AL and the AL's Milwaukee Brewers become the first team to switch leagues.

1994 The latest players' strike—baseball's eighth work stoppage since 1972—is by far the most severe. It wipes out half of the 1994 season, as well as the World Series, and delays the start of the '95 schedule. The major bone of contention is a proposed salary cap.

1995 Cal Ripken Jr. of the Baltimore Orioles plays in his 2,131st consecutive game to surpass Lou Gehrig's record streak.

From the Bench

One criticism of today's players is that they don't know the game's history. Well, I'm not so sure the guys in the 1940s knew all about the guys from the 1890s or the early 1900s, either.

Baseball has had a lot of money problems in recent years. Usually the complaint is that there isn't enough of it passed on to the players. It used to be the owners had all the power, but now the players hold the trump cards. And once you get legal people involved, who earn their money doing the best thing for whichever side they're working for, there will always be a conflict.

There are three sides running the game of baseball: the owners, the players, and the umpires. And I don't know that any of them share a common goal. Everyone's attitude is, "What's in it for me?" After work stoppages like baseball has had, you have to realize that it's like a breakup in a romance. To get back together, you have to send flowers and candy to try to win back your dear one—in this case, the fan.

Extra Innings

The Florida Marlins won the World Series in 1997, just their fifth year of existence. Of expansion teams in the four major team sports, only the NBA's Milwaukee Bucks built themselves into a world champion faster. Then, before the 1998 season, the Marlins stripped their club of almost all their star players to shrink their payroll and became the only "world champion" to ever have the worst record in the major leagues the very next year.

Sooner or later there has to be a unification of all sides. But I'm not sure if it will ever happen because of the money at stake—you see arbitrators deciding whether to give a certain player $1.8 million or $3.2 million, and the guy doesn't even have a .500 record. I see that as a failing. But now that the players have that power, they aren't going to give it back. And they've been more than willing to walk out and be damned by both the owners and the fans.

Top Players of the 1990s

Barry Bonds, left field, Pirates, Giants
Roger Clemens, pitcher, Red Sox, Toronto Blue Jays
Juan Gonzalez, right field, Texas Rangers
Ken Griffey Jr., center field, Seattle Mariners
Tony Gwynn, right field, San Diego Padres
Randy Johnson, pitcher, Mariners, Astros, Arizona Diamondbacks
Greg Maddux, pitcher, Braves
Mark McGwire, first base, A's, Cardinals
Sammy Sosa, right field, Cubs
Frank Thomas, first base, White Sox
Mo Vaughn, first base, Red Sox, Anaheim Angels

The Good Old Days?

I can appreciate the charm of baseball's bygone eras, but I wouldn't have wanted to play in any other time than when I did, from the late 1960s through the early '80s. It would've been fun in the days when the players rode from town to town on trains, but I wouldn't have wanted to be a catcher with the primitive gloves and equipment they had. I think I played at the right time—although my accountant wishes I was still playing today.

The Least You Need to Know

➤ To really appreciate the game of baseball, it's important to have at least a basic knowledge of the sport's long, rich history.

➤ Most historians agree that, contrary to popular legend, Abner Doubleday and Cooperstown played little or no role in the origin of baseball.

➤ The Black Sox scandal of 1919 and Jackie Robinson's breaking the major leagues' color barrier in 1947 were two landmark events in the 20th century.

➤ From 1901 to 1960 there were 16 major league teams. Since then, 14 have been added for a current total of 30.

Chapter 3

A Salute to Tradition

In This Chapter

➤ Why the game's traditions are so important

➤ Baseball's most famous poem and song

➤ Everything you need to know about nicknames

➤ Traditions you'll see at the ballpark

➤ Which teams have the winningest—and losingest—traditions

More than any other sport, baseball is a game of great traditions. As a fan, it's important that you have a sense of those traditions, because any time you watch a game—at the park or on TV—they'll be a part of it, whether you're standing up to sing "Take Me Out to the Ballgame" or watching Atlanta Braves fans do the Tomahawk Chop.

A Game for Fathers and Sons

Maybe it goes back to the traditional image of the father and son playing catch in the backyard. But for whatever reason, baseball has always been a game for fathers and sons, for families. The love of the game gets passed down from generation to generation. I know it was always that way in my family.

My dad's dream, his sole aspiration, was to play in the major leagues. But he joined the Army and served two hitches in World War II, and when he came out he was a little too old and his arm wasn't what it had been. He hoped that one of his sons would be a catcher like him, and maybe one day fulfill his dream. So he encouraged us to play. Neither of my older brothers fell in love with it, but I did.

That's why the movie *Field of Dreams* really hits home for me, as it did for a lot of people. There's a famous scene in which the son (played by Kevin Costner) plays catch with his father by the cornfield, and that really took me back. We had a cornfield in back of our house when I was a kid, and when we played ball, Dad could hit it all the way into that cornfield. That's how simple baseball can be, and how simple the idea of sharing time with your child can be. *"Come on, let's have a catch."*

Extra Innings

There are two sets of brothers in baseball's Hall of Fame (Paul and Lloyd Waner, and George and Harry Wright), but no father-son combinations, even though more than 100 father-son combos have played in the major leagues. While several Hall of Famers have had sons play in the majors, so far no member's father ever played in the big leagues.

Talkin' Baseball

"Baseball is continuous, like nothing else among American things, an endless game of repeated summers, joining the long generations of all the fathers and all the sons."

—Donald Hall in *Fathers Playing Catch With Sons*

Talkin' Baseball

"You're a hero one day and a bum the next."

—Babe Ruth on the fleeting nature of baseball stardom

"Casey at the Bat"

Baseball's most famous poem is more than 100 years old. Written by Ernest Lawrence Thayer, the son of a wool manufacturer, it first appeared in the San Francisco *Examiner* on June 3, 1888, under the title "Casey at the Bat: A Ballad of the Republic." The poem describes a dramatic confrontation between Casey, the star hitter for "the Mudville nine," and the opposing pitcher, as Casey comes to bat with his team behind, 4–2, and runners on second and third. The poem starts out:

> *The outlook wasn't brilliant for the Mudville nine that day;*
> *The score stood four to two, with but one inning more to play.*
> *And then when Cooney died at first, and Barrows did the same,*
> *A sickly silence fell upon the patrons of the game.*

Perhaps what makes "Casey at the Bat" so appealing is that it ends in an unexpected way. Here was the greatest of all hitters, failing. Some things are just not supposed to happen. Casey isn't supposed to strike out. But we find out that ballplayers are not infallible, that they do fail. Here's the final stanza of "Casey at the Bat":

Oh, somewhere in this favored land the sun is shining bright;
The band is playing somewhere, and somewhere hearts are light,
And somewhere men are laughing, and somewhere children shout;
But there is no joy in Mudville—mighty Casey has struck out.

Extra Innings

One of the better-known poems about baseball was written in 1912 by Franklin P. Adams. Called "Baseball's Sad Lexicon," it tells of the frustration of hitting into a double play against the Chicago Cubs' great infield of Joe Tinker, Johnny Evers, and Frank Chance. The poem begins:

These are the saddest of possible words:
"Tinker to Evers to Chance"

Team Nicknames: Official and Unofficial

Team nicknames have been an important part of baseball since the beginning—going all the way back to the Knickerbocker Base Ball Club of New York, the game's first club in 1845. But based on pre-Civil War newspaper stories that referred to some of the early professional teams as "the New Yorks" or "the Bostons," it's reasonable to conclude that many of the first pro teams' nicknames were not widely known, if they existed at all.

To increase fan appeal, as well as to avoid confusion in cities such as New York, Philadelphia, and St. Louis, where there were two teams, the use of team nicknames had become more common by the time the National League was formed in 1876. Some team nicknames, such as the Athletics (or A's) for the Philadelphia club or the Red Stockings (or Reds) for the Cincinnati team, were in use well before then.

From the Bench

Many teams' nicknames have a connection to their home city. Examples include the Baltimore Orioles, Colorado Rockies, Florida Marlins, Milwaukee Brewers, Minnesota Twins, and Seattle Mariners. The Dodgers are another— or at least they used to be. The team was so named in the late 19th century because residents of downtown Brooklyn, where a maze of trolley lines converged, had to be adept "trolley dodgers."

Over the years many teams have also acquired unofficial nicknames, which usually refer to their style of play. Some, such as the Bronx Bombers (for the power-hitting New York Yankees) are perennial. Others, such as the Gashouse Gang (for the St. Louis Cardinals of the 1930s) are used only for a period of a few years.

In the 1970s, the Reds team that I played for became known as the Big Red Machine, because we were so dominant we just rolled over other teams. A lot of people have taken credit for that nickname. I know I first heard it from Jim McIntyre and Frank McCormick, the Reds' radio announcers at that time. The upcoming table lists some of the more popular unofficial team nicknames.

It's surprising that the Atlanta Braves of the 1990s, as successful as they've been, haven't really developed a nickname. It's a sign of the times, I suppose, but it seems like they should have a moniker of some sort.

Popular Unofficial Team Nicknames

Nickname	Team
The Amazin' Mets	New York Mets
The Big Red Machine	1970s Cincinnati Reds
The Bronx Bombers	New York Yankees
Buccaneers/Bucs	Pittsburgh Pirates
Dem Bums	Brooklyn Dodgers
The Gashouse Gang	1930s St. Louis Cardinals
The Lumber Company	1979 Pittsburgh Pirates
The Miracle Braves	1914 Boston Braves
The Miracle Mets	1969 New York Mets
Murderers' Row	1927 New York Yankees*
The Mustache Gang	Early 1970s Oakland A's
The Southside Hitmen/ the Pale Hose	Chicago White Sox
The Tribe	Cleveland Indians
The Whiz Kids	1950 Philadelphia Phillies

* This nickname referred to the heart of the Yankees' batting order, which featured Tony Lazzeri, Lou Gehrig, Babe Ruth, Earle Combs, and Bob Meusel (all but Meusel are in the Hall of Fame). The nickname was also used for the meat of the 1919 Yankee lineup (Ping Bodie, Roger Peckinpaugh, Duffy Lewis, and Home Run Baker).

Johnny's Favorite Player Nicknames

They're not as popular today as they used to be, but player nicknames play a major role in baseball's colorful tradition. Some are pinned on players by sportswriters (such as High Pockets for George Kelly), others are conjured up by teammates (Blue Moon for John Odom), others have been used since childhood and simply follow a player to the big leagues (Peanuts for Harry Lowrey).

Many nicknames are derived from animal names (such as Hippo for Jim Vaughn) or from a player's appearance (Rusty for Daniel Staub). Others pay deference to a player's great skills (the Splendid Splinter for Ted Williams) or to his revered status in the game (Whitey Ford, the Chairman of the Board). A listing of every nickname in major league history would fill this chapter (and then some), so instead I've provided a list of my favorites in the following table.

Johnny's Favorite Player Nicknames

Nickname	Player
The Barber	Sal Maglie
Big Six	Christy Mathewson
The Big Train	Walter Johnson
The Brat	Eddie Stanky
Bullet Bob, Rapid Robert	Bob Feller
Captain Hook	Sparky Anderson
Catfish	Jim Hunter
Charlie Hustle	Pete Rose
The Chief	Allie Reynolds
The Commerce Comet	Mickey Mantle
The Flying Dutchman	Honus Wagner
The Iron Horse	Lou Gehrig
The Lip	Leo Durocher
The Meal Ticket	Carl Hubbell
Mr. Cub	Ernie Banks
Mr. October	Reggie Jackson
Old Aches and Pains	Luke Appling
The Old Perfesser	Casey Stengel
Old Reliable	Tommy Henrich
The Ryan Express	Nolan Ryan
The Scooter	Phil Rizzuto
Stan the Man	Stan Musial
The "Say Hey" Kid	Willie Mays
The Spaceman	Bill Lee
Wild Thing	Mitch Williams
The Wizard of Oz	Ozzie Smith
The Yankee Clipper, Joltin' Joe	Joe DiMaggio

Ernie Banks, Mr. Cub, was a power-hitting shortstop, and later a first baseman, for the Chicago Cubs of the 1950s and '60s. His philosophy of baseball can be summed up by his signature quote: "It's a great day for a ballgame— let's play two!"

I think in the old days there used to be so many more bench jockeys—guys who yelled from the dugout to get you riled up. The first time Mickey Mantle and Whitey Ford saw Pete Rose run down to first base—on a walk—Mickey scoffed and said, "Hey, look at Charlie Hustle." After that, Pete Rose became Charlie Hustle. Charlie Finley, the former Oakland A's owner, was probably the last guy who tried to put nicknames on people. Finley wanted John Odom to change his name legally to Blue Moon. He wanted to create personalities for people. I think he realized the value of what it meant when people came out to the ballpark and said, "Hey, there's Charlie Hustle." I miss the nicknames of the past in a lot of ways, but maybe those things are old hat.

Extra Innings

Some baseball nicknames are really a sign of the times. Walter Johnson, the Washington Senators' hard-throwing pitcher from 1907 to 1927, was known as the Big Train, because steam locomotives were the fastest form of transportation in those days. Roger Clemens, one of today's hardest throwers, is aptly nicknamed the Rocket.

Stan "The Man" Musial, the St. Louis Cardinals' Hall of Fame outfielder of the 1940s and '50s, began his baseball career as a pitcher. He was 18—5 in the Florida State League in 1940, but changed positions after suffering an injury in an off-season workout.

Pete Rose, a.k.a. Charlie Hustle, displays his trademark headfirst slide to beat the catcher's tag at home plate. Pete is baseball's all-time leader in hits.

The fireballing Walter Johnson was known as the Big Train. He won 416 games and threw a major league record 110 shutouts in his 21-year career.

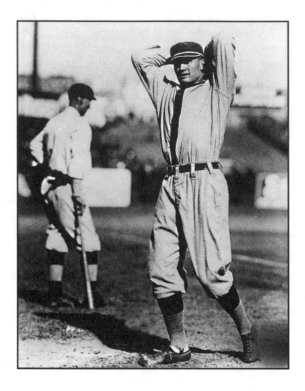

Pennants, Monuments, and Retired Numbers

An important facet of baseball is the honoring of great players and teams of the past. You'll probably see examples of it at your local major league park, provided you know what to look for.

Pennant is an important word in baseball. Literally speaking, it refers to a long, triangular flag, most often one bearing a team name and colors. Those small felt ones used to be quite popular—young fans would hang them on their bedroom walls—and you can still buy one at the souvenir stand at most ballparks.

More figuratively speaking, a pennant in major league parlance refers to a league championship (American or National). So if your team "wins the pennant," it means they're going to the World Series. And usually a team that wins a pennant will fly a "League Champions" flag in a prominent place in their stadium (usually out beyond the outfield wall). You'll also see similar flags flying in the parks of teams that have won the World Series, and even a division championship.

The New York Yankees do a great job of honoring their traditions. Behind the outfield wall at Yankee Stadium is Monument Park, which fans can visit before the game. There are monuments and plaques honoring Yankee greats like Babe Ruth, Joe DiMaggio, and Mickey Mantle. It's worth a visit if you ever make it to Yankee Stadium.

Something else you'll see—at Yankee Stadium and at many other major league parks—are retired uniform numbers. They're often large numbers displayed on the outfield wall (as they are at Shea Stadium, home of the New York Mets) or on the facade of the stadium somewhere. These are the uniform numbers once worn by great players of that team, and now, in honor of that player, no one on that club will ever wear that number again. The Cincinnati Reds paid me that honor by retiring my number 5 after my playing days were over.

This is a terrific tradition. A player who gives years of service and endears himself to the fans deserves it. For me, it was a tremendous honor, having played and given everything I had for 17 years, to know that it was appreciated and that it lives on.

The following table lists some of the more than 100 retired numbers in the major leagues. (The complete list is in Appendix D.) The Yankees lead the way with 15. (Keep in mind that most major league teams did not begin wearing numbers on their uniforms until the 1930s, so great players such as Ty Cobb, Walter Johnson, and Cy Young never had one.) You'll find more on the tradition of uniform numbers in Chapter 7.

Catching On

A **pennant** is a triangular flag, usually with a team name and colors. In the major leagues it's also used more figuratively to refer to a league championship. (For example, "the Giants win the pennant" means they've won the National League championship and will go on to the World Series.)

Important Retired Uniform Numbers

Number	Player	Team
3	Babe Ruth	Yankees
4	Lou Gehrig	Yankees
5	Joe DiMaggio	Yankees
6	Stan Musial	Cardinals
7	Mickey Mantle	Yankees
9	Ted Williams	Red Sox
14	Ernie Banks	Cubs
19	Bob Feller	Indians
21	Roberto Clemente	Pirates
24	Willie Mays	Giants
32	Sandy Koufax	Dodgers
41	Tom Seaver	Mets
44	Hank Aaron	Braves/Brewers
45	Bob Gibson	Cardinals

Extra Innings

The number 42 was retired for every major league team in 1997 in honor of Jackie Robinson, who wore that number for the Brooklyn Dodgers. Players who were wearing it at the time (such as Mo Vaughn of the Boston Red Sox and Butch Huskey of the New York Mets) were allowed to continue, but no new major leaguers will ever be issued that uniform number.

In baseball, you have to have pride in your organization—that goes for the players and front office as well as for the fans. Recently, for the first time in many, many years, the Reds put up plaques in the outfield for their retired uniform numbers and for the years in which they were world champions (1935, '75, '76, and '90). It's great—that's something that both parents and kids can be part of.

Throwing Out the First Ball—and the Presidential Connection

Another long-standing baseball tradition is the ceremonial first pitch, which dates back to the early days. It's simply a way to kick off the game with a little extra ceremony, having an honored guest toss the ball (either from the pitcher's mound or from the stands) to a player from the home team (usually a catcher).

U.S. presidents have been associated with this honor since April 14, 1910, when, before the Washington Senators' home opener, William H. Taft became the first president to throw out the first ball. Since then more than 40 games have begun with a ceremonial first pitch by a president, including Woodrow Wilson, Warren Harding, Calvin Coolidge, Herbert Hoover, Harry Truman, John F. Kennedy, Jimmy Carter, and Bill Clinton.

As a catcher, I caught some memorable first balls at All-Star Games and World Series from the likes of President Richard Nixon and Vice President Spiro Agnew. But on my retirement night, September 17, 1983, I caught the greatest first pitch of all—from my dad. We were out in the front yard warming up that afternoon so he could get his arm loose. For him, it meant everything. My dad was finally walking onto a major league field and being what he had so longed to be: a part of the major leagues. That was a tremendous honor for me to have my dad do that.

The National Anthem

You won't have someone throw out the first ball before every game, but one pregame ritual that you are guaranteed at a major league game is the playing and/or singing of "The Star Spangled Banner." Written by Francis Scott Key in 1814, the song was designated as America's national anthem in 1931. It was first sung during the seventh-inning stretch in Game 1 of the 1918 World Series, during World War I, and from then on it became standard practice to have the song played or sung before every game.

The Seventh-Inning Stretch and "Take Me Out to the Ballgame"

Something else you're guaranteed to experience at a big-league game is the seventh-inning stretch. It's exactly what it sounds like: In the middle of the seventh inning (before the home team comes up to bat), all the fans stand up and stretch their legs. This is usually accompanied by the playing and singing of "Take Me Out to the Ballgame." The song was written in 1908 by Jack Norworth (lyrics) and Albert von Tilzer (melody)—neither of whom had ever been to a professional baseball game. The part of the song that is sung at the park goes like this:

> *Take me out to the ballgame,*
> *Take me out with the crowd.*
> *Buy me some peanuts and Cracker Jack;*
> *I don't care if I never get back.*
> *So let's root, root, root for the home team* [or sing name of home team],
> *If they don't win it's a shame.*
> *For it's one, two, three strikes you're out*
> *At the old ballgame.*

There are a number of theories on how the seventh-inning stretch started. Many historians believe that President Taft—at the same 1910 game that saw him throw out the first ball—inadvertently started the tradition when he stood up to stretch in the middle of the seventh inning. Assuming the President was getting up to leave, the fans also stood up, out of respect. But when they observed Taft stretching, they did the same—and continued to do so at subsequent games as the practice caught on.

The New York Yankees: Baseball's Most Storied Team

Having read this far, you've probably already been struck by the number of references to the New York Yankees in this book. It's simply impossible to talk about major league baseball for very long without bringing up the Yankees. They are the best-known team, with the richest tradition of success, in baseball and quite possibly in the entire sports world.

The Yankee mystique starts with great accomplishments on the playing field: 24 World Series, 35 American League pennants, both more than double the number of any other major league team. The Yankees have also had so many great players—guys who transcended the game—such as Babe Ruth, Lou Gehrig, Joe DiMaggio, and Mickey Mantle. Two Yankees teams, the 1927 and 1961 editions, are arguably the two best in baseball history, and the 1998 version again made a claim for that honor.

Talkin' Baseball

"Rooting for the Yankees is like rooting for U.S. Steel."

—comedian Joe E. Lewis

Many people like me grew up with the Yankees of the late 1940s, '50s, and early '60s, when they were in the World Series just about every year, usually defeating their arch-rivals, the Brooklyn Dodgers. The Dodgers had to live in the shadow of the Yankee myth. The Yankees *were* baseball. You just couldn't hate the Yankees.

Teams That Just Can't Win

There are a few major league teams that just can't seem to win the big one. I don't know if they're cursed (many of their fans certainly think so), but the Boston Red Sox, Chicago Cubs, and Chicago White Sox each have streaks of championship futility that are unmatched in baseball—or in any other sport, for that matter.

The Red Sox won the first five World Series in which they appeared, but they haven't won one since 1918 (two years before they sold Babe Ruth to the Yankees), although they came tantalizingly close in 1967, 1975, and 1986. (You'd be well advised not to mention that most recent heartbreaker to a Red Sox fan.) Among Boston's recent litany of horrors:

➤ The Red Sox came within one win of a world championship in both 1967 and 1975.

➤ In 1978, they blew a 14-game lead in the American League East and were beaten by the Yankees in a one-game playoff—thanks to an improbable three-run homer off the bat of shortstop Bucky Dent. (Boston had also lost a one-game playoff to the Cleveland Indians 30 years before.)

➤ With a three-games-to-two lead over the New York Mets in the 1986 World Series, the Red Sox were ahead 5–3 heading into the bottom of the 10th inning of Game 6. In that inning Boston was one out away from a championship, but the Mets staged an amazing three-run rally—helped immensely when a ground ball went through first baseman Bill Buckner's legs—and won the game. They won the next game, too, and thus another World Series slipped away from the Red Sox.

Extra Innings

The Red Sox, world champs in 1918, fell to sixth place one season later. Strapped for cash, owner Harry Frazee sold his team's biggest star, pitcher-turned-slugging-outfielder Babe Ruth, to the Yankees for $125,000 and a $300,000 loan. It turned out to be a trade that would haunt the Red Sox for decades, as Ruth put up unprecedented numbers—including a record-shattering 54 home runs—the following season, and quickly became the game's greatest drawing card. Victimized by "the Curse of Babe Ruth," the Red Sox have yet to win a World Series since selling the Babe.

The Cubs have lost eight Series in 10 tries, and they haven't won a pennant since 1945. They won their last World Series in 1908. 1998 was a thrilling year for the Cubs, with Sammy Sosa chasing Mark McGwire for the home run record, leading the league in runs scored and runs batted in, and being named the National League's Most Valuable Player at season's end. The Cubs played an exciting wild-card playoff game against the San Francisco Giants, but, alas, the Braves brought the Cubs back to reality in the first round of the playoffs.

The White Sox, two-for-four overall in the Series, last won a pennant in 1959. Perhaps the baseball gods have frowned upon them because of the Black Sox scandal of 1919; they haven't won a Series since 1917. So even though these three teams have won 22 pennants and nine World Series between them, through the 1998 season they had gone a combined 251 years without a championship.

I don't know if there's a reason why these teams can't get over the hump. It would be so good for baseball to have them win. When the players' strike canceled half of the season in 1994 and they didn't have a World Series, the Red Sox and Cubs should have played a ceremonial series.

Talkin' Baseball

"It's not whether you win or lose, it's how you play the game."

—Grantland Rice

So now that you're up on baseball's traditions, we'll take a look in the next chapter at the game's best—those men and moments that have really stood out. And once we've covered that, you'll be ready to take the field.

The Least You Need to Know

➤ Every good fan should know baseball's traditions.

➤ Although they aren't as popular as they once were, team and player nicknames are a baseball staple.

➤ Pennants, retired numbers, and the seventh-inning stretch are examples of baseball traditions to watch for on a visit to the ballpark.

➤ While the New York Yankees are traditionally baseball's most successful team, the Boston Red Sox, Chicago Cubs, and Chicago White Sox are the game's hard-luck trio.

Chapter 4

Baseball's Best: Outstanding in the Field

In This Chapter

➤ Baseball's greatest players—and personalities

➤ The game's most memorable moments

➤ The pinnacles of pitching, hitting, and defense

What baseball is all about, really, is great matchups. Those are what create excitement, tension, and drama. And that's why people go to the ballpark: to see that one particular confrontation of pitcher and hitter. They want to see Willie Mays batting in the ninth inning against Bob Gibson. They want to see Mark McGwire come up against Greg Maddux with a chance to win the ballgame.

The greats of the game are the players who comprise these most memorable matchups—the guys who keep you in your seat when they're on the field. And the *immortals* are the guys who rise to the occasion most often when they're staring down a fellow Hall of Famer.

Just this past season, 20-year-old rookie Kerry Wood of the Chicago Cubs struck out 20 Houston Astros in a game—and all of a sudden a new legend was born. What a thrill that was—the people who saw that game will never forget it.

That's what this chapter is about: the great baseball players and the moments that stay with you forever.

The Greatest of All Time

Any list of the greatest baseball players of all time has to start with Babe Ruth (whose major league career spanned from 1914 to 1935), the legendary right fielder of the

New York Yankees. The Babe was amazingly big and strong, with an innate ability to hit a baseball a long way. His career record of 714 home runs stood for 39 years, until Hank Aaron broke it in 1974. And a lot of people forget that the Babe was also a heck of a pitcher for the Boston Red Sox before he became a home run hitter. He held the record for consecutive scoreless innings pitched in World Series play (29^2/$_3$), until Whitey Ford of the Yankees broke it in the 1950s.

The next name that comes up after the Babe's is Lou Gehrig (1923–39), the Babe's teammate from 1923 to '34, who hit behind him in the lineup and played in his shadow for all those years. Gehrig, baseball's Iron Horse, held the major league record for consecutive games played (2,130) until Cal Ripken Jr. broke it in 1995.

Talkin' Baseball

"The only real game, I think, in the world is baseball."

—Babe Ruth

But another Yankee was, without question, the greatest of all time: Mickey Mantle (1951–68). This is obviously a personal observation, but as a kid growing up in Oklahoma—the Mick's home state—I idolized him. He was undoubtedly the game's most powerful switch hitter; ten times he hit home runs from both sides of the plate (left-handed and right-handed) in one game. He also won three American League Most Valuable Player Awards and holds career World Series records for home runs (18), runs (42), and RBIs (40).

A 23-year-old Mickey Mantle is greeted at home plate by Yogi Berra after clubbing a home run in 1954. The Mick, my boy-hood hero, was from my home state of Oklahoma.

Beyond those greats, you have to include the following immortals:

➤ **Jimmie Foxx** (1925–45), a three-time AL MVP who hit 30 or more home runs in 12 straight seasons (1929–40) with the Philadelphia Athletics and Boston Red Sox.

➤ **Ty Cobb** (Detroit Tigers, 1905–28), the great Detroit Tigers center fielder, whose .367 career batting average is the best of all time.

➤ **Rogers Hornsby** (1915–37), who spent most of his career with the St. Louis Cardinals, Chicago Cubs, and St. Louis Browns, and whose .358 career average ranks second.

➤ **Napoleon Lajoie** (1896–1916), one of the game's most complete second basemen, and one of the few men to ever hit .400 (.426 in 1901 with the Philadelphia Athletics). His Cleveland club actually went by the nickname "Naps" in his honor in the early 1900s.

➤ **Honus Wagner** (1897–1917), who won eight NL batting titles with the Pittsburgh Pirates and played every position with equal skill.

➤ **Stan Musial** (1941–63), a three-time NL MVP with the St. Louis Cardinals who ranks second all-time in total bases (6,134).

➤ **Ted Williams** (1939–60), the Red Sox legend who was one of the greatest hitters ever, the last man to bat over .400 in a season and owner of baseball's highest career on-base percentage (.483).

➤ **Joe DiMaggio** (1936–51), who owns baseball's longest hitting streak (56 games in 1941) and played on nine championship teams in 13 years with the Yankees.

On the mound you couldn't do better than the five pitchers with the most career victories:

➤ **Cy Young:** 511 with the Cleveland Spiders, St. Louis Cardinals, Boston Red Sox, Cleveland Indians, and Boston Braves (1890–1911).

Catching On

On-base percentage is a statistic used to measure a player's offensive performance—it tells you how often a player gets on base. To compute on-base percentage, add hits plus walks plus times hit by pitch and divide that figure by the sum of at bats, walks, times hit by pitch, and sacrifice flies.

Talkin' Baseball

"There is always some kid who may be seeing me for the first or last time. I owe him my best."

—Joe DiMaggio, on why he placed such a high value on excellence

➤ **Walter Johnson**: 417 with the Washington Senators (1907–27).

➤ **Christy Mathewson**: 373 with the New York Giants and Cincinnati Reds (1900–16).

➤ **Grover Cleveland Alexander:** 373 with the Philadelphia Phillies, Chicago Cubs, and St. Louis Cardinals (1911 –30).

➤ **Warren Spahn**: 363 with the Milwaukee/Atlanta Braves and New York/San Francisco Giants (1942–65).

These were people who played the game with tremendous passion and flair. They wanted to give everything they could every time they took the field and to show people that they loved and respected the game.

The Greatest of My Time

The next names on my list of all-time greats would be guys who I played with—and against:

➤ **Pete Rose** (1963–86), best known as a Cincinnati Red, the game's all-time leader in hits with 4,256.

➤ **Willie Mays** (1951–73) of the New York/San Francisco Giants and New York Mets, third in career home runs with 660 and one of the greatest defensive center fielders of all time.

➤ **Joe Morgan** (1963–84), a two-time MVP with the Reds and one of the best second basemen ever, at the plate and in the field.

➤ **Mike Schmidt** (1972–89) the Philadelphia Phillies great who hit more home runs (509) as a third baseman than anyone and won 10 Gold Gloves for his excellence in the field.

➤ **Hank Aaron** (1954–76), baseball's all-time home run king with 755 for the Milwaukee/Atlanta Braves and Milwaukee Brewers.

➤ **Roberto Clemente** (1955–72), a classy, 12-time All-Star, who possessed one of the strongest throwing arms and was one of the greatest defensive outfielders the game has ever seen.

➤ **Willie McCovey** (1959–80), who hit 521 homers in his career and was the one batter I feared most—I think he was the only hitter I ever thought we couldn't get out.

Roberto Clemente won four batting titles with the Pittsburgh Pirates in the 1960s. His tragic death on New Year's Eve in 1972—in a plane crash while on a disaster-relief mission for earthquake victims in Nicaragua—shocked the baseball world.

As opposing hitters go, this guy was just plain scary: With the San Francisco Giants, Willie McCovey led the National League in home runs three times. You just didn't want to face him if the game was on the line.

Among pitchers from my era, I'd include:

➤ **Sandy Koufax** (Brooklyn/L.A. Dodgers, 1955–66), simply the game's best pitcher from 1962 to '66, when he led the National League in earned run average five times and won three Cy Young Awards.

➤ **Bob Gibson** (St. Louis Cardinals, 1959–75), one of baseball's most overpowering pitchers, who nine times struck out 200 or more hitters in a season.

➤ **Tom Seaver** (1967–86), best-known as a Met but also a teammate of mine with the Reds from 1977 to '82, who won 311 games in his 20-year career.

➤ **Nolan Ryan** (1966–93), the game's all-time leader in strikeouts (5,714) and no-hitters (seven) for the New York Mets, California Angels, Houston Astros, and Texas Rangers.

➤ **Steve Carlton** (1965–88), who has the most strikeouts (4,136, mostly with the Cardinals and Phillies) of any left-hander.

Extra Innings

Baseball requires very specific skills, but a few athletes were stars in other sports and were also gifted enough to make it to the major leagues. Two of the more notable ones are recent baseball/football standouts: Bo Jackson, a slugging outfielder and powerful running back in the late 1980s; and Deion Sanders, a fleet outfielder and explosive cornerback and return man in the early 1990s. Pro basketball legend Michael Jordan made headlines when he tried baseball in 1994, but he never made it to the majors. Two-sport success is nothing new, by the way: Ed (Batty) Abbattichio, a second baseman/fullback, first did it in the late 1800s.

The Best Teams of All Time

A pretty good measure of quality for a team is how many games it wins. But a great regular-season record isn't enough; you also have to win the World Series to qualify as one of the best teams of all time. The following table lists the World Series winners that won the highest percentage of their games in the regular season. (It's better to use winning percentage than total victories because the length of the season has varied through the years.) It's interesting to note that of the six teams with the best all-time regular-season winning percentages since 1903 (the year the first World Series was played), three lost the Series (the 1906 Chicago Cubs, the 1954 Cleveland Indians, and the 1931 Philadelphia Athletics).

Best Regular–Season Winning Percentages among World Series Winners

Team	Wins	Losses	Pct.
1909 Pittsburgh Pirates	110	42	.724
1927 New York Yankees	110	44	.714
1907 Chicago Cubs	107	45	.704
1998 New York Yankees	114	48	.704
1939 New York Yankees	106	45	.702

Note: In 1902, the year before the first World Series, the Pittsburgh Pirates had a 103–36 (.741) record.

The 1927 Yankees are widely regarded as the greatest baseball team of all time. They led the American League from wire to wire, finished in front by an unprecedented 19 games, and swept the Pirates in four straight games in the World Series. Babe Ruth led a powerful offense with a .356 batting average, 164 runs batted in, and a record-smashing 60 home runs—more than any other *team* in the league. Other big bats included Lou Gehrig (who had a league-record 175 runs batted in), Bob Meusel, Tony Lazzeri, and Earle Combs. The pitching staff, led by Waite Hoyt, Wilcy Moore, Herb Pennock, and Urban Shocker (each of whom won at least 18 games), had the league's lowest earned run average.

The 1961 Yankees (109–53), who hit a major league record 240 home runs, led by Roger Maris' individual mark of 61, are another club that comes up when all-time great teams are discussed. Mickey Mantle hit 54 homers that year, and four other Yankees (Bill Skowron, Yogi Berra, Elston Howard, and Johnny Blanchard) had 20 or more. All those home runs really made a difference in how this team was regarded.

I think the Cincinnati Reds teams that I played on in the mid-1970s deserve mention here as well. We had a terrific lineup, with guys like Joe Morgan, Pete Rose, Tony Perez, George Foster, Ken Griffey Sr., and myself; a solid starting pitching staff with Don Gullett, Gary Nolan, and Jack Billingham; and a terrific bullpen led by Rawly Eastwick and Will McEnaney. We were 108–54 in '75 and 102–60 in '76, and we won the World Series both years.

Along with the thrilling home run race between St. Louis Cardinal Mark McGwire and Chicago Cub Sammy Sosa, the biggest story in 1998 was the New York Yankees, who compiled a regular-season record of 114–48. Of the 10 teams with the highest winning percentages in history, only the '98 Yankees made the list *after* the game was integrated in 1947, when baseball finally included all of its greatest players. The Yankees' stellar pitching staff featured 20-game winner David Cone and David Wells, who threw the 15th perfect game in major league history on May 17. They might not have had a bona fide superstar, but they got offensive contributions from the top to the bottom of the batting order—and they did have 1998 American League batting champion Bernie Williams. With the 162-game season and the two additional playoff rounds, the Yankees won more games (125 total) than any team in history.

And the Winner Is...

Along with the team honors of making the playoffs and competing for a pennant and possibly a world championship, baseball honors individuals for their accomplishments each season in pitching, hitting, fielding, and managing, as well as promising rookies who made a big splash and beloved veterans who made a long trip back from the brink. Some awards are voted on by players, others chosen by a poll of coaches and managers, but most are voted on by the Baseball Writers Association of America, the BBWAA.

This has its pros and cons. In 1941, Ted Williams hit .406 and led the American League in home runs, slugging percentage, and runs scored—and didn't win the American League Most Valuable Player Award. The guy who did win, Joe DiMaggio, was certainly deserving, but Williams was hampered by the fact that one Boston sportswriter who voted for the award didn't even include Williams in his top 10—he omitted Williams from his ballot because he didn't like Williams personally. I think that guy should have had his voting rights revoked; the awards shouldn't be a popularity contest. A similar thing happened in 1995 when Albert Belle of the Cleveland Indians became the first man ever to hit 50 home runs and 50 doubles in a season but failed to win the MVP award, largely because of his surly attitude toward writers.

So as we take a look at the major individual awards for which baseball players compete each season, keep in mind that any time voting is involved, it's subjective and there's always plenty of room for debate.

➤ **Most Valuable Player (MVP)** Although this award was first given to American Leaguer George Sisler in 1922, it wasn't until 1931 that each league began regularly having its Most Valuable Player chosen by the BBWAA. Usually, the award is won by the position player or everyday player (though a few pitchers, like Detroit's Hal Newhouser, have won it) deemed to have made the most significant contribution to his team. So the award usually goes to a player from a good team. In some cases, though, a player on a bad team will have such impressive individual stats that he'll win the award anyway. The MVP is really the most prestigious award a player can win for a season. I was fortunate enough to win it twice, and I can tell you that it's a tremendous honor to be recognized as the best in your league.

There are also MVP awards given each year for the All-Star Game, League Championship Series, and World Series. Appendix D provides a complete list of all the MVP winners.

➤ **Cy Young** The BBWAA also votes to select the best pitcher in each league and awards him the Cy Young Award. It usually goes to a starting pitcher, but recently, as managers have begun to depend more and more on their bullpens, relievers have occasionally taken home the trophy. Appendix D lists all the Cy Young winners.

➤ **Rookie of the Year**   The Rookie of the Year Award, also voted on by the BBWAA, goes to the best first-year player in each league, whether he's a pitcher or a hitter. Players with very limited major league experience in previous seasons can still qualify as rookies in their first full year. That's how I won the award in 1968 even though I had played in 26 games the previous year. The complete list of Rookies of the Year is in Appendix D.

➤ **Gold Glove**   Rawlings, a major manufacturer of baseball gloves, hands out a Gold Glove award to the one player at each position (three outfielders are chosen) deemed to be the best fielder in each league. The awards, which were first given out in 1957, are voted on by coaches and managers. I'm proud to say that I won 10 Gold Gloves in my career, the most of any catcher.

➤ **Manager of the Year**   The BBWAA votes on the top skipper in each league. The Manager of the Year Award usually goes to the manager of a team that performed significantly better than expected.

➤ **Silver Slugger**   *The Sporting News* hands out the Silver Slugger awards to the best hitter at each position in each league, based on a poll of coaches and managers. Like the Gold Gloves, three outfielders are selected.

➤ **Comeback Player of the Year**   The Comeback Player of the Year award, handed out by *The Sporting News*, goes to the player in each league who has best bounced back, either from injury or just a bad season.

The Hall of Fame

The greatest honor that can be bestowed upon a professional baseball player is enshrinement in the Baseball Hall of Fame in Cooperstown, N.Y. As of 1998, out of the tens of thousands of individuals who have served the game, there were a total of just 237 men—former major league and Negro league players, managers, executives, and umpires—who had earned this great honor. Of the thousands of men who have played in the major leagues over the past 100-plus years, only 1 percent have a plaque in Cooperstown. When I received mine in 1989, it was one of the greatest days of my life.

The members of the Hall of Fame are elected by the BBWAA and specially appointed committees, such as the Veterans Committee and the now-defunct Committee on the Negro Leagues. Appendix D lists all the members of the Hall of Fame.

From the Bench

Baseball people are very superstitious, especially when a no-hitter is on the line. If a teammate is throwing a no-hitter, you don't want to jinx it by saying something about it, so many players won't talk to a pitcher or go near him in the dugout while his no-hitter is in progress. Often, even the TV announcers, especially the local ones, go out of their way to avoid referring to a developing no-hitter.

This is where every baseball player dreams of being immortalized: the National Baseball Hall of Fame and Museum in Cooperstown, N.Y.

Perfect Games

For a pitcher, the ultimate single-game achievement is a *perfect game*. That means simply that a pitcher started the game, he pitched a full nine innings (or more, if the game went extra innings), his team won the game, and he retired every hitter he faced. Twenty-seven up, 27 down—no hits, no walks, no errors, no hit batsmen, no baserunners—it doesn't get any better than that. But how hard is it to do? Well, in more than a century of major league baseball, it has been accomplished only 15 times—and not always by Hall of Fame-caliber pitchers (see the following table). The list of all-time greats who never threw a perfect game includes Christy Mathewson, Walter Johnson, Bob Feller, Warren Spahn, Whitey Ford, Bob Gibson, Steve Carlton, Jim Palmer, Nolan Ryan, and Tom Seaver.

Pitcher, Team	Opponent	Score	Date
John Richmond, Worcester Brown Stockings*	Blues*	1–0	June 12, 1880
Monte Ward**, Providence Grays*	Bisons*	5–0	June 17, 1880
Cy Young**, Boston Pilgrims	Athletics	3–0	May 5, 1904
Addie Joss**, Cleveland Naps	White Sox	1–0	October 2, 1908
Charlie Robertson, Chicago White Sox	Tigers	2–0	April 30, 1922
Don Larsen, New York Yankees	Dodgers	2–0	October 8, 1956 (World Series game)
Jim Bunning**, Philadelphia Phillies	Mets	6–0	June, 21, 1964

Pitcher, Team	Opponent	Score	Date
Sandy Koufax**, Los Angeles Dodgers	Cubs	1–0	September 9, 1965
Catfish Hunter**, Oakland Athletics	Twins	4–0	May 8, 1968
Len Barker, Cleveland Indians	Blue Jays	3–0	May 15, 1981
Mike Witt, California Angels	Rangers	1–0	September 30, 1984
Tom Browning, Cincinnati Reds	Dodgers	1–0	September 16, 1988
Dennis Martinez, Montreal Expos	Dodgers	2–0	July 28, 1991
Kenny Rogers, Texas Rangers	Angels	4–0	July 28, 1994
David Wells, New York Yankees	Twins	4–0	May 17, 1998

* Defunct National League teams: Worcester Brown Stockings, Cleveland Blues, Providence Grays, and Buffalo Bisons

** Hall of Famer (players are eligible five years after retirement)

Extra Innings

A lot has changed in the major leagues over the course of the century, but a perfect game has always been a big deal. Cy Young once recalled the aftermath of his 1904 masterpiece in Boston's Huntington Avenue Grounds, one of his three no-hitters:

"When the game was finished it looked like all the fans came down on the field and tried to shake my hand. One gray-haired fellow jumped the fence back of third and shoved a bill into my hand. It was five dollars."

No-Hitters

The next best thing for a pitcher, after a perfect game, is a no-hitter. It's similar to a perfect game, except that instead of not allowing a single base runner, a pitcher who threw a no-hitter did just that: allowed no hits. But he allowed at least one runner to reach base, probably via a walk, an error, or a hit batsman. All perfect games are also no-hitters, but a no-hitter is not a perfect game. See the difference?

It seems like a minor distinction, but it makes no-hitters much more common than perfect games. There have been more than 200 no-hitters in major league history. But

Catching On

A **perfect game** is a complete game victory in which a pitcher retires every hitter he faces (i.e., he does not allow a single baserunner). A **no-hitter** is a complete game victory in which a pitcher does not allow a single hit (i.e., there may have been batters who reached base via a walk or an error).

don't get the wrong idea—a no-hitter is a tremendous, extremely rare accomplishment, and you should consider yourself lucky if you ever have the opportunity to watch one, especially at the ballpark.

I caught one no-hitter in my career—from Jim Maloney. It was April 30, 1969, at Crosley Field in Cincinnati, against the Astros. Maloney threw the ball very hard, about 94 or 95 miles an hour, had one of the best curve balls, about 89 or 90 miles an hour, and had a great slider. I mean just *nasty*. That game was so intense. You knew what was on the board, and it was a 1–0 game to boot. Maloney was just overpowering that night. We wanted so badly for him to become a part of history, and I knew that, as the catcher, I would become a part of history, too. The amazing thing was, after Maloney threw his no-hitter against the Astros, Houston's Don Wilson came back the next night and threw one against us.

Extra Innings

Nolan Ryan is, quite simply, the master of the no-hitter. Ryan threw a major league-record seven no-hitters in his career (Sandy Koufax is second all-time with four), including one on May 1, 1991, against the Toronto Blue Jays, at the age of 44. However, Ryan never threw a perfect game.

Triple Crowns

For a hitter, the ultimate accomplishment in the course of a season is to win the *triple crown*. To earn that distinction, all you have to do is lead your league in home runs, runs batted in, and batting average. Sound easy? Well, in more than 100 years of major league baseball, only 14 players have done it (see the following table). Hall of Famers Babe Ruth, Joe DiMaggio, Willie Mays, Stan Musial, and Hank Aaron have a grand total of *zero* triple crowns among them. Only two players, Rogers Hornsby and Ted Williams, have done it more than once. And, through the 1998 season, it hasn't happened in the American League in 31 years, and in the NL in *61 years*.

Catching On

A player who leads his league in home runs, runs batted in, and batting average wins the **triple crown**. It's only been done by 14 players in history, and only Rogers Hornsby and Ted Williams have done it twice.

Triple Crown Winners in Major League History

National Leaguers, Year, Team	HRs	RBIs	BA
Paul Hines, 1878 Grays*	4	50	.358
Hugh Duffy, 1894 Beaneaters**	18	145	.438
Heinie Zimmerman, 1912 Cubs	14	103	.372
Rogers Hornsby, 1922 Cardinals	42	152	.401
Rogers Hornsby, 1925 Cardinals	39	143	.403
Chuck Klein, 1933 Phillies	28	120	.368
Joe Medwick, 1937 Cardinals	31	154	.374

* Providence Grays (defunct)
** Boston Beaneaters (now Atlanta Braves)

American Leaguers, Year, Team	HRs	RBIs	BA
Nap Lajoie, 1901 Athletics	14	125	.422
Ty Cobb, 1909 Tigers	9	115	.377
Jimmie Foxx, 1933 Athletics	48	163	.356
Lou Gehrig 1934 Yankees	49	165	.363
Ted Williams, 1942 Red Sox	36	137	.356
Ted Williams, 1947 Red Sox	32	114	.343
Mickey Mantle, 1956 Yankees	52	130	.353
Frank Robinson, 1966 Orioles	49	122	.316
Carl Yastrzemski, 1967 Red Sox	44	121	.326

Rogers Hornsby, the legendary second baseman of the Cardinals (and later four other teams), won seven National League batting titles in the 1920s and is second only to Ty Cobb in lifetime batting average (.358). The Rajah, as he was known, was also the only NL player in this century to hit .400 or better three times (1922, '24, and '25) and win two triple crowns (1922 and '25).

Triple Plays

A *triple play* occurs when three outs are made on the same play. For example, with runners on first and second and none out, you might have a hot smash hit to the second baseman, who catches it for one out, tags the runner off first base for the second out, and flips to the shortstop covering second base to get the other runner for the third out.

Much like hitting for the cycle, a triple play is something of a freak occurrence. But it happens less frequently, only a handful of times a season. The all-time record for triple plays in a season by a team is three (held by six teams).

Catching On

A **triple play** occurs when three outs are made on the same play.

An unassisted triple play is one in which all three outs are made by the same player. (Say that in the example above, the second baseman steps on second base himself; he would then have made an unassisted triple play.) Unassisted triple plays are extremely rare; there have been only 10 in major league history, and only one ever in a post-season game (see table). The next table shows how rare an unassisted triple play is relative to some other notable single-game achievements.

Unassisted Triple Plays in Major League History

Date	Player, Position, Team	Opposing Team
July 19, 1909	Neal Ball, SS, Naps	Red Sox
Oct. 10, 1920*	Bill Wambsganss, 2B, Indians	Dodgers
Sept. 14, 1923	George Burns, 1B, Red Sox	Indians
Oct. 6, 1923	Ernie Padgett, SS, Braves	Phillies
May 7, 1925	Glenn Wright, SS, Pirates	Cardinals
May 30, 1927	Jimmy Cooney, SS, Cubs	Pirates
May 31, 1927	Johnny Neun, 1B, Tigers	Indians
July 29, 1968	Ron Hansen, SS, Senators	Indians
Sept. 23, 1992	Mickey Morandini, 2B, Phillies	Pirates
July 8, 1994	John Valentin, SS, Red Sox	Mariners

* World Series

Some of the Major Leagues' Rarest Individual Feats

Feat	No. of Times Accomplished
Unassisted triple plays	10
Two grand slams in one game	9
Four-homer games	12
Perfect games	15

The Game's Most Unbreakable Records

It's often said that records are made to be broken. But a few baseball records aren't likely to fall anytime soon. Some are safe because they were set in an era that featured a livelier baseball, while others won't fall because players are used differently now than in the days when the records were set. Here are the single-season marks (post-1900) that are least likely to be topped any time soon:

➤ **Joe DiMaggio's 56-game hitting streak in 1941**   Since DiMaggio set the record in '41, nobody has come closer than my Cincinnati Reds teammate, Pete Rose, who hit in 44 straight games in 1978. If a player ever approached DiMaggio's streak—and in this era of increasingly specialized relief pitching, that's unlikely—the intense media pressure and scrutiny would make it almost impossible for him to break the record.

➤ **Hack Wilson's 190 RBIs in 1930**   Wilson's mark was set in the live-ball era. Since 1938, no player has come within 30 RBIs of the record.

➤ **Rogers Hornsby's .424 average in 1924** Another live-ball record that should stand forever. Since Ted Williams' .406 average in 1941, no player has hit better than .394.

➤ **Owen Wilson's 36 triples in 1912** It's been nearly 75 years since anybody has even hit as many as 25 triples. Earl Webb's mark of 67 doubles in 1931 looks pretty unapproachable, too.

➤ **Jack Chesbro's 41 wins in 1904** Chesbro pitched in an era when it was standard practice to send your best pitcher to the mound as often as possible. (He started a record 51 games—and completed a record 48—for the Yankees in '04.) Now, every team uses a five-man rotation, meaning that no starting pitcher throws more often than every fifth day. That translates into no more than 33 starts a year, so winning 31 games, let alone 41, is almost impossible. The same rationale means that Ed Walsh's 464 innings in 1908 and Vic Willis's 29 losses in 1905 will both almost certainly stand forever.

➤ **Johnny Vander Meer's Two Consecutive No-Hitters in 1938** Considering that a pitcher would have to throw three in a row to break it, I'd say that Vander Meer's mark is pretty safe.

➤ **Nolan Ryan's 383 strikeouts in 1973** Like Chesbro's mark, this will be tough to break because pitchers throw fewer innings these days. Ryan threw 326 innings in 1973, and averaged 10.6 strikeouts per nine innings. Several pitchers have bettered that number lately, but none have pitched enough innings to challenge Ryan's total of 383 whiffs. Bob Feller's mark of 208 walks in 1938 is similarly unassailable.

➤ **Rickey Henderson's 130 steals in 1982** Henderson's mark will be tough to top because fewer runners today have a green light to run any time they want. With home run totals soaring, most managers don't want to risk running themselves out of an inning, so they only call for steals in crucial stages of the game. Which means that Henderson's career total of 1,297 steals (through the end of the 1998 season) will also be tough to top.

➤ **Babe Ruth's .847 slugging percentage in 1920** Consider this: Mark McGwire hit 70 homers in 1998, and his slugging percentage was just .752. Ruth's career mark of .690 looks pretty safe, too—the next closest on the all-time list is Ted Williams at .634.

Speaking of which, there are also several career records that are likely to stand forever:

➤ **Cy Young's 511 wins** Look at it this way: Baseball's best pitcher, Greg Maddux, has averaged 18 wins over the past 10 seasons. At that rate, he'd have to pitch 18 and a half more seasons to catch Young. Young's streak of 16 consecutive 20-win seasons is also safe, as are his career totals of 7,377 innings, 751 complete games, and 313 losses.

➤ **Cal Ripken Jr.'s 2,632 consecutive games played**   The earliest this record could possibly be broken is 2112. Don't bet on it happening then—or ever.

➤ **Walter Johnson's 110 shutouts**   Even if a pitcher today is good enough to pitch eight scoreless innings, there's a good chance that his manager will pull him in the ninth and bring in the closer.

➤ **Ty Cobb's streak of hitting .300 in 23 consecutive seasons**   Through the 1998 season, Tony Gwynn had done it 16 times in a row. But Gwynn, who turns 39 in 1999, would have to keep hitting .300 till age 46 to pass Cobb. And if Gwynn can't break it, no one will. Cobb also holds the record for stealing home, which he did 50 times. The most by an active player as of 1998 was 10.

➤ **Sam Crawford's 312 triples**   No active player has more than 150 three-baggers.

➤ **Ed Walsh's 1.82 ERA**   These days it's pretty rare for a pitcher to even top this mark for one season, much less for an entire career.

➤ **Nolan Ryan's 5,714 strikeouts**   You may as well throw in his 2,795 walks as well. Ryan was an unbelievable workhorse who could throw close to 100 mph for 300 innings a year. They broke the mold when they made him.

Two men whose places in history are secure: Cy Young (left) and Cal Ripken Jr.

The Best Pennant Races of All Time

Few things in baseball are more exciting than the late-summer drama of two or more teams battling for a league title (although these days they're vying for division titles and wild card spots). In baseball, the fight down the stretch between teams for a league or division title is known as a *pennant race*. And there have been some thrillers in major league history. These are my picks for the all-time best:

➤ **1951 National League**   The Brooklyn Dodgers led the New York Giants by 13$\frac{1}{2}$ games on August 12, but the Giants went 39–8 down the stretch to finish in a dead heat with the Dodgers. A three-game series was played to break the tie, and after the teams split the first two, Bobby Thomson's dramatic three-run homer in the bottom of the ninth won the pennant for the Giants.

➤ **1978 American League East**   The Yankees were 14 games behind the Boston Red Sox on July 17, but rallied to first place after Bob Lemon replaced Billy Martin as manager. The Red Sox, who fell three games behind in mid-September, won 12 of their last 14 to force a tie. New York then won a thrilling one-game playoff, 5–4, thanks to a memorable home run by Bucky Dent.

Catching On

A late-season, down-to-the-wire battle between two or more teams for a division title (or in the old days, a league title) is known as a **pennant race**.

Extra Innings

Merkle's Boner happened like this: two outs, bottom of the ninth, the Polo Grounds. The Giants were up, Fred Merkle on first, Moose McCormick on third. Giant shortstop Al Bridwell hit a single and McCormick reached home. When Merkle saw the winning run score and Giant fans start pouring onto the field, he assumed the game was over and ran for the clubhouse—without touching second base. Knowing the play wasn't over until Merkle touched second, and that a force out would cancel the run, Cub second baseman Johnny Evers retrieved the ball and stomped on second base. After a week's deliberation, league president Harry C. Pulliam decided in the Cubs' favor: The game was declared a tie, to be replayed if the teams were tied at the season's end.

➤ **1908 National League**   The race went down to the season's final day: a replay of the September 23 game between the Chicago Cubs and New York Giants. That game had ended in a 1–1 tie because of Giant rookie Fred Merkle's infamous baserunning blunder. The Cubs won the replayed game, 4–2, to take the pennant, and the "Merkle Boner" was immortalized in baseball lore. (The Cubs won the World Series in five games over the Detroit Tigers—but haven't won one since.)

➤ **1914 National League**   The Boston Braves trailed the Giants by 15 games on July 4 (and were still in last place on July 19), but won 34 of their final 44 games to take over first place and pull off the greatest come-from-behind season in major-league history. Boston wound up 10$\frac{1}{2}$ games in front.

The Best Games of All Time

There have been so many great games in major league history that a list of the best would fill an entire book. But here are five of the most memorable:

➤ **The Shot Heard 'Round the World, October 3, 1951**   In the third and decisive National League playoff game, Bobby Thomson's three-run homer in the ninth inning capped an improbable Giants' rally to beat the Dodgers 5–4.

➤ **Mazeroski's Series Winner, October 13, 1960**
In the most dramatic finish in World Series history, Bill Mazeroski homered in the bottom of the ninth inning of Game 7 to lift the Pirates over the Yankees, 10–9—the first time a World Series ever ended with a home run.

➤ **Larsen's Perfection, October 8, 1956**   With the World Series tied at two games apiece, Don Larsen—who had been hit hard and taken out in the second inning of Game 2—pitched the only perfect game in Series history, mowing down the Dodgers with just 97 pitches.

➤ **Haddix's Heartbreaker, May 26, 1959**
Harvey Haddix of the Pirates threw 12 perfect innings against the Milwaukee Braves, only to lose 1–0 on a throwing error, a walk, and a Joe Adcock double. Milwaukee's Lew Burdette allowed 12 hits but no runs in 13 innings to earn the victory.

Warning Track

The sports memorabilia craze can get out of hand sometimes—and it isn't just a recent trend. After he hit his World Series-winning home run at Pittsburgh's Forbes Field in 1960, Bill Mazeroski had his glove and cap stolen in the postgame melee, and as he walked from the clubhouse door to his car, five different fans tried to sell him a baseball, each claiming that theirs was his homer ball.

One of the most enduring images in baseball history: Catcher Yogi Berra jumping into Don Larsen's arms after Larsen's perfect game in the 1956 World Series.

➤ **A Double-No-Hitter, May 2, 1917** Jim (Hippo) Vaughn of the Cubs and Fred Toney of the Reds hooked up in what was probably the greatest pitcher's duel of all time. Both allowed no hits for nine innings, before the Reds broke through to score a run in the 10th. (That run was driven in by Jim Thorpe.)

Extra Innings

Jim Thorpe, the football great and 1912 Olympic decathlon gold medalist, was also a major league baseball player. Thorpe, who was at one time known as "the world's greatest athlete," was an outfielder who played in parts of six seasons (1913–19) for the New York Giants, Cincinnati Reds, and Boston Braves. He was not a hit, however, compiling just a .252 career batting average.

The Best World Series

I played in the greatest World Series—1975—so I may be a little biased, but these are my picks for the five best of all time:

➤ **1975** Our Cincinnati Reds defeated the Boston Red Sox in seven thrilling games. The Series featured a memorable 12th-inning home run by Boston's Carlton Fisk in Game 6 that kept the Red Sox alive.

Carlton Fisk launches his dramatic home run off Pat Darcy that won Game 6 of the 1975 World Series (that's me behind the plate), and is then greeted by a jubilant group of Red Sox teammates. The mood in our dugout was, to say the least, a bit less celebratory.

➤ **1968** After St. Louis' Bob Gibson struck out 17 in Game 1 and won Game 4 to put the Cardinals up 3–1, the Tigers looked overmatched—it seemed that Gibson could win it by himself. But Detroit came back to win the Series in seven games.

➤ **1952** The New York Yankees beat the Brooklyn Dodgers in Game 7 to win their fourth straight championship in a classic Subway Series (as inter-New York City World Series are known) in which only one game was decided by more than two runs.

➤ **1912** The Red Sox beat the Giants four games to three, in what was the first Series ever decided on the last pitch. Boston scored the championship-winning run in the 10th inning of the final game, on a sacrifice fly by Larry Gardner, after a costly error by Giants center fielder Fred Snodgrass.

➤ **1924** The Washington Senators, led by rookie manager Bucky Harris, defeated the Giants, with John McGraw at the helm in his ninth Series. Walter Johnson pitched four scoreless innings of relief in Game 7 to earn the victory, which came when Earl McNeely's 12th-inning grounder took a bad hop over third baseman Fred Lindstrom's head.

Other Memorable Moments

By now you get the point that baseball history features a nearly infinite number of memorable moments. I've covered many of the major highlights above, but here are five more you should know:

➤ **Ruth's Called Shot** The 1932 World Series wasn't very dramatic—the Yankees swept the Cubs in four games—except for the mystique surrounding Babe Ruth fabled "called shot," his fifth-inning home run off Charlie Root that broke a 4–4 tie in Game 3. Some observers claimed that after taking two strikes, Ruth pointed to the center-field bleachers. But whether he was reminding the Cub bench jockeys that he still had one strike left, or he was really telling everyone that he was about to hit a homer to center—which he did on the next pitch—is a question for the ages.

Extra Innings

The legend of Babe Ruth's "called shot" in the 1932 World Series is widely disputed. Cubs third-base coach Woody English, along with pitcher Charlie Root, second baseman Billy Herman, and shortstop Billy Jurges, insist that Ruth was merely gesturing toward the Chicago dugout. "He held two fingers up above his head and said that's only two strikes," English told *Sport* magazine years later. "He didn't point." Most baseball historians believe the legend of the called shot was created by sensationalistic New York sportswriters.

➤ **Back-to-Back No-Hitters** In 1938 Johnny Vander Meer of the Reds accomplished something that no other pitcher in baseball history has ever done: He threw two consecutive no-hitters. The first beat the Boston Braves, 3–0, on June 11 and the second blanked the Brooklyn Dodgers, 6–0, four days later. More amazing than the feat itself is that Vander Meer has a career record of 119–121.

➤ **The Homer in the Gloamin':** The Cubs trailed the first-place Pirates by half a game when the two teams tangled on September 28, 1938, at Chicago's Wrigley Field. With the game tied, 5–5, in the ninth inning and darkness gathering (remember, this was more than 50 years before lights were installed at Wrigley), both teams knew the game would be called and declared a draw before it went to extra innings. But with two outs in the bottom of the ninth and two strikes on him, Cubs catcher Gabby Hartnett hit a famous home run into the darkening skies in left. Chicago took over first place and won the pennant, but lost the World Series to the Yankees in four straight.

➤ **Maris' 61 in '61** Roger Maris was disliked by many people in 1961. Not only was he making a run at the beloved Babe Ruth's single-season home run record of 60, he was competing for that record with his more popular Yankee teammate, Mickey Mantle. I remember every time I got a newspaper or heard a report on TV or the radio, and found out that Mantle hit one and so did Maris, I was thinking, "Please don't beat Mickey. He's the greatest!" Mickey would have beaten Ruth's record, but he was hampered by injuries and wound up with a career-best 54 homers. When he hit his 50th to pass Lou Gehrig's season-high, he told Maris, "I've caught my man, now you go get yours." I was 13 years old at the time and it meant a lot to me that Mickey was saying, "I'm not going to be able to reach it, you go after it. I'm pulling for you." It was a team thing. And Maris, as every baseball fan knows, hit No. 61 on the final day of the season.

One of the most historic swings of all time: In Yankee Stadium, Roger Maris connects for his record-breaking 61st home run of the season on Oct. 1, 1961, off Boston's Tracy Stallard.

Talkin' Baseball

"I don't want them to forget Ruth. I just want them to remember me!"

—Hank Aaron, as he closed in on Ruth's home run record

➤ **Hammerin' Hank Passes the Babe** Another memorable moment based on surpassing a record of Babe Ruth's was the breaking of the Babe's career home run record of 714. On April 8, 1974, in front of a standing-room-only crowd of 53,775 at Atlanta Stadium and a national television audience, Hank Aaron of the Braves clubbed homer No. 715, a shot over the left field wall off Al Downing of the Los Angeles Dodgers. Aaron finished his career in 1976 with 755 round-trippers; only he and the Babe have more than 700 career home runs. Willie Mays is third with 660.

Johnny's Most Memorable Moments from His Career

What were my most memorable moments as a player? Well, the first would have to be getting selected to play in the All-Star Game in 1968 as a 20-year-old rookie. (Even though I had played in some games late in the '67 season, I was still officially considered a rookie in '68.) Jerry Grote of the Mets was chosen as the starting catcher, but I was selected as a reserve.

I remember going into the locker room at the Astrodome in Houston, where the All-Star Game was played that year, and just sitting there at my locker. There's a rookie rule in baseball—or at least there was back then—that says you stay out of the way of the veterans. Here comes Bob Gibson. There goes Willie McCovey. There's Juan Marichal, Hank Aaron, Roberto Clemente. I'm just watching these guys when Willie Mays walks across the room, stops in front of my locker, and says, "You should have been the starting catcher."

That meant everything to me. I didn't even care if I played in the game—Willie Mays knew who I was! Obviously I respected Willie to begin with, but the fact that he made me feel like a major leaguer gave me an even greater admiration for him. I got to catch the ninth inning of that game, although I didn't get a chance to hit. I wound up being named Rookie of the Year after the season, which was another great honor.

In 1969 I was in the Army Reserves and the All-Star Game was played in Washington, D.C. As it happened, I was in Virginia at the time for two weeks of summer camp. The commanding officer released me to play in the All-Star Game, so I got to go up to Washington, visit the White House, and meet President Nixon. That was such a thrill—me, a kid from a town of 660 people in Oklahoma, in the White House.

The game got rained out, and it didn't look like I was going to be able to play. The Reserves gave me another day, though, and in my first at-bat I hit a home run off of Mel Stottlemyre. In my last at-bat I hit a deep fly to left field that Carl Yastrzemski jumped up over the fence and brought down, taking a home run away from me. (Twenty years later,

Yastrzemski and I wound up being inducted into the Hall of Fame together.) Willie McCovey hit two home runs and was named MVP of the game, as we National Leaguers beat our AL counterparts, 9–3.

Extra Innings

One of my professional baseball highlights came late in my career, when I broke the great Yogi Berra's career record for most home runs by a catcher, with a homer against the Montreal Expos. Yogi sent me a telegram to congratulate me, and it said, "I knew my record would stand until it was broken." I still have that hanging on my wall at home. Since then I've gotten to know Yogi, and he is one of the finest people I've ever known. He epitomizes the class of being a Yankee.

The Reds won the pennant and I was voted National League MVP in 1970 and '72, but we lost the World Series both years, so there was a feeling of unfinished business. That's why I'll always cherish the moment in Game 7 of the '75 Series—after Game 6 was rained out for three straight nights, and then we suffered that heartbreaking, 12-inning loss to tie the Series—when that fly ball finally landed in Cesar Geronimo's glove in center field, giving us our first championship. When I walked into our club-house after the game, I found out what winning really meant. The euphoria was unbelievable. It wasn't just the nine guys on the field who were world champions, it was all 25 players on the team, the five coaches, the manager, the trainer, the club-house guy—we were all going to get rings. We were the world champions and it was something we would have for the rest of our lives.

We came back the next year to sweep the Philadelphia Phillies in three straight to win the National League Championship Series, and then we won the World Series against the Yankees in four straight. I hit two home runs against the Yanks and was named Series MVP. I hadn't had a very good year offensively (my .234 batting average was a career low), so to contribute to the offense and make a difference in that World Series—which, as it turned out, would be my last as a player—was a great feeling.

Talkin' Baseball

"Baseball survives because guys like Clemente play it."

—Jimmy Cannon in the New York *Journal-American*

Of course, one of my greatest moments came in my final year, on September 17, 1983. That was my retirement night at Riverfront Stadium, when my Dad threw out the first pitch before our game against the Astros. The Reds expected a crowd of about 35,000 or 40,000, which was pretty good, because we were averaging around 20,000 or less that year. But when I walked out, through a gate in the outfield wall and onto a red carpet, 55,000 people had come to the game. That meant as much to me as anything in my career—because they came to see Johnny Bench. I hit a home run off of Mike Madden, and I don't think there was a dry eye in the house. It was so special to hear Reds radio announcer Joe Nuxhall's call of that home run—you could tell he was crying. That, in my baseball life, was everything. I played the game the way I was taught, with the greatest respect, and I performed at my best every time. It was gratifying to know all those people recognized that.

That, to me, is baseball at its best. And now that you have a sense of how great this game is, it's time to take a closer look at exactly how it's played.

The Least You Need to Know

➤ Babe Ruth is generally regarded as the greatest player of all time, and the 1927 New York Yankees are generally regarded as the greatest team of all time (but don't be surprised to hear dissenting opinions on both fronts).

➤ There are more great moments and colorful characters in baseball than we have space here to cover, but every fan should at least be familiar with the most memorable of each.

➤ The greatest single-game accomplishment for a pitcher is a perfect game (no runs, no hits, no errors—no batter reaches base); it has only happened 15 times in major league history.

➤ For a hitter, the ultimate accomplishment for a season is winning the triple crown (by leading the league in home runs, runs batted in and batting average); only 14 players in major league history have done it.

Part 2
Get Ready to Take the Field

One of the best things about baseball is walking out onto the field and seeing a giant expanse of green grass. There's also something special about putting on a jersey, hiking up your stirrups, and stepping into a pair of spikes. Once you've done this and grabbed your glove and a ball, you're ready to hit the diamond.

In this part of the book, we'll talk about where baseball is played and what it's played with. I'll explain what all those lines on the field mean, and I'll spin a nice yarn about how baseballs are made. We'll also look at the fashionable side of the sport when we examine uniforms. You'll also learn all about umpires, so you'll know more than just to boo them. And finally, we'll take a look at the major leagues, or "the show," which is the be-all, end-all destination for every kid who ever picked up a bat and ball.

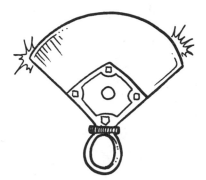

Chapter 5

The Playing Field: This Diamond Is a Gem

In This Chapter

➤ A tour of this field of dreams—and a look outside the lines

➤ Setting the defense

➤ Old school charm vs. modern amenities

➤ Rainouts: Weather or not?

If you could go back in time to a baseball game in the late 1800s when the sport was just becoming popular in America, you'd see a playing field that looks much like it does today. The *diamond*, as a baseball field is called, hasn't changed in shape or size since Alexander Cartwright devised the modern rules for the sport in 1845 (see Chapter 2).

That's one reason baseball has been so stable over the years—and one reason I treasure it so much. There's a continuity to the game, a sameness, that is refreshing. This is directly rooted in the constancy of the playing field, which we'll take a stroll around in this chapter.

The Lay of the Land

Imagine you're sitting in the stands of a major league stadium. You're in the upper deck, looking out at what look like four white squares that form the shape of a diamond in the dirt. Those white squares are called *bases*.

At the bottom of the diamond, closest to you, is home base, more commonly known as *home plate*. Home plate is a five-sided slab of white rubber. It is a 17-inch square with two of the corners removed: one edge is 17 inches long, two adjacent sides are 8^1/$_2$ inches long, and two 12-inch sides form the point of the pentagon. Home plate is set in the ground so it won't interfere with the flight of a pitched ball.

There are boxes drawn with white chalk in the dirt on both sides of home plate. Each is called a *batter's box*, in which the hitter must stand when he is up to bat. If the batter hits the ball while his foot is out of the batter's box, the umpire can call him out. The *umpire's box*, directly behind home plate and the catcher, is where the home-plate umpire stands—or, more accurately, squats—to call balls, strikes, and plays at the plate.

From home plate, look 45 degrees and 90 feet to your right and you'll see first base. Counterclockwise around the diamond are second base, third base, and then you'll come back to home plate. It's 90 feet between every base. The direct line between each base is called the *base path*. All the bases except home plate are 15-inch-square canvas bags set above the ground.

The infield consists of the home plate area, the base paths, and the *pitcher's mound*, which is the circular hill of dirt in the middle. Just beyond the bases where the outfield grass begins is the *outfield*, at the end of which is the *outfield wall*. Some outfield walls are set farther back than others. Major league rules state that the minimum distance from home plate to the nearest outfield wall must be 325 feet.

Now look back at home plate. Home plate is set with its point at the intersection of the two *foul lines* made of white chalk going toward first and third base and extending all the way to the outfield wall. At the end of the line, there's a tall, yellow *foul pole*. Any ball hit outside of the pole is ruled out of bounds and the batter is assessed a strike.

Catching On

The **batter's box** is the area on either side of home plate (defined with white chalk lines in the dirt) within which the hitter must stand during his time at bat.

From the Bench

Early in the game, a hitter may kick at the batter's box line with his cleats. Hitters want to get as far back in the box as possible, to get more time to see the pitch. If the line is obscured, the umpire can't see if his back foot is in the box. This is sort of a baseball tradition, and umpires tend to let hitters do it, although they give rookies a harder time about staying in the box.

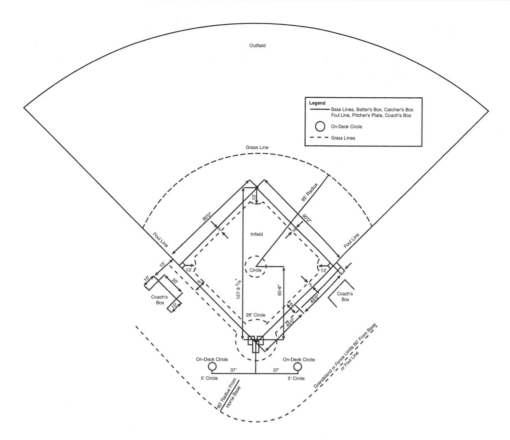

A major league field is laid out according to a tightly defined set of dimensions.

Who Plays Where?

Okay, you're in your seat behind home plate. You've sung "The Star Spangled Banner," you're working on your first hot dog and Coke, and nine players sprint out of the first-base *dugout,* where players sit when they're not on the field, to their respective defensive positions. Behind home plate, you'll notice a player wearing a face mask, a chest protector, and shin guards. This is the *catcher.* Moving counterclockwise along the base paths, you'll see the *first baseman,* just off first base; the *second baseman,* between the first baseman and second base; the *shortstop,* on the other side of second base; and the *third baseman,* between the shortstop and third base. In the middle of the diamond, standing on the dirt mound, is the *pitcher.*

Catching On

The **dugout** is where the manager and coaches sit, and where the players sit when their team's up to bat. The home team's dugout is usually along the first-base line; visitors sit along the third-base line.

75

In the area beyond the diamond—the outfield—from left to right, are the *left fielder*, the *center fielder*, and the *right fielder*. These players are also often referred to generically as *outfielders*, just as the first baseman, second baseman, shortstop, and third baseman are sometimes called *infielders*.

This is the normal positioning of the nine defensive players in the field.

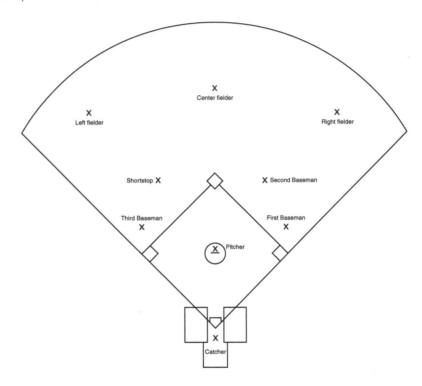

The Pitcher's Mound

The pitcher's mound rises 10 inches above the level of home plate. On top of the pitcher's mound is a rectangular strip of white rubber called the *pitching rubber,* or pitcher's plate. Like home plate, it is set in the ground. The pitcher uses the rubber both to help him maintain balance during his pitching motion and to push off from at the point of release to help him improve his velocity. He must have one foot in contact with the rubber at the start of his delivery.

Catching On

The **pitching rubber** is the rectangular (24-by-6-inch) strip of white rubber located 18 inches behind the center of the pitcher's mound.

Over the years, no feature of the playing field has changed more than the pitcher's station. As late as 1880, pitchers hurled from a rectangular box, the forward line of which was only 45 feet from home plate. By 1892, however, with league batting averages plummeting into the .240s, the mound was moved to its present distance of 60 feet, 6 inches from home plate. Although the pitcher is required to release the ball at this distance, the typical hurler finishes with his front foot about 55 feet away from home base—or only five feet farther away from the batter than the forward line had been in 1880.

The mound underwent another dramatic change in 1969, after pitchers had a banner year in 1968. To reduce the pitcher's dominance, the mound was lowered from 15 inches to its present-day height of 10 inches. By reducing the height of the mound, the angle from which the pitchers released the ball wasn't as sharp, making it easier for hitters to see and hit the ball. Not surprisingly, the American League batting average increased by 16 points from 1968 to '69, and the National League's increased by seven points.

Talkin' Baseball

"They're the only ones on the diamond who have high ground. That's symbolic. You know what they tell you in war: Take the high ground first."

—Hall of Fame center fielder Richie Ashburn on pitchers

Extra Innings

A 1986 game between the Los Angeles Dodgers and New York Mets saw a bizarre occurrence involving the pitching rubber. In the second inning of the Dodgers' 4–1 loss, Howard Johnson of the Mets lined a ball straight at the mound. The ball narrowly missed pitcher Bob Welch, caromed off the rubber, and rolled beyond the foul line. According to official baseball Rule 2.00: "A batted ball not touched by a fielder, which hits the pitcher's rubber and rebounds between home and first or between home and third base, is a foul ball." So Johnson's line drive, even though it went right up the middle, was called foul.

The Outfield

The outfield is covered with grass or artificial turf and bounded by the outfield wall. If a batter hits the ball over this wall, it's a home run. If a ball bounces over the wall, the batter is awarded a double, called a *ground-rule double*.

Outfield walls vary in texture and height. Some are made out of brick, others are composed of hard rubber. Some outfield walls, such as the left field wall in Boston's Fenway Park (known as the Green Monster), are exceedingly tall, others are as short as four feet.

In many major league parks a strip of grass lies just at the base of the outfield wall. Next to it is a swath of dirt, about six feet wide. This swath is called the *warning track*. It gets its name because it serves as a warning to outfielders that the wall is approaching. On a deep fly, for example, an outfielder will have his eyes on the ball as he runs toward the wall. The change in surface underfoot tells him that he's approaching the wall. When he arrives at the strip of grass at the wall's base, he knows he's out of running room.

Catching On

The **foul poles** are the two (usually yellow) vertical poles in the outfield (one in left field and one in right) that delineate between fair and foul territory. A ball that lands between the foul poles (or hits one of the poles) is fair (and good for a home run in most ballparks); a ball that falls outside the poles is foul.

Catching On

A **ground-rule double** is a hit on which the ball becomes dead (usually by bouncing into the stands or being touched by a fan), resulting in the batter being given a double.

On each side of the outfield wall are foul poles. In reality, these should be called "fair poles," because when a ball in flight hits one of these poles it is ruled fair and the batter is awarded a home run.

The Coaches' Boxes

On the foul side of both first and third base you'll see two incomplete rectangles, with one long side of the rectangle missing, painted in white on the grass. These are called the coaches' boxes, where the first- and third-base coaches for the batting team stand to advise both the hitter and the runners on base.

The funny thing about the coaches' boxes is that the coaches never seem to stay in them. For example, if a runner is on second and the batter hits a single to the outfield, the runner may have an opportunity to score. As the runner charges for third base, the third-base coach will drift out of the box toward home plate to get a better angle of the unfolding play in the outfield. Assessing the situation, the third-base coach will tell his runner to stop at third (if he thinks he can't beat the fielder's throw), or to proceed home (if he thinks the runner will make it). This is often called giving the runner "the red light" or "the green light."

The other function these coaches often serve is to tell the batter what to do. The third-base coach receives hand signals from the manager in the dugout that are coded instructions for the hitter. The coach then relays these instructions—whether it be to take a pitch, to bunt, or to swing away—to the hitter with more hand signals. Such signals are also used to communicate with base runners.

Extra Innings

The Astrodome in Houston, baseball's first domed stadium, has been home to some strange occurrences. On June 10, 1974, Philadelphia's Mike Schmidt hit a ball off a speaker that was suspended high above the field. The ball landed in shallow center field, giving Schmidt one of the most bizarre singles in baseball history. Similarly, a speaker suspended inside Seattle's Kingdome cost Willie Horton his 300th home run on June 5, 1979.

The On-Deck Circles

In the area between each team's dugout and home plate is a small circular plate in the ground, usually bearing a team insignia. These are called the *on-deck circles*.

The batter up next is on deck. To get ready for his at-bat, he'll loosen up in the on-deck circle. For some batters, the on-deck circle gives them a great vantage point from which to size up the opposing pitcher. You'll often see batters in the on-deck circle pretending to be at bat as the pitcher goes into his windup. The on-deck batter will even swing his bat as the ball crosses the plate, as he works on his timing.

The Fungo Circles

On either side of the field, close to the first- and third-base lines but in foul territory, you will see chalk or dirt circles called *fungo circles,* smaller than the batter's box, where a coach stands during fielding practice to hit ground balls to the infield and fly balls to the outfield. If you get to where you can use the word *fungo*—purely a baseball term, from the lightweight, aluminum fungo bats the coaches use—in a cocktail conversation, then you will have truly arrived as a baseball fan.

Catching On

Fungo is the name of fielding drill in which a coach or player, standing in one of the **fungo circles** (the two circular areas outside the baselines on either side of home plate), throws up a ball and hits ground balls and fly balls (or *hits fungoes*) to fielders with a *fungo bat*—a specially designed bat with a long, thin handle and a short, thick barrel. The practice dates back to the 1860s.

The Dugout

The *dugout* is the covered area where players sit when they're not out on the field. It consists of a long bench—definitely not the most comfortable seat in the ballpark—and houses all the equipment the players use, from bats to gloves to helmets to shin guards. Some newer parks have television sets telecasting what's going on in the bullpen, which helps the manager know if one of his relievers is warmed up and ready to go into the game. There's also a phone in the dugout that the manager can use to call the coach and players in the bullpen.

But what you really need to know about the dugout is that it's where all the strategizing and chess-playing occurs. The manager and his coaching staff make all the important decisions in the dugout, such as whether a pitcher should stay in the game, whether the team should hit-and-run, or whether a particular batter should bunt. The outcome of many games is decided not on the field, but in the dugout.

The Bullpen

Generally located beyond the outfield wall (but sometimes down the lines in foul territory), the *bullpen* is where relief pitchers sit during the game. It consists of a seating area and two mounds where the pitchers can warm up during the game. (Before the game, this is where the starting pitcher takes his warm-up tosses.) The bullpen coach sits here with his pitchers. There are also one or two backup catchers in the bullpen to help warm up the pitchers. When the manager in the dugout wants to get a relief pitcher ready to enter the game, he'll call on the bullpen phone and tell the bullpen coach.

Extra Innings

Relief pitchers are a rare breed. They don't know when or if they're going to play, and they have to endure the boredom of watching 162 games from some *really* bad seats. Sometimes they just go crazy. Bob Stanley, a longtime reliever for the Boston Red Sox, ritually destroyed beachballs with a bullpen rake nearly every night. I've heard of visiting bullpen pitchers burying things in the ground and then unearthing them when they return on their next road trip. Some guys light their teammates' shoes on fire. Other guys like to play poker. Some bullpen natives actually do constructive things with their free time, like grow gardens.

The Clubhouse

Also known as the locker room, the clubhouse is where the players dress and undress before and after games. It consists of locker stalls, couches, showers, an office for the manager, a trainer's room, and other normal things you'd expect to find in a locker room. Clubhouses are not, though, your average gym locker room. They are well-maintained, carpeted spaces where you can always find big buffets of food after the game. The clubhouse is also where the media speaks with the players after the game.

Talkin' Baseball

"The clubhouse is one of the seductions of baseball; it is a place where you don't have to grow up."

—Hall of Fame right fielder Reggie Jackson

The Friendly Confines

Surrounding it all is the atmosphere of the ballpark itself. Yankee Stadium, Fenway Park, Wrigley Field—these places are every bit as legendary as the men who played there. You can enjoy a game on TV or the radio, but to make a trip to the ballpark is to truly savor the baseball experience, whether it's a big league show or your local minor league park. No fan ever tires of walking up the ramp and into the glow of the stadium, with the beautifully manicured brown and green of the playing field spread before you, and the excited buzz of the crowd's anticipation filling the air.

Part of the beauty of baseball is the individual appeal of all the different major and minor league parks. What are the differences?

Outdoors or Indoors?

In terms of how an environment affects the game, there is considerable debate. Some people feel that the ball carries better indoors than outdoors. The theory is that there is no humidity or wind to slow the ball down as it flies through the air. Of course, places like Chicago's Wrigley Field, where the wind is famous for boosting home run totals when it's blowing out, or Coors Field in Denver, where the thin air and low humidity of the Mile High City give the hitters a great advantage, contradict that theory.

Real Grass vs. Artificial Turf

In the 1970s, when a wave of new stadiums were built, artificial turf (sometimes called AstroTurf) became very popular. Bob Howsam, a former general manager of the Reds, went on and on about how appealing artificial turf was. When you walked into a stadium as a fan everything looked beautiful, as if a gardener had just put the finishing touches on it. And as a player you knew that if it was raining before the game, there

Talkin' Baseball

"I don't know, I never smoked AstroTurf."

—Wacky relief pitcher Tug McGraw, when asked if he preferred grass or AstroTurf

was still a chance to play because the artificial turf fields drained so much better. If it rained heavily before a game on grass, it would be like a swampy marsh out there and pretty tough to play.

On artificial turf, the ball bounces truer. On grass the ball will sometimes hit a clump of dirt and take a weird bounce. But artificial turf has a major problem: It's much harder on the legs and knees of the players. Many careers have been shortened because of the "concrete carpet." The trend now is to go back to grass fields, which I think is nice because it moves the game closer to its pastoral roots.

Groundskeepers: Baseball's Unsung Heroes

Every ballpark has a crew of about 15 people responsible for the maintenance and upkeep of the field. These people are called the *grounds crew*. The person in charge is the *head groundskeeper*, a full-time stadium employee who oversees the care of the field. During games, the grounds crew comes out onto the field between certain innings and rakes the infield. At New York's Yankee Stadium, for example, the grounds crew rakes the dirt of the infield in the middle of the game. This is probably baseball's most colorful grounds crew—so colorful, in fact, that they lead the crowd in singing "YMCA" by the Village People as they rake.

Managers often ask the grounds crew to tailor the field to the home team's strengths and weaknesses. If a visiting team has an accomplished bunter, the grounds crew can build up the dirt along the infield foul lines so that a slow roller is funneled into foul territory. Artificial surfaces can be manipulated by pulling up a seam in the carpet and padding the proper places. The grounds crew can water down the base paths, making it harder to steal; replace the dirt in front of home plate with soft sand, to turn hard-hit choppers into weak ground balls; or let the infield grass grow longer, to slow down the grounders that their sinker-ball pitcher gives up. These practices may not seem to be in the spirit of fairness, but the tradition of "getting that extra little edge" is as old as the game itself.

The grounds crew's most important responsibility is to cover the infield with a tarp when the game is delayed because of rain—or sleet or snow. During the game, the tarp is rolled up in foul territory. Once the umpire decides that it has become too dangerous to play because of inclement weather, the crew will run onto the field and unfurl the tarp.

Rain Delays and Other Weather Hazards

Sometimes Mother Nature doesn't agree with the scheduling of major league baseball games and throws rain—or even snow—at us. But who decides what's playable what isn't? The answer is more complicated than you think.

The rules say that if the weather conditions are hazardous, the home team shall be the sole judge as to whether a game shall be started. This applies to all games except the second game of a doubleheader, when the responsibility falls to the chief umpire. If the game is already underway, the chief umpire decides if it can continue. This is logical because if the manager of the home team were to make the call, his decision would be influenced by the score of the game. (Once the team that is trailing has batted five times, the game is official.) If an umpire does delay the game, he can't *call* the game until at least 30 minutes after he has suspended play, but the suspension can continue as long as there is any chance to resume play.

One of the worst things for both a fan and a ballplayer is a rain delay. The fans have to scurry for cover, get out their rain gear, or just call it a night and risk missing the rest of the game, if it's played. The players have to wait around, sometimes for hours at a time, just trying to keep busy.

Extra Innings

One of the longest rain delays ever took place on July 30, 1988, when the Philadelphia Phillies and the New York Mets endured two delays totaling 3 hours, 25 minutes. The delay occurred in the second inning, and when the game was restarted, it was 11:26 p.m. The crowd of 34,192 had dwindled to a few hundred by the time the game ended at 2:12 a.m. Playing games late into the night is sometimes the only way they'll ever get played. "My first concern is to get the game played," said Frank Pulli, chief of the umpiring crew that worked that game. "I can't really be concerned with the inconvenience to the players and the fans."

Okay, so now you know your way around the playing field. Next up we'll take a look at the required tools of the trade.

The Least You Need to Know

➤ The four bases on the field, which are in the shape of a diamond, form the area called the infield; six defensive players are stationed there.

➤ The pitcher's mound is in the middle of the infield and the batter's boxes are on either side of home plate.

➤ The area beyond the infield is called the outfield; three defensive players cover this area.

➤ Be it an outdoor ballpark or a domed stadium, a field of natural grass or artificial turf, the basic field setup in the major leagues is always the same.

Chapter 6

Tools of the Trade

A.   B.

In This Chapter

➤ This ball's life: Quite a yarn

➤ Is that a real major league bat? You bet your ash it is!

➤ Glovin' every minute of it

➤ Why catchers aren't as ignorant as some might think

Baseball is a pretty simple game. Kids play it with a broomstick and anything round. But at the major league level, there's a lot more to the equipment than having something to throw and something to hit it with. Equipment has become more sophisticated and more well-made, and the game has become more well-played. Bats have become sturdier, helmets have made it safer to stand in against a pitcher throwing 95 miles per hour, and state-of-the-art gloves allow players to make beautiful catches.

Regulations prevent equipment from giving any one player an advantage. As you will see in this chapter, balls, bats, and gloves must conform to stringent regulations to keep the playing field level. Let's take a look at the gear that major league players use in their grown-up version of stickball.

How Far We've Come: The Evolution of Equipment

It's hard to believe that baseball players used to play without gloves, helmets, or catcher's equipment. Hard to believe, but true. Until 1864, bare-handed fielders were helped by a rule that made it an out if a ball was caught on the first bounce. In 1875, a first baseman named Charlie Waitt became the first player to use a glove in a game—although the glove he wore was a simple street-dress leather glove. Gradually, gloves became bigger, better-padded, webbed, and laced. The biggest advance in gloves came

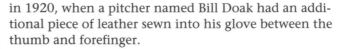

Talkin' Baseball

"There was no paraphernalia in the old days with which one could protect himself. No mitts; no, not even gloves; and masks, why you would have been laughed off the diamond had you worn one behind the bat."

—Hall of Fame outfielder Jim O'Rourke in 1913, recalling the good old days

Catching On

The portion of the glove that covers the palm of the fielder's hand is called the **pocket**. Players try to break their glove in by making the pocket deeper and rounder, making it easier to catch the ball.

in 1920, when a pitcher named Bill Doak had an additional piece of leather sewn into his glove between the thumb and forefinger.

As for the other two major pieces of equipment, well, the ball and bat have changed fairly little. The ball is still roughly the same size it was 135 years ago, although it's wound a little tighter and has significantly more bounce. The biggest change in the ball came in 1974, when the cover changed from cowhide to horsehide.

The bat has also changed very little. The maximum diameter in 1861 was two-and-a-half inches; now it is two-and-three-quarters inches. Players today generally favor lighter bats than their predecessors, and bats today tend to have a more defined taper, with a thinner handle. Beyond that, the two most basic pieces of equipment in baseball have remained fairly constant as the rest of the game has evolved.

The Baseball

You'll hear historians and old-timers talk about "the dead-ball era," a time when pitchers ruled the earth and batters were lucky to eke out a run on bunts and Baltimore chops. Actually, the ball wasn't that different, but pitchers used to scuff it, cut it, spit tobacco on it, rub dirt on it—anything to make the ball break more sharply and make it harder to see. In addition, the same ball was often used until it fell apart or was lost; in late innings, sometimes in fading daylight, batters squinted to see the dark, mushy lump whizzing towards the plate, hoping that if they didn't hit it, it wouldn't hit them.

All that changed in 1920, when the popular Ray Chapman of the Cleveland Indians was hit in the head by a pitched ball and killed. The baseball world was shocked, and Chapman's death—the major leagues' first on-field fatality—had a significant effect on how baseballs were used. Umpires prevented pitchers from scuffing and dirtying the balls, and replaced balls frequently, so that they were easier to see. Because they were always new, they were livelier, too. Suddenly, the ball was easier to see and easier to hit—far. This contributed to the "live ball" era of the 1920s and early '30s, in which hitters like Babe Ruth put up some awesome numbers.

But it's pretty much the same ball. Like the players themselves, a baseball travels a long, arduous road to the big leagues. All official major league baseballs are produced in Turrialba, Costa Rica, by Rawlings, the sole supplier of big-league balls. The core of the ball is a small, round piece of rubber, which is then wound tightly with wool and cotton thread. If the yarn used to make one baseball was stretched out in a straight line, it would be nearly a quarter-mile long.

After it is wound, the ball is covered with two pieces of bleached white horsehide that are sewn together with 108 stitches of red yarn. These seams serve an important purpose. They make the surface of the ball less smooth, and this added aerodynamic resistance makes it easier for pitchers to make the ball curve.

It looks like a baseball, but it's not quite ready for action. A ball must conform to certain weight and size restrictions. It must weigh between five and five-and-a-quarter ounces, and its circumference must be between nine and nine-and-a-quarter inches. After the balls are weighed, screened by metal detectors, and inspected 20 times, a sample of 144 balls is drawn at random and fired at a giant piece of wood to see how far they bounce back. If a ball bounces too far, it's too "lively," or "juiced." In recent years, as sluggers have hit more and more home runs, there has been much speculation that baseballs have become livelier, but there's no evidence that the ball is juiced.

If a baseball passes all its tests and inspections and is acceptable for use in the majors, it takes one final step. It must be rubbed down with special mud from the Delaware River, which takes the gloss off the ball. Then it is finally ready for the big time. And what is the baseball's reward for making this journey? Well, the lifespan of the average major league baseball is all of six pitches.

Extra Innings

"Baseball mud" is a concoction made of mud from the Delaware River and other secret ingredients that is rubbed on new baseballs to take the slick, glossy shine off them. Back in the early 1900s, Lena Blackburne, a third base coach for the Philadelphia Athletics, heard umpire Harry Geisel complaining about the slick surface on new baseballs. Blackburne grew up near a Delaware River tributary and recalled his boyhood practice of rubbing river mud on baseballs to make them easier to grip. So the next spring he showed Geisel a ball that had been rubbed down with his "mud." Geisel liked the idea, and convinced his fellow umpires to use the substance as well. Blackburne died in 1968, but the recipe has been handed down and is still used today.

Approximately 181,000 baseballs are used in a major league season, an average of about 80 per game. Here's what happens to them:

➤ Eighteen are scuffed and taken out of play by the umpire. These balls are kept for use as batting practice balls.

➤ Sixty get fouled off into the stands, where they become souvenirs for lucky fans. Most balls are fouled off behind home plate.

➤ Two get smacked out of the park for home runs.

The baseball hasn't changed much since 1954, when Spalding was the major leagues' official manufacturer.

The Bat

Except for Ted Williams, very few hitters are physics experts, but most of them can explain the concept of momentum. The momentum a bat imparts to a ball is a factor of two things: the mass of the bat and the velocity with which it is swung. As a result, hitters look for a bat that is heavy enough to provide them with some pop, but light enough for them to swing easily and quickly.

During my career, I started out using a 35-ounce bat, which is fairly heavy. Then I began using lighter bats. I worked my way down to $32^1/_2$ ounces, which I finally settled on because I liked the way the weight was distributed. I found that if the barrel was too heavy, the bat felt awkward to swing.

Of course, other hitters have different tastes. Some guys, like Tony Gwynn of the San Diego Padres, use really short, light bats. Babe Ruth, on the other hand, used bats as heavy as 52 ounces. It's simply a matter of feel. When you are at the plate, you have to be comfortable with your bat.

Bats used in the major leagues come in all weights and sizes, but they do have one thing in common: They are

Talkin' Baseball

"Your bat is your life. It's your weapon. You don't want to go into battle with anything that feels less than perfect."

—Hall of Fame left fielder Lou Brock

all made of wood. In most cases, the wood is white ash from the forests of New York or Pennsylvania. Batmakers take a block of wood and, using a lathe, sculpt out a bat to the exact specifications given to them by the player. So long as the bat is round, not more than 42 inches long and not more than two-and-three-quarters inches in diameter, it is legal for use in major league play.

In amateur baseball, non-wood bats are quite popular. Aluminum and other metal bats cost more than a $30 wooden bat, but they last for years, while a wood bat rarely lasts more than a month or so. Metal bats also allow batters to hit the ball harder and farther, because they are lighter and sturdier than wood.

Even though they make sense economically, metal bats will never be used in the majors. The game wouldn't be the same without the sound of the ball cracking off a wooden bat, and their use would turn the game into a home run-hitting contest. Can you imagine how far Mark McGwire would hit a ball with an aluminum bat? It might never come down.

Warning Track

The most common form of cheating is called "corking." To cork a bat, a player drills a hole in the end of his bat and fills it with a lighter substance, like cork. The lighter bat is easier to swing, but the face of the bat is just as hard and strong. If a team suspects an opposing player of corking his bat, they can have the umpire remove the bat from the game. The bat is then examined—often it is x-rayed—and if it has been tampered with, the player can be fined or suspended.

Extra Innings

Hitters can be very particular about their bats. Ted Williams, one of the best and most disciplined hitters who ever lived, once received a shipment of bats and decided that there was something wrong with the way the handle was tapered. He sent them back to the manufacturer. When the batmakers measured the grips on the bats, they found Williams was right. The handles were $^5/_{1000}$ths of an inch off.

Bats come in all shapes and sizes, but to be used in the major leagues, they must be made of wood like this one.

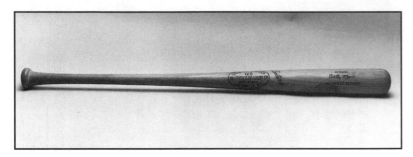

A Glove for Every Position

Baseballs can travel up to about 100 miles per hour when thrown and they can reach even faster speeds when they are hit. So before you jump in front of one and try to catch it, you'd better make sure you're wearing the right glove.

Common sense says that the bigger your glove, the better your chances of catching the ball. But using a big glove has its drawbacks. It's much easier to reach in and retrieve the ball from a small glove than a large one. So infielders, who often have to field a ground ball and then throw it in a hurry, tend to use smaller gloves. Outfielders, on the other hand, place an emphasis on simply catching the ball, so they use bigger gloves.

We've talked about *gloves*, but two players on the field use *mitts*, which, like mittens, don't have individual fingers. The first is the first baseman. He rarely has to make throws, but he's *always* catching fireballs from across the infield. His mitt has extra padding and is the biggest glove on the field, because he often needs to reach for throws or scoop low throws out of the dirt.

Talkin' Baseball

"It fits me like a glove."

—Anaheim Angels shortstop Gary DiSarcina, explaining why he has used the same glove for 10 years, when most players go through at least one glove per year.

The other player who uses a mitt is a catcher. A catcher's mitt has lots of extra padding. When you're catching a guy like Tom Seaver, who can fire the ball at more than 90 miles per hour, that helps. But I used to cut a lot of the extra padding out of my glove, because it was easier to break it in with less padding.

All baseball gloves are made of leather, and like a pair of leather shoes, they need to be broken in. There are now several creams on the market to treat new gloves, but the oldest trick in the book is to rub your glove down with Neat's foot oil, stick a ball in the pocket, tie a string around it, and let it sit for several days. The oil—which comes from the feet and shins of cattle—softens the leather and the ball molds and shapes the pocket.

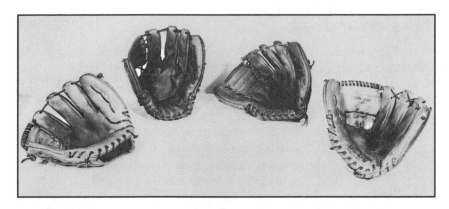

Four famous gloves from the Hall of Fame (from left): Third baseman Jim Gilliam's glove, used to make a key grab to secure the Los Angeles Dodgers' win over the Minnesota Twins in Game 7 of the 1965 World Series; Jerry Adair's glove, worn in 1964 while setting a record for fewest errors in a season (five) by a second baseman; Hoyt Wilhelm's glove, worn in his 907th game in 1968, when he broke Cy Young's all-time record for most games pitched; and Jim Maloney's glove, worn when he pitched his first no-hitter on August 19, 1965. (I caught his second one, in 1969.)

A catcher wears a large, round glove with extra padding.

The Hitters' Hardhat

It's hard to believe, but for the first 100 years of baseball, most players went to bat without wearing protective headgear. Even after Ray Chapman was killed, players refused to wear helmets because they feared their peers would make fun of them. Finally in 1941, after two of their players were hit in the head, the Brooklyn Dodgers became the first team to wear helmets. They looked a lot like the regular caps, except there was a pocket into which a piece of plastic could be inserted. Batting helmets weren't required in the major leagues until the mid-1950s.

Over the years, helmets have undergone quite an evolution. They are now made of plastic with padding inside them. They come with or without ear flaps, and if a player has a facial injury he needs to protect, the helmet can be outfitted with a faceguard. In fact, faceguards are required at many levels of amateur ball. Getting plunked in the noggin certainly isn't fun, but, with the proper helmet, it isn't as bad as it could be. I don't recommend stepping into the batter's box without a helmet.

Talkin' Baseball

"If we'd had them when I was playing, John McGraw would have insisted that we go up to the plate and get hit on the head."

—Casey Stengel on batting helmets and his tough-as-nails former manager

A plastic batting helmet makes standing in the batter's box a whole lot safer, so a major league team has one for every player.

Other Gadgets

Hitters arm themselves with all sorts of doodads. Many wear leather batting gloves to keep from getting blisters. Some players don't wear them, though, because they like the feel of the bat in their bare hands.

Some hitters step up to the plate looking like they're wearing suits of armor. A lot of guys wear plastic guards strapped to the inside of their front foot, because it is pretty common—and pretty painful—to foul a pitch off your instep. Other guys wear protective devices on their elbows, and some—like Jeff Bagwell of the Astros, who has been hit in the hand several times—even wear plastic guards on their hands. None of this makes swinging any easier or more comfortable, but it does make getting hit with the ball a lot less painful.

Many players today wear fancy designer sunglasses, but some don't like wearing shades all the time. They tend to use old-fashioned flip-up glasses. When they don't need sunglasses, they can turn the lenses up, so they can get a good, natural look around. If the ball is hit into the air, they can quickly flip the lenses down and block out the sunlight.

Most players also wear something called *eye black* under their eyes. Basically, this is just a black stripe painted under each eye, which serves to cut down the glare from the sun or the lights. At the end of a long, hot day, the eye black often gets mixed in with sweat and runs so it looks like these guys have been wearing mascara. But it's a whole lot better than squinting for three hours.

From the Bench

Sometimes you'll see a player running the bases clutching batting gloves in his bare hands. He's doing that because holding the gloves keeps his hands in a fist, so if he has to slide headfirst, he's less likely to jam or break his fingers.

Catcher's Gear

The only way to make it in the major leagues as a catcher is to remain injury-free, and the only way to do that is to expose as little of your body as possible to foul tips and errant pitches. Bumps and bruises are inevitable: Most catchers have hands that look like plumber's fittings, with their fingers pointing in every direction. And catching isn't a good idea if you like having nice toenails. You take countless foul tips off your feet, and even steel-toed shoes don't help.

Several pieces of equipment are invaluable to a catcher. The first is the mask, a plastic cage with

Talkin' Baseball

"The latest protection for catchers looks rather clumsy, besides delaying a game while the guards are strapped above the knee and around the ankle, and it is doubtful if the fad will ever become popular."

—A 1907 *New York Sun* article on Roger Bresnahan's use of shin guards foam padding attached. It has a strap on the back and can be slipped over a helmet, which catchers wear backwards. A few years ago, some catchers began wearing one-piece helmets made of state-of-the art, bulletproof material, like the masks hockey goalies wear. I tried on one of these and I loved it. The bulky padding on the traditional masks really cut down on my peripheral vision, but the sightlines in the new helmet are great.

Catching On

The equipment worn by catchers is sometimes referred to as **the tools of ignorance**. As a catcher, I naturally take great umbrage at this.

One piece of equipment that hasn't changed much over the years is the chest protector, a large piece of padding strapped to the chest. Catchers and umpires began wearing them in 1885, and while they have become less bulky, today's protectors are remarkably similar to those used decades ago. One thing I learned as a catcher: Chest protectors help, but if you have the choice, it's better to not get hit.

Catchers also wear shin guards made of hard plastic. They cover the side of the calf, and they also extend to the top of the foot. They were first worn in 1907 by Roger Bresnahan, who also was a pioneer in the development of the batting helmet.

Before climbing behind the plate, a catcher needs to put on a mask, chest protector and shin guards.

One of the biggest problems I had catching was that I often sprained the thumb of my glove hand. It was usually a foul ball, but if a pitcher threw an especially nasty breaking ball it might hit the thumb wrong and bend it back. One year, I got together with one of our trainers and we came up with a splint I could wear over my thumb in the glove, to keep my thumb from bending at an awkward angle.

Another recent minor invention that has become popular with catchers is a heavy pad strapped to the back of one of the calves (Sandy Alomar of the Cleveland Indians wears one). When the catcher squats down, the pad supports the area between the calf and the thigh, making it a lot more comfortable behind the plate—which still isn't saying much.

In the On-Deck Circle

When a player is waiting to come up to bat, he stands in the on-deck circle and takes some practice swings, often placing a metal weight called a *donut* over the barrel of his bat as he practices. This gets his muscles used to a heavier bat, so when he takes the donut off and goes up to the plate, his bat feels lighter.

A hitter will also do some minor tinkering with his bat in the on-deck circle. The circle will have a couple of rags covered in pine tar, which the hitter will apply to his bat to make the handle stickier.

Extra Innings

There's a rule against placing pine tar or anything else higher than 17 inches from the handle of the bat, but it isn't strictly enforced because pine tar doesn't aid the flight of the ball. In 1983, George Brett of the Kansas City Royals hit a home run in a crucial game against the Yankees but was called out for having pine tar too high on his bat. Brett stormed out of the dugout and his teammates had to restrain him from punching an umpire and ending his career. However, after an appeal, the American League ruled that Brett had violated the letter, but not the spirit, of the law. They restored his home run, and all was right with the world.

On the Pitcher's Mound

On the mound, a pitcher might feel like he's stranded on a desert island. To make sure he doesn't doctor the baseball by adding any foreign substances to it, he's not allowed

Talkin' Baseball

"I sometimes have to file my nails between innings."

—Minnesota Twins pitcher Joe Niekro, after his 1987 suspension for being caught on the mound with a nail file.

to take anything onto the hill but his cap, his glove, and his arm. Just about all you'll see out there is a large, white rosin bag. When a pitcher's hand gets wet from perspiration, he can pick up the bag and the rosin will dry his hand off.

The only other object you'll see on the pitcher's mound is a tongue depressor if the field is muddy. A pitcher needs good footing, and if too much mud collects in his spikes, it can throw off his mechanics. So, instead of using some hi-tech mud remover, he uses a good old-fashioned tongue depressor.

That's the lowdown on the tools of the trade, although there's one other vital piece of baseball equipment that we haven't covered yet: the uniform. So read on....

The Least You Need to Know

➤ Balls must meet stringent specifications to make it to the big leagues. They must be the proper size and weight, and they can't be too lively.

➤ Wood bats, which are used in the professional ranks, are less durable than metal bats, and they don't drive the ball as far. But they have a place in baseball's rich tradition.

➤ Fielders use gloves of different types and sizes, depending on what position they play. Infielders use small gloves, outfielders use bigger gloves, and catchers and first basemen use large mitts.

➤ Anyone brave enough to get behind the plate should be sure to don the proper equipment.

Chapter 7

Uniforms: Clothes Make the Man

In This Chapter

➤ The evolution of baseball uniforms: bagging the baggy look

➤ Dressing for success, from top to bottom

➤ Why changing styles can mean big-league dollars

➤ The major leagues' best- and worst-dressed teams

The Knickerbocker Base Ball Club of New York developed the game's first uniforms in 1849. They wore blue trousers, white shirts, and straw hats.

Pioneering baseball outfits were sportier versions of the office attire of the day, complete with long sleeves, stiff collars, and ties or bow ties. Baggy knickers and long stockings replaced trousers in the 1870s, but the collars and shirts remained.

Since then, uniforms have changed about as often as the weather. In the 20th century alone, major league teams have used more than 3,000 varieties of uniforms. Sack-like flannels have been replaced by aerodynamic double-knit polyester in virtually every color of the rainbow. In this chapter, we'll look at fashion on the baseball field.

Fashion Statement: The Evolution of Uniforms

Early baseball teams believed in the medicinal value of working up a good sweat. In the 1890s, some wore heavy, quilted knickers with hip-length wool sweaters even in warm weather. The uniforms were 100 percent wool flannel, or mostly wool with a hint of cotton—even the undershirts and socks!

Extra Innings

The original teams used solid colors, stripes, and even checks and plaids on their uniforms. The 1888 Detroit Wolverines wore white shirts with thin stripes, and the 1907 Chicago Cubs probably were the first to wear pinstripes in the 20th century. But baseball's most famous pinstripes arrived in the New York Yankees' (or Highlanders, as they were then known) home opener in 1912. By the mid-teens, half the teams sported pinstripes on their home uniforms, but, along with the classic "NY" logo, the pins are most closely associated with the New York Yankee dynasty, because they set the standard for winners.

The weight of the wool was gradually reduced by half by the 1940s, but not until the 1960s did teams start adding some orlon to the wool, and even then they were practically unbearable, particularly for pitchers and catchers, on the hot, sticky dog days of summer. I remember one day in the 1960s when Don Drysdale of the Los Angeles Dodgers lost 15 pounds pitching in Cincinnati's Crosley Field. On a humid, 90- to 95-degree day, that wasn't uncommon—those old wools didn't breathe.

Not until the 1970s did uniforms turn toward double-knit fabrics. Polyester and cotton were the greatest thing that ever happened to baseball uniforms. These new materials breathe, and they look good, feel good, and fit well. They're lighter, cooler, and more durable.

You could put two players in one uniform in the old days, they were so baggy. Now, they're more like leotards. The base-stealers especially like the lycra for speed, just as swimmers and sprinters do. They keep muscles warm, but they breathe enough that you're not sweating all the fluids out of your body the way you did in the all-wool days.

No longer do all the teams button their jerseys down the front. Some just use pullovers. They've tried the uniforms with and without belts. They've tried drawstrings. They've tried everything. Led by Charles O. Finley's Kansas City and Oakland A's, teams went through a stage of wild colors in the '60s and '70s. The 1976 White Sox, owned by Bill Veeck, even tried dark shorts that ended just below the knees topped off with a pullover shirt that wasn't tucked in. The shorts were nice on a hot day—but they just didn't look like a baseball uniform.

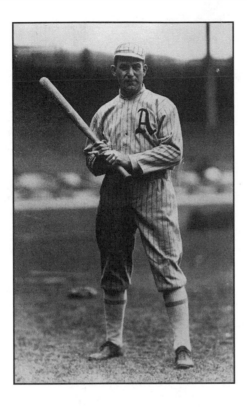

The uniforms from the major leagues' early days, such as this 1915 Philadelphia Athletics ensemble modeled by Hall of Fame second baseman Nap Lajoie (left), were made of looser-fitting wool, with long sleeves, high-button collars, and pants designed to roll up to just below the knee.

Today, a lot of teams hire fashion consultants to design uniforms with a winning look. New teams agonize over picking the "hot" color of the day; that's why the Marlins chose teal when Florida was awarded an expansion franchise. Old teams change uniforms not because of some great innovations that will help them win games, but because they make money. Every time the hometown team comes out with a new style, fans rush out and spend money to stay current—a diehard might buy every version of the team's hat, which is why you see teams using three or four styles these days.

The men-in-black look of the Oakland Raiders was so popular in football that some baseball teams have tried to emulate them. Even the Cincinnati Reds put some black in their uniforms, and they're going to add a little bit more. They sell white, red, gray, and pinstripe hats with the "C" logo on them. Like the players, the fans want to wear stuff that's stylish, looks good, and says, "This is my town and my team."

From the Bench

If you want to check out the evolution of uniforms in words and pictures, look for Marc Okkonen's book, *Baseball Uniforms of the 20th Century*. It's the definitive guide, with year-by-year illustrations of every team's styles.

Home Whites and Road Grays

Historians aren't certain when teams began using separate uniforms at home and on the road, but research shows that it was standard practice for all major league teams by the turn of the century.

Home uniforms are white, while road uniforms are gray or some darker hue. This continued to evolve when uniform colors became brighter—sometimes downright gaudy—in the late '60s and '70s. By the '70s, light blue replaced gray on many road uniforms—but most of them have gone back to gray. Also, the home jerseys usually have the team's name, and the away jerseys have the name of their home city—at home, the uniform says "Red Sox," and away, it says, "Boston." Today, many teams have more than just a home and road uniform—they have different variations of each look, such as an alternate cap or jersey style for certain games.

The Cap

Albert Spalding, a pioneering pitcher, manager, and businessman, outfitted his 1876 Chicago club with a different uniform for each position on the field, in hopes of selling more uniforms. A.G. Spalding & Brothers became the era's dominant sporting-goods firm—but not because of this innovation. A cynic said the club looked like a "Dutch bed of tulips," and the idea died until six years later. The 1882 Detroit Wolverines designated positions with different colors and stripes on caps, belts, and jerseys. But teams figured out that you could tell what position a guy played simply by where he stood on the field, and decided they looked a lot better with matching uniforms.

Extra Innings

The 1941 Brooklyn Dodgers experimented with the first batting helmet. Originally made of fiberglass, it was replaced by a stronger plastic. They didn't catch on quickly, but they became a pet project of Branch Rickey, the great general manager. After he left the Dodgers, he required all of his 1952 Pirates to wear them. The National League mandated them in 1955 and the American League in 1956, with a grandfather clause for veteran big leaguers who insisted upon not wearing them.

Many early teams wore *pillbox-style* caps with horizontal striping and flat tops. Others adopted the so-called *Brooklyn style*, with a higher, fuller, rounded crown than the *Boston style*, which was the forerunner of modern caps, with its rounded, close-fitting crown.

To commemorate baseball's 1976 centennial, many teams brought back the pillbox cap, and the Pittsburgh Pirates liked them so much that they wore them for several years afterward. The bills on old-fashioned caps were shorter than most of today's models. Otherwise, caps haven't changed too much in the past century.

The Jersey

Many original uniform shirts, or jerseys, were laced up the middle, but laces gave way to buttons fairly quickly. Many teams have dabbled with pullovers and a few even tried zippers. The original big, formal collars gradually evolved into small, "military" collars. John McGraw's 1906 Giants introduced the collarless V-neck shirt, but most wore the cadet look until the 1920s. By then, A.G. Spalding offered a V-neck collar and a choice of full, half, or three-quarters length sleeves and even a detachable sleeve that buttoned at the elbow.

Talkin' Baseball

"Progress brings complaints. Years ago, players squawked because numbers were put on their uniforms. Now, they're unhappy because I've put their names on, too."

—White Sox owner Bill Veeck in 1960

Extra Innings

Historians differ on when numbers first appeared on baseball jerseys. One source says the Red Stockings used them in 1883. Most point to the 1916 Cleveland Indians, who wore them on their sleeves, not their backs. The 1923 St. Louis Cardinals experimented with numbers. The 1929 Yankees wore large numbers on their backs, spurring some ridicule. Players and lineups didn't change much then, and the numbers corresponded to the player's spot in the batting order. Hence, Babe Ruth wore number 3 and Lou Gehrig number 4. Numbers quickly became a way to identify players, and by 1932, all major league teams were wearing them. The 1952 Dodgers added numbers to the front of their jerseys and many teams mimicked this look. Numbers were added to some teams' sleeves in the '60s and even on some pants in the '70s. The 1959 White Sox were the first team to put players' names on the back of their uniforms.

By the mid-1930s, nearly all teams were wearing elbow-length sleeves. The 1940 Chicago Cubs introduced a sleeveless vest worn over a blue undersweater. The look resurfaced in the '50s and '60s with the Cincinnati Reds, Pittsburgh Pirates, and Cleveland Indians. I always thought it was a great look—especially if you had big arms like Ted Kluszewski, a.k.a. Big Klu, the Reds' slugging first baseman.

By the '60s, teams were tweaking details such as logos and lettering, and in the '70s, they turned to better fabrics and brighter colors. Today, most teams favor the traditional look, with less garish colors and button-down fronts. Most jerseys feature V-neck collars.

Talkin' Baseball

"The funny thing about these uniforms is that you hang them in the closet and they get smaller and smaller."

—St. Louis Cardinal outfielder Curt Flood, before a 1989 old-timers game

Warning Track

Some people think that all a baseball player does on the field is spit and grab his crotch. Well, regarding the latter, a player does that probably because his protective cup is bothering him. When players wear a cup—and I recommend it for every position—they use the jock with the pouch; the cup fits inside the pouch, and they wear an undergarment or long-legged brief over it. But those briefs aren't always snug, so the cup moves around. I found that if I wore a tighter jock over the one with the cup holder, it held everything in place. I don't think we'll ever remedy the spitting, though.

The Pants

Baseball pants began much like conventional pants, some even with cuffs. Pants changed to knickers, supposedly to make running easier, in the 1870s, and remained loose-fitting wool until the 1970s, when the trend toward tight-fitting cottons and synthetics began. Pants usually came with a belt, but the new style made stretch waistbands popular.

Because the old-time players didn't make as much money as guys today, a lot of them had other jobs in the winter, so they didn't work out in the off-season. Now, there's so much money at stake, players work out year-round to maximize their earnings and success, and with more modern ideas about nutrition and fitness, they look a lot better in tight uniforms than the old-time guys did. This sleeker style doesn't exactly flatter a lot of old managers, coaches, and beer-guzzling players like the Yankees' David Wells, one of the few modern players who can wear a form-fitting poncho.

When ballplayers started pulling their pantlegs down to their ankles—sporting the pajama look—a lot of people said, "My God, look how awful this is." I thought, *"This is the ugliest thing in the world."* But it's been around for so long, when you see guys pull their pantlegs up the way they did in the old days, you think, *"Man, this really looks strange now. I'm not so sure I like this."* Black players such as Deion Sanders started showing their stirrups in honor of Jackie Robinson, but white players like Jim Thome and Chipper Jones do it, too.

Socks and Stirrups

The original stockings, or socks, were made of heavy wool and stretched from toe to knee. *Stirrups*, worn over what's called the *sanitary stocking,* were introduced around 1905. The stirrups are mostly just decorative, although they do offer an extra layer of protection against getting spiked. Striped and multicolored stirrups were popular until the late teens, usually, but not always, contrasting with the stockings. In a 1914 photo of "Shoeless" Joe Jackson, the lower part of the stirrups match the stockings, but from ankle to knee, the stirrups are dark.

Like skirt hemlines, the length of the stirrups goes up and down, depending upon the fashion of the day. When I started out with the Reds, we wore those old wool uniforms and wool socks and you couldn't have high stirrups. You could barely see the white socks underneath. Management thought it would set a good example for the kids—since they provide some protection—yet you'd go to a Little League game and every kid's stirrups were as high as he could get them. I loved that look when I was a kid: like Mickey Mantle, my pants down just below the knees, with those long stirrups and the socks showing. You could see the calves and the definition of the muscles.

By contrast, today's uniforms, such as this one worn by ex-Atlanta Braves outfielder David Justice, are made of lighter, more form-fitting material, with short sleeves, V-neck collars, and pants that are worn to about ankle level.

The Spikes

The original baseball shoes were handmade leather, high-topped so they looked a little like hiking boots. Steel plates with spikes were riveted to the soles. They dropped below the ankle by 1910, but the color—black—remained constant until the 1960s, when the Kansas City A's wore white. That created quite a controversy, but eventually teams began coordinating shoe colors with their uniform colors, so you don't see many all-black shoes today.

Now, athletic shoes are a billion-dollar business, and the shoe companies are constantly coming up with new ideas and new looks. They're paying athletes millions to wear their shoes, but I don't know how much better one is than the other. I mean, I think Kenny Lofton could play barefoot and still blow right by me.

Extra Innings

In baseball's early days, teams used a variety of nicknames, sometimes subject to change based on the whim of local sports writers, and they experimented with different versions on different uniforms. For instance, in 1919, the Chicago Nationals spelled out "Chicago Cubs" on one outfit, used a large "C" with a little cubbie bear inside on another, and used a rectangular "C" to enclose "UBS" on a third.

Talkin' Baseball

"I'll never forget September 6, 1950. I got a letter threatening me, Hank Bauer, Yogi Berra, and Johnny Mize. It said if I showed up in uniform against the Red Sox I'd be shot. I turned the letter over to the FBI, and told my manager, Casey Stengel, about it. You know what Casey did? He gave me a different uniform and gave mine to Billy Martin. Can you imagine that? Guess Casey thought it'd be better if Billy got shot."

—Longtime New York Yankees shortstop Phil Rizzuto

Stability vs. Change

Most teams change uniforms quite often these days. The Yankees and Dodgers are the exceptions, and that's good, because their uniforms are classics. Of course, Yankees and Dodgers merchandise still sells well. They'll probably be tempted to change styles if it ever stops selling, tradition be damned. I mean, let's face it, souvenir sales equal big bucks.

It used to be that you'd go into a sports shop and see the same Cincinnati Reds caps and t-shirts that we've seen forever and ever. But I was in an airport the other day and I saw a black hat with a red "C" and I thought, *"Wow, that's different. I like that."* Guys want a hat that fits their style when they're walking around town or playing golf. Maybe the red hat doesn't go with what they're wearing. But if they found a black or a blue hat with a red "C" on it, they might say, "I'm proud of the Reds, but I don't want to stick out like Rudolph the Red-Nosed Reindeer."

With the high salaries players make nowadays, teams look for every way they can to make more money, and the only way to do that is to put out something people will buy. I think that's the main reason why teams change styles more often than ever before.

Johnny's Best and Worst Uniforms

I always liked the Reds' cutout sleeves. When I came to my first spring training and got the pinstripe jersey with no sleeves, it was cool. It was really cool. The Yankees wore pinstripes. Mickey Mantle was a Yankee. Mickey was from Oklahoma. I was from Oklahoma. I loved Mickey, the Yankees, and their pinstripes.

The Dodgers were also a constant. When you thought of the Dodgers, you thought of their class, of their history, and that white uniform with "Dodgers" written across it. Maybe the simplicity made it look great. I like uniforms that make a statement without being gaudy, uniforms that are clean and crisp, not busy and garish. I like the current Reds, Indians, and Baltimore Orioles uniforms.

Extra Innings

Nicknames were rarely displayed on uniforms even into the early decades of the 20th century. The first team in the century to spell out its nickname on the jersey was Washington in 1905, when it wanted to replace Senators with Nationals. By the 1920s, the nickname or city name was usually displayed on team uniforms. The last original major league team to spell out its full nickname—Athletics—was Philadelphia in 1954. The A's moved to Kansas City the next year.

When we moved from Crosley Field to Riverfront Stadium in 1970, we changed to polyester uniforms and man, they looked great. They felt good and looked good. Looking good is part of marketing a baseball team and it also makes a statement: *We are the Reds. This is our uniform. Wear it proudly.* Once, the Reds changed the color underneath the bill of the cap from green to gray. Greens and dark colors supposedly made you angry and tense; the gray supposedly made you calmer and more focused. They're always trying to find something to improve the productivity of the athlete, but it's really pretty simple: If you think, *"Man, this uniform looks good, I'm proud to wear it,"* that can only help your confidence.

It would have been tough to proudly wear some of those loud uniforms of the 1970s. The Astros had some hideous rainbow-and-orange combinations, the White Sox abandoned their classic black-and-white look, and the Pirates and Padres wore all-yellow combinations that made the players look like Big Bird and all-brown uniforms that looked like they had rolled in a mud puddle. I didn't like the way the Pirates kept changing colors. They wore gold, then they wore black, then they wore brown, then they wore solids, then they wore pinstripes. They made you even dizzier by juggling different-colored caps, undershirts, socks, and stirrups. It was so far out that every night they had to list on the wall what outfit they were wearing.

Talkin' Baseball

"They look like Hawaiian softball uniforms."

—Pitcher Charlie Hough on the Houston Astros' new multicolored uniforms in 1975

And you know, it's called a uniform for a reason. I don't want to see some guy wearing a purple shirt underneath when his team colors are supposed to be blue. When guys dress as individuals, they don't look like a team. They look like a bunch of guys with no concept of teamwork, no respect for the history and tradition of the franchise. That uniform is a symbol that says, "We are a team." You've gotta dress like a team member and act like one.

The Least You Need to Know

➤ The original baseball uniforms were baggy and made of wool.

➤ Modern uniforms are designed for comfort, performance, and money–making reasons.

➤ Teams have one set of uniforms for home games and another for road games, and sometimes even more than that.

➤ The clean, traditional look of Yankee pinstripes and Dodger blue are still the best in baseball.

Chapter 8

Baseball 101

In This Chapter

➤ The object of baseball

➤ The basics of the game

➤ The rules: What you need to know

➤ A primer on terminology

"Are you *crying?!* There's no crying in baseball!" the gruff manager scolded in the movie, *A League of Their Own.*

Tom Hanks made it sound like a rule. It's not. Mark McGwire cried when he broke Roger Maris' home run record last year, and nobody claimed Big Mac wasn't acting manly. After all, he wasn't just a man, he was *the* Man, as Sammy Sosa liked to say.

But baseball does have a lot of rules, and while you don't have to rush out and buy the latest edition of the game's rule book, you do need to know the basics to understand and appreciate the game. In this chapter we'll start at the beginning and break down the game of baseball. If you know a little about the game you can probably skim through the first few sections, but stay tuned, because it gets tougher as we go along.

(You'll notice this chapter more than any other has a lot of the terms used in baseball italicized. Keep your eye out for them, and notice how they're used. The jargon of baseball is rich and colorful—learn to speak the language and you're well on your way to true fandom.)

Twenty-Five on a Side (But Only Nine—or 10—at a Time)

A major league team usually consists of 25 players. Those players constitute the team's *roster*. On September 1 teams are allowed to increase their roster to 40.

No matter how many players a team has on its roster, the most who can play at any one time is nine—or 10, in the American League, which allows a *designated hitter* (or *DH*) to hit in place of the weakest hitter in the lineup, the pitcher. For years baseball fans have been debating the pros and cons of the DH rule. We'll take a closer look at the controversy in Chapter 16.

Catching On

For most of the season, a major league team usually consists of 25 players. Those players constitute the team's active **roster**. On September 1, to allow for some experimentation before the postseason, teams are allowed to increase their roster to 40 players.

Catching On

Except for the National League, almost every league, including the American, allows the use of a **designated hitter** to hit in place of the weakest hitter in the lineup (the pitcher). During interleague play (including the World Series), the *DH* is used only in AL parks.

The two teams take turns playing offense and defense. The nine players are listed in the starting lineup by the positions they play when they line up on defense. They are: pitcher, catcher, first baseman, second baseman, third baseman, shortstop, left fielder, center fielder, and right fielder.

The Object of the Game

The ball is round. The bat is round and oblong. The object is to hit the round ball with the round bat— squarely. Not only squarely, but to a spot where the nine guys on defense can't catch it. Or, as Hall of Famer Wee Willie Keeler used to say, "Hit 'em where they ain't."

And unlike golf, where the ball sits on a tee, grass, or sand, baseballs are not stationary when you try to hit them. Pitchers throw them at speeds occasionally exceeding 100 miles an hour, using various techniques to make the balls rise, sink, and move inside and outside. No wonder many experts say hitting a baseball is the toughest task in sports.

The object of the game is to win, of course. You win if at game's end you have scored more *runs* than the other team. A run in baseball is like a point in football or basketball. A team scores a run when one of its players advances all the way around the bases and crosses home plate. (And no matter what those cute little kids do in pee-wee ball or on *America's Funniest Home Videos*, you can't just head from home plate to second or third base. You have to go from home plate to first base to second base to third base and *then* back to home.)

An offensive player begins his quest to score a run by taking a turn *at bat*. A *batter,* or *hitter,* can reach base in several ways, but the most common is via a *hit*. (You'll read more about the ways to get on base in Chapter 18, "Offensive Strategy.") His goal is to reach first base (or a subsequent base) before the defensive team can get him *out,* or *retire* him. A batter makes an out if:

➤ He hits a *fly ball* (fair or foul) that a fielder catches before it touches the ground (or the *infield fly rule* is called—you'll read about that later in the chapter).

➤ He hits a ball on the ground that a fielder picks up and throws to first base before the batter touches the base.

➤ He *strikes out,* by accumulating three strikes in his time at bat, or by bunting foul on a third strike, or if the catcher catches a foul tip on the third strike.

➤ He hits a *fair ball* that touches him before a fielder touches it.

➤ After hitting the ball, his bat touches the ball a second time in fair territory, or he throws his bat and it interferes with a defensive player in fair territory.

➤ He runs outside the baseline and is ruled to have interfered with a fielder's throw.

➤ He steps out of the batter's box to hit the ball, or steps from one batter's box to the other while the pitcher is in position to pitch.

➤ He interferes with the catcher's fielding or throwing.

➤ He uses an illegal bat, or bats out of order.

A baserunner makes an out if:

➤ A fielder *tags* him with the ball while the runner is not touching a base.

➤ In a *force* situation, he fails to reach the next base before a fielder tags him or that base.

➤ In the umpire's judgment, he runs out of the baseline to avoid being tagged.

Talkin' Baseball

"I love DH'ing. I think it's the greatest job in the world. It's like pinch hitting, except you get a second, third, and fourth chance."

—Minnesota Twins outfielder/DH Jim Dwyer, in 1989

Warning Track

A strikeout isn't always an out. If the catcher doesn't catch the third strike, the batter can try to run to first, provided first base is unoccupied, or occupied with two out. The batter is safe if he reaches first base before the throw. If a pitch gets by the catcher, the *official scorer* (more on him in the next chapter) decides whether to blame the mistake on the catcher (who would be charged with a *passed ball*) or the pitcher (who would be charged with a *wild pitch*).

➤ A ball that's hit in the air is caught and thrown to the base that he left before he can get back.

➤ He's hit by a fair ball in fair territory before the ball has touched or passed an infielder.

➤ He intentionally *interferes* with a thrown ball, or with a defensive player trying to field a batted ball.

➤ He passes a runner ahead of him on the basepaths.

➤ In the umpire's judgment, one of the base coaches physically assists him in returning to or leaving a base.

➤ He misses a base, or leaves a base early when tagging up, and the defense successfully appeals the play.

➤ He runs the bases in reverse order.

Extra Innings

Balls and strikes were first called in 1863. Before that, batters were expected to swing at all close pitches.

It (Usually) Takes 27 Outs to Win

Baseball games are divided into nine *innings*, just as football and basketball games are broken into four quarters and hockey games are sliced into three periods. But, importantly, baseball's innings aren't based on time, as quarters and periods are: Each team gets three outs in an inning, and there are nine innings per game. A baseball game usually lasts as long as it takes for each team to get the other out 27 times.

Each team gets to bat once per inning. The visiting team bats first, in the *top half* of the inning. The home team bats last, in the *bottom half* of the inning. Each out is sometimes referred to as a *third* of an inning. So if a pitcher starts an inning and gets two batters out before leaving the game, he is said to have pitched two-thirds of an inning.

A game begins with the visiting team at bat, trying to score as many runs as they can before the home team's defense can record three outs. Once the third out is made, the visitors take their position on defense and the home team bats until it makes three outs. That's one inning. In a regulation game the teams go back and forth until nine innings are played and each team has made 27 outs, with a few exceptions:

➤ If the home team is ahead after the visitors have batted in the top of the ninth inning, the game is over. The home team doesn't bother hitting in the bottom of the ninth, because they already have more runs than the visitors; the teams just play eight-and-a-half innings. Also, if the home team goes ahead in the bottom of the ninth, the game is over, even if they didn't accumulate three outs.

➤ If it's raining hard, the umpires can delay the game until the rain lets up. If the weather doesn't improve within what the umpires determine to be a reasonable amount of time, the umpires can cancel the game and start all over another day, if the teams haven't yet played at least half a game. But a game halted after four-and-a-half innings with the home team ahead, or five innings with the visiting team ahead, counts as a complete game.

Catching On

A baseball game is divided into nine **innings**. In each inning, both teams get a turn at bat. An inning lasts as long as it takes for each team to get the other out three times.

➤ If the teams have the same number of runs at the end of nine innings, they go into *extra innings*. They play until an inning ends with one team having more runs than the other. As soon as the home team takes the lead in the bottom of an extra inning, the game is over.

Terminology of a Run Scored

A team is run by a *manager* who is assisted by *coaches*. The manager makes out a lineup each day, deciding what position each player will take on defense and the *batting order,* or the sequence in which his players will hit throughout the game.

Here's an example of how your team might score a run:

The first batter, called the *leadoff man,* goes to home plate, and stands in the batter's box. The pitcher winds up and delivers the ball. If the batter swings and misses, that counts as a strike. If he doesn't swing, the home plate umpire calls it a *ball* if it's outside the *strike zone,* or a *strike* if it's in there. Sadly, the strike zone is not a hard-and-fast rule; it varies from league to league and umpire to umpire. Basically it's supposed to be an invisible rectangle over the plate between the player's knees

Catching On

The **strike zone** is "that area over home plate the upper limit of which is a horizontal line at the midpoint between the top of the shoulders and the top of the uniform pants [often called *the letters,* because that's where the team name is], and the lower level is a line at the hollow beneath the kneecap. The strike zone shall be determined from the batter's stance as the batter is prepared to swing at a pitched ball." That's what the rule says, but what major league umpires call a strike is often quite different. Sadly, the strike zone is not a hard-and-fast rule. It varies from league to league and from umpire to umpire.

and chest. Today's umpires have lowered the strike zone so that pitches not much higher than the waist are called balls and pitches as low as the bottom of the knee are called strikes, and widened it so that pitches that are as far as six inches outside the plate are called strikes.

If the batter hits the ball into *foul territory,* which is the area outside the white lines, it counts as a strike, too, unless he already has two strikes. A hit that is *popped up* and caught in the air in foul territory by a defensive player is an out. A third strike is not called on a foul ball unless it's a foul tip caught by the catcher on the fly. Otherwise, a batter who has two strikes can *foul off* (or hit foul) an unlimited number of pitches.

Anyway, as the saying goes, three strikes and you're out. If the batter takes four balls, he is awarded first base on what's called a *walk* or *base on balls*. To get a hit, the batter must hit the ball into *fair territory*—somewhere between the white foul lines.

If you watch a baseball game on TV, you'll frequently hear the announcers refer to *the count* when a batter is at the plate. They're not talking about a vampire—the count is simply the number of balls and strikes on the batter after each pitch, with balls listed first. Thus, a batter with a count of 2–0 (pronounced "two-and-oh," or simply "two-oh") has two balls and no strikes on him. A batter who has more balls than strikes—or a pitcher who has more strikes than balls on a hitter—is said to be *ahead in the count,* meaning that he has the advantage on his opponent. A count of 3–2 is called a *full count.*

Catching On

A batter draws a **base on balls**, or a **walk**, and is thus entitled to first base, when he accumulates four balls in his time at bat. It's been that way since the late 1800s, although in the 1880s, it took as many as nine balls to draw a walk. The current rule of four was instituted in 1889.

Okay, back to our example. Let's say the pitcher throws three balls and two strikes to the batter, and on the 3–2 pitch, he misses the strike zone and throws ball four. The hitter therefore reaches first base on a walk.

Now the second hitter comes up to bat. He swings at a pitch and hits it in the air, hard and on a level trajectory—that's usually called a *line drive,* or, in baseball slang, a *rope, frozen rope,* or *bullet.* The ball goes into left field and hits the ground before the left fielder can catch it. The hitter runs to first base, turns left, and takes a few steps toward second base—that is, he *rounds first,* or *takes a turn*—before quickly deciding that he won't be able to reach second base before the left fielder's throw gets there. He stays at first base with a *single,* because he doesn't want to get thrown out at second.

Catching On

A runner who's on either second or third base is said to be in **scoring position,** because he has a good chance of scoring on a base hit.

If he had reached second base on the hit, it would have been called a *double.* If he had reached third base, it would have been called a *triple.* If he had gone all the way around the bases and touched home on the hit, it would be have been called (no, not a quadruple) a *home run* or *homer.* Usually a home run comes on a ball that's hit over the outfield wall—then the batter just has to go through the formality of touching all the bases and showcase his *home run trot*—but occasionally a fast runner will hit a ball into a vacant area of the outfield and sprint around the bases for what's called an *inside-the-park home run.* A home run with runners on first, second, and third base—that is, with *the bases loaded*—is called a *grand slam.* (It's redundant to call it a grand slam home run—by definition, a grand slam is a four-run home run.)

Back to our example. The leadoff hitter, now called the *lead runner,* was on first base when the second batter hit a single. The lead runner advances to second base, where he is now said to be in *scoring position,* because major leaguers usually can score from second on a routine single. (A runner on third base is also said to be in scoring position.)

Warning Track

A player who can bat both right-handed and left-handed is called a **switch-hitter**. A hitter can change sides only from one at-bat to the next, or if the opposing team changes pitchers in the middle of his at bat. The rules state that "if he steps from one batter's box to the other while the pitcher is in position ready to pitch," he will be called out.

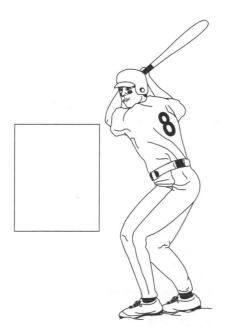

The boxed area shows the strike zone as defined by the rule book—but not as called by today's major league umpires.

Now the third batter hits a high-bouncing ball deep into the space, or *hole,* between shortstop and third base. The shortstop runs to his right, jumps up for the ball, and fires it to first base, but the speedy hitter just beats the throw. That's called *beating out*

Catching On

A **bunt** is hit with the bat held still, so the ball rolls slowly on the infield. A **squeeze bunt** is a bunt with a runner on third base. The riskiest is the **suicide squeeze,** in which the runner breaks for home on the pitch. The batter must make contact, even if it's out of the strike zone, because otherwise the runner will likely be tagged out. Less risky is the **safety squeeze,** in which the runner breaks for home after the bunt.

From the Bench

A complete listing of all the major league rules would be longer than this book. Even the hardest of hardcore fans probably don't know them all—if you watch baseball long enough, I guarantee you'll see some plays that will just absolutely stump you. If you want to really bone up on the complete rules, you can find them in the library or a bookstore, in the annual book called *Official Rules of Major League Baseball.*

an infield hit. On an infield hit, it's usually too risky to try to score from second base, so each runner advances just one base.

Now the bases are loaded (with no outs). The fourth hitter, called the *cleanup hitter,* comes to the plate. Let's say he hits the first pitch over the outfield wall, somewhere between the two foul poles. It's a grand slam, and all four men score.

Or, let's say he hits the ball in the air, far, or *deep,* into center field. The center fielder catches the ball on the warning track right in front of the wall. The runner on third base can then *tag up* by waiting on the base until the ball is caught, and then sprint to home plate. If he reaches home before the throw gets there, the hitter is credited with what's called a *sacrifice fly* and a *run batted in* (or *RBI,* or *ribbie*), because he sacrificed an out to drive in the run.

A hitter usually swings hard at a pitch, but sometimes he will *square around* to *drop down* (or *lay down*) *a bunt,* by turning his body, and his bat, toward the pitcher and trying to just tap the ball into fair territory, preferably about halfway down the first- or third-base line, where the infielders, pitcher, and catcher will have a hard time reaching it before the batter can run to first base. A hitter can bunt for the sole purpose of getting on base, or he can try a *sacrifice bunt* to advance a runner or runners. For instance, if the game is tied or the hitter is weak, the manager probably will order the hitter to try a sacrifice bunt to advance a runner on first base to second base. The manager is willing to sacrifice an out so that he can get the runner in position to score on a single. A riskier but more exciting play occurs when the manager calls for a *suicide squeeze,* a bunt with a runner on third base taking off for home. (You'll read more about the strategy of the bunt in Chapter 18.)

If a defensive player botches what is considered a routine play—either by not fielding a ball cleanly or by throwing it errantly to his intended target—he is said to have made an *error.* (More on that in the next chapter.)

Substitutions

There's no *free substitution* in baseball. That means managers can't pull players in and out of the game, like coaches do in football and basketball. Once a player is taken out of a baseball game, he cannot return.

A manager will replace a *starting pitcher* with *a relief pitcher*. And he'll replace a hitter with a *pinch hitter* or a baserunner with a *pinch runner,* if he wants a little extra speed on the bases. Sounds straightforward enough, but remember, if a slow runner with a great bat gets on base in, say, the top of the sixth, you can't just throw a faster guy in there; you have to consider how many at-bats you'd be giving up if you replaced that hitter, because once you pull him, he's done for the day. It's one of the most important factors in late-game strategy. We'll get into the strategic use of substitutions in the chapters that follow.

The Balk Rule

The *balk* rule, one of baseball's more esoteric, governs a pitcher's motion with runner(s) on base. Before a pitch is delivered a base runner is generally a few steps off the bag, in the direction of the next base; that's called *taking a lead.* The general idea is that a pitcher cannot use an illegal move, such as faking a pitch and then throwing to a base (usually first base) to try and *pick off* a runner. If, in an umpire's judgment, the pitcher uses an illegal movement to deliberately deceive base runners, the umpire can call a balk on the pitcher, and each runner is allowed to advance one base.

What's legal and what isn't? Even the most dedicated fans can't recite all 13 ways that a pitcher can commit a balk. There are some very gray areas here, and just how strictly they're enforced varies from game to game and umpire to umpire. The most common types of balks involve:

➤ Failing to come to a complete and discernible stop when throwing from the set position.

➤ While on the rubber, failing to step toward the base to which you're throwing.

➤ Faking a throw to first while on the rubber.

If you really want to learn them all, turn to Rule 8.05 in the *Official Rules of Major League Baseball.* And find a comfortable chair—you'll be reading for awhile.

Catching On

A **balk** is an illegal movement by a pitcher that results in all base runners being allowed to advance one base. The idea is to prevent a pitcher from deliberately deceiving a base runner—say, by faking a pitch and then whirling around and throwing to a base to pick off a runner. Without the balk rule, you'd almost never see a stolen base.

Extra Innings

Under official baseball rules, a batter is out if "after hitting or bunting a fair ball, his bat hits the ball a second time in fair territory. The ball is dead and no runners may advance." But, "if the batter drops his bat and the ball rolls against the bat in fair territory and, in the umpire's judgment, there was no intention to interfere with the course of the ball, the ball is alive and in play."

The Appeal Play

A team is allowed to *appeal* in certain situations when it thinks the opponent broke a rule. Players, managers, and coaches are given a limited amount of latitude in terms of arguing judgment calls—one that is never supposed to be argued is whether a pitch was a ball or a strike. But a manager can appeal a call—or the lack of a call—and ask for a correct ruling in a few specific instances.

For instance, a batter can be called out on appeal if he misses a base—even on a home run. That's why you might have noticed a jubilant McGwire make sure to go back and touch first base when he hit his record 62nd home run on September 8, 1998. A runner who tries to score on a sacrifice fly can be called out if he leaves third base before the fielder catches the ball. A batter can be called out on appeal when he fails to bat in his proper turn and another batter completes a time at bat in his place. The most common appeal, however, occurs when a manager or catcher asks the plate umpire to ask his partner for help on a half-swing, when the plate umpire has called the pitch a ball. If the hitter is judged to have gone more than halfway through his swing, it's said that he swung at the ball (and thus did not *check*, or *hold up* on his swing) and it's ruled a strike. But the only way a team is going to get any of these calls is to appeal them—the umpires will not make these rulings automatically.

To win an appeal, a team must hope that the umpire has seen the play the same way they did. And they must follow proper appeal etiquette, because if they botch the appeal, they don't get a second chance. For example, if

Catching On

A hitter has to have the discipline to lay off pitches that are out of the strike zone or that give him trouble. Often, he can't make that decision until he has started his swing, so he has to be quick and strong enough to **check** his swing before his wrists **break**, or the umpire will rule that he has **gone around** on his swing and charge him with a strike.

the pitcher throws to first base to appeal a hitter missing the base and winds up throwing the ball into the stands instead of to his first baseman, no second chance is allowed for the appeal.

Extra Innings

Here's one rule that I bet nine out of 10 avid baseball fans don't know: "If a pitched ball lodges in the umpire's or catcher's mask or paraphernalia, and remains out of play, the ball becomes dead and runners advance one base," according to baseball rules.

The Infield Fly Rule

The *infield fly rule* confuses some fans, but it's really not too complicated. Baseball rules define an infield fly as "a fair fly ball (not including a line drive nor an attempted bunt) which can be caught by an infielder with ordinary effort, when first and second, or first, second, and third bases are occupied, before two are out." An umpire invokes the rule under the appropriate conditions. Under the infield fly rule, the batter is automatically out—whether the ball is caught or not—but base runners may advance at their own risk.

The point of the rule is to prevent the defensive team from intentionally letting an easy fly ball or pop-up drop uncaught. Because the base runners in the infield fly scenario are in a *force play* situation—meaning that they're obligated to run on any fair ball that's not caught on the fly—the defense could get an easy *double-play* (or *triple-play*) (two or three outs on the same play) by letting the ball drop.

Pitching Deliveries

There are two legal pitching positions, as defined by Major League Baseball's Official Rules: the *windup* position, which involves a longer, more elaborate windup and delivery, and the set position, also known as *the stretch,* which is a quicker, more compact delivery. Either delivery may be used at any time, although most pitchers work from the set position only when there are runners on base. (More on these in Chapter 12.)

Quick Pitch

A *quick pitch* is an illegal pitch that occurs when the pitcher steps quickly onto the pitching rubber and, in the umpire's judgment, delivers the pitch "before the batter is reasonably set in the batter's box." With the bases empty, the penalty for a quick pitch is a ball awarded to the hitter; with runners on base, the penalty is a balk, meaning that all runners advance one base.

Extra Innings

The rules state that, "If the impact of a runner breaks a base loose from its position, no play can be made on that runner at that base if he had reached that base safely. If a base is dislodged from its position during a play, any following runner on the same play shall be considered as touching or occupying the base if, in the umpire's judgment, he touches or occupies the point marked by the dislodged bag."

Warning Track

A base runner is automatically out if he is "touched by a fair ball in fair territory before the ball has touched or passed an infielder." The ball is dead and no runner may advance. The exception: "If a runner is touching his base when touched by an infield fly (as defined by the Infield Fly Rule), he is not out; although the batter is out." If a runner is *not* touching base, he *is* out.

Interference and Obstruction

The major leagues define several types of *interference,* all of which result in a dead ball.

Offensive interference occurs when the team at bat "interferes with, obstructs, impedes, hinders, or confuses any fielder attempting to make a play." If an umpire calls a base runner out for interference, all other runners must return to the last base that they had legally touched at the time of the interference.

A base runner is called out for interference and the ball is dead when, "in the judgment of the umpire, the base coach at third base, or first base, by touching or holding the runner, physically assists him in returning to or leaving third base or first base."

➤ **Defensive interference** is "an act by a fielder which hinders or prevents a batter from hitting a pitch" (usually *catcher's interference*).

➤ **Umpire's interference** occurs "when an umpire hinders, impedes, or prevents a catcher's throw attempting to prevent a stolen base, or when a fair ball touches an umpire in fair territory before passing a fielder."

➤ **Spectator interference** occurs when a fan "reaches out of the stands, or goes on the field, and touches a live ball."

➤ **Obstruction** is "the act of a fielder who, while not in possession of the ball and not [in the umpire's judgment] in the act of fielding the ball, impedes the progress of any runner."

Extra Innings

Of course, some players have their own personal rules as well. These were Negro League legend Satchel Paige's rules for "How to Keep Young":

1. Avoid fried meats, which angry up the blood.
2. If your stomach disputes you, lie down and pacify it with cool thoughts.
3. Keep the juices flowing by jangling around gently as you move.
4. Go very light on the vices, such as carrying on in society. The social ramble ain't restful.
5. Avoid running at all times.
6. Don't look back. Something might be gaining on you.

If you feel like your head is spinning a little, don't worry—you've just gotten through the most complex chapter in the book. The rules of baseball can be complicated, and the same goes for the world of the men who enforce them, as you'll see in the next chapter.

The Least You Need to Know

➤ A team wins a baseball game by scoring more runs than the opposition.

➤ A run is scored by a player who advances all the way around the bases.

➤ A regulation game consists of nine innings, and each team gets three outs per inning.

➤ The basics of the game are pretty easy to understand, but baseball has plenty of obscure rules and terms, too.

Chapter 9

Men in Blue (and Gray): The Umpires

In This Chapter

➤ The men who enforce the rules

➤ Why the best are nearly invisible

➤ Rhubarbs and controversies

➤ Who determine hits and errors

Hall of Fame manager Joe McCarthy liked to tell about the time he dreamed he had gone to heaven, where God asked him to put together a baseball team. He gathered Babe Ruth, Lou Gehrig, Honus Wagner, Tris Speaker, Christy Mathewson, Cy Young, Walter Johnson, and all the other early superstars. Nobody could beat his team. It was the best ever.

The Devil proposed a game with Heaven's team.

"But you don't have a chance," Joe said. "I've got all the ballplayers."

"I know," Satan said. "But I've got all the umpires."

In this chapter we'll take a close look at the "men in blue" and how they can bedevil managers and players alike.

The Role of Umpires

The *umpires,* or *umps* for short, who make the calls and enforce the rules on the field, are the most reviled men in baseball. Fans shout, "Kill the umpire!" Managers call them blind. Players call them arrogant—and a lot of other, unprintable names.

They're an indispensable part of the game, perhaps more important than the on-field officials in any other sport. They determine who's safe and who's out. They call balls and strikes. They enforce the rules. Still, they're not supposed to be the stars. They're not even supposed to be a sideshow. The best umpires are taken for granted. You only notice them when they screw up.

When it comes to deciding who's safe and who's out, they're almost always right. But a lot of their calls on balls and strikes are debatable. When they botch a close call—*kick* one, as an umpire would say—or make up their own strike zone instead of going by the rules, they get noticed. I remember one time our first-base coach Tommy Helms told an umpire, "Fans don't come out here to see you guys." The umpire considered it inflammatory and threw him out of the game, but it's true.

Talkin' Baseball

"My favorite umpire is a dead one."

—Hall of Fame second baseman
Johnny Evers, Chicago Cubs

The best umpires are models of respect and decorum. They know the rules, they enforce them, and their judgments are nearly always right. They don't abuse their power. They don't play favorites. They're anonymous, virtually invisible, because they don't call attention to themselves. Seven umpires have been enshrined in the Hall of Fame:

➤ **Bill Klem**, known as "The Old Arbitrator" and regarded as the best ever, was a pioneer who recast the umpire's image from the object of scorn to the object of respect.

➤ **Cal Hubbard**, who made the Pro Football Hall of Fame as a player, made the Baseball Hall of Fame as an umpire.

➤ **Jocko Conlan**, an average outfielder, became a Hall of Fame umpire.

➤ **Tom Connolly** was known as a strict disciplinarian and yet went 10 years without ejecting a player.

➤ **Billy Evans** was a sportswriter who began umpiring because of an absent arbiter. The youngest to ever be employed as a major league ump at age 22, he umpired for 22 years before running the front offices of both baseball and football teams.

➤ **Bill McGowan** umpired for 30 years and never shied away from making a tough decision.

➤ **Al Barlick** umpired a record seven All-Star Games, spanning four decades, including the famous 1970 game in which my teammate, Pete Rose, flattened Cleveland catcher Ray Fosse on a play at the plate.

The Problem with Umpires

However, we seem to have an increasing number of bad umpires in the major leagues today. Umpires are supervised and evaluated (and occasionally even fined for transgressions) by the leagues, but their powerful union makes it difficult to weed out the bad ones. Since 1993, only four major league umpiring positions have turned over; compare that to an average attrition rate of about 10 percent for officials in the National Football League. And the umpires' lopsided collective-bargaining agreement doesn't even allow the leagues to choose their best umpires for the playoffs and World Series. Some of them make better money than players do. They've been featured on trading cards. They've written books.

Talkin' Baseball

"He's so incompetent, he couldn't be the crew chief on a sunken submarine."

—Manager Billy Martin on crew chief Jerry Neudecker

Umpires' temperaments started changing in the late 1970s. The old umpires tolerated more. You could argue your case and they would say, "That's enough." You blew off some steam and you went on your way.

The strike zone itself has changed dramatically—it's gotten lower and wider, and frequently is up to the whim of the individual ump. I don't know that we'll ever see balls and strikes called accurately. The umps have influenced the outcome of post-season games by making up their own strike zones.

The umpires were particularly controversial in the 1998 post-season, especially in Game 2 of the American League Championship Series between Cleveland and New York. There was a memorable play in which home plate umpire Ted Hendry failed to call the Indians' Travis Fryman out for interference after Fryman ran outside the base path (in fair territory, instead of outside the foul line where he should've been) on his way to first. Fryman was hit by the throw from Yankee first baseman Tino Martinez, who had run up to field Fryman's bunt, to second baseman Chuck Knoblauch, who was covering first. New York fans were, predictably, up in arms, but, objectively speaking, that call was debatable: If, in the umpire's opinion, Fryman beat the throw, that would nullify the interference, because he's *allowed* to be in fair territory when touching base, because that's where the base is.

However, Hendry's strike zone in that game was a much bigger problem—literally, as it incorporated a "big" area, far outside the plate. Unlike the Fryman play, that affected the game from start to finish. Nine Indians struck out, eight of them looking, and 11 Yankees went down on strikes, four of them called third strikes. "You couldn't have reached some of those pitches with bamboo poles," New York manager Joe Torre said afterward.

But umpires are rarely held accountable by the media. They play an integral part of the game, and yet while every player is grilled after the game by every media outlet in the country, an umpire can go into his locker room and never be questioned. Instead of facing all the questions, they face one "pool" reporter, if that. Nobody should be above the game.

We'll continue to see certain umpires who still believe that the fans came out to see them. I long for the umpire of long ago, who made his very best effort and was never afraid to say, "I missed it."

Extra Innings

Richard Higham of Troy, N.Y., a former manager and National League player, was banished in 1882 for advising gamblers how to bet on games that he umpired. That's notable because he's the only umpire ever judged guilty of dishonesty on the field.

The Golden Rules for Umpires

Major League Baseball's official rulebook includes a series of general instructions to umpires that serve as valuable advice to baseball arbiters at any level. Here they are, verbatim. Read them and decide if you think today's umpires meet these standards:

➤ Umpires, on the field, should not indulge in conversation with players. Keep out of the coaching box and do not talk to the coach on duty.

➤ Keep your uniform in good condition. Be active and alert on the field.

➤ Be courteous, always, to club officials; avoid visiting in club offices and thoughtless familiarity with officers or employees of contesting clubs. When you enter a park your sole duty is to umpire a ball game as the representative of baseball.

➤ Do not allow criticism to keep you from studying out bad situations that may lead to protested games. Carry your rule book. It is better to consult the rules and hold up a game 10 minutes to decide a knotty problem than to have a game thrown out on protest and replayed.

➤ Keep the game moving. A ball game is often helped by energetic and earnest work of the umpires.

➤ You are the only official representative of base-ball on the ballfield. It is often a trying position which requires the exercise of much patience and good judgment, but do not forget that the first essential in working out of a bad situation is to keep your own temper and self-control.

➤ You no doubt are going to make mistakes, but never attempt to "even up" after having made one. Make all decisions as you see them and forget which is the home or visiting club.

➤ Keep your eye everlastingly on the ball while it is in play. It is more vital to know just where a fly ball fell, or a thrown ball finished up, than whether or not a runner missed a base. Do not call the plays too quickly, or turn away too fast when a fielder is throwing to complete a double play. Watch out for dropped balls after you have called a man out.

➤ Do not come running with your arm up or down, denoting "out" or "safe." Wait until the play is completed before making any arm motion.

Talkin' Baseball

"It's the only occupation where a man has to be perfect the first day on the job and then improve over the years."

—Umpire Ed Runge

➤ Each umpire team should work out a simple set of signals, so the proper umpire can always right a manifestly wrong decision when convinced he has made an error. If sure you got the play correctly, do not be stampeded by players' appeals to "ask the other man." If not sure, ask one of your associates. Do not carry this to extremes, be alert, and get your own plays. But remember! The first requisite is to get decisions correctly. If in doubt don't hesitate to consult your associate. Umpire dignity is important but never as important as "being right."

➤ A most important rule for umpires is always "BE IN POSITION TO SEE EVERY PLAY." Even though your decision may be 100 percent right, players still question it if they feel you were not in a spot to see the play clearly and definitely.

➤ Finally, be courteous, impartial, and firm, and so compel respect from all.

Training Umpires

Major league umpires are supposed to be the best of the best. Many played the game for years and/or worked their way up through the ranks, beginning as low as youth leagues and needing certification annually by the high school level. The road to the big leagues usually requires 10–15 years of experience at the lower levels, and even then there are no guarantees. Because there are only 64 umpires in the major leagues and 180 in the minor leagues, and very little turnover, umpires face an even tougher road to the top than players.

"First and foremost you have to love the game," says Dutch Rennert, who umpired in the National League for 20 years after toiling for 15 years in the minors, seven at the Triple-A level, before earning a spot in the majors in 1973. "No one ever said it was going to be easy, but you have to set your goals to be the best."

Accredited umpire schools are run by former major league umpires: Joe Brinkman/ Bruce Froemming, Jim Evans, and Harry Wendelstedt. The schools are in session for five weeks in January and February and usually enroll a combined total of about 350–400 prospective umpires. Umpiring students who finish in the top 10 percent of their class are invited to Major League Baseball's Umpire Development Evaluation

Course. Those who finish in the top half are offered a job in the short season or rookie leagues, whose season begins in June and runs for two-and-a-half months. From there they work their way up the ladder through the minor leagues, just as the players do.

Rennert says baseball umpires have the most difficult job of any sport's field officials. "As [a home plate] umpire, you're making more than 300 split-second decisions a game," he says. "Your concentration level has to be at its best one hundred percent of the time for you to call a good, consistent game."

Extra Innings

Attorney William R. Wheaton umpired the first recorded "modern" game on October 6, 1845. J.L. Boake umpired the first professional league game in 1871, Billy McLean the first National League game in 1876, Tommy Connolly the first American League game in 1901, and Hank O'Day and Connolly umpired the first modern World Series in 1903.

The Umpiring Crew

Organized baseball used only one umpire for most games in the 19th century. He frequently took up his position behind the pitcher, so as to see the whole field to make pitching and baserunning calls. The National League allowed two in 1898, but it wasn't standardized for several years. Both the National and American leagues added a third umpire in 1933, and in 1952 the majors instituted the current setup of four umpires in each of the major leagues' 16 crews.

Catching On

The **crew chief**, or umpire-in-chief, has sole authority to forfeit a game and final say on any controversies.

For each game, one crew member is assigned to home plate (called the *home plate umpire,* or simply the *plate umpire;* he's the only one who wears a mask), and one to each of the other three bases, collectively called the *base umpires* or *field umpires.* The umpires rotate positions for each game. The major leagues add two additional umpires down each outfield line for post-season games. Each crew has a *crew chief,* or umpire-in-chief, who has sole authority to forfeit a game and final say on any controversies.

The plate umpire stands behind the catcher and calls (and counts) balls and strikes, signals fair and foul balls, makes calls at home plate, and makes all decisions on the batter. The other three umpires stand in the vicinity of first, second, and third bases. The following figure shows the normal positioning of the four umpires, as well as the additional two umps that work the lines for post-season games. The base umpires make all calls at their bases unless the plate umpire has a better view. They help decide issues such as calling *time* (or timeout), balks, defacement or discoloration of the ball by the pitcher, the use of an illegal pitch, when a fly ball is caught, and ejection of any coach or player for flagrant unsportsmanlike conduct.

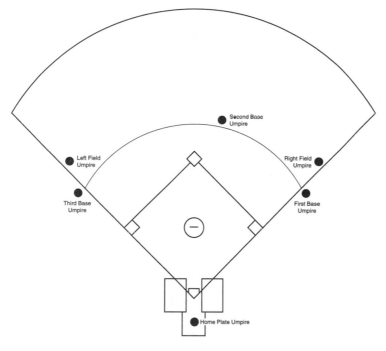

Second Base
Umpire

Left Field
Umpire

Right Field
Umpire

Third Base
Umpire

First Base
Umpire

Home Plate Umpire

This diagram shows the normal positioning of the umpires for a major league game. (The two extra umpires down the lines are added for post-season games.) The base umpires will move around depending on the game situation—always trying to be in the best possible position to make a call.

Extra Innings

In the early days of baseball, the lone umpire worked either behind the batter or behind the pitcher and did not shift. In 1888, John Gaffney, The King of the Umpires, moved behind the plate when the bases were empty. When a second official was added, the umpire moved behind the plate for good.

Umpire Signals

Umpires have a basic set of hand signals that they use to convey their calls to participants and fans. Some, such as the extending of the arms straight out to indicate "safe," are pretty standard. Others, such as the "out" call and the "strike" call, vary a bit from umpire to umpire, and from situation to situation—for instance, you'll often see an ump make a more emphatic "out" call on an exciting, close play. Sometimes, like when a pitch is called a ball, there's no signal at all. The following figures show some of the common umpire signals.

Umpires' out calls vary a bit, but most involve a punching motion with a fist—and an accompanying shout ("OUT!") just in case there's any question on a close play.

The safe call is more standardized: a quick, outward, sweeping motion that ends with both arms fully extended to the sides.

The strike call usually involves a pumping motion with the right hand. Some plate umps will turn to the side and sort of point to indicate a strike. You'll know the strike call when you see it, because there's no hand signal for a ball.

To signal for time, an umpire extends both arms skyward, with the palms facing forward. It's important that this signal is immediately noticed by everyone on the field, so an umpire will usually shout, "Time!" as well. An umpire follows a similar procedure to signal interference—because this is also a dead ball, or timeout, situation.

To indicate a foul tip that may be difficult to detect from the dugouts and stands, a home plate umpire extends both arms upward and strikes the right hand with the left, then follows with his normal strike signal.

To signal obstruction on the defensive team, an umpire places his hands on his hips.

The Most Difficult Calls

According to *Make the Right Call: Major League Baseball's Official Rules and Interpretations plus League Umpire's Guide and Instructions*, the umpire's toughest decisions include:

➤ Judging whether or not a batter checked his swing to avoid a strike

➤ Determining when a balk has been committed

➤ Calling consistent balls and strikes

➤ Getting in proper position to make calls at home plate

➤ Maintaining concentration throughout the game

➤ Determining whether long fly balls are fair or foul

Warning Track

If you're at a major league game and want to know if an umpire blew a call, you'd better be recording the game at home, because you won't see a replay at the ballpark. Under agreement with the umpires' union, which doesn't want to show up its members or start riots, Major League Baseball doesn't allow teams to use instant replay on the scoreboard for controversial calls.

Talkin' Baseball

"I couldn't see well enough to play when I was a boy, so they gave me a special job—they made me the umpire."

—President Harry S. Truman

With instant replay there to second-guess every call, and with the speed of runners today, there will always be controversial "bang-bang" plays on the bases. Safe or out? On a grounder to the shortstop, the umpire can't watch the ball as it's thrown over to first base and the runner at the same time, so he has to listen for the ball hitting the glove while watching the runner's foot hit the bag. That can be extremely difficult, but I think they do a pretty good job on those calls.

Calling Balls and Strikes

I found throughout my career—and I think you'll always find—that umpires have different ideas of where the strike zone is. Some guys call the low pitches and some guys don't call the high pitches. There are guys who call strikes along the edges of the plate, even if they're an inch or two outside that black border.

But I don't have a problem if they're close—and if they're consistent. Lee Weyer was a big old guy who would bend over and scrape the dust off the black edges and everybody knew that he called the edges. He was consistent, which is exactly what you want. Being able to make adjustments is critical in baseball, and as long as you know an umpire's strike zone, whether you're pitching or hitting, you should be able to adjust.

The strike zone is supposed to be from the letters to the knees, according to the rule book. I think the old American League umpires made better ball/strike judgments because they wore the old foam chest protectors (sometimes called balloons or mattresses) and stood directly behind the catchers and could see both sides of the plate when they were judging balls and strikes. But when Bill Klem became the boss of National League umpires, they went to a more compact chest protector and called balls and strikes from just over the catcher's shoulder nearest the batter.

Today, both leagues use that style, and I don't think umpires have the best perspective on all of home plate. They peer around the catcher from one side or the other. If it's a right-handed hitter, then the umpire is on his inside corner and can't make the best of judgments on the outside corner. He's too far away, and his view is blocked. He loses all consistency in calling balls and strikes and he makes calls that you just shake your head at. These days pitches that are six inches outside are being called strikes.

The Post-Season Controversy

The umpires' association's current contract, which runs through 1999, stipulates that no umpire can work more than one special event (All-Star Game, Division Series, League Championship Series, or World Series) in a season. (There's one exception: An umpire can work both a Division Series and the World Series in the same year.) No ump can be assigned to two World Series in a row.

The idea is to give everyone a crack at the highest-profile—and most lucrative—assignments. Besides their regular salaries, which range from $75,000 to $225,000 with a $7,500 bonus for crew chiefs, umps receive an additional $12,500 for working a Division Series, $15,000 for a League Championship Series, and $17,500 for a World Series.

I'm all for spreading the wealth—and this system does that, guaranteeing that three quarters of all major league umpires will work one of the year's biggest events. As of the end of the 1998 season, out of the 64 full-time major league umpires, 45—that's 70 percent—had been assigned either to an All-Star Game or to a post-season series.

The problem with this setup is that it doesn't guarantee that the best umpires will work in many of the most important games of the year. (And it showed in the 1998 playoffs, where there were several questionable calls.) Compare that to the other three major pro sports, all of which regularly evaluate and rate their officials and assemble post-season crews based on merit alone. For example, the National Basketball Association, which ranks its referees from 1 to 58 based on performance evaluations, assigns the top 32 refs to work the playoffs, and chooses from among the best 11 for its finals crew. It makes sense: You have the best teams in the playoffs—you should have the best officials, too.

Talkin' Baseball

"This must be the only job in America that everybody knows how to do better than the guy who's doing it."

—Umpire Nestor Chylak

When the Men in Blue Make You See Red

Disagreements with umpires often start out heated. From his vantage point in the dugout, the manager thinks the play wasn't even close. He wonders, *"How could the umpire not see that? Where was he? Was he blocked out? Why doesn't he ask his crew for help?"*

The really nasty arguments come when there's a history of problems between a team and an umpiring crew. You feel they either have a grudge against you, or they don't make their best effort, and when that resentment is already there, it just builds and builds and then it explodes.

If it's a tie game or a one-run game and you think the ump blew the call, you can't believe they don't understand how important that call is to the outcome of the game. So you get worked up and it becomes confrontational—and when that happens, the manager or the player always lose. He's out of order and he's out of the game. The guy has to leave the field and the dugout. If he pushes his luck any further—say, by bumping the umpire—he's risking a fine or suspension.

Catching On

A **rhubarb** is a baseball term for an argument—and sometimes a fight—between teams or one team and the umpires.

The good umps will listen to your argument and say, "Okay, you've had your say and that's it." You can tell yourself, "Okay, he let me say my piece. I'll relax." I was always frustrated by the umpires who would leave you standing there with nobody to argue with. Then there are the guys who keep going at you and instigating more. The ump confronts you and inflames you and you wind up extending the argument. Then comes anger and profanity. And then the showers.

Extra Innings

Sometimes a manager isn't really arguing with the umpire, even though it looks that way. The manager may have another agenda, such as buying time for his relief pitcher to get warmed up before replacing a starter. I remember one time when Tommy Lasorda, managing the Los Angeles Dodgers, went out to the mound and dilly-dallied around until the umpire, Tom Gorman, came out and told him to hurry up and make a decision.

Tommy stalled. "What do you think I ought to do here? Should I take him out?" he asked.

"Well, I don't care," Gorman said. "Do whatever you want to do."

"Well, I don't know. What do you think? Should I take him out? I mean, how is he throwing?"

"Come on, Tommy," Gorman said. "I don't know this stuff. Just make a decision."

"Okay," Tommy said, knowing he couldn't stall any longer. "I'll take him out." And he motioned for his reliever, finally ready, to come in the game.

Memorable Arguments in My Career

My Cincinnati Reds were playing the Baltimore Orioles in the 1970 World Series when Bernie Carbo scored—or so we thought—on a close play at the plate. The Orioles catcher, Elrod Hendricks, had the ball in his hand, but he appeared to tag Bernie with the glove, not the ball. Ken Burkhart, the home plate umpire, called Bernie out. Everybody in the ballpark saw it except Burkhart, because he was in a bad position and couldn't see it. Our manager, Sparky Anderson, was never vicious or mean, but he went crazy that time.

When we played the Boston Red Sox in the 1975 World Series, there was a famous bunt by Eddie Armbrister that helped us win Game 3 in extra innings. Red Sox catcher Carlton Fisk bounded out from behind the plate to field the ball, and he thought he was bumped or interfered with by Eddie, who was starting to run to first base. Fisk picked up the ball and threw it to second base. If he'd gotten the out at second, it would have been a double play, because Eddie was just leaving home plate. But Fisk threw the ball away, and Boston's manager, Darrell Johnson, screamed for interference on Eddie. We believed Eddie didn't interfere, and this time the umpires sided with us. We went on to win the Series in seven games. I'm still amazed we had such controversial calls in two different World Series.

The Official Scorer

When a guy reaches base and you're not sure if it's a hit or an error, a display on the scoreboard—sometimes it's just an "H" for a hit or an "E" for an error—as well as the public address announcer will usually tell you. A lot of these calls are obvious. But some are controversial—especially if the pitcher is throwing a no-hitter and a tough play is ruled a hit instead of an error. Or if a hitter is vying for a batting title and feels he was "robbed" of a base hit that was called an error.

Who makes these decisions? The *official scorer*, who sits upstairs in the stadium's press box. Chances are, you'll never know his name, unless, like the umpire, he provokes a big debate.

Official scorers can be college coaches, retired writers or baseball publicists, or anyone who's witnessed a lot of major league games over the years. Scorers used to be mostly baseball writers, but in the past decade or so, some newspapers, citing a conflict of interest, barred their writers from scoring the same game that they were writing about. The papers don't want to be put in a situation where a player doesn't talk to a writer because of a decision he made as a scorer.

A scorer has to be truly committed to know the rules, be alert at all times, and make judgment calls

Catching On

The **official scorer** is the scorekeeper or statistician of record, and makes rulings such as whether a play is a hit or an error.

on things that happen in a split second. Sometimes at a game I'm talking to someone or I turn my head and I miss a play: "Man, I didn't see it. What happened?" But the official scorer has to pay close attention all the time. They have to turn in long, detailed reports after every game, and for all the hours and scrutiny, they make less than $100 a game.

It's a tough job. They can't let players' ulterior motives influence them when they know they're right. There have always been "homers," guys who give the benefit of the doubt to the hometown pitchers. For instance, if a scorer calls what could have been a hit an error, his pitcher might wind up with no earned runs charged against his record, even though he gave up five or six runs. Rule it a hit, however, and all the runs are earned, and the pitcher's ERA really skyrockets. So maybe one of his infielders gets stuck with an error instead. Big money is tied to personal statistics, and scorers can get nasty looks and even phone calls from irate pitchers and hitters when decisions don't go their way.

Talkin' Baseball

"The worst thing that can happen to a man is to be born without guts and be an umpire."

—Umpire Cal Drummond

Official scorers are allowed to review plays on instant replay and in conversations with managers and players, but their decisions are final 24 hours after the game.

I think the system is as good as it can be. I think the scorers are usually fair. Over the course of a year, a player might get the benefit of three or four calls and lose the benefit of three or four calls. For the most part, things balance out.

Well, we've covered the field, the equipment, the rules, the umpires, and the scorers. Looks to me like we're ready to go to "the show"—baseball's major leagues.

The Least You Need to Know

➤ Major league crews consist of four umpires for regular-season games (one at each of the four bases) and six for post-season games.

➤ The best umpires are so accurate and cause so little controversy that you forget they're even there.

➤ The worst umpires take a belligerent attitude toward players, throw them out of games too quickly, and make up their own interpretation of the strike zone.

➤ The official scorer fills out the official record of each game and decides issues such as whether a batter reached base on a hit or an error.

Chapter 10

Hitting It Big: The Major Leagues

In This Chapter

➤ America's best off-Broadway show

➤ Who plays where and who plays who

➤ Why you've gotta watch what you say in Boston

➤ What it takes to win it all

To many kids, major league players are the first heroes they have. As a kid growing up in Oklahoma, I remember watching Mickey Mantle and dreaming that someday I, too, would play in the major leagues.

While it's true that baseball in the major leagues is the same game you can see played in the minor leagues, college, high school, and even Little League, there's no doubt that big-league baseball is different. And it's not just the quality of play. They call the majors "The Show," and to baseball players and fans it's the greatest show on earth. In this chapter, we'll take a look at the major leagues, from the teams that make them up to the rivalries, the pageantry, and the rites that make the big leagues the greatest show on earth.

The Leagues and Divisions

The major leagues are comprised of two separate leagues, the *American League* and the *National League*. The NL, which has been in existence since 1876, is the older of the two and therefore sometimes known as the *Senior Circuit*. The AL was formed in 1901.

You Call This Organized?

You can really trace organized baseball back to—would you believe it—Cincinnati, where the Red Stockings, baseball's first professional team, were formed in 1869. For an eight-month season of barnstorming, Harry Wright paid his players salaries ranging from $600 for a reserve to $1,400 for the team captain and star shortstop George Wright, Harry's brother. The total team payroll was $9,300—today's superstars earn more than eight times that much *per game*.

The undefeated Red Stockings won 56 games in their first season—playing before an estimated total of 200,000 fans—and didn't suffer their first loss until June 14, 1870, at the hands of the Brooklyn Atlantics. Fans lost interest when the streak was over, and ensuing losses both on the field and in the bank book led to the club's demise after that season.

However, other cities took notice of the notoriety that the Red Stockings had brought the city of Cincinnati, and businessmen started envisioning the profits to be made in fielding their own pro teams. The National Association of Base Ball Players (the game's name was still two words in those days), which had been organized in 1858 to govern the sport at the amateur/club level, had essentially died out by 1871. Into its place stepped the National Association of Professional Base Ball Players, formed in March of 1871.

The National Association, baseball's first professional league, began its inaugural season with 10 teams: the Boston Red Stockings (Harry Wright's team had moved there), Chicago White Stockings, Cleveland Forest Citys, Fort Wayne Kekiongas, New York Mutuals, Philadelphia Athletics, Rockford Forest Citys, Troy Haymakers, Washington Nationals, and Washington Olympics. Considering the venture too risky, the Brooklyn Eckfords opted not to pay the $10 initiation fee; they later replaced the Fort Wayne club, which dropped out of the league at midseason.

Philadelphia won the first National Association championship, and Boston took the next four. But those two clubs, along with New York, were the only ones that lasted even five years. More than 25 teams floated in and out of the National Association during its brief existence. By the end of the 1875 season, amid financial losses, competitive imbalance, and allegations of gambling and game-fixing, the National Association was on the ropes.

Talkin' Baseball

"There is something electrifying about the big leagues. I had read so much about [Stan] Musial, [Ted] Williams, and [Jackie] Robinson... I had put those guys on a pedestal. They were something special.... I really thought that they put their pants on different, rather than one leg at a time."

—Hank Aaron

The National League

Chicago owner William A. Hulbert still felt that professional baseball could be a moneymaker, but he wanted a better-managed league. With the support of the National Association's three other Midwestern clubs—Cincinnati, Louisville, and St. Louis—Hulbert was able to convince four other teams—Boston, Hartford, New York, and Philadelphia—to pull the plug on the National Association and join his new National League of Professional Base Ball Clubs. This is the same National League that exists today.

Hartford president M.G. Bulkeley was elected league president, and the National League adopted a no-nonsense, business-minded approach to the game, instituting strict player contracts and banning gambling, Sunday games, and liquor sales at the ballparks. They also instituted a "reserve clause," which meant that a team "reserved" a player's services for the next season—other teams in the league couldn't hire him, and he could not offer himself to teams at a higher salary.

If you attended a National League game back in those days, you would've seen the same basic game you see today, with a few important differences: Most fielders played bare-handed, the catcher stood directly behind home plate only when there was a runner on base, and a batter had the right to request a high or low pitch—pitchers didn't try to outsmart the batter; their job was just to serve up the ball.

The National League struggled through the 1870s, facing challenges from three other leagues in its first 15 years of existence. The most serious came from the American Association of Base Ball Clubs, which cut ticket prices from 50 cents to 25 cents, allowed liquor sales (it was called the "Beer and Whiskey League"), and played Sunday games. The National League and the American Association were bitter rivals at first, and player salaries climbed as the upstart AA, not bound by the NL's reserve clause, started drawing fans as it raided the NL's rosters with promises of more money. Eventually the two leagues signed the National Agreement of 1883, which provided for the mutual observance of the reserve clause (i.e., no luring away each other's players) and a post-season championship series between the two leagues.

Two other leagues were formed in the late 1800s, but each lasted only one season. The Union Association of Base Ball Clubs, which tried to entice players from the other two leagues by proclaiming its opposition to the reserve clause, played only the 1884 season. The Players League, formed by the Brotherhood of Professional Base Ball Players because of the players' objections to the reserve clause and the owners' threats to institute a ceiling on salaries, lasted only for the 1890 season.

Soon after the Players League went under, the National League and American Association were at war again (over distribution of players from the PL), and this time the latter didn't survive. The newly named, 12-team National League and American Association of Professional Base Ball Clubs, which added the defunct AA's teams in Baltimore, Louisville, St. Louis, and Washington to the NL's eight clubs (Boston, Brooklyn, Chicago, Cincinnati, Cleveland, New York, Philadelphia, and Pittsburgh), served as baseball's sole major league from 1892 until the turn of the century.

The American League

In January 1900, a minor league called the Western League announced that it was renaming itself the American League and reorganizing, by planting franchises in Baltimore, Chicago, Cleveland, and Washington. The league also requested—and was denied—recognition by the National League as a second major league.

In December of that year, AL president Bancroft Johnson, having announced his league's intention to plant a team in Boston for the 1901 season, was granted a meeting with National League executives at their winter meetings. But the NL owners stood Johnson up, slipping out a back door while the AL president waited outside the meeting room for hours. Furious, Johnson proceeded with the AL's planned Boston entry, making that the third city, along with Chicago and Philadelphia, in which the two leagues would go head-to-head. By offering significantly higher salaries, the American League convinced about 30 NL regulars, including Cy Young and Nap Lajoie, to defect.

For two years the leagues waged war over players. Finally, the National League, suffering from poor leadership among its owners, was forced to make peace on Johnson's terms. As part of a peace agreement signed in January 1903, the American League gained recognition as a major circuit, and the National Commission was formed to oversee all of organized baseball, which consisted of the AL, NL, and the National Association of Minor Leagues. Ban Johnson was the most powerful man in Major League Baseball.

The AL and NL agreed to respect each others' player contracts (upholding the reserve clause throughout organized baseball) and territorial rights, and establish a common body of rules. The AL installed a team in New York, and the structure of major league baseball was set for the next 50 years. They also agreed to stage a World Series between the champions of each league at the end of every season. The two major leagues have existed unchallenged in the 20th century except for 1914–15, when the short-lived Federal League tried unsuccessfully to establish itself as a third major league.

Some of the nicknames changed, but the following table shows the structure of Major League Baseball for those first 50 years.

The Major Leagues: 1903–1953

National League	American League
Boston Braves	Boston Red Sox
Brooklyn Dodgers	Chicago White Sox
Chicago Cubs	Cleveland Indians
Cincinnati Reds	Detroit Tigers
New York Giants	New York Yankees
Philadelphia Phillies	Philadelphia Athletics
Pittsburgh Pirates	St. Louis Browns
St. Louis Cardinals	Washington Senators

Stability and Expansion

For half of the 20th century, baseball was centered in the northeastern quarter of the country, with St. Louis the most western city with a team and Washington, D.C., the most southern. Several cities were represented by more than one team. At one time, Chicago, Philadelphia, St. Louis, and Boston had one team in each league, while New York City had one AL and two NL franchises (the New York Giants in Manhattan and the Brooklyn Dodgers).

Baseball began to move after the 1952 season, when the Boston Braves moved to Milwaukee and started drawing record crowds. The St. Louis Browns moved to Baltimore and became the Orioles, bringing back the name of the old National League team that had folded in 1899. The Philadelphia A's moved to Kansas City in 1954 (then to Oakland in 1968). Most shocking of all, New York lost both its National League teams in 1957, when the Brooklyn Dodgers and the New York Giants moved their ancient rivalry to the West Coast (Los Angeles and San Francisco, respectively). In 1961, the Washington Senators moved to St. Paul and became the Minnesota Twins, and in 1966 the Braves moved to Atlanta.

In the '60s the leagues also began adding new franchises, known as *expansion teams*. A new version of the Senators moved into Washington in 1961, only to move 10 years later and become the Texas Rangers. Seven more teams were created: the Kansas City Royals, Montreal Expos, San Diego Padres, Houston Colt .45s (later the Astros), Los Angeles (later the California) Angels, and Seattle Pilots, who lasted one season and moved to Milwaukee to become the Brewers. And the National League came back to New York: The luckless, lovable Mets took the Yankees old manager (Casey Stengel), the Dodgers' old color (blue), and the Giants' old logo (the orange "NY").

By 1969, each league had 12 teams, and for the first time the leagues split into East and West divisions. By 1994, there were 14 teams in each league, so each league added a Central Division. In 1998, two more teams were added to the majors, bringing the total to 30.

When the Arizona Diamondbacks and Tampa Bay Devil Rays were added to the majors in 1998, the powers that be were faced with a dilemma. They didn't want to put both new teams in the same league, but splitting them up would leave 15 teams in each league, meaning that on any given day of the season, one team in each league would have an off-day. The solution they came up with was to put Tampa Bay in the AL, Arizona in the NL, and have Milwaukee switch from the AL to the NL, giving each circuit an even number of teams. While several teams have moved from city to city, the Brewers became the first major league team to switch leagues. Milwaukee didn't mind: They'd been an NL town when the Braves were there from 1953 to 1965. The following table shows the current alignment of the major league teams and their divisions.

The Major Leagues Today

National League	American League
East Division	
Atlanta Braves	Baltimore Orioles
Florida Marlins	Boston Red Sox
Montreal Expos	New York Yankees
New York Mets	Tampa Bay Devil Rays
Philadelphia Phillies	Toronto Blue Jays
Central Division	
Chicago Cubs	Chicago White Sox
Cincinnati Reds	Cleveland Indians
Houston Astros	Detroit Tigers
Milwaukee Brewers	Kansas City Royals
Pittsburgh Pirates	Minnesota Twins
St. Louis Cardinals	
West Division	
Arizona Diamondbacks	Anaheim Angels
Colorado Rockies	Oakland Athletics
Los Angeles Dodgers	Seattle Mariners
San Diego Padres	Texas Rangers
San Francisco Giants	

The Schedule: A Mere 2,430 games

A major league team plays 162 games in a *regular season* (not including preseason games or playoff games). It's a long and sometimes tedious grind, but playing that many games is the best way to find out who the strongest teams in the league are.

The toughest part of the schedule are the *doubleheaders*—back-to-back games, with about a half-hour of rest in between. The first professional doubleheader was played way back on September 25, 1882, when Providence played Worcester. They aren't as common now, but I still think this is the ultimate test for any young player. If you can play as hard as you can for 18 straight innings and still want more, then you have the desire a big leaguer needs.

The schedule that's used now is slightly weighted so that each team plays more games against teams in its own

Catching On

If one team wins both games (or **ends**) of a doubleheader, it is called a **sweep**. If each team wins one game, the doubleheader goes down as a **split**.

division than against other teams. This makes sense, because ultimately these are the teams you're competing against for the division title and a spot in the playoffs.

Interleague Play

The 1996 season brought us an unprecedented scheduling quirk. For the first time ever, regular-season interleague games were played. Up until that season, National League teams played American League teams only in the World Series. Predictably, a lot of purists were upset by interleague play. But the fans loved it. It was finally a chance for fans in New York to see the Mets play the Yankees. Chicagoans got to see the White Sox play the Cubs. And Ohioans finally got to see my old team, the Cincinnati Reds, play the Cleveland Indians.

Every team still plays 162 games, as they did before interleague play was instituted, so the interleague games just replace games against teams in your own league. Although many newspapers list each team's interleague record separately in the standings, there's no difference in the standings—a win is a win, a loss is a loss, they all count the same towards your record. When two teams are tied, either for a division championship or a wild-card berth, those situations are always resolved with a one-game playoff.

Interleague play has been popular with fans, but there's one legitimate argument against it that needs to be kept in mind. Interleague games are scheduled as follows: Teams from each league's East division play each other, while Central division teams go head-to-head and the same holds for the West. So schedules are no longer of uniform toughness.

For example, in 1998, the Mets had to play 16 games against the AL East, which is full of tough teams like the Yankees, Boston Red Sox, and Toronto Blue Jays. The Cubs, on the other hand, played 13 games against the AL Central, which had only one team—Cleveland—with a winning record. At the end of the season, the Cubs had a better record than the Mets by one game, thanks in part to the fact that they played an easier schedule. This gave the Cubs an advantage in the battle for a National League playoff spot.

Warning Track

If you're used to watching teams from only one league play, don't become alarmed when watching interleague games if it seems like the game is being played by different rules than you're accustomed to. The American League uses a designated hitter to bat for the pitcher, the NL doesn't. During interleague play (and the World Series), the DH is used only in AL parks.

Catching On

Before each season, major league teams spend five or six weeks—from mid-February until Opening Day in late March or early April—in **spring training**. Spring training is a chance for established players to get back into regular-season shape, and an opportunity for young players to impress the coaches. Teams train in Florida or Arizona, because of their mild climates.

Spring Training: Working the Kinks Out

Before each season, major league ballplayers spend five or six weeks—from mid-February until Opening Day in late March or early April—training, working out the rust and the cobwebs. *Spring training* is a chance for established players to get back into regular-season shape, and an opportunity for young players to make an impression on the coaches. It's the closest thing the major leagues have to a tryout.

Teams either train in Arizona or Florida, because of their mild climates. For the first two weeks or so, spring training is just calisthenics and working on fundamentals. Then the exhibition games start. Early on, established players will only play a few innings, then they'll head out for the golf course. As the regular season nears, though, the games get more serious, the good players play more, and the pretenders are sent down to the minor leagues. By the end of March, the games feel almost real and everyone's attention turns to the start of the regular season.

For major leaguers, spring training means lots of calisthenics and drills.

Opening Day was always special for me, because I played for the Reds, and the first major league game of the season used to be played in Cincinnati every year. There would be a parade with floats, bands, and even elephants. Everybody would be optimistic about the upcoming season, and the players, especially the younger guys, would experience a rush that's hard to describe. The new uniform, the smell of the ballpark, the buzz of the crowd … that's what Opening Day is all about. Spring training—and all of its wind sprints and games that didn't count—become a thing of the past, and we begin playing for real.

Catching On

The teams that compete in spring training in Florida play in what is known, unofficially, as the **Grapefruit League.** The teams in Arizona play in the **Cactus League.**

Extra Innings

The best Opening Day pitching performance in major league history was turned in by Bob Feller of the Cleveland Indians on April 16, 1940. Feller didn't give up a hit against the Chicago White Sox, making it the only game in major league history in which every player on one team ended the game with the same batting average (.000) he had when it began.

The All-Star Game: A Midsummer Night's Dream

Once a year, baseball takes a break in mid-season (early to mid-July) to honor its best players. The *All-Star Game,* featuring a team of National League stars against the American League's best, is a thrill for players and fans alike.

Fans can pick up ballots at any professional ballpark and vote for one player at each position (except pitcher). These days, you can even vote online, at Major League Baseball's official web site: **http://www.majorleaguebaseball.com**. The votes are tallied up, with the top vote-getters winning the opportunity to start the All-Star Game. The reserves and pitchers are then selected by each team's respective manager, who must make sure that each team has at least one representative.

Being named an All-Star is a great honor. It's a great feeling to know that fans all over the country know your work and appreciate it. The game is played on a Tuesday night, and the majors shut down on the day before the game and the day after. Some players consider it a grind to have to travel to the site of the game (which alternates each year between an AL park and an NL park) when most other players are home relaxing. But I

From the Bench

You'll know about nine months before the game who will serve as managers in the All-Star game. That's because the All-Star teams are managed by the managers of the previous season's league champions.

Catching On

Four teams make the playoffs in each league: the three division winners and one **wild card** team, which is the second-place team with the best record in each league.

wouldn't miss it for the world. When you're retired, being an All-Star becomes a badge for you. People remember you as a three-time All-Star or a six-time All-Star. Even being a one-time All-Star is special. It's a great thing to be remembered for.

The Playoffs: Who Gets In—and How You Win

When the AL and NL split into divisions in 1969, it led to something unprecedented: playoffs. Up until then, the team with the best regular-season record in each league was that league's representative in the World Series. Divisional play meant that another round of playoffs had to be added. So the East and West Division winners began meeting in '69 in the *League Championship Series (LCS)*. They played a best-of-five series, meaning the first team to win three games won the series, and the winner would advance to the World Series.

The first change to the playoff structure came in 1985, when the League Championship Series were expanded to best-of-seven. The next change came in 1995. Since each league now had three divisions, another round of playoffs, the Division series, was added. But you can't have a playoff with just three teams, so to fill out the field, the second-place team with the best record in each league were given playoff spots as *wild-card* teams.

This is how the playoffs now work in each league: In the first round, the division winner with the best record plays the wild-card winner and the other two division winners play each other. These *Division Series* are best-of-five. The winners then meet in the LCS, which are best-of-seven. The winners then meet in the World Series. That means a team has to win 11 games to win the world championship, and the playoffs go on for almost a month. But if you're a fan, it's a great, tension-filled, dramatic month.

Today's playoff format is better than ever. Talk about excitement—now you've got three rounds of action. But it makes it that much tougher for a team to get through and maintain focus and intensity, particularly a team like the 1998 Yankees, who clinched their division so early. In the playoffs, every game is so crucial you can't afford a mistake.

The extra round of playoffs also increases the importance of quality starting pitching. If you've got a guy like Kevin Brown or David Wells who can go out and win two games in that first round, all you have to do is figure out a way to win one more game and you've won the series. That was exactly what the Astros had in mind when they acquired Randy Johnson last summer, and Johnson did his part in his two first-round starts—he just got outpitched.

As you get deeper into the playoffs, with longer series, the bullpen becomes more important. But pitching is still the key—the team whose pitchers come up big is almost always going to win a post-season series. Look at the Padres in 1998: Their bullpen was superb in beating the Braves in the LCS, then it fell apart as they were swept by the Yankees in the World Series.

Extra Innings

In 1997 the Florida Marlins, who finished second in the NL East to the Atlanta Braves, became the first wild-card team to win the World Series, defeating the Cleveland Indians in a seven-game thriller. The Marlins, who were born as an expansion team in 1993, also set a record by winning a championship in just their fifth year of existence.

The World Series: Truly a Fall Classic

The first World Series—the showdown between AL and NL champs—was played in 1903, when the American League's Boston Pilgrims (as the Red Sox were once known) beat the Pittsburgh Pirates of the National League. No series was played in 1904, because of bad blood between John McGraw, manager of the NL's New York Giants and American League president Ban Johnson, but the following year the series resumed and it has continued almost uninterrupted since. The only year since 1903 in which the Series wasn't played was 1994, when labor strife caused it to be canceled. Fans could deal with regular-season games being wiped out, but there was something almost sacrilegious about seeing the Fall Classic scrubbed. It led to a lot of ill-will between fans, players, and owners.

The Series itself is simple: Two teams play until one wins four games. That team wins a nice trophy, a ring for everyone on the club, and, most importantly, the right to call itself baseball's best team for the next year. The regular season might sometimes seem to drag on, but in the World Series every pitch is crucial and everyone hangs on it.

Every single move a player or manager makes will be scrutinized, and if a player makes one amazing play or one horrible play, people will remember him for that play for the rest of his life. There's a lot of tension, but it's good tension. It's no wonder they call the World Series the Fall Classic.

The Least You Need to Know

➤ The 30 major league teams are divided into two leagues of three divisions each.

➤ Despite the fact that franchises have been moving for years, several great rivalries have survived the unrest.

➤ Interleague play is good for fans, but not necessarily good for competition.

➤ To win the world championship, a team has to win 11 games and three different series.

Part 3
The Name of the Game Is Pitching and Defense

I spent most of my career as a catcher. Before every pitch, I'd signal to the pitcher which pitch he should throw, then I'd make sure all of our fielders were positioned properly. Each one of those responsibilities was crucial, because the hallmark of any successful team is good pitching and solid defense. You simply can't win without them.

In this part of the book, we talk about pitching and defense. You'll be amazed how many different types of pitches there are, and the variety of dances these pitches can perform. I'll also tell you about strategies that pitchers employ when facing hitters. It's the catcher's job to tell the pitcher which pitch he should throw, so we'll take a look at the role played by these masked men, as well as the rest of the guys in the field.

Chapter 11

Pitchers: Armed and Dangerous

In This Chapter

➤ How a pitcher throws the ball

➤ Which types of pitches—and pitchers—are the toughest to hit

➤ The different roles for pitchers

➤ Baseball's best men on the mound

Twenty-five players make up a baseball team. Nine take the field at a time. But the essence of the game is in a one-on-one confrontation: pitcher versus hitter.

The one player on the field who can truly control a baseball game is the pitcher. To win the game, you have to beat the guy on the mound. If he's throwing well, you've got your work cut out for you. In this chapter we'll take a close look at exactly how a pitcher does his job.

Baseball's Most Valuable Players

Some experts claim that pitching is 75 percent, or even 90 percent, of the game. The malaprop-a-minute Yogi Berra figured it this way: "Baseball is 90 percent mental. The other half is physical." Like Yogi, I don't know much about mathematics, but I do know that if your pitcher can hold the opposition to one or two runs, your chances of winning improve enormously.

For example, when my Cincinnati Reds played the New York Yankees in the 1976 World Series, we held the Yankees to two runs per game, and we swept them in four straight. With the powerful lineup we had, I'd take that situation every time, because our team could always put at least three runs on the board.

But a few years earlier, in 1970, although we'd won 70 of our first 100 games, Wayne Simpson and a few of our other top pitchers got hurt. We went just 32–30 down the stretch and sort of limped into the World Series, while the Baltimore Orioles were totally in sync, having won their last 13 or 14 in a row. They were confident their pitchers would hold us and all they had to do was play solid defense and scratch out a few runs. And they were right: We were totally overmatched by their pitching—guys like Jim Palmer, Mike Cuellar, and Dave McNally—and we lost in five games.

Even more than a quarterback in football or a goalie in hockey, a pitcher can single-handedly dominate a baseball game. Look back in history and you can see what a pitcher like Sandy Koufax, Bob Gibson, or Tom Seaver can do. Or watch what Randy Johnson does today. They intimidate the opposition and inspire teammates.

Extra Innings

They call it America's game, but Ferguson Jenkins proved that Canadians can play baseball, too. A native of Chatham, Ontario, Fergy won 284 games between 1965 and 1983, more than 100 in both the American League and National League. He defeated 24 teams at least six times each; the only two he never beat were the Chicago Cubs and Texas Rangers, the teams with which he spent the bulk of his career. The Hall of Famer is also the only pitcher in big-league history to surrender home runs to all three Alou brothers: Jesus (San Francisco Giants) in July 1967, Felipe (Atlanta Braves) in April 1968, and Matty (St. Louis Cardinals) in September 1971. (No pitcher ever gave up home runs to all three DiMaggio brothers.)

Mixing It Up: Different Types of Pitches

To a novice watching his first baseball game, all the pitches might look the same, like those blurs going by at the Indianapolis 500, and you wonder how the guys sitting way up in the broadcast booth can identify them. But sit behind home plate or in front of your television screen, watch closely, and you'll start to see the different pitches:

➤ **Fastball**   The most common pitch; it comes in straight and fast.

➤ **Breaking ball**   The name for a *curveball, slider, screwball,* and anything else that's a little slower and tends to move more, darting inside or outside, rising or sinking.

➤ **Change-up**   The "change of pace": A slower pitch designed to throw off a hitter's timing.

If his fastball has enough speed and movement, a major league pitcher can succeed with just one pitch for a few innings or even a few games. But if he wants to stick around in the bigs for more than a cup of coffee, he needs at least three pitches in his repertoire: a fastball, some sort of breaking ball, and a change-up.

Successful pitchers know the secrets: *changing speeds* constantly and making the ball move in *the hitting zone,* the area right out in front of home plate, where most good contact is made.

Talkin' Baseball

"Good pitching will always stop good hitting and vice versa."

—Casey Stengel

Even the great Nolan Ryan wouldn't have survived if he had simply thrown every pitch 100 miles an hour, with no movement, because major league hitters can time a jet plane and hit it if it comes in at the same speed every time. The good pitchers are simply "sneaky fast." They have a great *motion*—their windup and delivery looks the same every time, whether they're throwing the ball 100 mph or 70 mph, whether it's a fastball or a breaking ball. They disguise their pitches, so the batter can't tell until it's too late to react. That way a hitter can't simply anticipate, or *sit on,* the fastball.

When I say a pitch *moves* or has great *movement,* I'm not talking about it streaking across the plate in a straight line. I mean balls that slice inside or outside, that rise or sink. A breaking ball that doesn't break, that *hangs* on one plane, is a *mistake* that usually winds up in the cheap seats—a home run. A pitcher wants a ball that doesn't hang but continues to break, to bite and rotate down or *away* from the normal pattern of flight.

If a pitcher is able to change speeds and throw a pitch that looks like it's headed for the hitting zone but breaks away at the last second—or moves just as it enters the hitting zone—he can throw off the batter's timing and reduce his chances of hitting the ball with the *sweet spot* of the bat.

How does a pitcher make the ball move? By changing the way he holds the ball. It varies based on the pressure placed on the seams, the number of seams gripped, the number of fingers used, the position of the ball in the hand. To change speeds, certain pitchers grip the ball with three fingers, other guys choke it—or hold it tighter—with the palm, certain guys change how deep they hold it in their hand. Choke it a little bit and it comes out slower, but you keep the same motion, so the batter thinks it's a fastball but it's really a change-up. By putting more pressure on one part of the seam than the other, a pitcher makes his ball sink or run away from the hitter.

When a pitcher has everything working well, he's said to have his *good stuff.* "Stuff" is baseball shorthand for quality, effective pitches. If I say a guy "has his good stuff today," I mean his fastball is really buzzing and his breaking balls are moving well.

Some pitchers come by movement naturally and some learn it. Greg Maddux has developed it. Maddux doesn't throw that hard, but he has pinpoint *control,* or accuracy, with his pitches. Tom Glavine, Maddux's teammate on the Atlanta Braves, has also created a lot of movement and variation in the velocity of his pitches. He chokes it, he cuts it, he beats you off-speed. These guys don't have to overthrow and tire their arms; they've practiced until it's a natural movement, and they do it with finger pressure rather than doing it all with their shoulder and their arm. Here's a breakdown of the different types of pitches:

Four-Seam Fastball (or Basic Fastball)

The basic pitch is a *four-seam fastball,* or *four-seamer,* which means that the pitcher is throwing it with two fingers across the wide part of the seam. If you look at a baseball you'll notice that it has that big round circle at the end of the seam, kind of like a lightbulb. The four-seamer is thrown with the index and middle finger across the wide part, with the first finger joints right on top of the seam. When the pitcher's arm comes down on his follow-through, it's like pulling down a window shade. If he pulls down on it and gets the seams rotating, he can get quite a bit of velocity. Then it's *mano-a-mano* time: *"Here's my fastball. See if you can catch up with it."*

The grip for a four-seam fastball.

Two-Seam Fastball (or Sinker)

In the old days, they called this pitch a *sinker,* or *sinkerball.* Now they call it a *two-seam fastball.* Whatever you call it, if you watch this pitch on its path from the pitcher's hand to home plate, it drops, sinks, or dives more than a basic fastball. The two-seamer is thrown with the fingers between the narrowest part of the seams. A pitcher can force the ball to sink more by putting a little bit more pressure on the inside finger, the index finger. The more pressure he puts on it, the air currents hit those seams in a different fashion, and the more it sinks.

The grip for a two-seam fastball.

Curveball

A curveball is thrown with the fingers along the lightbulb side of the seam. It's cocked so that if I pointed it toward you, my knuckles would actually be pointing toward home plate. The pitcher creates pressure downward on that seam with his middle finger. He starts at the very top of the arc and snaps it down to create movement.

Sandy Koufax, the great Dodger pitcher, once told me that a so-so curveball makes nine complete rotations on its way to home plate. A good curveball rotates 11 times, and a great curveball rotates 13 times. Few pitchers have ever reached 13 rotations. But the idea in throwing the curveball is that, from the time the pitcher's arm reaches the high point of his delivery until he releases the ball, he creates so much pressure and so much snap that the ball whooshes out of there with as much spin as possible.

Extra Innings

Hall of Fame pitcher Candy Cummings is credited with inventing the curveball in 1867. Cummings pitched professionally from 1866 to 1878.

A right-hander's curveball breaks down and in on a right-handed hitter (which makes it tougher to hit) and away on a left-handed hitter (which means it breaks out over the plate and is easier to hit). A left-hander's curveball breaks the opposite way. That's why managers are always trying to create righty-lefty matchups—to improve their odds. (More on that in the next chapter.)

The curveball is sometimes referred to as *the deuce* (because the most common catcher's sign for it is two fingers) or *the hook,* because of the movement it makes. Another nickname for the curveball is *Uncle Charlie,* and you might hear an outstanding curveball referred to as *Lord Charles.*

The grip for a curveball.

Slider

The slider is thrown with two fingers across the seam. Some guys throw it with the fingers along the lightbulb side of the seam as they release it, and they create just a little bit of an angle to the right with the hand and force down on the seam to get it to cut, so that the ball comes out pushing off of that seam and it actually breaks to the left. And the more the pitcher creates the angle and turns his hand to the right in a counter-clockwise fashion, the wider the break on the slider.

A slider breaks late, and in the opposite direction of a curveball. A left-hander's slider breaks down and in to right-handed hitters, and away from left-handed hitters. A right-hander's slider breaks the opposite way.

The grip for a slider.

Split-Fingered Fastball and Forkball

Bruce Sutter, the outstanding closer for the Chicago Cubs, St. Louis Cardinals, and Atlanta Braves in the late 1970s and early '80s, threw the *split-fingered fastball,* or *splitter*; another great reliever, Elroy Face, threw the *forkball* for the Pittsburgh Pirates in the late '50s and early '60s. They're very similar pitches—the splitter is just held lower between the fingers. The pitcher grips the ball by splitting his fingers as wide as he can across the outside part of the seam. The ball rests in a V between his index finger and his middle finger. It kind of slips out of his hand with a little more rotation than a knuckleball and a little less rotation than a fastball. It tends to sink and it can go in different directions depending on how much pressure is applied with the fingers and what angle the fingers are at when the ball is released.

The grip for a split-fingered fastball.

Change-up

A change-up or *off-speed pitch* takes longer to reach the plate than the aforementioned pitches. That makes it sound like it might be easier to hit, and it is—if the hitter isn't fooled. But the idea is to throw off the hitter's timing and get him to start his swing before the ball reaches the plate. If a pitcher went through a deliberate windup and delivery and lobbed the ball, it would be easy to hit. So he disguises it by using the same motion as on his other pitches, but the change-up is slower because the pitcher grips the ball further back in his hand or spreads his fingers out.

Some pitchers throw the *circle change-up* (or *circle change)* by putting their index finger inside, against the joint of their thumb. The ball is held in the three outside fingers. Because there's no pressure from the fingertips, it just comes out of their hand dead, with very little velocity. Instead of pulling down, the pitcher just sort of pushes the ball out of his hand. Others throw the *three-finger change-up,* by gripping the ball with the three middle fingers across the seam.

The grip for a circle change-up.

The grip for a three-finger change-up.

Knuckleball

Pitchers used to press their knuckles against the ball to throw a *knuckleball,* which is how it got its name. Now they actually dig the fingernails of their index and middle fingers into the lightbulb side of the ball and they push as they throw. It's as if they just extend their arm and force the ball to come out so the seams don't rotate. And if the ball doesn't rotate, then the air currents carry the ball in whatever direction the air currents are going at that particular moment. That's why not even the pitcher, let alone the catcher and hitter, knows where a good

Talkin' Baseball

"If you want to know how it feels to catch the knuckleball, ask the backstop, not me."

—Cleveland Indians catcher Sandy Alomar Jr.

knuckleball is going. Bob Uecker once quipped: "The way to catch a knuckleball is to wait until the ball stops rolling and then pick it up."

It takes years of practice to learn to throw the knuckleball effectively, which is why there are only a handful of knuckleball pitchers in the major leagues. But when it's working, this pitch can be truly baffling to hitters because of how slowly it travels and how drastically it breaks.

The grip for a knuckleball.

Screwball

The screwball, or *scroogie,* is the reverse of the curveball. Only a few pitchers throw it, because it's hard on the arm. The grip is similar to that of the four-seamer, but the pitcher rotates his index finger in an inverted manner, so that his hand actually points outward as he comes over the ball. That's why the screwball breaks the opposite way of the curveball.

The grip for a screwball.

Palmball

The *palmball, as* the name suggests, is thrown by holding the ball tightly in the palm, with two fingers across the seam, so as to slow down the pitch's speed while maintaining a consistent delivery to a fastball. It's not a particularly difficult pitch to throw, but it doesn't have a whole lot of movement. Not a lot of major leaguers throw it.

The Toughest Pitches to Hit

Some hitters crush fastballs but can't hit breaking pitches. When pitchers find out— and the way teams scout and research opponents these days, it doesn't take long—

those hitters will be fed a steady diet of breaking pitches until they prove they can hit them. And if they can't, they won't last long in the show.

Other hitters can handle breaking balls but don't have the short swing or bat speed to get around on a really hard fastball. So if you ask what's the toughest pitch to hit, different hitters will have different answers. I think the pitchers who are hardest to handle have two nasty pitches: a split-fingered fastball and a really good, live fastball.

The difference between the speed and the motion of the two pitches really puts a hitter at a disadvantage. The secret of hitting is being able to home in on one pitch. If a pitcher didn't have a top-notch fastball, I would look for his curveball, and then if he threw a fastball, I could still hit it because he didn't have the velocity to throw it by me. But a guy who has two really good pitches can be deadly, because you can't be ready for both on one offering. For instance, if a guy has a 95-mph fastball and an 85-mph split-finger that darts down in different directions, it's hard to prepare for both. So you're up there on the defensive, and the pitcher is on the offensive.

> **Talkin' Baseball**
>
> *"We need three kinds of pitching: left-handed, right-handed, and relief."*
>
> —Manager Whitey Herzog

Different Types of Pitchers

The beauty of pitching is, you can win with all different styles. Take the top relief pitchers. You've got power pitchers such as Billy Wagner of the Houston Astros today and Terry Forster in the 1970s and '80s. They threw 94 or 95 miles an hour and dared you to catch up with it. Rollie Fingers, the closer for the great Oakland A's teams of the '70s, would come out with that big handlebar mustache, a great fastball, a great slider—and that's all. He could run the fastball and move it just a little bit; he had good enough velocity and got his fastball just far enough up in the strike zone, just out of the hitting area, and you couldn't get good wood on the ball. Then he'd mix in his slider and finish you off. Bruce Sutter, probably the best reliever ever, basically threw one pitch. He threw the splitter, he threw the splitter, and he threw the splitter. But the thing dropped like a rock when it got near the plate, and he got save after save after save.

Now look at the best starters. Tom Seaver had a great fastball. He threw it 94, 95 miles an hour. His breaking ball was only decent, but he could throw his fastball right by you and then keep you off balance with his curveball. Jerry Koosman, Seaver's team-mate with the New York Mets in the late 1960s and '70s, had a really good rising fastball and a *big* (really great) curveball. Steve Carlton had a tremendous slider, a great curveball, and a wonderful fastball. Lefty's slider was nasty. Bob Gibson threw 94, 95 miles an hour, and his pitches moved. He had a little curve, but mostly he threw fastballs and sliders. He came right at you, and he had great location. Sandy Koufax had one of the greatest curveballs you'll ever see.

Rollie Fingers, the great closer for the Oakland A's teams of the 1970s, in his pre-mustache days.

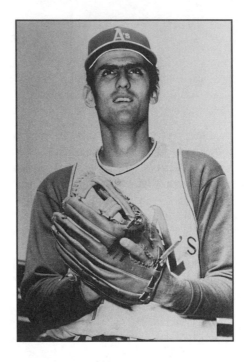

Today, Randy Johnson (now with the Arizona Diamondbacks) has a wicked fastball and slider, but not great control, which actually works to his advantage because hitters go up there a little afraid. Greg Maddux won four Cy Young Awards in a row even though he doesn't have a top fastball or slider. Anybody in the stands who's ever played the game would say, *"I can hit this guy."* But he wins with movement and location and changing speeds. He gets you off balance.

Then there's Roger Clemens, who's a lot like Nolan Ryan was: all power. A big—really big—fastball. A good curveball, a *roundhouse* with a really big break to it. Later in life, Nolan became a better pitcher because he tightened up his curveball and could change speeds and throw sinkers and splitters. Clemens continues to amaze me, winning Cy Young Awards in his mid-30s because he has learned to really *pitch*. He can still challenge hitters with his fastball when he needs to, but he can change speeds and leave them swinging at air because they're anticipating another blazer.

What makes one pitcher an effective starter and another more suited to a relief role? To a large extent, it's stamina. Some guys have great arms but can't sustain quality pitches for six, seven, eight innings. They can throw hard for a couple of innings, but if they try to back off a little bit to preserve their arms, they end up giving up too many hits.

Others who are better suited to relieving are the one-trick ponies, who only have one or two really good pitches. Typically, they have great fastballs or sliders and little else. They can dominate one or two innings when they face only six or seven batters, but if they have to go through the lineup more than once, they can't keep going on power. Their arms get tired, and hitters watching them for awhile get their timing down for their next at-bats. These power pitchers often aren't effective if they have to worry about mixing in breaking balls and change-ups.

Bob Gibson, the overpowering pitcher for the St. Louis Cardinals of the 1960s and early '70s.

Sandy Koufax, arguably the greatest left-handed pitcher ever, was a three-time Cy Young Award winner for the Los Angeles Dodgers in the 1960s.

Starters

A *starting pitcher,* or *starter,* is exactly what he sounds like: the pitcher who starts the game. Anyone who comes into the game after him is called a *relief pitcher,* or *reliever.* In the mid- to late 1900s, all the best pitchers were starters. They often pitched all nine innings, a *complete game.* Other pitchers—usually starters themselves—came on in *relief* only if the starter was injured or having a bad day. But over the past 30 years, relievers

Catching On

The four or five pitchers who regularly start games for a team make up what is called the **starting rotation** or simply the **rotation**. A dominant, No. 1 starter is called an **ace.** The pitchers who make up the relief corps referred to collectively as the **bullpen,** because that's the part of the field where they watch the game and warm up before they are called upon to pitch.

have grown in importance and in degrees of specialization. Today, starters rarely pitch all nine innings, and it's expected that two or three relievers will pitch in the same game. Each relief corps is broken down into *long relievers, middle relievers, setup men,* and *closers*—which we'll get to in a moment.

Starters used to pitch eight or nine innings every four days. Today, managers are happy if they can get six or seven innings out of their starters every fifth day. Most have switched from four-man to five-man *starting rotations* and rely more heavily on their *bullpens.* Why? Some old-timers grumble that today's pitchers haven't spent a lifetime throwing rocks and balls the way we used to as kids, and so their arms aren't strong enough to pitch as often as the old-timers did. But it's got more to do with strategy: Most managers figure they're better off using fresh arms, using matchups to their advantage, and making sure they don't wear out arms that are worth so much money and so many victories.

Long and Middle Relievers

Talkin' Baseball

"I'm throwing twice as hard but the ball is getting there half as fast."

—Lefty Grove on the aging process

If a starter gets rocked in the first two, three, or four innings, he'll be replaced by a long reliever. This is typically a guy who has challenged for a starting job but isn't quite good enough. Maybe he's a kid who needs to learn on the job and prove himself, or a veteran whose arm is starting to wear out. If the starter is replaced in or before the fifth or sixth inning, a middle reliever comes in. Depending on the score and situation, a middle reliever might face one batter or work two or three innings.

Setup Men

A setup man tries to keep you in the game in the seventh and/or eighth inning before your relief ace, or closer, comes in to save the game and close out the victory. Usually, the manager has a left-handed setup man and a right-handed setup man, and he chooses which one to use depending on the matchup. For example, a left-handed pitcher usually fares better against a left-handed hitter than against a right-handed hitter. (More on that in the next chapter.)

Closers

Today, even if a guy has the ability to start, he might wind up as the closer because that job has become so important. A closer typically pitches in 60–80 games a year, versus 30–35 for a starter. Managers typically turn to their closer when they're ahead in the ninth inning. Sometimes they go to the closer in the eighth inning of a tight game, especially if runners are on base, if the setup man is struggling, or if the closer hasn't pitched for a few days and needs the work. Give him the ball and the lead and a good closer will save the victory at least 90 percent of the time. But a bad closer can blow a game that you thought you had won.

That's why a top-quality closer is so important. If he's almost certain to shut out the opposition, the opposition in effect gets only seven or eight innings to score and you get nine. Teams knew if they didn't get a lead before facing Bruce Sutter, maybe the greatest relief pitcher ever, they almost surely weren't going to win. And that was intimidating. Managers usually save their closer for save situations—that is, with a lead of three runs or fewer late in the game. Why waste your savior in a blowout?

The Benchmarks of Excellence

What statistics do you look at to see if a pitcher sets himself apart from the competition? Well, it depends on the pitcher's role.

Twenty victories in a season used to be the benchmark for a top-notch starter, but that standard became more difficult to achieve when pitching staffs went from four- to five-man rotations. Still, you know Roger Clemens is going to win around 20 every year. You can pretty well book him to win 17 to 21 games. Pedro Martinez of the Boston Red Sox has proven he has the stuff to win 20.

But even the greatest pitcher's win-loss record—the number of his victories and losses—depends on how well his club hits behind him. He could have a great year, could allow three earned runs for every nine innings pitched (which would give him an

From the Bench

Most fans prefer high-scoring games to pitchers' duels. I want to see good defense, but I also want to see runs. I'd rather see a game that's 9–7 and see the closer just get bombed. Pitching has become tougher, because the good, young arms that could've been starters now get put in the bullpen. They come in and they throw it 96 mph nine times and they close the door. The managers are relieved, but as a fan, it's exciting to see a great ninth-inning rally.

Catching On

A starter gets a **win** if he throws at least five complete innings, at the end of which his team holds the lead, and his team wins. Regardless of how many innings a pitcher throws, he will take a **loss** if he surrenders the run that put his team behind. A reliever gets a **save**, but not a win, when he finishes a game his club won and meets one of these conditions: 1) He enters the game with a lead of no more than three runs and pitches at least one inning, or 2) He pitches effectively for at least three innings, or 3) He enters the game with the tying run on base, at bat, or on deck.

161

earned run average, or *ERA,* or 3.00), but he won't win many games if his club only scores a run or two every time he's on the mound.

Catching On

Earned run average, or **ERA**, is the average number of earned runs a pitcher allows per nine innings. It's the most common measure of a pitcher's effectiveness. To compute ERA, multiply the total number of earned runs by 9, then divide that figure by the total number of innings pitched.

Curt Schilling could win 20 games if the Philadelphia Phillies were a better club. Maybe he's the best pitcher because he's going to strike out 275 to 300 hitters a year, but strikeouts can be misleading. For years, Nolan Ryan struck out anywhere between 250 and 300—or more—yet he didn't always have a winning record. You could book 250 to 300 strikeouts a year for Tom Seaver and Steve Carlton, but you could also book 20 wins.

You can expect 15 to 17 wins—20 if things go right—from guys like the Baltimore Orioles' Mike Mussina and the New York Yankees' Andy Pettite and David Cone, when he's healthy. Other guys will step up one year and win 15 or 17 games and lose only six or seven. Can you depend on them the next year? Maybe not. If your two best starters go 16–6, those two have put your team 20 games over .500. You hope you can get a couple of others to win three or four more than they lose, and all of a sudden you're 26 games over .500 and you're in the playoffs.

Extra Innings

You need more than an ace to go far in the major leagues. Just look at the Washington Senators of the early 1900s. From 1910 to '19, Walter Johnson averaged 26 wins a year, led the American League in victories five times, and never won fewer than 20 games. But in those 10 seasons the Senators finished in seventh place four times, and never wound up higher than second. People said Washington was "First in war, first in peace, and last in the American League." Johnson didn't win his first pennant until 1924—his 18th year in the big leagues. The Senators finally won a World Series that year, and got Johnson one more pennant the next year.

Closers are judged on their save totals. Guys like Mariano Rivera of the New York Yankees, John Franco of the New York Mets, Rod Beck of the Chicago Cubs, Trevor Hoffman of the San Diego Padres, and John Wetteland of the Texas Rangers should get anywhere from 30 to 45 saves, depending on the opportunities they have. If his club isn't ahead going into the ninth inning very often, a particular closer obviously isn't going to get as many chances as a closer on a powerhouse team.

Power and Finesse: Johnny's Picks

I've talked a lot about the best pitchers in baseball's storied history in previous chapters, so I won't repeat myself. But, for the record, I'll say a few words here about the toughest pitchers I faced and the toughest today.

The Best Pitchers Johnny Faced

In my early 20s, I felt superhuman. I didn't think there was a pitcher who could get me out. But I had lung surgery two days after I turned 25, and I never was as quick, never had the same muscles, never had the same nerves again.

I had some success, but not much, against the greatest pitchers of my era: **Bob Gibson**, **Tom Seaver**, and **Nolan Ryan**. Oddly enough, the pitchers who gave me the most trouble were journeymen named **Rick Reuschel** and **Bill Singer**. They'll never make the Hall of Fame, but I could never pick up the rotation on their pitches to judge what was coming. They had sweeping, breaking sliders and they could run the sinker in and then locate the fastball away. It seemed like they threw the ball right out of their uniforms and I could never judge the rotation, the speed, or the break of the ball. If you can pick up the ball, you always figure you have a chance to get a hit. The guys you never can pick up are the ones who always frustrate you.

The Best Today

I've already mentioned **Greg Maddux**, **Randy Johnson**, and **Roger Clemens**. When **David Cone** is healthy, he's a marvelous pitcher. The Dodgers just signed **Kevin Brown** to a record-setting contract because he's a relentless battler with an iron arm. In 10 years, he's been on the injured list only four times, and never with an arm problem. **John Smoltz** and **Tom Glavine** join **Greg Maddux** to give Atlanta the best pitching staff in baseball. Those guys have proven their mettle year in and year out. **Pedro Martinez** is probably the best young pitcher in baseball, and the Chicago Cubs' **Kerry Wood** may be in the near future. I like to watch them because they know how to pitch in every situation, they've got the stuff to make it work, and they've got guts.

The Least You Need to Know

➤ The pitcher is the most important player on the field.

➤ A starting pitcher needs at least three different pitches for long-term success.

➤ A good pitcher can make the ball move different ways based on his grip and how much pressure he applies to the ball.

➤ The importance of relief pitchers, especially closers, has increased dramatically over the years.

Chapter 12

Pitching Strategy: Throwing with Your Head

> ## In This Chapter
>
> ➤ How pitchers use their brains
>
> ➤ Variety is the spice of life on the mound
>
> ➤ When it's time for a farewell to arms
>
> ➤ Special delivery: the windup and the stretch

Have you ever seen the movie *Bull Durham*? In it, Tim Robbins plays "Nuke" LaLoosh, a young pitching phenom with "a million-dollar arm but a five-cent head." Kevin Costner is "Crash" Davis, a cagey veteran catcher brought in to tutor Nuke on the differences between throwing and pitching: To throw, all you need is your arm. But to pitch, you've gotta use your head.

Crash taught Nuke how to use the right pitch in the right situation. He showed Nuke that he couldn't just blow the ball by every hitter he faced. And it was that advice that helped Nuke become a pitcher in the big leagues—or, as Crash reverently called it, "the Show." In this chapter we'll offer a similar crash course (sorry, couldn't resist) in pitching strategy.

Pitch Selection: Reading the Signs

As I mentioned in Chapter 11, a major league pitcher has to be able throw a fastball, a change-up, and some sort of breaking ball—usually a curveball or a slider, and often both. But a pitcher can't just rear back and throw whatever pitch he feels like—he has to be in agreement with his catcher (and in fact, the infielders are usually also aware of what pitch is coming next). So either on his own, or by relaying a signal from his

Talkin' Baseball

"He's temperamental all right. But it's ninety-eight percent temper and two percent mental."

—Hall of Fame pitcher Lefty Gomez on a teammate

Catching On

In baseball, a **sign** is a strategic instruction, usually made with a gesture or hand signal, from a manager, coach, or player, to a player on the field. A catcher uses his fingers—one for a fastball, two for a curve, or whatever—to *put down the signs* or *flash the signs* for his pitcher, to tell him which type of pitch he wants to be thrown next.

manager or pitching coach, the catcher will *flash a sign* to his pitcher to tell him which type of pitch he wants to be thrown next.

The catcher squats down in his stance, putting his right hand (or throwing hand) between his thighs and extending one or more fingers downward. The signs can vary from team to team and from situation to situation—especially if a catcher suspects that the opposing team might be trying to *steal the signs,* but traditionally the catcher flashes one finger for a fastball, two for a curveball, three for a change-up, and four for a slider (or whatever the pitcher's fourth pitch is). The catcher might pat his right or left thigh, depending on which direction (inside or outside) he wants the pitcher to aim. Just before the pitch, the catcher will usually shift his feet or his body weight a few inches, setting up inside or outside to present a better target for the pitcher—and hopefully to influence the umpire to call a borderline pitch a strike.

If the pitcher wants to throw a different pitch than what his catcher's calling for, he *shakes off* his catcher, shaking his head "no." And the catcher will keep flashing signs until they agree on the pitch selection. It's imperative that a pitcher and catcher be on the same page before the pitch is thrown—because the catcher will have a tough time handling a pitch he's not expecting.

The idea, obviously, is to throw a pitch that the batter will have a difficult time hitting, but that doesn't mean a pitcher with a great fastball will just throw fastballs. He wants to mix up his pitches so that the hitter can't simply wait on a fastball. He wants to keep the hitter guessing about:

➤ **The type:** Fastball? Curveball? Change-up? Slider?

➤ **The movement:** Rising fastball? Sinking fastball? Curve barreling inside or slider breaking outside?

➤ **The speed:** Is it his hardest 95-mile-an-hour fastball? Or an 80-mile-an-hour change-up?

➤ **The location:** Low and inside? Low and outside? High and tight? High and outside? Right down the middle?

The hitter has just a split second to process all these possibilities in his brain and react. Two-thirds of the time, he's wrong.

Setting Up Hitters

It's important for a pitcher to *set up* hitters, to try to fool them about what pitch he's going to throw next, but I think a lot of teams in the major leagues go about it the wrong way.

Every team charts every pitch—the type of pitch and the result. But to me, it's mostly a waste of time. I never looked at a chart. I never understood the value of it for a catcher; I called the pitch that I thought would get the hitter out in that situation. After a game, a pitching coach might say to the pitcher, "You used too many curveballs in this situation. You threw a breaking ball every time on 2 and 1, a fastball every time on 3 and 1, a breaking ball every time on 2 and 2." Or maybe he'll say, "You threw 112 pitches, 73 of them fastballs, 34 curves, and a few change-ups. You really need to balance it out."

I'm not sure a pitcher needs balance. I'm looking for this: How many outs did he record? How many hits did he give up? If he gave up 10 hits and they scored only two runs, that's all right. Maybe we'd change our approach if a batter wound up hitting the breaking ball or always looked for a breaking ball in certain situations.

From the Bench

As a catcher, you have to make sure your pitcher can see your signs, but you also have to shield them from the opposing players and coaches. It's especially tricky with baserunners; that's when a catcher will usually switch to a more complicated set of signs. And depending on how bad the shadows are—and how the pitcher's eyesight is—a catcher may tape his fingers to make them more visible.

Extra Innings

Cy Young, who pitched from 1890 to 1911, owns the major league record for victories with 511. No one else is even close—Walter Johnson is next with 417, followed by Grover Alexander and Christy Mathewson with 373 each—and because today's pitchers don't start nearly as often, probably no one will ever come close again. That's why the Cy Young Award, given to the best pitcher in each league, is named in his honor.

I just went by feel. If I thought the batter was looking for a curveball, I wanted to throw a fastball. I went by memory. If the batter liked to sit on (wait for) the curveball in a certain situation, then I tried to fool him. I gauged every hitter every time I faced him. I'd think, *"He did such-and-such the last time, but this situation is a little different...."* Or, *"They have a guy hitting behind him that I know we can get out, so I'm going to pitch carefully to this hitter...."* Or, *"He's a fastball hitter, so I'm not going to throw him a fastball unless it's a 'waste' pitch—way out of the strike zone."* If the batter wants to swing at bad pitches and strike out, okay. Otherwise, let's walk him and get the next guy out instead.

Changing Speeds

Nowadays every major league pitch is clocked with a radar gun. One common type is called a Jugs gun. The speed is recorded by coaches and scouts, and even posted on the stadium scoreboard and on television.

How fast is *fast* for a major league pitcher? Nolan Ryan and a few other pitchers throughout history have been known to top 100 miles an hour, but normally, 94 would be considered a real good fastball. But sometimes 94 with no movement is not as good as 92 or 91 with movement.

It's fun for a fan to see how fast different pitchers and pitches are. But during the course of a game, the manager and pitching coach are more interested in seeing whether their starter is maintaining his velocity. When he starts losing several miles per hour off his fastball, it means he's getting tired, and they better get him out of there before he gets shelled.

As a catcher, I wanted my pitcher to keep changing speeds so he could foul up the hitters' timing. It's a lot better to throw one pitch 94 mph, the next 89, the next 96, the next 79, the next 92, than to throw five in a row at 98 mph. A good hitter can eventually catch up to the fastballs of Nolan Ryan—or even Nuke LaLoosh—if they throw at the same speed all the time. But if the pitcher is always changing speeds, the hitters usually swing a little early or a little late.

Catching On

When baseball people say a pitcher **throws hard**, they don't necessarily mean that he uses a lot of effort. They mean that his pitches are fast. Or they use a 25-cent word for speed: **velocity**. And you'll often hear baseball people talk about the difference between *throwing*—which just means rearing back and firing the ball—and *pitching*—which means using your head and mixing things up in terms of location and speed.

But don't get me wrong. A pitcher with a really good fastball has an advantage over a pitcher with an average fastball. When a guy only threw 88 or 89 miles an hour, I knew I could look for his breaking ball and still have time to adjust and hit the pitch if it was a fastball. But when I faced J.R. Richard in his heyday with the Houston Astros, I had to go to the plate with a defensive attitude. He threw a 97-mile-an-hour fastball and a 92-mile-an-hour slider. He put me at a severe disadvantage. He threw both pitches so hard, I couldn't get my bat around fast enough to really connect with an outside pitch, so I had to narrow down my strike zone and swing only at pitches over the inside half of the plate. If he made a mistake in there, I could hit it. And if he didn't? I walked back to the dugout, shaking my head.

Extra Innings

A pitch by the Cleveland Indians' Bob Feller was clocked at a record 107.9 miles an hour in a 1946 game. But Ted Williams, the Boston Red Sox's Hall of Fame hitter, swears that there was a pitcher even faster than Feller. His name? Not Sandy Koufax, Nolan Ryan, or Roger Clemens. It was Steve Dalkowski, a Baltimore Orioles' minor leaguer who reportedly could "bring it" at nearly 110 miles an hour. But Dalkowski never made it to the majors: In a 1963 spring training game, shortly after striking out Roger Maris of the New York Yankees, the left-hander suffered a career-ending elbow injury.

The Importance of Control

In pitching, as in real estate, there's a simple mantra: *Location, location, location.*

The best pitchers know where they want to throw the ball, and they have enough *control* to put it there. They not only can throw the ball over the plate for strikes, but they can throw it to specific parts of the plate. They target pitches to the *hole* in a hitter's swing, a spot where the batter struggles to hit the ball with authority. Maybe one hitter can't handle pitches that are low and inside. Maybe another guy can't get good wood on pitches that are low and outside. Maybe another can't hit pitches that are high and tight. That's the location a pitcher goes for.

Catching On

Location usually refers to where a pitcher's pitches are going—one of the key measures of whether a guy is throwing effectively. The best pitchers know where they want to throw the ball, and they have enough **control** to put it there. They not only can throw the ball over the plate for strikes, but they can throw it to specific parts of the plate.

The Right Pitch at the Right Time

The fastball is the staple of most pitchers' repertoires, and most throw more fastballs than anything else. Out of 100 pitches, you'll probably see around 70 fastballs and 30 off-speed pitches, be they change-ups or breaking balls or whatever the pitcher throws best.

The percentage varies from pitcher to pitcher and game to game. Don Gullett, my hard-throwing teammate with the Reds, might throw 85 fastballs and 15 sliders. Fellow

Red Gary Nolan might throw 50 fastballs, 35 curveballs, and 15 change-ups. Or 25 curveballs and 25 change-ups. What's the pitcher's most effective pitch today? What's he throwing consistently for strikes? If he's having trouble on certain days getting his breaking ball to work, then I have to call more fastballs. I may use four fastballs in a row, get the guy out, and go on to the next hitter. I might call for a fastball on the first pitch to get ahead in the count, then call for two breaking balls just to break up the pattern. Or maybe the batter is a dead low-ball hitter and I've got a low-ball pitcher. So I may call for pitches up in the strike zone and low-ball sinkers that are way down and out of the strike zone, hoping that he'll *chase* a pitch in the dirt.

It's not an exact science. It's part head game and part guessing game. If I were catching Tom Seaver, I might have him throw nine fastballs and one curveball in an inning, because Tom had a terrific fastball. But the next inning, we might face guys who hit the fastball well and couldn't touch the curveball, so we'd throw four curves, three fastballs, and then more curves. You just have to go by your gut feeling, by how your pitcher is throwing that day, and by the competition. When we faced a free-swinging team like the Philadelphia Phillies with Mike Schmidt and Greg Luzinski, I called for more breaking balls and change-ups just to get them to chase balls. We had to get three guys out every inning. If I knew we'd have a tough time getting two of them out, I'd just try to make sure we didn't let those two guys beat us or hurt us to the point that we couldn't get out of the inning alive.

Talkin' Baseball

"Trying to sneak a pitch past Hank Aaron is like trying to sneak the sunrise past a rooster."

—Joe Adcock, Milwaukee Braves first baseman and Aaron's teammate

Hall of Famer Tom Seaver was one of the most talented and most intelligent pitchers ever. He is best remembered for his success with the New York Mets (including a World Championship in 1969), but he was also my teammate with the Cincinnati Reds for five-and-a-half years.

Righty vs. Righty and Lefty vs. Lefty

As a right-handed hitter, you have an inherent advantage against a left-handed pitcher, because his curveball breaks toward you, not away from you. A hitter can drive inside pitches better than outside pitches, so a left-hander's curveball always moves toward a right-handed hitter's power. But a right-hander's curve breaks outside on a right-handed hitter, so the pitcher has the built-in advantage in that matchup.

Big-league managers play these percentages all the time. When they use a pinch hitter, they try to send up a right-handed hitter against a lefty pitcher and vice versa. When they change pitchers, they might bring in a lefty just to face one tough left-handed hitter. Or they might use the lefty instead of the righty if two of the next three hitters are lefties. And managers sometimes *platoon* two players at one position, starting a right-handed outfielder against left-handed starting pitchers and a left-handed out-fielder against right-handed starters. Because more pitchers are right-handed, the lefty hitter gets a lot more at-bats. And because he lines up in the batter's box a little closer to first base, the lefty can get to first a shade quicker than a right-handed hitter. (You'll read more about platooning in Chapter 18.)

Starting out in Little League, you don't see that many left-handed pitchers, so it's hard to get conditioned to hitting against them. But by the time he reaches the bigs, a right-handed hitter has seen enough lefties that he should have the advantage.

The Intentional Walk

A manager orders an *intentional walk* when he doesn't want to give a particular batter a chance to hit. The manager signals for the walk, and the catcher extends his arm way outside, usually stands up, and takes a stride outside. The pitcher lobs four balls and the batter draws the automatic base on balls.

This is a common strategy late in a game when the opponent has a runner on second base and first base is *open*. A walk puts men on first and second, so that if a ground ball is then hit to the infield, the defense has a chance to force out the runners at second and third. Say there's a grounder to shortstop. If there's no runner at first base, the man on second doesn't have to try for third if he's afraid the shortstop might tag or throw him out. But if there's a runner at first, the man on second must head to third and risk being forced out. This strategy increases the probability—but also the importance—of getting a double play to help the pitcher and his defense get out of a *jam*.

A manager usually won't put the winning or tying run on base intentionally, but sometimes this unwritten rule is broken when facing a really

Talkin' Baseball

"You know you're having a bad day when the fifth inning rolls around and they drag the warning track."

—Former Baltimore Orioles pitcher Mike Flanagan

171

dangerous hitter. In a most unusual case in a game in 1998, Arizona Diamondbacks manager Buck Showalter walked San Francisco's Barry Bonds with the bases loaded and an 8–6 lead in the ninth inning because he would rather walk in one run than take his chances on the Giants' left fielder driving in two, three, or four runs with a hit. (The strategy paid off: The next hitter, journeyman catcher Brent Mayne, lined out to right field to end the game.) It marked the first time a major league batter had been intentionally walked with the bases loaded since July 23, 1944, when New York Giants manager Mel Ott put the Chicago Cubs' Bill "Swish" Nicholson on base in the second game of a doubleheader. Nicholson had hit four home runs that day.

Often, a walk doesn't officially go down in the books as intentional, but for all practical purposes it was. A pitcher might not want to risk throwing, say, Mark McGwire any strikes that Big Mac could hit out of the park, so he'll fire pitches far out of the strike zone. He's hoping that McGwire might chase some bad pitches and strike out, but realistically expects to walk him and take his chances with a lesser hitter.

The Pitchout

If the defense suspects that a runner is about to try to steal a base—usually we're talking about second base—the manager might call for a *pitchout.* A pitchout is a fastball delivered to a spot far outside where the catcher can snare it (and the batter can't hit it) and quickly throw to second or third base in hopes of nabbing the would-be thief. This can give a catcher a split-second advantage, and sometimes that's all you need. Of course, if the manager is wrong and the opposing runner doesn't take off, the pitch is a ball instead of a strike, and now the hitter and runner have the advantage.

Brushbacks and Inside Pitches

Brushback or *purpose pitches* are thrown high and tight, often tight enough to clobber a batter if he doesn't jump back, to make him a little scared and a lot less aggressive. You want him to back off the plate far enough that his bat will be less likely to reach—or at least make solid contact with—an outside pitch.

If some guy is hitting a pitcher exceptionally well, the pitcher thinks, *"Wait a minute, pal. You need to be a little less comfortable up there."* Some hitters just get too comfortable at home plate; they dig in, and their whole mentality is that they're in command. To be successful, a pitcher has to put the hitter on the defensive. That's why you change speeds. That's why you pitch inside. You remind him that he'd better not get comfortable and lean over the plate. You take him out of his comfort zone. You make him think about the negatives—namely getting hit with a pitch. You want the hitter to think you're nasty enough to hurt him. You're trying to tell him, *"You're taking part of my plate. You're taking part of my living. Back off."*

If the pitcher plunks someone, you end up with a stare-down. And sometimes a hitter charging the mound. And often the opposing pitcher retaliates later in the game. It used to be part of the game; your pitcher had to defend his teammates or he was considered gutless. But it led to a lot of *beanball* wars and bench-clearing brawls, and the rules have been changed. Now, baseball tries to protect the hitter more, and the umpire has the discretion to eject a pitcher if he thinks he threw at a batter intentionally.

That's good because it doesn't allow guys to go crazy and do something that could, indeed, ruin somebody's career. But pitching inside has always been essential, and there are still guys today who know how to do it—Roger Clemens, Greg Maddux, Tom Glavine. Pitching inside doesn't mean throwing at the guy's head—or throwing behind him, which is even more dangerous, because he instinctively ducks backward into the ball. Pitching inside means a ball that does not cross the plate but rather misses it inside by four to six inches. You can't allow guys to lean over the plate and try to hit that outside pitch. A pitcher has to own the outside part of the plate to be successful.

Catching On

A **pitchout** is a pitch that's intentionally thrown wide of home plate, out of the batter's reach, to give the catcher a better chance to throw out a runner stealing or going on a hit-and-run. A pitchout is a gamble that can give a catcher a split-second advantage, and sometimes that's all you need. Of course, if the manager is wrong and the opposing runner doesn't take off, the pitch is a ball instead of a strike, and now the hitter and runner have the advantage.

Extra Innings

Over the past 30—and especially the past 10—years, pitchers have become less likely to throw brushback pitches because hitters are more likely to fight them and umpires more likely to eject them. The trend dismayed Don Drysdale, a Hall of Fame brushback artist. "If the game becomes any more namby-pamby," he once said, "they may have to put the ball on a batting tee."

The Windup and the Stretch

The basic mechanics of a pitcher's motion have changed little in a century. Standing on the mound, a right-handed pitcher wants to be as close to the batter as possible while still keeping his right foot in contact with the pitching rubber. After he and the catcher agree on the type of pitch, the right-handed pitcher who is working from the

Catching On

The **full windup**, or **windup**, is the delivery usually used by a pitcher when there are no runners on base. Pitchers usually throw from **the stretch** when runners are on base. The stretch is a shorter version of the windup, used so that base runners don't have as much time to steal a base or take as big a lead.

Talkin' Baseball

"[The manager] had to take me out. The outfielders were getting tired."

—Pitcher Rick Sutcliffe

full windup brings his hands together, rocks sideways, brings his hands over or near his head, lifts his left leg, rocks backward, and then flings his arm forward while striding toward the plate to get his weight behind the pitch. He releases the ball with a snap of the wrist and makes a complete follow-through.

Pitchers usually throw from what's called *the stretch* when runners are on base. The stretch is a truncated version of the full windup, so that baserunners don't have as much time to steal a base or take as big a lead. The leg kick isn't as high and the other motions are neither as deliberate nor as long.

A pitcher's ability to hold runners on base is an important facet often overlooked by fans—at least we catchers think so, because we usually get blamed for giving up a stolen base. Most experts say that bases are stolen more on the pitcher than on the catcher. The pitcher has to do a good job of holding the runner close to the base. He can look that way, fake a throw, or throw over to the defensive player who's covering that base. The pitcher can shorten or mask his delivery, so that the runner isn't quite sure if he's throwing to first base or to home plate. After guys like Lou Brock and Rickey Henderson turned base stealing into an art form, pitchers started finding ways to cut the time it takes to deliver the ball to the plate, so the catcher will have that extra split second to fire the ball to second.

On the Defensive: Get Ready for Some Rockets

Whether he throws from a full windup or the stretch, the pitcher can't relax once he releases the ball. He must quickly regain his balance and be prepared in case the hitter belts a line drive right back at him. By the time he's done with his follow-through, he can be as close as 50 feet from the batter, who can slug a ball more than 100 miles an hour. That gives the pitcher virtually no time to react, and the scariest injuries in baseball occur when a pitcher is nailed in the head by one of these bullets.

The pitcher has to be ready not only in the interest of *self*-defense but also for defense. A good-fielding pitcher can save himself a lot of runs—and losses. Two great ones who come to mind are Jim Kaat, who won a record 16 consecutive Gold Gloves for his fielding excellence in the American and National leagues, and Greg Maddux, who won his ninth in a row in the National League in 1998.

The pitcher must be prepared to glove line drives and ground balls hit hard up the middle. When teams use the strategy of the sacrifice bunt to advance a runner or runners into scoring position, the pitcher can turn the tables in a hurry by quickly pouncing on the ball and throwing a strike to gun down the lead runner. Also, if a ground ball is hit to the first baseman, the pitcher must cover first base in a hurry, sprinting across the diamond to catch the throw before the runner reaches first.

Greg Maddux, the Atlanta Braves' unassuming right-hander, beats opposing hitters with his arm, his head, and his glove.

The Call to the Bullpen: Making a Pitching Change

A manager calls for a new pitcher when the opposing batters have figured out the guy on the mound and start hitting him, or when the pitcher's tiring and the manager wants to get him out of there before he starts getting hit. In the National League, when his team needs some runs, a manager may send up a pinch hitter to bat for his pitcher and start getting someone else warmed up in the bullpen. In any case, once a pitcher leaves the game, he can't return.

Even if the starting pitcher is throwing well, the manager will usually think about replacing him once he has thrown around 100 or 120 pitches, because he doesn't want to wear out the pitcher's arm. Using a phone in the dugout, the manager or pitching coach will call the bullpen to say which

From the Bench

You'll often see a manager or pitching coach visit the mound and talk with the pitcher, but return to the dugout and leave him in the game. The manager and coaches are only allowed one such trip to the mound per inning, per pitcher. The second time out, the pitcher must be removed. A manager also may not make more than one visit to the mound during any one hitter's time at bat.

pitcher(s) should start warming up. There are only two mounds in the bullpen, so only two relief pitchers can warm up at one time. Sometimes a manager will warm up a right-hander and a left-hander. Then, when he's ready to make a move, the manager will get timeout from the umpire and walk out to the mound, signaling for the righty with his right hand or for the lefty with his left hand. He'll talk with the departing pitcher for a few seconds, give some instructions to the new guy, and walk back to the dugout. The reliever will get his warm-up pitches in and then the game will resume.

Starting pitchers can take as long as they want to loosen up their arms in the bullpen before a game. So can relievers in the bullpen during games. But once they enter the game, relievers are allowed only eight warm-up pitches (which must be completed in one minute), unless they're replacing an injured player—then they are allowed unlimited warm-up pitches.

Catching On

A top relief pitcher, or closer, is sometimes called a **fireman**, because, in a manner of speaking, he's called upon to come in and "put out the fire," or bail his team out of a jam.

Warm-ups usually consist of some basic stretching and lobbing a few throws before heading to the mound. The pitcher progressively throws faster and goes through his whole repertoire of pitches, trying to make sure each one is breaking properly and going where he wants it to.

So now that you have a better understanding of the importance of a pitcher mixing up his pitches, changing speeds, and varying location, as well as staying in sync with his catcher (more on that in Chapter 13) and his fielders, wouldn't you agree that there's a whole lot more to pitching than just rearing back and firing the ball in there?

The Least You Need to Know

➤ Good pitchers rely on both their arms and their brains.

➤ Pitchers need to mix up types of pitches, location of pitches, and speeds of pitches.

➤ It's just as important—and effective—to fool a hitter as it is to overpower him.

➤ A good pitcher also must be able to hold runners on base and play good defense.

Chapter 13

Catchers: The Men Behind the Mask

In This Chapter

➤ Mamas, don't let your babies grow up to be catchers

➤ The importance of avoiding injuries

➤ The chess game of calling pitches

➤ The many roles of the catcher

When Jim Maloney, a pitcher and teammate of mine with the Cincinnati Reds, started to lose a little off his fastball, he decided to try throwing an illegal *spitball* (which means just what it sounds like: doctoring the ball with a little saliva to make it break more sharply). Hall of Famer Gaylord Perry got away with throwing *spitters* all the time, but Jim was afraid of getting caught, so he threw his only when he really needed to. He always signaled me beforehand, but a spitball moves so much that it still was like trying to catch the wind. A spitter can break six inches or two feet. You never really know where it's going. So every time Maloney threw it, I never even let my eyes blink, because I knew how nasty it was, and I didn't want to miss it and get clobbered.

One time we were playing the Pittsburgh Pirates at Forbes Field when one of Jim's spitters started chest high and then just exploded down. It barely touched the bottom of my glove and crashed right into my cup (the rock-hard plastic piece that's supposed to protect your groin)—crashed so hard, my cup shattered. For three weeks after that, some of my favorite body parts were black and purple and other unnatural colors.

And you know what? That was just one of seven cups that shattered on me in my career. I got hit lots of times, and every time, I went through the same instant pain and the same long-lasting rainbow tattoo. And I was considered one of the best defensive catchers ever—I won 10 Gold Gloves—so you can imagine how much abuse a catcher would endure if he didn't know what he was doing. I don't like it when people call our protective gear *the tools of ignorance,* but I can sort of understand why. Maybe you have to be a little dumb or a little crazy to choose the pain and suffering of life as a catcher.

But the thing I liked most about catching was that there were four ways I could have a good game: I could call a good game for my pitcher, I could throw runners out on the bases, I could block runners at home plate, and I could get base hits.

Extra Innings

Cleveland Indians catcher Sandy Alomar Jr. once had a reputation for being injury-prone, but his manager, Mike Hargrove, predicted the Alomar would stay healthy and emerge as an All-Star catcher. Why? "There's nothing left to fix," Hargrove said.

Get Ready to Take a Beating

A catcher, or *receiver* or *backstop,* as they're sometimes called, gets beaten up like a crash-test dummy. We get bumps and bruises and aches and breaks in places that most players don't even think about. Here's a quick inventory on my battered body after 17 years in the majors:

Talkin' Baseball

"A good catcher is the quarterback, the carburetor, the lead dog, the pulse taker, the traffic cop, and sometimes a lot of unprintable things, but no team gets very far without one."

—Manager Miller Huggins

➤ Six broken bones in each foot
➤ One broken thumb
➤ One split thumb
➤ One broken little finger
➤ One broken ankle
➤ One acromio-clavicular joint removed (shoulder)
➤ One part of a lung removed

Late in 1972, two days after my 25th birthday, I contracted what they call Valley Fever. I got it in Fresno, California, and I had to have part of my lung removed. A doctor performed the operation without cutting my back muscles, but my career was never the same. I had just made MVP and had hit 40 home runs for the second time in three years, but after the lung surgery, I never had the same power. I still made the Hall of Fame, still rang up some good numbers, but who knows what I could have done if I had stayed healthy.

But that's the thing. Not many catchers are able to stay healthy. Of course, the Valley Fever had nothing to do with catching, but that's a pretty long list up there even without it. You get the idea—injuries are part of the job description behind the plate.

I Can Do This with One Hand Behind My Back!

As a catcher, you know the only way you can have success and longevity—and make money—is to avoid injuries. So many times, a batter gets just a little bit of the bat on the ball, and his foul tip nails you right in the hands. That happens so often, a lot of catchers' fingers are swollen up and pointed in every direction, and catchers are in and out of the lineup for a laundry list of injuries.

I was playing for the Peninsula Grays in the Carolina League when I got called up to Buffalo in July 1966, and in the first inning of my first Triple-A game, I got a foul tip off my thumb and broke it. The next year I started the season with Buffalo before I was called up to play for the Reds. With about three games left in the season, I reached up to try to pick a baserunner, Glenn Beckert, off first base just as the batter barely foul-tipped the ball. My right thumb was exposed, and the foul tip just split it wide open.

Two years in a row I had thumb injuries, and I thought, *"I can't stay in the lineup and produce numbers this way. The only way I can do this is to keep my hands safer."* I also didn't like thinking I was going to look like all the old catchers with hands that looked like bags of walnuts.

Extra Innings

There've been only about three or four left-handed catchers in baseball history. Dale Long and Mike Squires were lefty catchers I remember—they were mainly first basemen but they could catch in a pinch. I guess most hitters were right-handed, and a lefty catcher couldn't easily throw over the batter. But I don't know why a left-handed catcher couldn't do the job. Tag plays at home plate would be a little more difficult—it would be tough to make a sweep tag—but if you're a good enough athlete it shouldn't matter what position you play.

In 1968, Randy Hundley (father of Mets and now Dodgers catcher Todd Hundley) caught 160 games for the Cubs—an incredible feat, just unheard of—and it was because he was catching one-handed, with his throwing hand protected behind his back. I made up my mind to go to the one-handed style of catching. I kept my right hand behind my back, out of harm's way, until I needed to throw the ball, and it changed everything. I wasn't trying to create a style, but all catchers started to follow us, and it cut down on injuries considerably.

I was pretty good at squaring up and blocking pitches in the dirt with my body, and when I wasn't in position, I would just backhand them—reach across my body with my left arm and catch the ball with the pocket of my mitt facing the playing field. Longtime big-league catcher Joe Garagiola always said I ruined more catchers because I could do that and nobody else could. Some catchers were so bad at it, their pitchers wouldn't throw their best curveball or split-fingered fastball in a tight game with runners on base, because they were afraid it'd get by the catcher and cost them a run.

Stayin' Alive

Back in 1966, when I was an 18-year-old minor leaguer, I had a bit of a temper, and I would throw my batting helmet when I made an out. Sometimes I'd fire it against a concrete wall, and I broke something like three helmets that year. It cost me $35 every time. Then I'd go out to play defense with a catcher's mask over my cloth baseball cap, and about once a week I'd get a foul tip right off the little bead on top of the hat. It stung like hell and it made me mad.

Finally, I told myself, *"I can't keep breaking helmets. It's not right, and it's costing me money. Plus, these foul tips hurt! Why don't I wear my helmet while I'm catching, too?"* I stopped throwing my helmet—now I was going to use it—and all of a sudden those foul tips hitting me in the head didn't hurt so much. I put the helmet on backward, slipped my mask over it, and pretty soon, catchers were mimicking me on that, too.

Extra Innings

I don't recommend that other catchers try this, but I once caught a pitch barehanded. It wasn't a macho thing, it was motivational. In a 1969 game against the Los Angeles Dodgers, our pitcher, a big lefty named Gerry Arrigo, was just laying it in there—throwing it like it was an orange. I tried everything to get him to put something on his fastball. Finally, I just reached out with my bare hand and caught the damn thing like it was a tennis ball. Nearly everybody in the ballpark saw it, including the Dodgers, most of whom doubled over laughing. Gerry was pretty flustered, but his good fastball suddenly returned.

But a catcher anticipating a play at home plate—where he would have to tag out a runner trying to score—always threw off his mask to make sure he could see the ball coming toward him. You could see better, but your head was exposed and in danger when guys tried to score by running over you. Nowadays, they make the helmet and mask all in one piece. The visibility is better, so you can leave it on at all times, protecting yourself not only from foul tips but from home-plate collisions.

I was always trying to find ways to protect myself. Earlier I mentioned the thumb guard that I designed with the Reds' trainer, Larry Starr, to try to prevent my left thumb from getting sprained. If a catcher sprains his glove thumb, it doesn't heal until the season ends, because every sinker and every foul tip just aggravates the injury. We molded a plastic splint that I stuck right inside my mitt.

Steve Yeager of the Dodgers introduced another safety measure during my era. He started using a little flap that hung over the throat from the bottom of the catcher's mask to guard against balls that hit in the dirt and ricochet up, or even foul tips that caught you in the throat. If you ever had it happen to you, you'd remember it a long time. A blow to the Adam's apple could almost be fatal.

Shin guards have evolved now, too; they have a little more padding on the side to protect against the spikes of runners sliding into home. Metal-toed shoes protect against foul tips—very few catchers have a nice pedicure—and now they extend flaps from the shin guards to cover more of the foot.

From the Bench

I wore out two or three mitts a year, and I was always breaking one in. I'd have a backup or bullpen catcher use one of my new gloves in the bullpen so it was game-ready when needed. Infielders and outfielders don't abuse their gloves nearly as much. I've known guys who used the same glove for 10 or 12 years.

Baseball's Iron Men

So they've made a lot of strides in protecting the catcher. Still, you get beat up by errant pitches, by foul tips, by guys running you over trying to score. You get worn out by injuries, by doing 100–200 squats a day, by spending hours in a crouch. That's why a lot of catchers are streak hitters. You can be hitting the ball pretty well for a while and then you get a foul tip off the shoulder, another one off the foot, another off the hand, and you're trying to swing around the injuries.

Catching is tough on the knees, too. You're crouching down, handling about 150 pitches a night, and games usually last three hours or more. And you're up and down in your stance a lot, which also takes its toll. Catchers aren't generally fast runners to begin with—your prototypical catcher is more the fireplug type, stocky and strong—and years of playing the position don't exactly make your legs suited to zippy baserunning.

You see an outfielder run into a wall and the manager runs 400 feet to see if he's all right. You see a pitcher take a line drive off his shin and the manager sprints to the mound with a trainer to make sure he's okay. But a catcher can take a foul tip that's so wicked it breaks his cup and leaves him breathless, laying on the ground in agony for 10 minutes, and the manager looks the other way because he doesn't want to take his catcher out of the game. The only guy who'll come over is the umpire, and he just says, "Come on, get up. We've got a game to play."

The attitude is, *"He'll be all right; he's a catcher."* Catchers are expected to shrug off pain that would put other position players on the disabled list.

A Full Plate

So now that I've explained why mamas shouldn't let their babies grow up to be catchers, let me explain why a kid might *want* to.

The catcher is the second most important player on the field, right behind the pitcher. The catcher not only has to pull down every pitch, he has to call every one. That means he has to remember the strengths and weaknesses of every pitcher on his team and every hitter in his league, and he has to be smart enough to call the right pitch at the right time. He has to stop a runner from advancing on a stolen base, a *passed ball* (a pitch that, in the official scorer's judgment, the catcher should have caught but didn't), or a *wild pitch* (a pitch that gets by the catcher but is ruled the pitcher's fault). The catcher has to block home plate, positioning himself directly in front of the plate, sacrificing his body when a runner trying to score barrels over him or scoots around

Catching On

A **passed ball** is a pitch that, in the official scorer's judgment, the catcher should have caught but didn't; a **wild pitch** is a pitch that gets by the catcher but is ruled the pitcher's fault.

him. And like every other position player, the catcher has to hit.

But unlike a lot of position players, particularly outfielders and cornermen (first and third basemen), a catcher can go 0-for-4 and still have a great game. That's what I always liked about playing the position. There are so many ways to contribute to a victory. You can call a good game and help your pitcher throw a shutout. You can preserve a victory by blocking the plate when the tying run tries to score. You can cut down basestealers. You can save a wild pitch in the dirt. Or you can hit a home run. A lot of catchers dwell on the negatives and the pressures of the position, but I always enjoyed the positives.

Calling the Shots

A smart catcher knows his pitcher, his opposition, and how to work the matchups to his team's advantage. Every team compiles scouting reports to create a "book" on every hitter, and, as a catcher, I had my own scouting reports. We'd put all this information together and draw up a game plan, keeping it in mind from the moment the leadoff hitter walks into the batter's box. As you're calling pitches, you're figuring out the psyche of the hitter and what pitch he's looking for. You go by gut feeling, by how he's standing at the plate, by whether he's swinging the bat well.

The game plan may change as the game goes on—your pitcher isn't getting anybody out, or he's having trouble with his location, his breaking ball, whatever—and then you do what you have to do. Sometimes in the first or second inning I'd tell our manager, Sparky Anderson, to get somebody throwing in the bullpen, because I knew the pitcher didn't have his stuff that day. If it was early in the game, I'd try to nurse him along as far as I could. When his fastball wasn't there, I'd call for his curve and mix in his change-up. I'd go away from his normal pattern to try to get the most out of him before the hitters figured out he didn't have anything.

The real chess game occurs with a pitcher who never has overpowering stuff. Jim Merritt won 20 games for us in 1970 despite a 4.08 ERA. There were guys he just couldn't get out, who'd hit the ball out of the park. People looked at the number of walks he gave up and never understood that we were walking people we wanted to avoid so we could get to the batters that we could get out.

If we were facing Hank Aaron for the Atlanta Braves or Willie McCovey and Willie Mays for the San Francisco Giants, and I didn't think we could get them out, I would try to *pitch around* them, to get to another hitter who I was pretty sure we could get out. I'd go after the guy who couldn't handle the breaking ball, because Jim threw good breaking balls and off-speed pitches. You're always looking for the guy in the lineup who can't beat you—he winds up being your out man. Tom Seaver was a dominating pitcher, yet he was notorious for pitching around people until he got to the guy he knew he could get out.

Bob Gibson was so overpowering, it wouldn't have mattered if he was facing Babe Ruth, Ted Williams, or Hank Aaron: He could go right after them. With my best pitcher throwing, I'd go right through the lineup without a lot of fear. If I'm catching a decent right-handed pitcher, and I've got a great left-handed hitter at bat with a base open, I probably won't give him anything to hit. I'm going to give him borderline pitches that he might chase and get himself out. You try to keep him off-balance, try to make him swing at your pitch.

Now, you might be wondering, "What about the pitcher? Doesn't he have some say? Doesn't he know himself better than anybody?" Well, if the pitcher trusts his catcher to call the right pitch, it takes pressure off him, and I think you get a much better performance.

Talkin' Baseball

"You gotta have a catcher or you'll have a lot of passed balls."

—Casey Stengel

Extra Innings

The most famous—or infamous—catcher's gaffe of all time occurred in Game 4 of the 1941 World Series. Leading 4–3 with two outs in the ninth inning, the Brooklyn Dodgers were on the brink of evening the Series with the New York Yankees at two games apiece. Brooklyn's Hugh Casey threw a third strike past Tommy Henrich that would have ended the game, but the ball got past catcher Mickey Owen for a passed ball, allowing Henrich to reach first base. The Yankees made the most of the opportunity by staging a four-run, game-winning rally, and wrapped up the Series with a 3–1 win the next day.

Tom Seaver had already established himself as a Hall of Fame-caliber pitcher when he was traded by the New York Mets to the Reds in 1977, so I called the pitches that I thought he wanted. But he didn't want that. He trusted me to call the pitches I wanted. So it was easy to work with him. Shoot, I don't think Don Gullett shook me off 10 times in the seven years that we played together. He got the sign, he threw the pitch. He had good enough stuff and it worked.

It never bothered me if a pitcher shook me off—as long as I trusted him to judge the situation and not try something he shouldn't. If he was confident that he could throw a certain pitch and get away with it, if he had enough on that pitch and some history with it, fine. After he hurt his arm, Gary Nolan shook me off all the time because he never again trusted his fastball. He'd throw curves and change-ups, and as much as you wanted him to throw a fastball in certain situations, he didn't want to, because he had lost confidence in it. We'd been together since the instructional league when we were 18, so I trusted him and let him call his game to a certain extent.

That should be the job of a catcher. Now, it seems like more and more pitching coaches are involved, calling pitches from the dugout. And unless your catcher is dumb or inexperienced, I don't think that's right. From the dugout, a manager or pitching coach can't get the feel of a pitcher or the flow of the game as well as a catcher. They can't see the movement of the pitches as well as a catcher. They might think, "Here's a perfect place to call for a curveball," but the catcher can see how the pitcher's curve is breaking and decides, "I can't trust him to throw a curve here."

The Catcher's Couch

A catcher has to play chess when calling pitches, and play psychiatrist when dealing with a staff of 10 or 12 pitchers with all different types of personalities. Head cases, flakes, future doctors and lawyers—catchers see all types of pitchers.

There's the pitcher who gets in trouble and you have to walk out to the mound and just calm him down and tell him, "Remember your mechanics. You're really rushing. Just stay back and relax and follow me." You try to get him to focus totally on you and the hitter. His mind might be all over the place—on the hitter, on the on-deck hitters, on the dugout, on the fans and what they're yelling—and you have to put his mind at ease and get him to focus.

Extra Innings

Backup catchers are some of the funniest guys in baseball. Bob Uecker and Joe Garagiola parlayed humor into long broadcasting careers. I once got into a running gag with backup Pirates catcher Junior Ortiz when he went on a rare hot streak and jokingly compared himself to me. "He's the best I've ever seen," I agreed. "He had three hits the other day, so I guess he's taken care of April and May." Rich Donnelly, a wise-cracking Pirates coach, said Junior was better. "John was a great Hall of Fame catcher, but anybody can play every day. To have no talent at all and play once a week like Junior—that's incredible." Outfielder Andy Van Slyke chimed in, "I think if Junior played with a Morgan, a Bench, a Perez, a Rose, a Griffey, he might get—who knows?—thirteen, fourteen RBI a year." I said Junior reminded me of two Reds backups, Pat Corrales and Bill Plummer. They became major league managers, so the writer asked me if Junior could, too. "I think he's got a good chance," I said. "As long as there's a Little League team down in Puerto Rico that needs some help."

There's the pitcher who's rattled and you know you can't shake him out of it entirely, but you just remind him of the situation and tell him he has good enough stuff to handle this hitter. Say the bases are loaded and you know the pitcher is excitable. "Keep the ball down on this hitter," I'd say. "If he hits it back to you, throw it home and we'll get the guy at the plate."

And then there's the pitcher you have to challenge. You have to put your spikes right in the middle of his back (so to speak) and say, "Look, you've got to gut it out. You've

185

got to step it up a notch." And you might not be that polite, because you want to get him a little mad so he'll concentrate and get the most out of himself.

Talkin' Baseball

"When Steve and I die, we're going to be buried in the same cemetery, 60 feet, 6 inches apart."

—Tim McCarver, Steve Carlton's "designated catcher" in the late 1970s

Warning Track

Don't judge a catcher's defense based on fielding percentage. The guy with the great fielding percentage who doesn't commit many errors usually isn't taking many chances. One time I tried to pick off a runner at first base, threw it down the right-field line, and the runner went all the way to third. But on the next pitch, I picked him off at third. So you have to take some chances as a catcher. That means you throw down to second even when you have no shot unless you throw a perfect peg: 127 feet, three inches, and put it six inches above the bag—to catch a guy who runs the 100 in 9.5 seconds.

So every pitcher is different. The catcher's job is to get the very most out of each one. You really have to work the whole time, using a different psychology and a different mentality on each pitcher, trying to get their best out of them.

The Recipe for the Ideal Catcher

The ideal catcher has to endure the bumps and bruises, catch balls in the dirt or over his head, throw out basestealers, and block the plate when runners try to score. He has to be smart enough to get inside the heads of his pitchers and opposing hitters. He has to be an extension of his manager, like a quarterback in football or a point guard in basketball. When I played they called me "the Little General," and I took pride in that: It meant that I was doing my job.

A catcher has to do all this and hit, too. Because if he doesn't hit, he won't stay in the lineup, no matter how valuable he is defensively. But if he's terrific defensively and hits even .250, he is one of a team's most valuable players. And if he can hit the way Yogi Berra did in the 1950s, the way I did in the late '60s and '70s, the way Gary Carter did in the '70s and '80s, and the way Mike Piazza does in the '90s, he's going to make a lot of All-Star teams and his team is going to win a lot of games.

Johnny's Best Behind the Plate

Yogi Berra, Roy Campanella, Mickey Cochrane, Gabby Hartnett, Bill Dickey, Josh Gibson, and **Ernie Lombardi** are all Hall of Fame catchers (along with myself)—the best ever. They were before my time, so you don't need me to tell you about them. Instead, I'll focus on the best defensive catchers of the past 30 years.

Randy Hundley of the Chicago Cubs and **Jerry Grote** of the Mets were real take-charge catchers. Every catcher should play like them: control the pitcher, control the field. A lot of bench coaches maneuver players in the field based on computer-generated charts, but it's better if the catcher can shade the outfielders based on whether they're working inside and the hitter is likely to pull the ball, or pitching outside and the hitter is more likely to go to the opposite field. The catcher is that much more in touch with the game at the plate. Those two guys were just outstanding in those areas.

Yogi Berra of the Yankees was one of the greatest of all time behind the plate, both offensively and defensively.

Other contemporaries I admired were **Steve Yeager** of the Dodgers, **Carlton Fisk** of the Boston Red Sox and Chicago White Sox, and **Gary Carter** of the Montreal Expos and the Mets. **Paul Casanova** of the Washington Senators and the Braves didn't spend a lot of time in the majors, but he had one of the best arms I've ever seen. **Thurman Munson** of the Yankees didn't throw very well, but he compensated with his quickness. **Ted Simmons** of the St. Louis Cardinals was so gutty and gritty that he made himself into an exceptional catcher. Had we not been in the same league, **Manny Sanguillen** of the Pirates would have gotten more attention as a top catcher. **Bob Boone** of the Philadelphia Phillies and California Angels was short on offense, but excelled defensively and set the record for games caught— an incredible feat for a guy who had to ice down his knees two hours before the game and two hours afterward. That's what it takes to be a catcher sometimes; nobody sees how hard it is on you.

Among today's players, **Ron Karkovice**, who spent most of his career with the White Sox, has never put up great offensive numbers, but everybody

Talkin' Baseball

"They say he's funny. Well, he has a lovely wife and family, a beautiful home, money in the bank, and he plays golf with millionaires. What's funny about that?"

—Casey Stengel on Yogi Berra

respects his exceptional defensive abilities. **Dan Wilson** of the Seattle Mariners also has developed into an outstanding defensive catcher.

Ivan "Pudge" Rodriguez ("Pudge" was his idol Carlton Fisk's nickname) of the Texas Rangers is exceptional. And he's built for it. A catcher should be around six foot, six-foot-two, and have mobility and strength. With the new workout machines, today's players can develop strength and durability. Pudge's quickness sets him apart, and that's the key for any catcher. He releases the ball so quickly and accurately when guys try to steal. Pudge loves to throw guys out; it's a point of pride with him. He's like I was: He's not afraid to take chances.

The Least You Need to Know

➤ Catching is risky; catchers get hit by a lot of pitches and foul balls, and they can also get run over during plays at the plate.

➤ I and a few others have developed a number of equipment innovations to prevent injuries at the position.

➤ The catcher is like a coach on the field in terms of how he calls pitches and handles his pitchers.

➤ Seven other famous catchers and I are enshrined in Cooperstown, but I'd include a few other lesser-known catchers in my personal Hall of Fame.

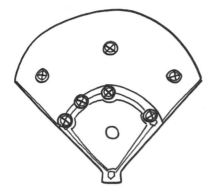

Chapter 14

The Other Defensive Positions: Who Does What

In This Chapter

➤ The value of good defense

➤ Which positions are the most important

➤ The job description for each spot in the field

➤ Where managers turn for defense in a pinch

Roger Clemens of the Toronto Blue Jays and Kerry Wood of the Chicago Cubs have each struck out 20 batters in a single game. That's a phenomenal feat. And yet each pitcher still needed his defense to get seven outs. Over the course of a season, even the strikeout kings will average only about one strikeout per inning. That means they need good defense behind them to get a lot of outs. Groundball pitchers like the Atlanta Braves' Greg Maddux are even more dependent on the fielders behind them. "You can have good defense without good pitching," Hall of Fame manager Earl Weaver once said, "but you can't have good pitching without good defense."

A team builds a good defense *up the middle*—catcher, shortstop, second baseman, center fielder—because that's where most balls are hit. Catcher and shortstop are so important to defense—and success—that a team will carry exceptional defenders at those positions even if they're only mild threats with the bat. Second basemen and center fielders are expected to provide more offense, but not as much as players at the corners—first and third base, and right and left fields. Even the best hitters cannot be total stiffs in the field, though. As another Hall of Fame manager, Casey Stengel, reasoned, "I don't like them fellas who drive in two runs and let in three."

As you'll see in this chapter, defense is a vital part of the game, even if it doesn't earn as much recognition as hitting and pitching. Great defense doesn't earn a player too many invites to the All-Star Game or the Hall of Fame, unless he's truly one in a million. But it will earn his team a lot of victories.

First Base: Footwork Is Important

First base often provides a rest home for guys who can still hit but can't run, clumsy slowfoots whose lack of *range* (the amount of area that they can safely cover defensively) and quickness are liabilities at other positions. Dick Stuart, so prodigious a slugger he once hit 66 home runs in a minor league season, was known as Dr. Strangeglove because he booted so many plays. By contrast, defensive standouts like Wes Parker, Steve Garvey, George Scott, Don Mattingly, and Keith Hernandez made all the routine plays—and a lot of great ones—for their clubs.

A first baseman can save a lot of runs for his pitcher, and a lot of errors for the other infielders, by scooping up in-the-dirt, one-hop, and off-target throws. He can save a lot of extra-base hits by spearing line drives down the right-field line. He can transform game-turning sacrifice bunts into inning-ending double plays by charging hard for the ball and making an accurate throw to the correct base. He needs good footwork to find the bag and *stretch* for infielders' throws, to hold runners on base, to decide which balls to chase and which ones to let the second baseman or pitcher handle. And, of course, he has to catch the ball. If a first baseman can't handle the tough throws, his infielders start aiming the ball, giving the runners an extra step, and often wind up throwing even less accurately.

Guys who throw left-handed often are stationed at first base. Their gloves are a tad closer to their fielders when stretching on bang-bang plays, and they don't have to turn awkwardly to make throws to second and third on grounders and bunts.

Talkin' Baseball

"If you don't catch the ball, you catch the bus."

—Infielder Rocky Bridges

Catching On

A defense gets a **double play** when it records two outs on the same play. **Triple plays** are rare, but a good defense can turn several double plays in a game. In the most common double play, a runner is on first and the batter grounds the ball to the shortstop or third baseman, who flips the ball to the second baseman who **forces out** the runner, then fires to first base to **double up** the batter.

Yankee great Lou Gehrig was well known for his prowess with the bat, but he was pretty handy with the glove, too. Here he shows off his stretch at first base.

Extra Innings

You see quite a few right-handed first basemen, but you hardly ever see a left-hander at the other infield positions or at catcher. Throwing angles make it awkward for lefties at those positions. Since 1902, only Dale Long (1958), Mike Squires (1980), and Benny Distefano (1989) have caught even a single game left-handed.

Second Base: The Acrobats of Baseball

Shortstops generally have more range and a stronger arm than second basemen. From pee-wee through high school ball, the best, most athletic players usually play shortstop, but only the cream are found at the top levels. The rest end up at second base. So people often think of second base as, well, secondary.

Which I don't understand. Personally, I think the second baseman has the second-toughest job on the field—after the catcher, of course. He has to do so many things:

Catching On

A **relay** is a throw from one fielder to another, who then throws the ball to a third player. For example, say there's a runner on first, and the batter hits the ball off the wall in right field. The second baseman has to hustle into shallow right field to take the relay from the right fielder, then whirl around and throw quickly and accurately to cut down the lead runner at the plate.

From the Bench

Double plays are said to be a pitcher's best friend because they can get him out of so many jams. Two outs, two runners gone—what a relief!

Talkin' Baseball

"A great catch is like watching girls go by. The last one you see is always the prettiest."

—Hall of Fame pitcher Bob Gibson

cover first base on bunts, cover second base on steals and pickoff plays, hustle into the outfield for the *relay* from an outfielder and then whirl around and throw quickly and accurately to cut down the runner. He has to range up the middle to flag down would-be base hits and, even though his momentum is carrying him in the opposite direction, do a 180-degree turn and throw over his body in time to get the runner at first base.

He's the cornerstone of the double play. As he scrambles to second base to take the throw from the shortstop or third baseman, his momentum is carrying him away from first base. He doesn't always have time to catch the ball, turn, and step toward first base as he throws. He has to stand in at second base with a runner barreling in, spikes high, trying to break up the double play—coming at him from his blind side, or just in his peripheral view, and that's the scariest part for any fielder. Every other fielder can see a runner advancing toward him. But the second baseman has to catch the ball, avoid the runner, pivot, and throw at the same time—and still get enough on his throw to get the runner at first base.

I marvel at the acrobatic way the best second basemen get out of harm's way on a double play, jumping over the runner or quickly sliding off to one side. On a slow-hit ball to third, the second baseman knows the runner is bearing down on him and is going to cream him, but he hangs in there anyway.

Longtime Pittsburgh Pirates second baseman Bill Mazeroski set the standard for turning the double play. Probably the slickest second baseman ever, "Maz," who retired after the 1972 season, has been overlooked for the Hall of Fame because he was just an average hitter—except for the day in 1960 when he beat the mighty New York Yankees in the World Series with a home run in the ninth inning of Game 7. Joe Morgan, my Cincinnati Reds teammate, made the Hall of Fame for his greatness on offense and defense. Frank White of the Kansas City Royals and Ryne Sandberg of the Chicago Cubs were also terrific defensively. Today, Craig Biggio of the Houston Astros and Bret Boone of the Atlanta Braves set the standard.

No second baseman was more sure-handed—or better on the pivot—than Pirates star Bill Mazeroski, who goes airborne here to avoid a sliding runner.

Shortstop: The Ballerinas of Baseball

Because most hitters are right-handed and attempt to pull the ball toward left field or up the middle, the shortstop generally fields more grounders and line drives than any other player. He must have a stronger, quicker arm than the second or third baseman because he plays deeper and further from the first baseman. He must quickly retrieve and deftly flick balls to the second baseman to start double plays, or scoot to second and take the second baseman's throw and fire to first to complete the *twin killing,* as a double play is sometimes called. The best shortstop/second base combos, called *double play combinations,* feature telepathic precision borne of years of practice, communication, and study.

Like second basemen, shortstops have to charge slow grounders, time high hoppers, take away base hits up the middle, and make good relay throws from the outfield. What's more, they must range deep in the hole toward third base and have strong enough arms to fling the ball to first base in time. My Reds teammate Dave Concepcion developed a revolutionary play for balls hit deep in the hole at Riverfront Stadium in Cincinnati. He purposely threw the ball so it would bounce on the artificial turf once and go directly to the first baseman. People who didn't know better would think it was a bad throw. Actually, it was brilliant. To throw that far while off-balance is very difficult. But if he bounced it, the turf (it only worked on artifical turf) gave it a bounce that was fast and true enough that the first baseman could handle it easily.

Catching On

Infielders throw the ball **around the horn**—from first to second or short and then to third—after an out when there's no one on base and at the end of their warmups between innings. Outfielders **hit the cutoff man** when they field a base hit and throw back to the second baseman or shortstop, who tries to spin and throw out the runner or keep him from advancing another base, depending on the situation.

Shortstops who hit, like Cubs Hall of Famer Ernie Banks and future Hall of Famer Alex Rodriguez of the Seattle Mariners, provide big bonuses. Managers often will sacrifice offense—playing a shortstop who hits .200 to .250 with little power—because his defense is so important.

We've seen a wide range of brilliant fielders at shortstop over the years, from Pee Wee Reese to Phil Rizzuto to Luis Aparicio to Mark Belanger to Dave Concepcion to Ozzie Smith. Larry Bowa and Cal Ripken Jr. didn't have Concepcion's silky-smooth range, but they were as consistent as the sunrise. Smith, the St. Louis Cardinals' Wizard of Oz, set a standard for ballet-like plays, range, and grace. He was poetry in motion, the Michael Jordan of shortstops. Every day, you'd swear, "I never saw a shortstop do *that* before!" And then he'd one-up himself the next day.

Today, we have a bountiful crop of promising young shortstops—including Rodriguez, Nomar Garciaparra of the Boston Red Sox, Derek Jeter of the Yankees, and Omar Vizquel of the Indians—many of them as brilliant with the bat as they are with the glove.

Ozzie Smith's wizardry with the glove at shortstop will one day land him in the Hall of Fame.

Third Base: They Call It the Hot Corner

Third base is all about reactions. A strong pitcher can throw a ball 100 miles an hour, and a quick bat can boomerang it back even faster. If a ball is hit 120 or 140 miles an hour, it only takes a split second to reach a third baseman just 90 feet away. Someday one of them is going to wind up like a cartoon character who tried to catch a cannon-ball—with a big hole where his belly used to be.

Third base is called *the hot corner* for a reason. Sometimes you've got no chance at all, like when a left-handed pitcher throws a breaking ball and a right-handed power hitter smokes it down the left-field line.

A third baseman must have quick reactions to get in front of scorching liners—and the courage and pain threshold to handle the inevitable shots off his shins, chest, and sundry other body parts. No flinching allowed. On bunts and topped balls, he has to be able to charge in, bare-hand the ball, and throw quickly to first without breaking stride. He has to react to the sharply hit ball, turn, and throw to second base to start the double play. He has to dive and reach across his body to backhand balls behind the bag and come up throwing. Sometimes momentum carries him into foul territory and he still has to make that long throw. He has to cut off balls in the hole that the short-stop can't reach. He doesn't need the range and agility of the middle infielders, but he'd better have quick reflexes—and be able to hit with power. Maybe not as much power as the first baseman, but most clubs look for a third baseman who can hit 20-plus home runs and drive in 80 or more runs a year.

Brooks Robinson of the Baltimore Orioles, Mike Schmidt of the Philadelphia Phillies, Graig Nettles of the New York Yankees, and Ron Santo of the Chicago Cubs were the best I've ever seen. They could really *pick it,* as they say in baseball parlance. Unfortunately, I learned all about Robinson's skills in the 1970 World Series, when he made more brilliant defensive plays against my Cincinnati Reds than most guys make in a lifetime. The St. Louis Cardinals' Ken Boyer would have gotten more notoriety for his defense if he hadn't played in the same era as Brooks. Today, I like Ken Caminiti of the Houston Astros.

Brooks Robinson flashed plenty of leather in his day. Unfortunately, he did plenty of that in the 1970 World Series, when his Orioles beat my Reds.

Left Field: Bring Your Glove

Fans sometimes think of outfielders as lumbering sluggers who stand around, catching one or two balls a game. That's true some of the time, but good defensive outfielders are fast and athletic. They can make up for speed by positioning themselves where each hitter is likely to go and by reacting quickly at the crack of the bat and getting a good jump. Sometimes they have to time their leap to snare the ball before it goes over the wall, and other times they have to sacrifice their bodies and bang into the wall to take away an extra-base hit.

Outfielders don't field as many balls as infielders, but their muffs are more costly. An infielder's error usually gives the opposition one extra base. If an outfielder drops a sure catch or lets a ball go between his legs, the batter could wind up with a triple or an inside-the-park home run. So while an outfielder makes his money on his hitting, he'd better not be daydreaming out there, thinking about his last at-bat or some girl up in the stands.

A key to playing well in the outfield is being able to hit the *cutoff man*. Nothing is more important than the coordination between the outfielder and infielder. Before the ball is even hit, the outfielder has to know where to throw, based on the number of outs and the positioning of runners on base. The cutoff man has to hustle into the shallow outfield and get in good position to catch and throw the ball to the infield. The other infielder has to judge the strength of the throw and the speed of the runners and yell directions to the cutoff man either to catch the throw or to let it go through. If the cutoff man is going to relay the ball—let's say to try to stop a runner from scoring—he has to get in good position, turn, and fire to the right man without hesitating or even really looking. That takes coordination and practice, because he's always in a little different position on the field, and he has to throw quick, hard, and accurately.

Of the three outfielders, the left fielder can get by with the weakest arm, because he has the shortest throw when trying to nab a runner at third base. (No left fielder ever has to throw the ball all the way across the field to first base, but a right fielder does have to make the long throw to third base on occasion.) However, on average, more balls are hit to left field than to right, so you can't have a guy out there who's a defensive liability. So you'll see a guy like the San Francisco Giants'

Talkin' Baseball

"The secret of my success was clean living and a fast-moving outfield."

—Hall of Fame pitcher Lefty Gomez

Catching On

A key to playing the outfield is hitting the **cutoff man**, who makes the relay. Before the ball is even hit, the outfielder has to know where to throw, based on the number of outs and the runners on base. The other infielder has to judge the strength of the throw and the speed of the runners and yell to the cutoff man whether to catch the throw or to let it go through.

Barry Bonds, who has the speed but not the arm to be a great center fielder, playing left, where he is a perennial Gold Glove winner.

One other thing: This isn't as important in a symmetrical ballpark, but in a stadium like Fenway Park, with balls bouncing off the Green Monster (the high left-field wall) and the ballpark's scoreboard and the funky angles in left field, an outfielder has to know how to play caroms off the wall. Red Sox Hall of Famers Ted Williams and Carl Yastrzemski threw out a lot of runners because they mastered the Green Monster's idiosyncrasies.

Talkin' Baseball

"He has a glove contract with U.S. Steel."

—Teammate Charlie Hough on defensively challenged outfielder Pete Incaviglia

Center Field: You Gotta Have Wheels

There are probably more balls hit to center field than anywhere else in the outfield, so your center fielder has to have the good judgment, the gazelle-like speed, and the great glove to rush in and take away singles, go to the warning track and take away extra-base hits, and cut off balls hit in the gap. A good, fast center fielder can make up for the lack of range of the guys next to him. For instance, when lead-footed Greg "The Bull" Luzinski played left field for the Phillies and Garry Maddox played center, they used to say two-thirds of the Earth was covered by water and the rest by Garry Maddox.

In the outfield, the center fielder is the captain, the general, the traffic cop, making decisions on balls hit in the gap: Does he *call off* the guy next to him (wave his arm and shout, "Mine!" or "I got it!" to let the players around him know that he'll take the catch), or is he too far away and should let someone else make the catch? The center fielder has to make same decision on short fly balls hit into that "no-man's land" between the middle infielders and the outfield. Because he's running straight at the ball and doesn't have his back turned to the plate, those are his plays if he can get there. He's in the best position after the catch to gun out a runner trying to advance. However, on balls hit into the gap, another outfielder might have a better throwing angle, and the center fielder has to be smart enough to back off.

With all that responsibility, the center fielder has the biggest role out there. Often, it's a glamour position. Hall of Famers Joe DiMaggio, Mickey Mantle, and Willie Mays all played center field. You can watch ESPN highlights all summer long, but you'll never see a better catch than Willie, playing for the New York Giants against the Cleveland Indians in the 1954 World Series opener at the Polo Grounds, chasing an impossibly long drive to the warning track and catching it with his back to the plate.

Talkin' Baseball

"They had better defense at Pearl Harbor."

—Center fielder Andy Van Slyke on his team's sub-par fielding

Extra Innings

Glen Gorbous, a Canadian outfielder born in Drumheller, Alberta, set a world record by throwing a baseball 445 feet, three inches in 1957 at an exhibition in Omaha, Nebraska. But the long-distance throw is more for the circus than for baseball; Gorbous played in just 115 major league games with the Reds and Philadelphia Phillies from 1955 to 1957, retiring with a major league batting average of .238.

Right Field: It Helps to Carry a Gun

The right fielder usually has the strongest arm in the outfield. It can be a macho thing: Do baserunners dare test his arm and try to go from first to third on a single to right?

Warning Track

It's important to get a good jump on fly balls, but even Gold Glove outfielders like Andy Van Slyke have been known to turn the wrong way. One such misplay gave Delino DeShields an inside-the-park home run in an April 1992 game. "Somebody told me after the game that the shortest distance between two points is a straight line," Van Slyke said. "But I was very poor in geometry. I always thought it was an isosceles triangle."

Some outfielders say right field is a little more difficult to play than left. Other than the longer throw to third base, I'm not sure why. It may be the way a right-handed hitter's ball cuts away from the right fielder. The left fielder faces the same thing with left-handed hitters, but there aren't as many left-handed hitters.

When you talk about the great right fielders, you talk about guys with guns for arms. Pirates Hall of Famer Roberto Clemente was probably the best there ever was in right. Today, Raul Mondesi of the Los Angeles Dodgers reminds me a little of Clemente.

Defense off the Bench

When a manager has a terrific hitter who's something of a liability in the field, and he can't use the guy as a designated hitter, he often will replace him with a defensive specialist in the late innings, going for defense to assure the win. If he's losing, he'll bring in his pinch hitters in hopes of generating offense. Say he has two shortstops, neither of whom can hit, but both of whom can really play defense. He'll start one, pinch hit for him in a key situation, then turn to the other shortstop when the team goes back on defense.

A lot of defensive specialists make their living not just on their good gloves, but on their versatility. Take a look at the Yankees of the last couple years. In Luis Sojo, they've had a valuable *utility infielder* who can play first, second, short, or third. Similarly, with Chad Curtis they've had a good gloveman who could fill in at any outfield spot.

Defensive subs don't get much credit when they play an inning or two and make just one or two plays. They only get noticed when they screw up—or when the manager screws up and doesn't use them. A manager who doesn't play the percentages in crucial games often pays a high price. In the third game of the 1977 National League Championship Series, Phillies manager Danny Ozark didn't replace Luzinski in the late innings with Jerry Martin, as he had all year, and the Bull botched a play in the ninth to cost Philadelphia the game. Philadelphia was eliminated the next game. In Game 6 of the 1986 World Series, Red Sox manager John McNamara broke his late-inning habit of replacing aging first baseman Bill Buckner with Dave Stapleton, and Buckner let a ground ball go through his legs to help the New York Mets win the game and, having forced a Game 7, the World Series.

Catching On

A player who can play several positions is called a **utility** man or a utility player. A lot of defensive specialists make their living not just on their good gloves, but on their versatility.

Talkin' Baseball

"Amazing strength, amazing power. He can grind the dust out of the bat. He will be great, super, wonderful. Now if he can only learn to catch a fly ball."

—Casey Stengel on new Met outfielder Ron Swoboda

Extra Innings

Kansas City Athletics' shortstop Bert Campaneris gave new meaning to the word versatility when, on September 8, 1965, he became the first major leaguer to play all nine positions in one game. Against the California Angels, Campaneris started one inning at each position, in this order: shortstop, second base, third base, left field, center field, right field (where he committed his only error of the game), first base, pitcher (where he gave up a run on one hit and two walks), and catcher (he left the game in the ninth inning after hurting his shoulder in a home-plate collision with Ed Kirkpatrick). Cesar Tovar of the Minnesota Twins matched Campaneris's feat in a September 22, 1968, game against the Oakland A's.

The Least You Need to Know

➤ Defense is a vital but often overlooked part of the game.

➤ The most important defensive positions are catcher, shortstop, second base, and center field.

➤ Left-handers often play first base but rarely are found at the other infield positions or at catcher because of awkward throwing angles.

➤ The center fielder is the traffic cop who covers the most area, but the right fielder usually has the best arm in the outfield.

Chapter 15

The Thinker's Guide to Defense

> ## In This Chapter
>
> ➤ Why defensive players are always moving around
>
> ➤ Dissecting different defensive strategies
>
> ➤ The D-lingo: shifts, bunts, steals, cutoffs, and relays
>
> ➤ The science of blocking the plate

Albert Einstein—the physicist, not the bagel guy—was as brilliant a man as the world ever knew. But even he was stumped by baseball's intricacies. One time he was talking with Moe Berg, a backup catcher in the 1920s and '30s and a man of letters. Moe took espionage photos in Japan and spied on a German atomic scientist for the U.S. before and during World War II. He was a mathematician, a graduate of three universities, a lawyer, and a linguist. They used to say Moe could speak a dozen languages—but couldn't hit in any of them. Einstein suggested he could teach Berg the fine points of mathematics if Berg would teach him baseball. "But," Einstein added, "I'm sure you'd learn mathematics faster than I'd learn baseball."

It *can* take years to learn all of baseball's subtleties and nuances. But that's what makes it fun. No matter how many games you play or watch, you can always learn new wrinkles. I obviously can't discuss every conceivable situation in one chapter, but in the pages that follow I'll offer some valuable lessons on various defensive schemes. And I promise you don't have to be a rocket scientist to understand them.

Getting in Position

The guys on defense aren't just standing around daydreaming out there (or at least they're not supposed to be). They're supposed to be thinking before every pitch, *"OK, what's the situation? How many outs? What's the count? Are there any baserunners? What's my pitcher likely to throw here? Where's their batter most likely to hit the ball? What am I going to do with the ball if it's hit to me—in the air, on the ground?"*

If the batter is a right-handed pull hitter, the fielders will shade toward left field. But if he's an opposite-field hitter—or if the scouting report says the pitcher should throw everything outside—the defense will probably take a step or two the other way. If the pitcher is ahead of the hitter—say the count is no balls and two strikes, or one ball and two strikes—then the defense figures that the hitter will have to *protect the plate,* or go

on the defensive to prevent a strikeout, and thus become more likely to spray the ball around the field. But if the hitter is ahead—say the count is 2–0 or 3–0—then he's more likely to take a full rip and pull the ball.

Say you're the shortstop and there's a man on first with one out and a 1-and-0 count on the hitter. Might their manager tell the runner to steal, because the pitcher isn't likely to pitch out and let the hitter get ahead 2 and 0? Might the manager ask the hitter to bunt, so he can advance the runner to second and eliminate the risk of grounding into a double play? Might the manager ask the hitter to swing away since he's ahead in the count? It depends on the score, the inning, the speed of the baserunner, and the ability of the hitter and the men who follow him in the batting order. But a good player, manager, and fan mulls over *all* of these possibilities before every pitch.

Even if the ball isn't hit to a particular fielder, he still has to think and react. You rarely just stand there. Oh, if it's a line drive to an infielder there's not much time to react or do anything, but defenses have to choreograph a bunch of schemes based on situations and managerial preferences. Most moves are automatic, based on experience and spring training drills. Even on a simple ground ball, you'll see a lot of defenders moving around.

Say it's a grounder toward third base with no runners on. Both the third baseman and shortstop go after the ball, with the one who's closer fielding it and the other backing him up. The first baseman gets in position to take the throw, with one foot on the bag, and the catcher and right fielder hustle toward first to *back up* a possible errant throw. The left fielder moves in to back up in case the ball gets through the infield.

Talkin' Baseball

"It's like church. Many attend, but few understand."

—San Francisco Giants coach Wes Westrum

From the Bench

Watch how the fielders move a bit from batter to batter and even from pitch to pitch. They do so from experience and intuition, but also because teams employ advance scouts to watch the opposition and keep statistics on where each batter hits the ball most often. These "eye in the sky" scouts will mark each hit (or out) on a diagram of a baseball field to determine tendencies, and then managers and coaches will use these charts to help position their fielders.

Cutoffs and Relays

The choreography is more complex on base hits with men on base. But the No. 1 priority for an outfielder is always *hit the cutoff man.* Here are a few examples of cutoff and relay plays.

Single to left, no runners on

The second baseman covers second base, where the throw will arrive. The first baseman backs up the play there. The catcher backs up first.

The first baseman makes sure the hitter touches first and is prepared if the ball gets by the second baseman, if the runner takes a big turn around first base and the defense tries to throw him out, or if the defense gets the batter caught in a *rundown* (or *pickle*) between first and second.

The shortstop lines up between the left fielder and second baseman to serve as the cutoff, or relay, man. The center fielder backs up the left fielder. The left fielder throws the ball to the shortstop on a routine single, but he may fire the ball straight to second if the batter tries to stretch it to a double. The third baseman covers his base in case an error gives the batter a chance to try for third.

Catching On

A baserunner who gets caught between two bases—and two or more defensive players with the ball—is said to be caught in a **rundown**.

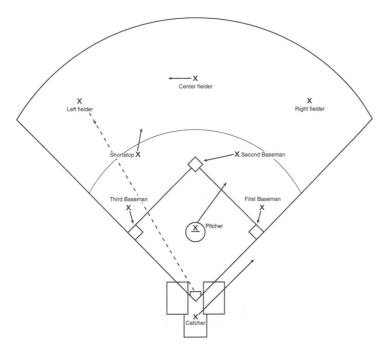

On a single to left with the bases empty, the shortstop can act as the cutoff man, or the left fielder can just throw right to second base.

Single to left, runner on second

The fielders make essentially the same movements as the last hit, except: The catcher stays home and the pitcher heads toward home to back up in case there's a play at the

203

plate. The left fielder has to hustle more, and with the help of his teammates, decide where to throw: to the cutoff man, who could fire to home, third, or second; straight home, if, as is probably the case, the runner is trying to score; or straight to second base, if the hitter is assuming the throw will go home and figures he can take an extra base. The outfielder needs to hit the cutoff man when the cutoff man is providing a directional target for the throw in.

On a base hit to left with a runner on second, the cutoff man, in this case the shortstop, can serve a vital role in terms of deciding whether or not to throw home.

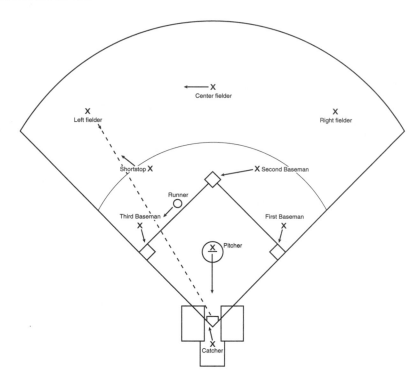

Talkin' Baseball

"Catching a fly ball is a pleasure, but knowing what to do with it after you catch it is a business."

—Outfielder Tommy Henrich

Drive down the left-field line, runner on first, less than two outs

The left fielder sprints toward the ball. The pitcher moves midway between second and third, ready to back up either base. The second baseman could cover second, backed up by the first baseman, or leave the base to the first baseman and hustle into the outfield to shout directions to the left fielder and the shortstop, who positions himself between the left fielder and home.

A runner on second will usually score on a single to left, but it's 50-50 whether a runner on first will score on a double to left. The left fielder wants to prevent a run from scoring, of course, but if he has little chance of nabbing the runner at the plate, he doesn't want to throw there and allow the hitter to advance to third, where he can score much more easily (on, say, a sacrifice fly, a passed ball, or a wild pitch). So he must use proper fundamentals: Throw the ball strongly and accurately, so the shortstop can catch it—or cut off the throw—if there's little chance of getting the runner who's trying to score, or let it go straight through to the catcher for a play at the plate. The second baseman sizes up the possibilities and shouts to the shortstop to let the ball go or to cut it off and fire to second or third base.

And you thought these guys were just standing there spitting tobacco juice and adjusting their jockstraps?

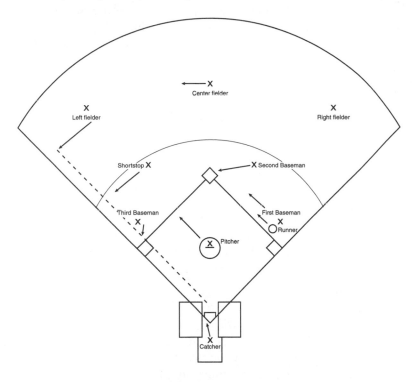

On a ball hit down the left-field line with a runner on first and fewer than two outs, it's essential that the left fielder hit the cutoff man, who then must decide whether there's time for a play at the plate.

Bringing the Infield In

The number of outs and baserunners determine the position of the infielders. With no one on base, the infielders stay back far enough to give themselves the most time to get to a ground ball and still throw out the batter at first base. With a man on second and two outs, they will play even deeper, because if they cannot prevent a hit, they can at least try to stop the ball from going through the infield for a run-scoring single. If it's a slow hitter or the ball comes right to them, they can still make the play at first for the third out. With a man on first and fewer than two outs, the second baseman

Catching On

A manager makes a **double switch** when he replaces two players at once, usually when he wants to substitute for an ineffective pitcher who's scheduled to bat in the next half-inning. For example, say his shortstop, batting eighth, struck out to end the previous inning, and the pitcher is scheduled to lead off the next inning. In a double switch, the manager brings in a new shortstop, who will change spots in the batting order and lead off the next inning, and a new pitcher, who will now take the eighth spot in the order.

Catching On

In certain situations a manager will station his first and third basemen closer to the foul lines to **guard the lines**, in hopes of flagging down hard-hit balls that could be doubles or triples if they get past the infield. Managers often guard the lines in the late innings of a close game.

and shortstop *cheat* toward second base, trying to get in better position to turn a double play.

A manager will sometimes *bring the infield in* in a close game with the bases loaded or a runner on third, or if his team is behind by two or three runs and one more would spell real trouble. The idea is that by having the infielders move in, closer to home plate, they can quickly get to a ground ball and throw home to prevent the tying or winning run from scoring. But this can be risky. Playing the infield in can "turn a .200 hitter into a .300 hitter," as Casey Stengel used to say, because a ground ball is more likely to get past the infielders for a single. So if you have a good lead, you keep your infielders back and give up a run or an infield hit and try to stop the opponent from a big inning.

Guarding the Lines

In certain situations a manager will station his first and third basemen closer to the lines in hopes of flagging down hard-hit balls that could be doubles or triples if they get past the infield. Managers often *guard the lines* in the late innings of a close game. Sometimes they do it with two out and nobody on. Batters hit a lot more balls to the middle of the field than down the lines, but those are more likely to be singles; hits down the line can be damaging extra-base hits.

Managers used to go by baseball's unwritten book and guard the lines a lot. They don't do it quite as much now, maybe because they've figured out that you have to consider who's hitting and who's pitching and how they're doing before you make that decision. If the pitcher is throwing 95 miles an hour, chances are the hitter isn't going to pull the ball down the line, but he could be late swinging at the pitch and send it down the opposite line. So for a right-handed batter, you wouldn't have the third baseman guard the line, but you might have the first baseman do so. But if the hitter is a notorious pull hitter, guard the third-base line no matter the pitcher, the score, or the inning.

The Shift

Managers occasionally use *the shift* or *the infield shift* when a batter has a strong tendency to hit the ball to one side of the field or the other. For example, say a right-handed batter comes up to hit, and throughout the season he's shown a tendency to pull the ball, or hit it between second and third base. The manager of the defensive team, aware of the batter's tendency, might opt to move his third baseman closer to the third-base line (guarding the line), his shortstop closer to third base (into the hole between his normal position and third), and his second baseman behind second base or even a bit toward third. The manager now will have three infielders on the left side of the infield. The outfielders often move a few steps to the right of their normal positions, too.

Ted Williams of the Red Sox, known as the greatest hitter who ever lived, was shut down in the 1946 World Series by the St. Louis Cardinals, who employed a shift first conceived by Cleveland Indians manager Lou Boudreau. Moving their four infielders to the right, stretching from first to a little left of second base, they held the left-handed, pull-hitting Williams to five singles in seven games. Williams was too proud to hit into the wide-open spaces in left field; he batted .200, 144 points below his career average, in what would be his only World Series.

Talkin' Baseball

"I've got nothing against the bunt—in its place. But most of the time, that place is at the bottom of a long-forgotten closet."

—Longtime Baltimore Orioles manager Earl Weaver

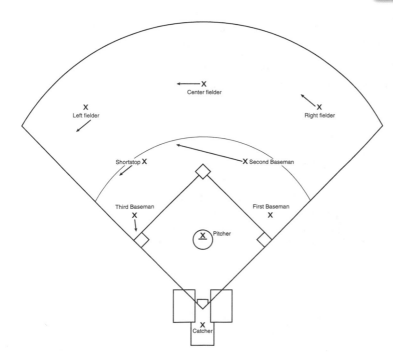

For a right-handed pull hitter, the defense will occasionally swing so far to the left side that there are actually three infielders between second and third base.

Defending the Bunt

To bunt, a hitter doesn't swing; he merely puts his bat in front of the pitch and tries to direct a little roller in the infield—usually about halfway down the baselines, but sometimes in no-man's land between the pitcher and infielders. Sometimes you bunt in the hopes of beating out an infield single. More often, it's a sacrifice bunt, with the hitter giving himself up as an out to advance a runner from first to second—into scoring position—without risking a double play.

Sometimes with nobody out in a close game, a manager will call for a hitter to sacrifice a runner from second to third in hopes of then scoring him with a sacrifice fly. And in really rare cases, a manager will call for a suicide squeeze, with the runner taking off from third with the pitch and trying to slide home before the defense can make a play on the bunt. If the hitter misses the ball, though, the runner is dead, and if the hitter pops the ball up, it's probably a double play. So you don't see many suicide squeeze plays.

Some managers vary the strategy, but the most common way to defend the sacrifice bunt is the *rotation play*. The first and third basemen charge toward the plate when the pitch is released, the second baseman heads to cover first base, and the shortstop to cover second or third, wherever the runner is headed. The pitcher and catcher also chase the bunt, but the man who gets there fastest and has the best throwing angle makes the play.

Let's take the most common scenario: trying to sacrifice a runner from first to second base. The fielder tries to wipe out the lead runner if he can, but if the odds aren't good, he must throw to first and settle for the sure out. The priority for the defense is: *Make sure you get one.* You always have to get the sure out. Never give a team more than three outs in an inning. If the fielder who picks up the bunt hesitates or throws late to second, the opposition winds up with men on first and second and no outs. Even major leaguers botch this play more often than they should—which is why managers use it.

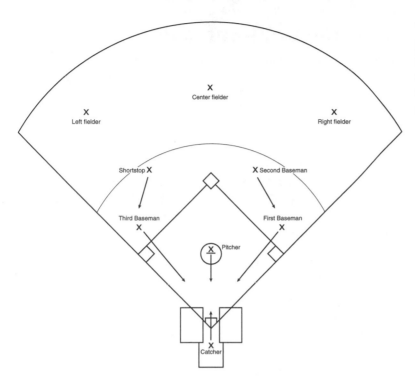

The most common strategy for defending the sacrifice bunt involves the cornermen charging while the middle infielders cover the appropriate bases.

Pickoff Plays

When a runner is on base, the defense will try a variety of ways to hold him close to the base and, better yet, pick him off the base. It takes a little nerve for a catcher, but after a pitch, I used to love to gun the ball down to first base or third base and nail a runner who had taken a big lead and was lollygagging back to the base.

More commonly, the pitcher tries to *pick off* the runner before the pitch. The mechanics, footwork, and eye contact vary on whether the pitcher is right-handed or left-handed and which base is occupied. Sometimes the pitcher tries to *look the runner back.* Sometimes he steps off the rubber. Sometimes he wheels around and fires to a middle infielder sneaking in behind the runner at second. Sometimes the first or third baseman sneaks in behind the runner and they pick him off or get him in a rundown. The most common pickoff play comes with the first baseman standing on the bag and the pitcher making a variety of *pickoff moves* toward first. Sometimes he'll show the runner a bunch of bad, slow moves, entice him to go, and then use his best move and fastest strike to nail the guy. A pitcher with a great *pickoff move* can really help himself and his catcher, and a pitcher with a lousy pickoff move allows a lot of stolen bases—which are charged to the catcher's statistical record as an allowed stolen base even though they're mostly the pitcher's fault. (Do I sound a little biased here?)

Gunning Down a Would-Be Basestealer

To throw out a good basestealer, a catcher needs a quick release and a strong, accurate arm. But even more than that, he needs a pitcher who holds the runner close to the base and then delivers the pitch quickly, without a lot of wasted motion. Maybe it's a cliché, and maybe it was started by a frustrated catcher, but it's true: Runners steal more on the pitcher than the catcher.

A good runner with a decent lead can get to second base in between 3.1 and 3.3 seconds. To nail him, the pitcher needs to throw his best fastball (which arrives quicker than a breaking ball), then the catcher must catch the ball in his glove, transfer it to his throwing hand, grip it across the seams, throw it past the pitcher's head 127 feet and 3 inches to a target area about one foot above and two or three feet to the right of the bag, so that the infielder can drop down and tag the runner in time. That takes the catcher about 1.5 seconds. If the pitcher and catcher combined take three seconds, that leaves only 0.1 to 0.3 seconds for the guy covering second to catch the ball and apply the tag—and that's really not enough time.

So a slow pitcher needs to pare some time off his delivery, or they'll be running on him all the time. The difference between "fast" and "slow" is amazingly slim: If a pitcher has a 1.5-second delivery, he's slow and you can run on him. If he delivers in 1.3 seconds, though, only the best baserunners make it, and even then they need a real good jump.

Throwing from *the stretch,* as opposed to the full windup, or using the *slide step* helps pitchers get rid of the ball faster when men are on base. These are truncated pitching deliveries, used so that baserunners don't have as much time to steal a base or take as big a lead. The leg kick isn't as high and the other motions are neither as deliberate nor as long.

It's become a real science. You see coaches today with stopwatches timing how fast a batter gets down to first after he hits the ball. They time how fast a runner gets to second base on a steal attempt. They time how long it takes a pitcher to throw to first base—how good is his move?—and to deliver the ball home. The coach can say, "Pitcher A goes to home in 1.2 seconds. Pitcher B goes to home in 1.5 seconds." Then they calculate how fast the catcher gets the ball to second base and how fast their runner can get to second base. That's how they decide whether or not to flash the steal sign.

Talkin' Baseball

"When you steal a base, 99 percent of the time you steal on a pitcher."

—St. Louis Cardinals Hall of Famer and former stolen base king Lou Brock

They always say the triple is the epitome of a timing play: The runner sprinting around the bases, the outfielder chasing the ball and hitting the cutoff man, the cutoff man turning and firing to the third baseman, and the third baseman sweeping his glove to touch the runner's foot or hand. But nabbing a basestealer is just as much a timing play. You break it down in slow motion on television and see the pitcher release the ball. And you shift to the shot of the runner pivoting, digging, and running toward second base. You see the pitch go outside and the catcher reach across his body with his left (glove) hand, transfer the ball to his right (throwing) hand and throw a strike to second base. It's an incredible move, and hard to do. That's how a catcher earns his Gold Glove.

Lou Brock knew a thing or two about stealing bases—when he retired after the 1979 season he had 938, which still ranks second all-time to Rickey Henderson.

Blocking the Plate

When one of his teammates is trying to gun down a runner at home plate, a good catcher tries to make it difficult for the runner by *blocking the plate*, and then tagging him out. Now, to block the plate, a lot of catchers think they have to be squarely in front of it. Well, if you're blocking the plate from the time that ball's hit, a runner coming around third base can't see home plate. He has two choices: go around you and try to come back and touch his hand on the plate, or go right through you. The mentality of most runners is to run over you.

So I learned to let that runner see home plate so they'd think, "*Okay, I can slide and catch the corner of the plate with my foot.*" I wanted him on the ground, not in the air, banging into my shoulder. Besides, blocking the plate before I had the ball didn't serve any purpose. So I always positioned myself with my foot inside the third-base line, and as soon as I knew I was going to catch the ball, I stepped with my left foot in front of the plate, down the line, and made sure my toe was pointed toward the runner. Getting that left foot in position is the most important thing in blocking the plate. When you point your toe toward the runner, your shin is protected from the runner's spikes by your shin guard; the side of your knee isn't exposed, and he can't fly into your knee, tear it up, and put you on the disabled list. Your knee has the strength to divert his slide so he never reaches the plate. He hits you and slides away, and you catch the ball and put the tag on.

Of course, when the ball is hit down the right-field line, and the right fielder is throwing from one side and the runner is coming from the other, you're stuck. You have to focus on where the ball is coming from and catching it. You have to peek a little or use your peripheral vision on the runner and just go by timing and instinct. You still have to get that left toe pointed out, and be prepared to accept a blow while at an awkward angle. On throws from right field, I developed the *sweep tag,* reaching across my body to catch the ball and then sweeping my glove back to the other side to tag out the runner.

From the Bench

Major League Baseball's official rules define defensive obstruction as "the act of a fielder who, while not in possession of the ball and not in the act of fielding the ball, impedes the progress of any runner." For example, a catcher has no right to block home plate unless he has the ball or is fielding the ball. Whether or not a defensive player is "in the act of fielding the ball" is a judgment call that's up to the appropriate umpire.

Talkin' Baseball

"Pitching is the art of instilling fear by making a man flinch."

—Pitcher Sandy Koufax

Then there's the throw that flies in from foul territory or the left-field line and arrives at the same time as the runner. You're stuck. More than once I was hit in mid-air by runners. Once, you could see an entire cleat print on my left thigh; fortunately, players had just started wearing rubber cleats, but you could see every one of those rubber cleats in my thigh. I've had cleats get stuck in my shin guard. I had my shin guard ripped on the side. On the back of my right hand, I still have the scar of a spike mark from the day Lou Johnson tried to steal home and I didn't have time to block the plate with my feet. I had to catch the pitch and dive forward into the runner, exposing my hands in the glove. He was out. I still have the scar to prove it.

Those bang-bang plays can really rack you up. A lot of times you have to improvise. There's never a set bounce, never a set runner, never a set slide. There's no Spalding Guide to instruct you on this. You just have to catch the ball, react, and make as quick a tag as you can.

Well, now you have a better understanding of how a defensive team tries to shut down the team that's up to bat. In the next few chapters we're going to switch sides, take our turn at the plate, and see how we can try to put a few runs up on the board.

The Least You Need to Know

➤ Defensive players vary their position by a step or two—and often more—based on the batter and the game situation.

➤ Strategy dictates a complex choreography of player movement on virtually every pitch.

➤ The pitcher is frequently more responsible for giving up a stolen base than the catcher.

➤ *Blocking the plate* and *hit-and-run* are important—though not completely accurate—baseball terms.

Part 4

You Still Have to Score Runs to Win

Baseball's most exciting play, without a doubt, is the home run. Every time a big slugger like Mark McGwire or Sammy Sosa comes up to the plate, everyone in the park pays a little extra attention. But there's more to scoring runs than hitting homers. Good offensive teams can scratch out a run or two by mixing timely hitting with quality baserunning.

This part of the book is all about offense. I'll give you a quick primer in the mechanics of hitting, which should give you some idea of just how tough it is to hit a baseball. We'll talk about strategies managers use when their teams are up to bat—making out the lineup, having the batter bunt, calling for the stolen base. I'll also talk about the importance of a good manager, and what attributes the good ones should have, and then we'll take a look at some of the game's greatest hitters. You'll see that there's a lot more to scoring runs than hitting the ball over the fence.

McGwire

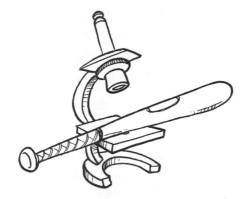

Chapter 16

The Science of Hitting

> **In This Chapter**
>
> ➤ The toughest feat in sports
>
> ➤ The mechanics of hitting
>
> ➤ Getting out of slumps
>
> ➤ Why hitters have to avoid the bail and the bucket

Anybody can pick up a basketball and hit a jump shot. And while I admire the way hockey players skate and maneuver and take cross checks, the toughest thing to do in sports, without question, is to hit a baseball.

When a pitch is speeding toward a hitter, he doesn't know how fast it's coming or which way it's going to break. It's not like a receiver in football who can say, "The quarterback is throwing the ball *to* me, with a nice spiral." A pitcher is trying to make a hitter *miss* a pitch, by throwing it with different rotations and at different speeds. Being able to analyze all of this within microseconds and then swing the bat with the perfect timing in the perfect location so you can hit a round ball *square* with a round bat, as they say, and hit it well enough that nobody can catch it, is a phenomenal feat.

Slumps and Soft Beds

"Slumps are like a soft bed: They're easy to get into and hard to get out of." I borrowed that quotation from the great Ty Cobb years ago, but writers often credited me with coming up with it.

No matter who said it first, it's true. Any little bad habit can plunge you into a batting *slump*—but it can take a lot longer to pull yourself up. Move your head, drop your hands, lose proper eye focus—any of them can cause a slump. Your eyes send all the

Ty Cobb, nicknamed the Georgia Peach, holds the record for career batting average with an awesome .367 mark.

Catching On

A prolonged period of subpar hitting is called a **slump**. Any little bad habit can plunge you into a batting slump—but it can take a lot longer to pull yourself up. When a hitter is struggling at the plate, trying too hard and just not relaxed, he's said to be **pressing**.

signals to the brain about how to react to a pitch. If your eyes don't tell the brain where the pitch is, your brain malfunctions and doesn't send the signal to your body. Your head starts moving or you start dropping your hands or moving them forward, your body isn't coordinated, and nothing you do seems to help. You fall into a funk. You start *pressing*, trying too hard.

Hitting a baseball is hard enough when you have everything working. You're successful when you get three hits out of 10 tries. The guy who's in the slump gets two hits out of 10. It doesn't seem like a whole lot—20 hits as opposed to 30 hits in 100 at bats—but even a short slump can ruin your batting average and your stature in the game.

In 100 at bats, the guy who hits .260 has four fewer hits than the .300 hitter. And we say, "This guy can't hit—he only hit .260." He only had four less hits; he may even have driven in more runs. Still, when you're not banging out hits you always feel like you're in a slump. One year I had three different slumps—1 for 28, 1 for 24, and 1 for 22—and still hit .293 for the season. Take away any of those slumps and I hit .300.

Coping with Failure

Since even the great hitters fail in seven of 10 at bats, it's important to learn to handle failure. Some hitters, like Cal Ripken Jr. of the Baltimore Orioles, are always tinkering with their swings. Others feel consistency is more important and only make adjustments when they're slumping.

A hitter also has to adjust as his nerves slow down and his muscles wear out. The wear and tear of playing every day—especially when you're a catcher and your body's getting beat up—takes a toll on you.

As a player ages, he has to admit to himself, "OK, I've slowed down some. I have to change a little bit, do a few different things, and coordinate my swing a little quicker. I have to start my hands sooner." Instead of holding the bat up high and counting on quick timing, he may have to put it down in a hitting position so he can just start his hands, not his body. You compensate. And if it still doesn't work, hitters keep looking until they find something that does.

The Mind-Body Connection

As a hitter, you don't want to get too stressed out about slumps. You want to keep believing in yourself—remember, it's a long season; remember, good hitters end up hitting. I learned that from Lee May, the first baseman for the Reds in the late '60s. When Lee went into a slump, he'd always say, "When the leaves turn brown, I will be around." And when September came, his numbers were always good. That's the beauty of baseball. It takes six months to produce a season. You can start out in April and May hitting .167, and wind up reaching .300—as long as nobody panics and you're still in the lineup in September.

From the Bench

A hitter has to see the ball when it leaves the pitcher's hand. He doesn't want a bunch of distracting colors, especially whites, on the center field wall or the center field stands. Major league stadiums have a dark background in center, without a lot of signs or advertisements on the fence, so the hitters can pick up the ball. Sometimes they raise the fence. Sometimes, like in Pittsburgh's Three Rivers Stadium, they put a dark tarp over the center field seats.

Talkin' Baseball

"I feel like the team that plays the Harlem Globetrotters every night."

—Shortstop Gary Disarcina after an 11-game losing streak

Part of hitting is simply confidence. It's inner conceit. It's *knowing*—not just hoping—that you can beat that pitcher. It's the power of positive thinking. And it's developing techniques and styles that give you confidence.

Talkin' Baseball

"Hitting is timing. Pitching is upsetting timing."

—Pitcher Warren Spahn

Catching On

A **switch-hitter** can hit from both sides of the plate—right-handed or left-handed—giving him an edge over whoever's pitching. He bats right-handed against left-handed pitchers and left-handed against right-handed pitchers. Mickey Mantle, Pete Rose, and Eddie Murray were all great switch-hitters.

Talkin' Baseball

"Young man, when you throw a strike, Mr. Hornsby will let you know."

—Umpire Bill Klem, to a pitcher who complained that he'd thrown Rogers Hornsby strikes, not balls

But first, a hitter has to have some physical skills. He needs strong hands, strong forearms, and a great eye for picking up the speed and rotation of the pitch. Some guys are "born hitters." They're naturally gifted athletes with the physical abilities, the motor sensor nerves, the motor skills, the great coordination, the timing, the eyes.

A lot of them were born to hit but didn't learn the techniques and style and the right way to hit. Once they were given the right way to do it, they developed into good hitters. They learned to hit by trial and error, by learning better techniques. You can teach a talented athlete how to hit better.

Different Types of Hitters

Some guys bat right-handed, some left-handed, and some *switch-hit*. Some hit for power and some hit for average. There'll always be guys who hit the ball farther and other guys who succeed with timing. There will always be naturals like Mickey Mantle and self-made players like Pete Rose.

Baseball fans always get into arguments about who's more valuable: the slugger who hits .250 but drives in 100 runs, or the pure hitter who hits .320 but drives in 70 runs. The object is to create runs, and I drove in a lot of runs despite just a .267 career average, whereas Pete Rose scored a ton of runs thanks to his .303 average and great baserunning.

Guys like Tony Gwynn, Wade Boggs, and Paul Molitor are the purest of hitters. They're not just naturals, they've studied the science of hitting. It's fun to watch them hit, talk with them, and hear their approaches to hitting. One thing that all three share is a great batting eye. They're very patient at the plate, selective in the pitches they swing at, and they know the strike zone well—so well, in fact, that they probably influence a home plate umpire's call from time to time: If a hitter of this stature doesn't swing at a particular pitch, an umpire is more inclined to call it a ball. The same could certainly be said of Ted Williams, arguably the greatest hitter of all time.

Ty Cobb certainly knew the strike zone well enough to draw a walk, but he preferred to be aggressive at the plate. He didn't strike out often, and with his quick bat he was very adept at getting the ball in play, which is why he has the number one lifetime batting average, .367—a commendable *season* average for anyone—and is second only to Pete Rose in career hits (4,191). Cobb was the first player to swing several bats at once in the on-deck circle, so that when he came up to the plate his bat would feel lighter. This practice, or the use of a weighted bat, is common today.

The Mechanics of Hitting

Entire books have been written on the many fine points of hitting. Rather than turn this into an instructional manual, we'll provide an overview of the basic mechanics.

The Bat

Old-time sluggers like Babe Ruth and even more recently Willie McCovey and Dick Allen used to carry 40-ounce bats. Most of today's hitters lean toward bats of around 31 to 33 ounces for greater bat speed. Ted Williams, who gave hitting a lifetime of study and successfully hit for both power and average, determined that bat speed was more important than weight, so he chose a lighter bat.

Even Mark McGwire, who launches some unbelievable long balls, uses a pretty run-of-the-mill bat. He's an incredibly strong guy, but he's not up at the plate with a club. The key to his power is his bat speed—he's got that stick flying through the hitting zone. It's the same reason that Tiger Woods hits a golf ball such a long way. It's not the size of the club, it's the speed.

The Grip

Power hitters grip the bat close to its bottom, or *knob.* The dominant hand, which generates the *bat speed,* is on top. Gripping the bat further up the handle, or *choking up,* offers more control but less power. Ty Cobb choked up on the bat, with his hands wide apart, so he could jab at the ball and aim hits where he wanted.

The hitter grips the bat just tightly enough that it doesn't fly out of his hands. He doesn't want to grip it so tightly that he's tense and wasting energy. Ted Williams used to say that his grip should be relaxed enough that someone could walk up and take the bat right out of his hands. The angle of the bat varies, but most hold it more vertical than horizontal, with the knob tilted forward.

Catching On

Choke up means to hit by gripping the bat further up the handle, toward the barrel (the thickest part of the bat) and away from the knob at the other end. By choking up a hitter gets better bat control and a faster swing, but less power.

The Position

A hitter can line up anywhere within the batter's box, which is four feet wide and six feet deep. The chalk line is considered within the box, but a lot of guys like to stand a few inches deeper than the back line. So early in a game, you'll see them sweeping the chalk off the back line with their feet and setting up with their back foot just out of the box, buying a tad extra time to watch the pitch. Most umpires will give them a few inches, but a batter can be called out if he hits a ball with one or both feet on the ground entirely outside the batter's box. A batter cannot jump or step out of the box to hit an outside pitch, even one that's lobbed in for an intentional walk.

Hitters learn early on to step into the box and tap the outside of the plate with the bat or take a practice swing over the plate to make sure they're close enough to hit a strike on the outside corner. But you don't want to get too close, or crowd the plate, and then get hit or *jammed* by an inside pitch. Each hitter finds a happy medium where he's comfortable—and that can change from pitch to pitch depending on how the pitcher is working him.

The Stance

Stances vary widely. The most basic is parallel with the batter's box and plate, but some hitters employ an *open stance* and others use a *closed stance*. A righty with an open stance stands with his right foot close to the plate and his left (front) side further away. Arizona Diamondbacks infielder Tony Batista has such a wide, open stance, he seems to be facing parallel rather than perpendicular to the pitcher. Andres Galarraga of the Atlanta Braves is a more famous example. A righty with a closed stance has his front foot closer to the plate than his back foot, and his shoulders will be opened up a bit as well. Exaggerated stances can work for some individuals, but they mess up the mechanics of most. A hitter with an open stance has to bring his front side around before going forward with the swing and has a tougher time reaching the outside strike. A hitter with a closed stance can struggle with the inside pitch.

Some hitters stand very upright, while others, such as Pete Rose, Stan Musial, and Rickey Henderson, go into a crouch. Most are somewhere in between, with their knees flexed and upper body leaning slightly inward. Texas Rangers slugger Juan Gonzalez holds his hands way up in the air and cocks the bat back towards the pitcher, while Baltimore Orioles slugger Albert Belle holds his hands in near his body and keeps his bat nearly perpendicular to the ground.

Talkin' Baseball

"I'd rather hit than have sex."

—Hall of Famer Reggie Jackson

One thing all of these hitters have in common, though, is that when they start their swings and bring their bats through the hitting zone, they'll all be in almost exactly the same position. We'll get to that in a minute. But first, we'll talk about what to look for before you start your swing.

One thing to remember with your grip of the bat is that when you hold the bat directly in front of you, you should be able to see the label branded on the bat. The reason is that bats are branded where the grain is widest, which is the weakest part of the bat. So if you hold the label up, the strongest part of the bat will come in contact with the ball.

The Look

You're now ready and waiting for the pitch. It takes about four-tenths of a second from the moment the pitcher releases the ball until it crosses the plate. So you have two or three tenths of a second to decide if you want to swing, and if so, how hard and where. In that split-second, you watch the ball intently, hoping to determine how fast it's traveling and where it's going. You're looking for a pitch worth swinging at—you must have the eye focus and bat control to swing only at pitches you can drive. Watch the ball from the time the pitcher releases it until contact is made. Obviously, the longer you can wait, the better you can determine where the pitch is headed and whether you should swing.

One reason Ted Williams was a Hall of Fame hitter was that his 20-10 vision enabled him to see pitches more clearly than most other players. Another great hitter, Rod Carew, said by training his eyes to watch the pitcher's release point and how his hand moved in the follow-through, he could tell if a fastball or breaking ball was coming. Carl Yastrzemski checked for the ball's color; if Yaz saw mostly white when the ball left the pitcher's hand, he anticipated a fastball, because the backspin blurred the red seams, whereas curves and sliders featured topspin and more red.

The Stride

Baseball players aren't generally into physics, but there's one law they should be interested in. It tells us that force is directly proportional to acceleration. Think about that. The quicker you accelerate the bat, the harder (and farther) you hit the ball. When you're kicking a football or a soccer ball, you take a running start to get maximum distance. You can't do that in baseball, though. You have to accelerate the bat from a standstill. So it all starts with the stride, or the step you take towards the pitcher as he releases the ball and you begin your swing.

The length of the stride is in direct correlation with how far apart your feet are when you set up in the box. Obviously, the further apart you set your feet originally, the shorter the stride you can naturally take. Some hitters spread their legs to cut down their stride and assure a more compact swing. Jeff Bagwell of the Houston Astros, for instance, has his feet spread so far apart that instead of taking a step, he just lifts his front foot and puts it right back in the same spot. Most stride forward with their foot barely off the ground, but some, such as Darryl Strawberry and Ruben Sierra, use a high leg kick. That's not recommended, though, because even though a high leg kick gives you a little more power (think of how much harder you can punch a punching bag when you take a big stride into it), it tends to encourage overswinging. It's no coincidence that Strawberry and Sierra are known for striking out a lot.

The Swing

Although I separate the stride and the swing, the two happen together. Begin with your hands held chest high, near the back shoulder, then take them back to trigger the swing, while twisting backward with your weight on your rear foot. Then stride forward, uncoiling your hips, shoulders, and arms, lower your head, turn your wrists, extend your arms, snap and turn your wrists at contact with the ball, and follow through. You want to get the bat on the ball in front of the plate, not as it crosses the plate. Some hitting coaches advocate taking the top hand off the bat at the end of the follow-through.

Some hitters, such as Tony Gwynn, have "quiet hands," meaning they don't cock them back very much before bringing them forward. Other hitters, such as Albert Belle, bring their hands way back before they start in at the ball. This is dangerous, because if your hands aren't fast enough you'll be late on every pitch. The reward, however, is that the bathead will accelerate faster through the hitting zone. Belle is so incredibly strong that he can start his hands in front of his face, then cock them way back as he strides, then explode through the ball.

The best thing is to go for something in between the two. As you stride, you should take your hands back a little (they should move back a little naturally as you stride), allowing you to get them back through the ball but giving you a little pop as well.

You have to lay off pitches that are out of the strike zone or that'll give you trouble, and often, you can't make that decision until you've started your swing. Then you have to be quick enough and strong enough to stop, or *check*, your swing before your wrists break, or the umpire will rule that you've gone around on your swing and charge you with a strike. That's why quick hands and wrists are so important, and why a lighter bat can work better. A short, quick stroke gives you an extra split-second to try to identify the pitch, its speed, and its likely path, and decide whether to swing, and if so where.

If you have two strikes on you and the pitch is in the strike zone, you can't just check your swing. You must have the bat control to foul it off and wait for a pitch you can handle.

Talkin' Baseball

"When you're swinging good, it's the easiest thing in the world. When you're swinging bad, it's the hardest thing in the world."

—George Brett on hitting

The best hitters don't lunge at the ball. They use their hands and lower body, not just their arms, to generate power. They keep their front shoulder locked in, aiming toward the pitcher, not bailing out, away from the pitch. In other words, a right-handed hitter who *pulls out* is opening his shoulder toward third base too soon. (A lefty bails out toward first base.) When the shoulder opens, the hips open, the head goes up, and the hands come forward too soon, and the batter is hitting with his arms instead of his whole body. You have to keep that front shoulder in until your follow through opens it up naturally.

Hank Aaron was said to have the fastest wrists in baseball history. He could wait until the ball was almost on top of him before committing himself, then snap his bat so fast that he almost took the ball out of the catcher's glove. Yaz, in his book on hitting, wrote that he decided whether or not to swing when the ball was about 25 feet in front of him. Some current guys with exceptionally quick bats, such as Ken Griffey Jr., Barry Bonds, and Tony Gwynn, can wait even longer—till the pitch is about 10 or 15 feet from the plate. Those hitters generate terrific bat speed. It's not just a matter of athleticism; Michael Jordan is one of the greatest athletes ever, but he couldn't hit major league pitching because he lacked quick hands and perfect mechanics, and had a long, slow swing. Some players with looping swings, like Darryl Strawberry, can wallop long home runs, but they're also more prone to strikeouts and cold streaks.

Catching On

A hitter is said to **bail out** when his front foot strides away from the pitch. This is also called **opening up** or **stepping in the bucket**, and it's common among timid hitters who are afraid of getting hit. They end up opening up their hip and shoulder and costing themselves power and the chance to drive an outside pitch.

Hammerin' Hank Aaron is major league baseball's all-time home run king with 755.

So, to sum up, here are the elements of hitting:

➤ **The Bat** Pick the bat that's right for you: the right combination of weight and ease of swing.

➤ **The Position**   Line up in the box in a place where you feel comfortable: not too close to the plate, and not too far away.

➤ **The Stance**   The most important thing to remember as you stand in the box is to be comfortable, and ready to swing.

➤ **The Look**   Watch the ball from the moment it leaves the pitcher's hand, and try to visualize the path the ball will take and where it will be as it crosses the plate.

➤ **The Stride**   Take a step toward the pitcher with your front foot. At the same time, cock your hands back a bit.

➤ **The Swing**   Bring your hands forward as you uncoil your hips and shoulders. Keep your eye on the ball and try to make contact with it just before it reaches the plate. Be careful not to open your shoulder up too soon.

Pulling the Ball vs. Going to the Opposite Field

When I was a kid, I used to play home run derby with my friends. The object was to try to hit every pitch out of the park. I did that by pulling every pitch I saw—that is, as a right-handed hitter, I hit every pitch to left field. The reason I did that was simple: to hit the ball far, I needed bat speed. And since my bat was accelerating as I swung it, the way to get bat speed was to have a long swing. Think about driving a nail into a board with a hammer. If you start the hammer six inches from the nail, you won't drive it very far into the board. But if you swing the hammer a couple of feet, you'll build up some speed and really wallop that nail.

Now, to get a really long arc, I had to meet the ball early, when it was still out in front of the plate, and my swing was starting to come back to the left. As a result, the ball would go to left field. By the time I reached the majors, I could pull just about any pitch, even a good hard fastball.

Sometimes pulling the ball isn't in your best interest, though. We just said that to pull the ball you have to meet it out in front of the plate. That's easy to do when a pitch is on the inner part of the plate. But sometimes the location of the pitch makes it tough. Say, for instance, the pitch comes in low and on the outside part of the plate. It's awfully tough to pull a pitch out there, because you have to reach too far for it.

It's not easy to visualize, so try this exercise: Stand near the edge of a table or desk. Place your left foot right up against the corner. Now take your right hand and touch the corner of the desk. Notice how your natural inclination is to open your hips a bit—kind of like a baseball swing—and reach across your body. Your hand should be facing right about where left field would be. If your hand was the bat and the corner of the desk was the ball, the ball would go to left field. Now you see why it's natural to pull an inside pitch.

Talkin' Baseball

"The pitcher has got only a ball. I've got a bat. So the percentage in weapons is in my favor and I let the fellow with the ball do the fretting."

—Hank Aaron on hitting

Now take a big step back and try to touch the corner of the desk. You can't do it, not in the same way. You have to lunge to reach it. If you try to open your hips and reach it, you'll either come up short or fall down. Now you see how difficult it is to pull an outside pitch.

So what do you do? Well, you do the same thing you had to do to touch that desk corner. You keep your hips closed, your hands back, and you reach out to make contact. As a result, you're almost slapping the ball into right field (assuming you're a right-handed hitter). This is called *hitting to the opposite field,* or *going the other way.* It's hard to generate a lot of power hitting like this, which is why hitting a home run to the opposite field requires a lot of raw strength.

A lot of times, you'll hear hitters talking about hitting the ball where it's pitched. This simply means that if a pitcher throws you an inside pitch, you should pull it. If he throws you a pitch outside, take it the other way. Keep that in mind: Go with the pitch.

Why Pitchers Can't Hit

From Little League through high school, the best players are often pitchers, and they're usually good hitters, too. But as they work their way from the minors to the majors, they become the worst hitters. Why? Pitchers aren't selected for their hitting. It's the one position where you don't have to hit at all to make it to the majors. Most pro leagues, including the American League, use designated hitters in place of pitchers, so the pitchers never hit in games and don't practice.

Even National League pitchers don't take very much batting practice. Teams don't seem to care too much about whether they can hit or not. Sometimes hitting is even discouraged, because teams don't want their pitchers risking injury, or expending their energy as hitters and baserunners, then being gassed when they get back to the mound.

Maybe it's a self-fulfilling prophecy, but you see that a lot: A pitcher gets on base, maybe has to run hard for a few seconds to go from first to third or second to home, and he gets out on the mound a few minutes later and he's still dead. You'd think they'd be in better shape than that. And you'd think they'd realize how much they can help themselves as a pitcher if they hit .250 instead of .150 when they got to the plate.

Having pitchers hit does introduce more strategy into the game, though. If a pitcher who has thrown well comes up to bat in a situation with men on base late in a tight ball game, a manager has to decide whether or not to remove him for a pinch-hitter or keep him in the game to pitch. This also puts some strain on the bullpen, because someone will have to warm up any time it's possible that a pitcher will come to the plate in a pivotal situation.

Talkin' Baseball

"I knew I was in for a long year when we lined up for the national anthem on Opening Day and one of my players said, 'Every time I hear that song I have a bad game.'"

—Manager Jim Leyland

227

The Quest for 70 Home Runs

Before Babe Ruth's heroics in the 1920s, home runs were a rarity. The league-leading totals were often in the teens at the turn of the century. The National League leader had six in 1902, and nine each in 1903, 1904, and 1905. They called him "Home Run" Baker when Frank Baker led the American League with 11 in 1911, 10 in 1912, 12 in 1913, and nine in 1914.

Professional Players with 60 or More Home Runs

Player	Year	Team	League	HRs
Joe Bauman	1954	Roswell, NM	Longhorn	72
Mark McGwire	1998	St. Louis	National	70
Joe Hauser	1933	Minneapolis	American Association	69
Bob Crues	1948	Amarillo, TX	West Texas-New Mexico	69
Sammy Sosa	1998	Chicago	National	66
Dick Stuart	1956	Lincoln, NE	Western	66
Bob Lennon	1954	Nashville	Southern Association	64
Joe Hauser	1930	Baltimore	International	63
Moose Clabugh	1926	Tyler, TX	East Texas	62
Ken Guettler	1956	Shreveport, LA	Texas	62
Roger Maris	1961	New York	American	61
Tony Lazzeri	1925	Salt Lake City	Pacific Coast	60
Babe Ruth	1927	New York	American	60
Frosty Kennedy	1956	Plainview, TX	Southwest	60

Then the Sultan of Swat changed everything. In 1919, the first season in which the pitcher-turned-outfielder played more than 100 games, he belted 29 homers. Then he blew away everyone with 54 and 59 homers in back-to-back years, and his style changed the way the game was played. Others started aiming for—and clearing—the fences. But nobody was as good as the Babe. When he hit his 60th in 1927, he crowed, "Sixty, count 'em, sixty! Let some other son of a bitch match that!"

No major leaguer ever did in a 154-game season. It was considered an unbreakable record, the greatest in all of sport. When Roger Maris finally hit 61 in 1961, the season had been lengthened to 162 games, and the commissioner, an old friend of the Babe's, put an asterisk by Roger's record. Not until the 1990s was the asterisk removed.

Finally, in 1998, the unbreakable record was shattered. Mark McGwire reached 62 home runs in less than 154 games, and he finished with an unfathomable 70. The achievement was made even more remarkable because of his months-long duel with Sammy Sosa, who finished with 66. They captivated the nation. Now you wonder: How high can they go? Is anything possible?

The Quest for .400

Not too many major league hitters hit under .200—not if they want to stay major leaguers. But not too many top .400. That mythical mark was reached several times in baseball's early days, but it hasn't been attained since Ted Williams hit .406 in 1941.

Extra Innings

Mario Mendoza stuck around in the big leagues for nine years despite a career batting average of .215. He was a slick-fielding shortstop, but his name would have been forgotten if not for a somewhat cruel tag given him by George Brett. George looked in the Sunday sports section, where they published every hitter's batting average, and said anyone hitting worse than Mario was below "The Mendoza Line." The Mendoza Line thus became famous, representing struggling hitters batting under .200. As you can imagine, Mendoza was none too thrilled about his place in history.

Several hitters have taken a run at the standard. Williams hit .388 in 1957. Stan Musial hit .376 in 1948. Carew hit .388 in 1977. Brett hovered around .400 until late September before finishing with a .390 average in 1980. Tony Gwynn hit .370 in 1987, .394 in 1995, and .368 in 1996. Andres Galarraga hit .370 in 1993. The 1998 batting champs were, in the National League, Larry Walker of the Colorado Rockies, with .363; and in the American League, Bernie Williams of the New York Yankees, with .339.

Will anyone reach .400 again? After watching McGwire and Sosa smash the home run record, I can't say no. But it's going to take a pure hitter who goes all season without a slump or an injury. Gwynn was probably the best candidate we've had in recent memory, but he'll be 39 this year, and his shot is probably gone. The most likely candidate will be a fast left-handed hitter who can lay down some good bunts and beat out some infield hits.

It's kind of funny that they say bad pitching helped McGwire and Sosa hit all those home runs, but no one has been able to hit .400 off those same bad pitchers. There are a couple of possible explanations: First, travel has become rougher since Ted Williams hit .406 in '41. Sure, players today travel

Talkin' Baseball

"Tommy Henrich, no question. Henrich could hit me at midnight with the lights out."

—Bob Feller on the toughest hitter he ever faced

by plane instead of by train, but they have to go to a lot more cities, and make several coast-to-coast trips each season. Second, the increasing infatuation with the home run has placed an emphasis on power, so I don't think kids grow up wanting to hit .400. They grow up wanting to hit 50 or 60 (or 70) home runs. But I think the biggest reason no one has hit .400 in so long is that hitting a baseball, even against so-so pitching, is just so dang hard.

The Benchmarks of Excellence

Hitters' benchmarks come in round numbers. A .300 batting average. One hundred runs batted in or scored. Three thousand career hits. The guy who can combine power and speed and reach 30 home runs and 30 stolen bases in a season is a top player. Last year Alex Rodriguez of the Seattle Mariners became a rare 40-40 player, with 42 home runs and 46 stolen bases.

Thirty home runs used to be considered a good season. With more guys lifting weights and watching their diets, and expansion diluting the quality of pitching, the bar has been raised to 40 home runs nowadays. Fifty is still a rarity, but Big Mac and Sammy proved that 60—and now, even 70—are no longer out of the question.

The Least You Need to Know

➤ Hitting a baseball is the most difficult feat in sports, requiring exceptional mental and physical skills.

➤ Some players are born with quick wrists and the right athletic attributes; others develop into good hitters with attention to the right mechanics—but *every* player has to work at it.

➤ A quick, short stroke is almost always better than a swing-for-the-seats rip.

➤ A good hitter keeps his eye on the ball, his front shoulder in, and uncoils his entire body to generate power.

Chapter 17

Batting Around the Order

In This Chapter

➤ The ideal order: a perfect mixture of power and speed

➤ Johnny's greatest lineup

➤ The designated hitter: a boon or bane for baseball?

As definitions go, *batting order* is pretty simple to understand: It's the order in which the players on a team must come to bat. If a player bats out of turn, deliberately or otherwise, he's called out—provided that the other team recognizes the transgression and appeals to the umpire immediately after the player's at-bat. The only way a batting order, or *lineup*, can be changed is by the use of a substitute batter. Once a player has been substituted for, he's out of the game and not allowed to return.

Before each game, the managers of each team fill out a form that the league provides, called a *lineup card*. Each manager makes three copies of the card: One goes to the opposing manager, one goes to the home plate umpire, and the manager keeps a copy.

Back in the early days of baseball, a team almost always finished a game with the same nine that it started with. But in the modern era the game has become much more specialized. Now teams use substitutes liberally, and very rarely do teams finish a game with the same nine players that started. So these days, as you'll see in this chapter, it's not just how a manager puts his starting lineup together that matters, it's also what changes he makes during the course of the game.

Putting Together the Lineup

The best teams in baseball have lineups that feature a combination of power hitters, contact hitters, and hitters who have exceptional speed. A *power hitter* hits home runs and deep fly balls on a regular basis, but often lacks speed. A *contact hitter* puts the ball in play a lot, doesn't strike out, handles the bat well, and hits for a high average. A *speed player* may not consistently drive the ball deep into the outfield but has enough speed that he's a threat to steal once he's on base. With a lineup that features these different types of players, a manager has the opportunity to score runs in a variety of ways.

Let me give you an example of how a balanced lineup can be effective in scoring runs. Say your first hitter in the inning is a speedy player. He hits a high chopper to third and, because of his quickness, beats the throw to first. The next batter is an excellent bunter who lays down a sacrifice bunt, allowing the speedster at first to advance to second. Then the runner at second, who's been watching the windup of the pitcher closely, steals third. The next batter, a power hitter, hits a deep fly to center field, allowing the runner on third to tag up and score.

If the first batter had been a power hitter, he might not have even gotten on base in the first place, much less moved around to score. Similarly, if only speed players had come up to bat, you might not have gotten the deep hit to score the runner on the sacrifice fly.

Tailoring the Lineup to the Ballpark

Whenever possible, a manager will try to tailor his lineup to the ballpark—especially his home park. The manager tries to use the dimensions of the ballpark to his advantage. For example, Yankee Stadium in the Bronx has a very short right-field wall, often called a short *porch*. This makes it easier for left-handed batters to hit home runs than right-handed batters, because a hitter tends to pull the ball when he's swinging for power. Therefore, the Yankees have traditionally had great left-handed power hitters in their lineup over the years, from Babe Ruth to Roger Maris to Reggie Jackson to, most recently, Tino Martinez and the switch-hitting Bernie Williams. Colorado's Coors Field is a larger park, but because the ball carries so well, the Rockies try to stack their lineup with big boppers—home run hitters like Vinny Castilla, Dante Bichette, and Larry Walker.

The Leadoff Hitter

The first man up in the lineup is called the *leadoff man.* He's usually a fast runner and a good contact hitter. He typically doesn't have much power, but his on-base percentage is high because he can hit singles and draw a lot of walks. Once on base, he should be a threat to steal. Ideally, your leadoff batter should score the most runs for your team.

The best leadoff hitter I played with in my career was Pete Rose. Once he was on base, I don't think there was a better guy going from first to third than Rose. On practically any ball hit to right or center field, Pete would make it all the way to third base because he was such an aggressive baserunner, which is precisely what a good leadoff hitter should be.

Catching On

Porch refers to the depth of a ballpark's outfield. For example, the distance from home plate to the right field wall in Yankee Stadium is relatively short, so that stadium is said to have a **short porch** in right. This makes it easier for left-handed batters to hit home runs than right-handed batters, because a hitter tends to pull the ball when he's swinging for power.

Extra Innings

A leadoff hitter usually isn't called upon to hit home runs, but throughout major league history there have been a few leadoff men with extraordinary power. No No. 1 hitter has hit more round-trippers than Rickey Henderson, who'll lead off for the New York Mets starting in 1999. Playing for the A's, the New York Yankees, the Toronto Blue Jays and the San Diego Padres during his career, Henderson has hit a major league record 73 (and counting) leadoff home runs.

The Second Spot

The No. 2 man in the batting order should also be a good contact hitter. He needs to be disciplined, too, because often the manager will ask him to take a lot of pitches to give the leadoff man a chance to steal. He should also be a good bunter and be prepared to sacrifice when asked to. Some managers feel there is an advantage in having a

From the Bench

An effective lineup has a balance of left- and right-handed hitters, making it more difficult for the opposing manager to go to his bullpen in the late innings and create multiple matchups in his favor. Right-handed pitchers fare better against right-handed batters, so if a right-handed hitter is up and a lefty is on the mound, the manager might bring in a righty. But if the next hitter up is a lefty, the manager might not change, because the matchup will only last for one batter, and he only has five or six relievers.

Catching On

The fourth batter in the lineup is called the **cleanup hitter**, because he often comes up with runners on base and is asked to "clean the bases" with a big hit. He's also expected to deliver hits in the **clutch.**

left-handed swinger in the No. 2 spot. If he's a lefty, the thinking goes, he can hit the ball through the hole between first and second base when the first baseman is holding the runner on. No matter which way he bats, his main responsibility is to advance the leadoff man into scoring position for the power hitters coming up behind him.

The Third Spot

The No. 3 and 4 batters are your money players, the guys who should be the two best hitters on the team. Most managers believe that the third hitter should be the best overall hitter on the team. He should hit for a high average, but also have enough power to produce extra-base hits to score a runner from first base and to put himself in scoring position. Ideally, he should have enough speed to stay out of inning-ending double plays, but, more than anything, he should produce at the plate—especially in the clutch.

The Cleanup Hitter

The fourth batter—called the *cleanup hitter,* because he often comes up with runners on base and is asked to "clean the bases" with a big hit—should be your best power hitter, capable of driving in runs with the long ball. He should be a *clutch hitter,* because he and the fifth batter in the lineup will have more RBI opportunities than any other hitters.

It used to be that you worried about a No. 4 hitter who struck out a hundred times in a season, but now there are power hitters who strike out 170-plus times in a season, players like Sammy Sosa of the Chicago Cubs and Mark McGwire of the St. Louis Cardinals. These guys hit enough home runs to make up for their strikeouts, because the bottom line is that they drive in a lot of runs. They both are also .300 hitters.

The Fifth Spot

The fifth-place hitter has to be able to *protect* the fourth-place hitter by making it undesirable for the opposition to pitch around the cleanup man. He's similar to the fourth hitter in that he has to have power, preferably to all fields; he has to be able to produce in the clutch, with runners on base; and he's often prone to striking out. Because they're the biggest run producers, the third, fourth, and fifth hitters are often referred to collectively as *the meat of the order.*

Protection

When Roger Maris hit 61 home runs in 1961, he was never walked intentionally the entire year. When Mark McGwire broke Maris's single-season home run record in 1998 by smacking 70 round-trippers, he was intentionally walked 28 times. The difference? In baseball-speak, it's called *protection.*

Simply put, Maris was never put on base intentionally because he had Mickey Mantle, one of the best hitters to ever play the game, hitting behind him in the cleanup spot. Mantle offered protection to Maris, meaning the pitchers had to try to get Maris out. No manager would deliberately put anyone on base with Mickey Mantle coming up! If Maris had been intentionally walked just a few times, perhaps one or two of his home runs in '61 never would have been hit.

Which makes McGwire's accomplishment in 1998 all the more incredible. He shattered Maris's record even though he had Ray Lankford hitting behind him in the lineup for the majority of the season. (Lankford's no slouch—he hit .293 with 31 home runs and 105 RBIs—but he's no Mickey Mantle, either.) Walking McGwire was reasonable to opposing managers—they were willing to take their chances against Lankford. If McGwire had had someone as talented as Mantle batting behind him, his home run total would have been even higher.

Catching On

A good hitter needs another good hitter behind him—someone who also strikes some fear in the other team—for **protection**. For example, the fifth-place hitter protects the fourth-place hitter by being another threat, making it tough for the opposition to pitch around the cleanup man.

From the Bench

As baseball gets more specialized, managers utilize a *platoon* system at certain positions. When a manager has two position players of nearly equal talent, one who bats right and the other left, he'll use the left-handed hitter when the opposing starting pitcher is a right-hander, and vice versa. When a player is a gifted hitter but a defensive liability, the manager may, if he has the lead, replace the poor fielder in late innings with one who's more reliable with the glove but is not as good with the bat.

Extra Innings

In baseball, a *Texas League single* is a little looping fly that just clears the infield, falling in front of the outfielders for a base hit. How did it get its name? Well, as the story goes, during the late 1800s, cowboys wore their six-shooters when they went to Texas League (minor league) ballgames, and one such cowboy whipped out his revolver and angrily shot at an untimely pop fly as it sailed through the air. Fearing for their lives, none of the players moved to field the ball, which fell in for a hit. From then on, pop-ups that dropped in for base hits were called Texas Leaguers.

The Bottom of the Order

You also have to have players at the bottom of the order who can create offense. The sixth, seventh, eighth, and ninth hitters will typically be the weaker batters in the lineup, but they often will still be counted on to produce runs during the game.

From the Bench

Managers sometimes try something different to shake things up. In 1998, St. Louis Cardinals manager Tony La Russa began batting his pitcher eighth and his catcher ninth. La Russa believed that this gave him an advantage by adding an "extra leadoff hitter"—someone else ahead of the meat of the order who could get on base. La Russa also hoped that a position player batting ninth could provide another baserunner for Mark McGwire, who batted third.

The sixth batter, because he will lead off many innings, should have similar skills to the leadoff man: He should have speed, be a good contract hitter, and be able to work deep into the count. The sixth batter will have many more RBI opportunities than the leadoff hitter, so generally he should hit for a fairly high average.

The seventh batter is similar to the second batter, but he won't be called on to sacrifice as much. He needs to be a good hit-and-run man since he will often have to advance the fifth batter, who will generally be slow on the basepaths.

The eighth and ninth hitters are the two weakest hitters on the team. You know a team is good when they have good hitters to fill these spots. The fastest of the two last batters in the order should hit ninth, since if he gets on base he has the top of the order coming up behind him, and that helps create another opportunity to score a run.

The National League is the only major professional league in which pitchers hit. Since they don't play every day, or practice the art of hitting as much as the other players, pitchers are placed ninth in the batting order. If any runner is on base and there are fewer than two outs when the pitchers comes to bat, he will almost always bunt. In the American League, and throughout the minor leagues, a designated hitter bats in place of the pitcher.

The Designated Hitter

In 1973, the American League adopted the Designated Hitter Rule. The rule states, "A hitter may be designated to bat for the starting pitcher and all subsequent pitchers in any game without otherwise affecting the status of the pitcher(s) in the game."

Since the rule was introduced, the designated hitter, or DH, has produced an average of about .270. Run production, home runs, slugging percentage—every conceivable offensive category is up since the introduction of this rule. And not only does it insert another powerful bat into the lineup, the rule also allows managers to hide a player's defensive liabilities by taking him out of the field and making him a full-time DH.

Many people, including nearly everyone in the National League (in which the pitchers still hit), don't like the rule. Those opposed to the DH say that because of the rule, managers aren't forced to make difficult decisions over whether or not to remove a pitcher who's still doing well for a pinch-hitter late in the game when his spot in the batting order comes up. Regardless of your preference, it looks like the DH is here to stay.

Talkin' Baseball

"I've changed my mind about it. Instead of being bad, it stinks."

—Cincinnati Reds manager Sparky Anderson in 1976, on the designated hitter rule

The Greatest Lineup of All Time

The Cincinnati Reds of the mid-1970s had, in my opinion, the greatest lineup of all time. "The Big Red Machine," as we were known, had it all: speed at the top of the lineup, power in the middle, and consistent hitters at the bottom. We had good pitching during the '75 and '76 seasons when we won back-to-back world championships, but I think the key to our success was our daily lineup.

Pete Rose, who has more hits than any other player in major league history, was our leadoff hitter, our catalyst. He would do whatever it took to get on base, whether taking a walk or bunting or slapping a single between second and third. And once he got on base, there was no one better on the basepaths. I still believe he is the greatest baserunner to ever play the game.

Rose was followed by Ken Griffey (yes, the father of Ken Griffey Jr.). The elder Griffey was a terrific contact hitter, but his greatest virtue as a hitter was that he was patient, willing to give Rose time to feel out the pitcher and steal a base if he so desired.

Our third hitter was Joe Morgan. It's unusual for a second baseman to hit in the third slot, but Joe usually hit around .300, with good power, so he wasn't your typical second baseman.

Joe Morgan could do it all—hit for average, hit for power, produce in the clutch, draw a walk, steal a base—which made him a great No. 3 hitter.

I hit behind Joe, and when I came up, it was rare that one of the guys ahead of me wasn't on base. I was followed by Tony Perez, who would have been a No. 3 or 4 hitter for probably any other team in the majors—he was that good. Then came George Foster, who was a great power hitter, evidenced by the fact that he hit 348 home runs during his 18-year career.

I like to think that we did a great job of producing runs, but I think one fact speaks for itself: The first six hitters in this lineup were Hall of Fame–caliber players, or close to it. I don't know of any other lineup in history that can make that claim.

Our No. 7 and 8 hitters—Cesar Geronimo and Dave Concepcion—made us a truly unique team. With them, we were almost as capable of creating runs at the bottom of the lineup as we were at the top. In 1974, for example, Geronimo hit .281 and drove in 54, while Concepcion also hit .281 and drove in 82 runs. Moreover, both of these guys could steal a base when needed.

You want protection from the fifth spot? There was nobody better than Tony Perez, who drove in 100 or more runs seven times and kept other teams from pitching around me.

Batting Order for the Big Red Machine of the Mid–1970s

Spot	Player, Position	Batted	Key Career Stat(s)
1.	Pete Rose, 3B	Switch	All-time leader with 4,256 hits
2.	Ken Griffey, RF	Left	.296 batting average
3.	Joe Morgan, 2B	Left	.271 batting average, 268 homers
4.	Johnny Bench, C	Right	389 homers, six 100-RBI years
5.	Tony Perez, 1B	Right	379 homers, seven 100-RBI years
6.	George Foster, LF	Right	348 homers, .274 batting average
7.	Cesar Geronimo, CF	Left	.258 batting average
8.	Dave Concepcion, SS	Right	.267 batting average
9.	Pitcher	—	—

So you can see that there's a lot more to putting together a lineup than just writing down everybody's name. Now that we've got our lineup put together, we're ready to take a closer look in the next chapter at the various strategies once the game starts.

The Least You Need to Know

➤ The batting order is the order in which the players on the offensive team must come to bat.

➤ Every player in lineup has a particular role.

➤ The ideal lineup features a balance of right-handed and left-handed hitters, as well as a combination of power hitters, contact hitters, and speedsters.

➤ The DH is used in the American League but not in the National League.

Chapter 18

Offensive Strategy: Baseball's Chess Game

In This Chapter

➤ Seven ways to leave home

➤ Bunting isn't just a festive decoration

➤ What teams do when they're in a pinch for offense

➤ Why crime pays and breaking up is hard to do

If a team can score in three or four different innings, then it has a really good chance of winning.

Score in four innings and that's a minimum of four runs. Put up "crooked numbers"—more than one run—in half of those innings and you've got at least six runs. If you score six or more runs, you're going to win most games.

Conversely, a pitcher and his defense must limit not only runs but *opportunities*. Every out is important. You know the other team is going to get some hits, but you can't give away outs. You put yourself in a heap of trouble if you hand the other team three walks and a couple of errors. All of a sudden, their third, fourth, and fifth hitters have a chance to bat not only four but five times in the game. If you let good hitters bat that many times, they're going to beat you. You don't want to face the heart of the batting order in the ninth inning with the lead at risk.

So any way it can, the offense is looking for ways to create runs against a defense that's trying to stop them. The quickest way is to clobber the ball over the fence. But only two teams are blessed with Mark McGwire and Sammy Sosa in their lineups, and even the most prolific home run hitters only go deep once every two or three games. So you need ways to *manufacture* runs, and we'll talk about some common strategies in this chapter.

The Seven Ways to Get on Base

A hitter has seven ways to reach base, and only one of them is by way of a hit. How many can you name without sneaking a peak ahead? Here they are:

➤ **base hit**   He hits a single, double, triple, or home run.

➤ **base on balls**   He takes four balls before the pitcher can throw three strikes.

➤ **error**   The defense misplays a ball that he hits; the umpire judges that it would've been an out if played correctly.

➤ **fielder's choice**   He hits a ground ball and the defense opts to force out another runner instead of the batter.

➤ **hit by a pitch**   He's awarded first base because a pitch hits him.

➤ **catcher's interference**   He's awarded first base because the umpire rules that the catcher has inhibited him (almost always by reaching forward and nicking the batter's swing with the glove).

➤ **muffed third strike**   A third strike gets past the catcher, who can't throw the batter out before he reaches first.

Getting on base, somehow, some way, is the first step toward scoring a run. There are plenty of ways to reach the final step—home plate—beyond a simple base hit.

Bunting: Drags, Sacrifices, and Squeezes

In politics—and on Opening Day—bunting is the fabric used for flags and festive decorating. In bird watching, bunting is a stout-billed bird. In baseball, it's a strategy employed for a variety of purposes; the perfectly placed bunt allows the defense little or no time to field the ball and throw to the correct base. You can also catch a break if the fielder tries to gun down the lead runner and his throw is late or errant.

➤ **drag bunt** No, it isn't a bunt in women's clothes, it's an attempt to get a base hit via a bunt, usually to start a rally or break out of a slump. It's most often employed by speedsters, especially if they see the third baseman and/or first baseman playing fairly deep. Maury Wills of the Dodgers earned a lot of hits this way, but bunting for a hit seems to be a lost art these days.

➤ **sacrifice bunt** An attempt to advance a runner with the hitter himself expecting to get thrown out. He sacrifices himself, and an out, to move a runner or runners closer to scoring. It's most often employed by pitchers and mediocre hitters, especially in close games where one run is significant. A manager rarely asks his best hitters to bunt, because he doesn't want them to surrender an out; he wants them to swing away and try to drive in the runner(s) themselves. And, of course, you don't sacrifice with two outs because you'd be making the third out unless the defense botches the play.

Catching On

A **drag bunt** is one on which the hitter is trying to get a base hit. A **sacrifice bunt** is an attempt to advance a runner while the hitter himself is expecting to get thrown out. A **squeeze bunt** is used to try to score a runner from third base.

➤ **suicide squeeze** This can score a runner from third when a base hit or sacrifice fly seem less likely. It's most often employed with one out when the runner is fast and the hitter isn't likely to drive the ball deep enough into the outfield for the runner to score on a sacrifice fly.

To bunt, a hitter doesn't so much swing as stick his bat in the strike zone. He wants to keep the top of the bat above his hands and let the bat almost catch the ball; he doesn't want to punch at the ball, because he'd hit it too hard. A right-handed hitter angles the head of the bat upward, toward first base, and slides his top hand near the label, guiding the bat so the ball hits somewhere between the sweet spot and the end of the bat, directing the ball just out of the reach of the infielders, pitcher, and catcher. He tries to deaden the velocity of the pitch by letting the ball hit the bat and guiding the ball into the ground, preferably into the dirt along the third base line. Sometimes he'll try to push the ball into the gap between the pitcher, first baseman, and second baseman. Lefties will try to go down the third-base line or push the ball into the no-man's land on the right side.

If the batter is trying to get on base, he'll try to bunt while taking a full stride toward first base. That's why it's called a drag bunt—he kind of "drags" the ball as he runs. On a *push bunt,* he pushes the ball between first and second.

If he's trying to sacrifice, a batter often can't afford to miss on a bunt attempt and get his runner thrown out, so he *squares around,* bringing his back leg forward and facing the pitcher just in front of the plate. He doesn't want to try to bunt while staying in his stance, afraid of getting his body and his top hand in front of the pitch, because he'll be more likely to miss, especially on outside pitches. He doesn't run until ball and

243

bat collide, increasing the chances of making contact but almost assuring he won't get away from the plate quick enough to beat out the throw. Sometimes a hitter will square around even before the delivery. It telegraphs the sacrifice, but so what? The defense is usually expecting it anyway.

If the batter is trying to get a runner home via the suicide squeeze, he has to make contact in any way possible, even if the pitch is far out of the strike zone, because otherwise his runner will likely be tagged out at the plate. And if he pops the ball in the air, to the pitcher or maybe the third baseman playing shallow, he's out and the runner is probably doubled up, too. That all-or-nothing risk element is why it's called a suicide squeeze, but when everyone executes correctly, it can't really be defended. The runner is crossing home before a fielder ever reaches the ball. It's not used that often because it's so risky, but the suicide squeeze is one of the most exciting plays in baseball.

From the Bench

Watch how often your team's manager uses the sacrifice. With a weak or slumping offense, they may scratch out runs any way they can. In an NL game, watch for the pitcher to sacrifice bunt with a runner on first and under two outs, or runners on first and second with no outs. If a team is way behind, one run at the cost of one out isn't a good tradeoff. Rule of thumb: The closer the game, the later the inning, the weaker the hitter, the more likely the bunt.

In a less-risky variation called the *safety squeeze,* the runner on third breaks only after the ball is bunted. That way the runner isn't hung out to dry if the bunt fails—but the bunt had better be a good one, because the runner's getting a later break from third.

Every once in awhile, when everyone in the ballpark is expecting a bunt and the infielders are charging hard toward the plate, you'll see the batter square around to bunt, sucker them in, then pull his bat and body back, take a short swing, and chop the ball past them for a hit. (You don't see this very often, either.)

Fundamentals never change: Here Hank Bauer of the New York Yankees attempts a sacrifice bunt in a 1959 game against the Chicago White Sox.

The Sacrifice Fly

The idea of a sacrifice fly is to hit the ball deep enough into the outfield that a runner can tag up at third base, wait for the catch, and then take off, crossing home before the defense can get the ball there. A sacrifice fly doesn't count as an at-bat, so it doesn't affect a player's batting average, but it does earn the hitter an RBI.

Hitting Behind the Runner

Another way to advance a baserunner is to *hit behind the runner*. This is why a lot of managers try to have a lefty hitting second behind a good leadoff man. The lefty pulls the ball to the right side of the infield and the runner can more easily advance to second on a ground ball, or go to third if the ball gets through for a single.

A sacrifice bunt or sacrifice fly doesn't affect a player's batting average, but if he makes an out other than a sacrifice, it counts as an at-bat—because he's presumed to be trying to get a hit—and will lower his average if he grounds out. So he must be a real team player to give himself up and hit behind the runner. An unselfish No. 2 hitter can help his leadoff man score a lot of runs but end up costing himself 20 or 30 points in batting average—and maybe a lot of money, because those subtle skills don't show up in the stats, and are often overlooked at contract time.

The Hit-and-Run (and the Run-and-Hit)

As I mentioned earlier, the *hit-and-run* is something of a misnomer, because the running precedes the hitting. The idea again is to advance a runner. The manager signals the play to his base coaches, who relay it to the hitter and the runner. If one of them doesn't get the sign—or if the hitter fails to make contact, or there's a pitchout—the play backfires. A little subterfuge helps.

As the pitcher delivers, the runner on first takes off like he's stealing second, forcing the second baseman or shortstop to rush to cover the base. The batter then tries to hit the ball on the ground, into the just-vacated gap between first and second or second and third, depending on which infielder is covering second. If the batter can't connect, he still has to swing to slow down the catcher, who'll try to grab the ball quickly and fire it to second to throw out the runner. At all costs, the hitter must avoid hitting it in the air to an infielder or outfielder, because the runner will be too far away to scramble back to his original base and tag up before the fielder can throw the ball there and double him up.

A manager usually doesn't call a hit-and-run with two strikes because he doesn't want to risk a strikeout. He likes to call it when the hitter is ahead in the count—usually 1–0, 2–0, or 2–1—and the pitcher is trying to throw a strike. He usually won't call it if it's 3–0 or 3–1: He doesn't want his hitter to swing at ball four, and, since the pitcher needs to throw a strike, the batter should take a big cut, not a little chop, if he gets a pitch he can drive.

A properly executed hit-and-run puts men on first and third without sacrificing an out. But even if the hitter grounds out, he usually can advance even a slow runner to second, thus avoiding a double play. Maybe they should call it the *run-and-hit*, but in baseball parlance that actually means something a little different: It's a similar play, except that the batter doesn't have to swing unless the pitch is a strike, nor is it as crucial for him to hit the ball through the vacated hole. If he doesn't swing, the play just becomes a straight steal attempt.

Talkin' Baseball

"Go up and hit what you see. And if you don't see it, come on back."

—Manager Bucky Harris to his Senators before facing Bob Feller

Coming Through in a Pinch

A player can spend most of the game in the dugout—some managers will even let him sneak off to the clubhouse—and yet still win a game for you. In a key situation, the manager will call upon a good hitter to *pinch hit* for a pitcher or a weak hitter, and because it often happens with men on base, a good *pinch hitter* can really help his club.

A good pinch hitter doesn't goof off during a game. He prepares himself, watching closely. What is this pitcher throwing? What are his tendencies? Which pitches are working for him today and which aren't? How much is his ball moving today? The hitter compares today's effort with the book he's kept on the pitcher in the past.

From the Bench

A pinch hitter doesn't officially enter the game until his name is announced, so a manager will send someone on deck, see if the opponent changes pitchers, then decide who to use. That's why the manager on defense doesn't change pitchers until the hitter's name is announced. If there's a pitching change and the manager on offense wants to change hitters again, the guy whose name was just announced is out of the game—without ever coming up to hit.

He has to think, *"He got me out last time with a curve ball. Bet he tries it again."* Or, *"He's going to try to get ahead in the count with a fastball because his breaking pitch isn't consistent today."* Or, *"This pitcher likes to get guys out with his slider; I'm going to look for him to start me off with a slider."*

A pinch hitter has one chance. He can't waste an at-bat. He can't put too much pressure on himself, but he must be totally focused and confident. He must be zoned in, anticipate the way the pitcher will work him, and trust his own ability.

Who Pinch Hits?

Anyone who didn't start the game is eligible to pinch hit—a regular getting the day off, any bench player, even a decent-hitting pitcher. Maybe a manager *platoons* at a position and starts his right-handed second baseman against a left-handed pitcher, but when a right-handed reliever comes in, he plays the percentages and pinch hits his left-handed hitter, who then takes over at second. When a manager picks a team, he usually keeps a couple of good hitters on the bench to pinch hit. Some might be fading regulars. Some might be promising prospects. Many aren't quite good enough to play everyday—maybe they're lousy in the field or on the basepaths, maybe they struggle against lefties, maybe their weaknesses would be exposed playing everyday—but they excel in their role as pinch hitters.

The best pinch hitter of my era was Manny Mota of the Dodgers. He was just outstanding. He wasn't a power hitter, but he knew what his job was. He was a contact hitter, and he could start a rally or drive in a key run with a base hit. He holds the career record for pinch hits with 150.

Manny set himself apart, but the Reds had some good pinch hitters in Jimmy Stewart and Ty Cline. The average fan might not have heard of them, but we could always say, "All right, grab a bat. Be ready to hit." And they were ready. They knew what the situation was, what they had to do, and they produced. They worked hard at their skill, and their job was to be prepared at all times. They knew they were going to start only occasionally, but they had to be ready for every situation.

Speed in Reserve

It's a luxury now that many teams keep 11, and sometimes 12, pitchers and only 13 or 14 position players, but sometimes a manager will keep a guy around just because he's fast and can steal a base. Especially if you have a slowpoke slugger, it's a great luxury to send in a *pinch runner* for him in the ninth inning and let the speedster steal second or even third. That way you don't have to sacrifice an out by bunting him over to scoring position. This strategy is more commonly employed in September, when rosters are expanded from 25 to 40.

Catching On

Managers sometimes **platoon** two players at one position, using the right-handed hitter against left-handed pitchers and the left-handed hitter against right-handed pitchers. Because more pitchers are right-handed, the lefty hitter gets a lot more at-bats. As baseball has grown more specialized, managers have become more reliant on the platoon system in deciding on their starters and pinch hitters.

Talkin' Baseball

"You can't hit what you can't see."

—Ping Bodie after striking out against the legendary Walter Johnson

Extra Innings

In 1974, Oakland A's owner Charlie Finley signed Herb Washington, who held the world indoor track records in the 50- and 60-yard dashes, as a "designated pinch runner." Without ever batting, Herb appeared in 104 games and stole 30 bases—but he hadn't played baseball since high school, so he didn't know enough about the nuances of the game to be as good as his speed might suggest. In fact, in the ninth inning of Game 2 of the 1974 World Series, Herb pinch ran after Joe Rudi's single cut Oakland's deficit to 3–2—and promptly got picked off first. That was the only game the A's lost en route to beating the Dodgers for the world championship.

Base Coaches: Can't You Read the Signs?

When a team is at bat, it stations coaches in foul territory next to first and third base. As a batter reaches first base on a potential extra-base hit, the *first base coach* shouts

Talkin' Baseball

"If I'm looking at you, you're hitting.... If I'm walking away from you and spitting, you're hitting.... If I'm looking at you and spitting, you're NOT hitting.... If I'm walking away and not spitting, you're NOT hitting."

—Casey Stengel's signs when he was managing the Brooklyn Dodgers, as recalled by third baseman Frank Skaff, who added, "They give you an idea of why some of those guys were missing them."

advice on whether he should try for a double or a triple. If a batter stops at first, the coach relays instructions from the manager on anything from a potential hit-and-run to how big of a lead to take. The *third base coach* is busier. He relays advice to runners stationed on third and, more importantly, he makes split-second decisions on whether to send home a runner rounding second on close plays—plays that can make the difference between winning or losing.

What's more, the third base coach relays intricate hand and body motions to pass instructions from the manager to the hitter, and the hitter had better get the signals right and follow them, or he's going to get in trouble. The coach can flash a dozen signs before every pitch—most of them merely decoys—and the hitter has to watch them and know what play is "on" and whether he's *hitting* (swinging away) or *taking* (not swinging). Coaches use a variety of systems so opponents can't decipher the strategy and use it against them. For example, the third sign might be the one that counts, or the first one after the coach touches the bill of his cap, or a more elaborate combination. How does the hitter know which signal is real and which is a dummy, a decoy? Those are reviewed in pregame meetings, and as a player you'd better know them.

Life on the Basepaths

A fast, aggressive runner is an overlooked but valuable commodity, because he can stretch a single into a double or a double into a triple. He can go from first to third on a single and from first to home on a double. He can break up double plays and keep his offense alive. He can steal bases and he can steal runs. He can get a multi-run rally going.

He's quick to take advantage of even short, wild pitches and passed balls. He runs hard out of the batter's box even when it looks like he'll probably be out, because you just never know—even major leaguers make errors, especially when they're forced to rush their throws. Even on long drives, he races out of the box, because if he stops to admire them, a few will end up hitting the wall instead of clearing it, and he'll cost himself a base. He takes a wider turn at first base on singles hit to left field than to right or center (because the left fielder is unlikely to pick him off at first) in case the ball is bobbled and he can go to second.

He takes the extra base, takes the risk, but has the smarts and judgment to know when to run and when not to. He doesn't get doubled up on line drives, or picked off taking foolish or lazy leads. He doesn't take silly chances, but he also doesn't clog the bases with safety-first, one-base-at-a-time running. He anticipates whether a fly ball will fall in for a base hit or get caught, and he makes sure to tag up on automatic outs, tear around the bases on sure hits, and play it somewhere in between on the debatable plays. He doesn't dive into first base or stop at it; it's faster to run through the base. And it should go without saying, but I'll say it: He touches every base.

So why is good baserunning overlooked? Maybe because taking the extra base doesn't show up in any stat column except one: victories.

The Cardinal Rule

You never want to make an out, but this is one of baseball's cardinal rules: Never make the first or third out at third base. In other words, don't try to steal third, or go from first to third on a single, or push a double into a triple, with no outs or two outs.

Why? With nobody out, it's not worth the risk because you're still in scoring position at second base and your team has plenty of ways to get you home. With two out, it's not worth the risk because you can't tag up at third and score on a sacrifice fly. But with one out, it's worth the risk because you can score a cheap run on a sacrifice fly, suicide squeeze, ground ball, wild pitch, passed ball, or a hit.

Taking a Lead

Before each pitch, a runner takes a *lead,* trying to get as far away from the base as he can and still close enough to get back before the pitcher can pick him off. The quicker the runner, and the better he can recognize when the pitcher is throwing to first or throwing to the plate, the bigger the lead he can take. And the bigger the lead, the more likely the runner can steal second, break up a double play, or take an extra base on a hit. Smart runners concentrate on getting their jump, not talking with a first baseman who's trying to distract him with smiles and idle chit-chat.

Portrait of a thief: All-time stolen base king Rickey Henderson, now with the New York Mets, is a master at sizing up a pitcher's pickoff move and getting a good jump.

Sliding

Some guys are just more comfortable sliding into bases hands—and face—first, as my old teammate Pete Rose used to do and Rickey Henderson still does. But you risk getting spiked and beating up your hands, which are every hitter's livelihood. Most runners are better off sliding in feet first, then popping up on the bag as soon as they reach it. The *pop-up slide* has proven itself for a hundred years.

A runner should slide on the side of the bag furthest from the throw, so the fielder has to go as far as possible to tag him. So if he's trying to stretch a single, he keeps his body to the inside of the bag, away from the outfielder's throw. If he's trying to steal second, he wants to slide to the center field side of the bag, occasionally evading the tag by just touching the base with his left hand. Similarly, if the right fielder is trying to throw him out at home, he should go left of the plate, making the catcher sweep around to his left as far as possible.

The Art of the Steal

I didn't make the Hall of Fame for my *stolen bases;* I averaged just four a year. But one reason I did make it was I knew how to gun down thieves. The top basestealers have more than just speed. As I explained earlier, even though it goes against a catcher's stats, runners steal more on a pitcher than a catcher. They study each pitcher's mechanics so they can tell when he's going to throw to first and when he's delivering a pitch to the plate. It's not just an art, it's a science. There are so many fast players today and so many players studying the steal that stolen-base percentages have risen steadily over the years.

A good runner will take progressively bigger leads off first base, daring the pitcher to throw over, hoping to see his best pickoff move so he can gauge how far he can lead off safely. He bends his knees, hangs his hands low (and off his knees), gets on the balls of his feet, pivots smoothly on his right foot, crosses over with his left foot, and sprints toward second. He can't be oblivious, however.

By his second or third stride, he has to take a peek back toward the plate to see what happened. If it's a fly ball, he has to stop and determine whether it will be caught. If it's a grounder, he has to determine whether he'll slide into second base to break up a double play or whether the ball will get through for a hit and he'll have a chance to go to third. He wants to see for himself and not let a middle infielder fake him out.

The Double-Steal

A *double-steal* is exactly what it sounds like: two runners trying to steal. If they're on first and second, the trail runner takes off as soon as he's sure the lead runner is going (and not just bluffing toward third), and the catcher has to decide where to throw. He can throw out only one, if that. I used to get some steals this way. Pete Rose or Joe Morgan would take off and draw the throw to third, and I'd skeedaddle into second easily.

Talkin' Baseball

"He had larceny in his heart, but his feet were honest."

—Writer Bugs Baer on plodding Ping Bodie

Warning Track

It's common for a pitcher to try to sandbag a runner by first using a slower, less-threatening version of his pickoff move; then, once the runner thinks he has the pitcher's move timed, the pitcher unveils his "A" move and nails the guy.

Talkin' Baseball

"He's like a little kid in a train station. You turn your back on him and he's gone."

—Pitcher Doc Medich on stolen base king Rickey Henderson

251

If men are on first and third, you use a *delayed steal*. The man on first takes off, hoping to entice the catcher to throw. Sometimes he'll even stop midway between the bases. The catcher has a quandary: Does he throw to second and risk letting the man on third score before the infielder can fire the ball back? Does he hold onto the ball and risk letting a man reach scoring position without even trying to throw him out? The split second he spends deciding may be all the time the runners need.

Extra Innings

The year 1866 marked both the professional ranks' first slide on a stolen base attempt (by Rockford's Bob Addy) and the first bunt (by Brooklyn's Tom Barlow).

Stealing Home

It takes 3.0 to 3.5 seconds for a pitcher to throw home and the catcher to fire the ball to second or third and nab the runner. It takes 1.0 to 1.5 seconds for a pitcher to throw home. So to steal home, a runner needs a tremendous jump, tremendous speed, tremendous courage—and a pitcher with a long windup who isn't paying attention to holding him on base. Very few managers or runners today will risk stealing home. Managers don't want to lose a runner who's gotten to third base. Players don't want to risk a collision at home.

The most famous steal of home came in the 1955 World Series, when Jackie Robinson of the Brooklyn Dodgers caught New York Yankees pitcher Whitey Ford by surprise in Game 1. Ty Cobb and Pete Reiser also mastered this rarity.

One attempt to steal home that I'll never forget came in a game against the San Diego Padres in the mid-1970s. A young Dave Winfield was on third base with two outs, the batter was the great Willie McCovey—and Dave tried to steal home! Of course, McCovey was a left-handed hitter, so I saw Dave all the way, and the throw was there in time and I tagged him out.

I'll never forget the look on Willie's face. Here's one of the greatest hitters in the history of the game—he hit 521 home runs in his career, tenth best in history! He stood there at the plate with his bat on his shoulder, in utter disbelief, just glaring down at Dave. He was still standing there when I left home plate. Finally, he just dropped his bat, laid his helmet down, somebody handed him his glove, and he went to first base.

The point is: You don't steal home when the man at the plate can knock you in.

Breaking Up the Double Play

If you're on first base and your teammate hits a ground ball to the infield, you have to hightail it to second as fast as you can. Even though you know you're going to be forced out, you want to make it as difficult as possible for the shortstop or second baseman to flip the ball to first base for the double play.

Runners with speed obviously have a better chance to *break up the double play,* but there's more to it than just speed. There's aggressiveness and attitude. As soon as contact is made and the ball is on the ground, you have to charge toward second. You have to find the infielder who's taking the relay and slide as hard as you can into him, run into his legs with yours, get him off-balance so he can't throw to first, or at least can't get anything on the throw.

Some guys are legendary for the way they broke up the double play. Pee Wee Reese and Dizzy Dean always talked about the way Bob Cerv, an out-fielder in the 1950s and early '60s, slid into second base. He was feared, because he was going to take you out. I never had the speed to get there and effectively take out the guy at second, but I still tried. You have to try!

Even the middle infielders accept that it's part of the game—usually. But there are exceptions, like the 1973 National League Championship Series between the Reds and Mets. Pete Rose barreled into the Mets' shortstop, Bud Harrelson, and Bud thought Pete slid too hard, and the next thing you know, a fight breaks out on the field. That's intensity. That's what the long season and the playoffs do. Unfortunately, Bud's reaction incited the Mets' fans to the point of rage. They were like rabid animals. Even with security trying to prevent it, they were throwing stuff on the field. It was scary.

In the next chapter, we'll step off the diamond and into the dugout for a look at the men and minds behind baseball strategy.

From the Bench

Even if the announcers call it a "routine" double play, watch the play at second base. The runner can be vicious. The infielder can be balletic. It's amazing at how athletic he can be, particularly if you ever got a chance to see the Wizard of Oz, Ozzie Smith. One time Lenny Harris flew in, body high, and Ozzie catapulted over him and turned the double play anyway. Lenny asked him how he managed to get out of the way and Ozzie replied, "Son, you were on the third floor, so I went up to the sixth."

In an attempt to break up the double play in a 1959 game, Norm Siebern of the Yankees goes barreling into Washington Senators shortstop Ken Aspromonte—but Aspromonte is too quick with the throw to first.

The Least You Need to Know

➤ A hitter taps a little bunt that never makes it out of the infield in an effort to get a base hit or sacrifice himself so a runner can advance.

➤ Offenses also can move runners ahead with the sacrifice fly, hit-and-run, and hitting behind runners.

➤ The best baserunners help their team by running hard and aggressively, by taking the extra base, and by breaking up double plays.

➤ Thieves who steal bases are considered great assets in baseball.

Chapter 19

The Brains in the Dugout

In This Chapter

➤ The book: a must-read for every manager

➤ Do statistics lie?

➤ How teams catch themselves good managers

➤ How to survive when your underlings make $12 million a year

Baseball is the only sport in which the managers and coaches wear the same uniforms as the players. It's also the only sport in which a member of the coaching staff can run out onto the field of play, kick dirt on another grown man, scream like a madman, get ejected from the game—and no one will think twice about it.

Being the manager of a baseball team is a unique job. It requires intelligence, interpersonal skills, a thick skin, a strong baseball background, and the patience of a saint. If you have all of those things, you'd be perfect for the job. Just know this before you run off and apply: In this day and age, it's extremely rare for even the most qualified applicants to last four years without getting fired. Still interested? Let's examine the job a little more closely.

The Manager

The guy who runs a baseball team isn't called the head coach, like he is in other sports. He's called the *manager,* which is a pretty good word for what he does. A baseball team is comprised of 25 players, from all different backgrounds, with all different personalities, who spend the better part of eight months together. The manager has to manage these disparate personalities, deal with the press, and act as a liaison between the players and the front office.

Oh, yeah. He also has to call all the strategic shots during the game, subjecting himself to second-guessing from fans, writers, his boss, and sometimes even his own players if a move doesn't pan out. He has to keep an awful lot of people happy. If you ask me, anybody who simply survives 162 games as a major league manager has done a pretty good job.

The Book

They've been playing baseball for more than 100 years, so no matter how bizarre the situation a manager finds himself in, chances are dozens of other managers have been in the exact same position. And the most common scenarios are played out so frequently that there is a generally accepted strategy to use in most situations. A manager who applies that generally accepted strategy is said to be managing by *the book*.

Extra Innings

While *the book* is unwritten, some managers and coaches keep their own written books. When Earl Weaver managed the Baltimore Orioles, he was known for being knowledgeable in the rules of the game. One of his coaches, Ray Miller, kept detailed notes in his copy of the rule book. Miller figured one day he would become a manager and it might come in handy. Well, Earl had quite a temper, and one night in Cleveland he was arguing with an umpire over the balk rule. Weaver stormed into the Orioles dugout for a rule book, so he could show the ump he was wrong. He grabbed Miller's annotated copy. Before Miller could stop him, Weaver took the book onto the field and pled his case with the umpire. When the man in blue failed to see things Weaver's way, Earl tore the rule book to shreds as Miller looked on, stunned. Years of note-taking, down the drain. Maybe that's why no one has ever written down all the tenets of *the book*.

The book is unwritten, but every manager has it memorized. For example, as we've explained earlier, a right-handed pitcher tends to be more effective against right-handed hitters, because his curveball will break away from a righty. (The same holds true for left-handed pitchers against left-handed hitters.) So if a manager is in the late innings of a tight ballgame and the opposing team has a tough right-handed hitter coming up, the skipper—assuming he's going by the book—would want a right-handed pitcher available to face him.

There are other unwritten rules that comprise baseball's book. For instance, if it's late in a tie game and the first batter up in an inning gets on base, the manager is expected to have the next hitter bunt the man over to second. The best count on which to call a hit-and-run is two balls and one strike. There are plenty of others, and every manager knows these components of the book by heart.

Baseball Is a Numbers Game

With the advent of computers, managers and coaches have every conceivable statistic at their fingertips. They know how each hitter on their team has fared against each pitcher on the opposing team, as well as how their pitchers have done against each opposing hitter. They know how every player in the league has performed in certain situations—with no outs, two outs, bases empty, etc.

Most managers have this information in a folder on the bench, so they can consult it when deciding which hitter to send up or which pitcher to bring in the game. With all of these stats at their fingertips, today's managers play hunches far less often than when I was playing. They'll examine the relevant stats and go with the matchup that's most likely to turn out favorably.

Talkin' Baseball

"A manager's job is to always anticipate the worst things that can possibly happen. Consequently, your job is built on paranoia."

—Mike Hargrove, Cleveland Indians manager

Talkin' Baseball

"Most ballgames are lost, not won."

—Former manager Casey Stengel, on how mistakes can cost a team

Does a Manager Really Matter?

Right now you're probably asking yourself, if there's a book and you have access to all of these statistics, how hard can it be to manage? Well, it's not that easy. Linus always used to tell Charlie Brown that statistics don't lie. They don't, but they don't always tell the full story. Let's say a certain player is 2-for-16 (a .125 average) against a certain pitcher. That .125 average just tells you how many hits and outs the hitter made. It doesn't tell us anything about the outs. What if six of those 14 outs were hard-hit balls that just happened to be caught? That would mean that half of the time the hitter faced the pitcher, he hit the ball hard. So numbers can be deceiving.

Managers can also fall victim to information overload. When presented with two choices, a manager will often have strong statistical backing for either option. For example, a certain potential pinch hitter might be hitting .600 against the pitcher, but he also might be hitting .125 over the past two weeks. The manager has to decide which information is more relevant, keeping in mind that no matter what he chooses to do, if his move backfires, the second-guessers will have a field day.

To me, a manager's job is simply to get his team in the most favorable situation possible. He can't be expected to do any more than that. Ultimately, success or failure is determined by whether or not his players do their jobs. A manager can do his job flawlessly but his team can still lose if the players don't come through. A lot of times when a manager gets fired, it's really not fair, because he did everything he could. But there's an old adage in baseball: You can't fire all the players. So when it's time to hold someone accountable for the team not winning, fair or not, it is going to be the manager.

A Matter of Style

The more time that a manager puts in on the job, the more he takes on his own style. Former Orioles manager Earl Weaver was known for favoring strong pitching and waiting for his hitters to come through with three-run homers, as opposed to trying to scratch out a run here and there. A manager's style is influenced by several factors. First is his personnel. Weaver wouldn't have survived long playing for the big inning if he didn't have sluggers like Ken Singleton and Eddie Murray on his teams.

Next is the skipper's personality. Houston Astros manager Larry Dierker is known for giving his starting pitchers the benefit of the doubt when deciding whether or not to take them out. Dierker used to be a starter himself, and he knows how hard it is for a pitcher to be pulled from the game when he wants to stay in.

A final factor in determining a manager's style is his environment. When Lou Piniella managed the Yankees and Cincinnati Reds, his teams ranked around the middle of the pack in stolen-base attempts. But now that he manages the Seattle Mariners, Piniella doesn't run as often. It's not that he doesn't have fast players; it's largely because the Mariners' home stadium, the Kingdome, is a home run hitter's park. So Piniella is more inclined to sit back and play for the big inning instead of potentially running himself out of a rally.

Why Bad Players Make Good Managers— and Vice Versa

Rogers Hornsby was one of the greatest players ever to step on the diamond, a terrific hitter and a true student of the game. "Baseball is my life, the only thing I know and can talk about, my only interest," he once said. Sounds like the ideal manager, right? As it turned out, Hornsby wasn't a very good manager at all. The fact that he knew the game as well as anyone didn't matter. What held Hornsby back was that he couldn't accept the fact that not every player was as good as he was. His players complained that he held them to ridiculously high standards and lost his temper when they made mistakes.

Hornsby isn't the only great player to fail as a manager. More often than not, the best managers are guys who had mediocre—at best—playing careers, journeymen who have bounced around and seen everything there is to see in the game. You can learn a lot by sitting on the bench and paying attention. And getting a great effort out of a superstar isn't that hard. But to get the lesser players to contribute, you have to understand them and empathize with them. And I think that's a big reason why so many of the game's top managers—Casey Stengel, Sparky Anderson, and more recent guys like Bobby Cox of the Atlanta Braves and Terry Collins of the Anaheim Angels—were never great players.

Casey Stengel (left) and Sparky Anderson were kindred spirits.

Hall of Fame Players

	Major League Player			Major League Manager	
	HRs*	RBIs*	BA*	Win %*	Postseason Appearances
Luke Appling	45	1,116	.310	.250	0
Mordecai Brown**	(239–129, 2.06 ERA)			.442	0
Ty Cobb	118	1,961	.367	.519	0
Eddie Collins	47	1,299	.333	.521	0
Larry Doby	253	969	.283	.425	0
Johnny Evers	12	538	.270	.485	0
Burleigh Grimes**	(270–212, 3.53 ERA)			.432	0
Ted Lyons**	(260–230, 3.67 ERA)			.430	0

continues

continued

	Major League Player			Major League Manager	
	HRs*	RBIs*	BA*	Win %*	Postseason Appearances
Rabbit Maranville	28	884	.258	.434	0
Eddie Mathews	512	1,453	.271	.481	0
Christy Mathewson**	(373–188, 2.13 ERA)			.482	0
Kid Nichols**	(360–203, 2.94 ERA)			.465	0
Mel Ott	511	1,860	.304	.467	0
Frank Robinson	586	1,812	.294	.491	0
George Sisler	100	1,175	.340	.475	0
Joe Tinker	31	782	.263	.497	0
Ted Williams	521	1,839	.344	.429	0

* In regular season
** Pitcher (Win-Loss, ERA)

Non-Hall of Fame Players

	Major League Player				Major League Manager	
	HRs*	RBIs*	BA*	Win %*	Postseason Appearances	World Series Wins
Walter Alston	0	0	.000	.558	7	4
Sparky Anderson	0	34	.218	.545	7	3
Bobby Cox	9	58	.225	.553	8	1
Leo Durocher	24	567	.247	.540	3	1
Whitey Herzog	25	172	.257	.532	6	1
Ralph Houk	0	20	.272	.514	3	2
Miller Huggins	9	318	.265	.555	6	3
Tony La Russa	0	7	.199	.523	6	1
Tommy Lasorda**	(0–4, 6.48 ERA)			.526	8	2
Connie Mack	5	265	.245	.484	8	5
Billy Martin	64	333	.257	.553	5	1
Joe McCarthy	Did not play			.615	9	7
Casey Stengel	60	535	.284	.508	10	7
Earl Weaver	Did not play			.583	6	1
Dick Williams	70	331	.260	.520	4	2

* In regular season
** Pitcher (Win-Loss, ERA)

Why Catchers Make Good Managers

You might think I'm being biased when I say that catchers make the best managers, but look at the proof: Six of the 30 major league managers—one out of every five—in 1998 were former backstops, including the World Series winner and winningest skipper, the Yankees' Joe Torre. Maybe you do have to be smart to wear "the tools of ignorance" after all.

Catchers have to pay attention to a lot of the same things managers do. They have to know the scouting reports on the opposing team's hitters so they can call the right pitches and help position the fielders accordingly. They also have to keep their pitcher calm and focused, and they must be able to detect when a pitcher no longer has his best stuff and communicate that to his manager. So, in a way, the catcher is something of a coach on the field.

The Coaches: Increasing Specialization

Managers have help, and I don't mean the armchair experts who voice their opinions in letters to their local newspaper editor and on sports talk radio. A staff of *coaches* assists the manager. Each coach focuses on one aspect of the game, and in recent years the degree of specialization has increased.

The most visible coaches are the first base and third base coaches. As we covered earlier, their job is to advise runners on the basepaths. These coaches also usually have another responsibility, such as serving as the staff's *baserunning coach* or as a *fielding coach*. The *pitching coach* works with the pitching staff on their mechanics as well as the mental aspect of the game. The *hitting instructor,* as you probably guessed, works with the hitters, usually during batting practice or in the batting cage. Most managers have a *bench coach,* whose primary function is to discuss strategic options during the course of the game. Then there's the *bullpen coach,* who oversees the pitchers as they warm up before entering the game. Having so many coaches allows the manager to not have to focus too much time and attention on any one area of the game.

Talkin' Baseball

"Nice guys finish last."

—Brooklyn Dodgers manager Leo Durocher

The Scouting Report

Another group of guys who contribute to the team's success are the scouts. *Advance scouts* watch a team's upcoming opponents and prepare reports on what to expect, both in pitching and in hitting. This is especially handy if a team has a new player, such as a pitcher who has just come into the league and who no one on the team has faced before. For me, like most players, knowing a pitcher and knowing what he

Catching On

Advance scouts watch a team's upcoming opponents and prepare reports on what to expect, such as hitting and pitching tendencies of certain players.

Talkin' Baseball

"They've played on grass, they've played on AstroTurf. What they should do is put down a layer of paper in Candlestick Park. After all, the Giants always look good on paper."

—San Francisco disc jockey Don Rose in 1984, complaining about the chronically underachieving Giants

throws and what he likes to throw in certain situations was important. Also, if a team is considering trading for a particular player, it will often send a scout to watch that player in action for a few games and file a report.

A lot of times you can tell just from reading the paper which hitters are swinging the bat well. But when you're playing a team for the first time, the reports from advance scouts are particularly useful—like in the World Series, when you usually have two teams who haven't faced each other all year (although interleague play has changed that somewhat). They tell you that you don't want to pitch to this guy in this situation, or this guy likes the ball out over the plate, or this guy hates the inside pitch, or this guy loves swinging at high pitches.

When it comes to the hitting report, sometimes the scouts are only as good as the catcher. As a catcher, I'm trying to get the best I can out of my pitcher, so sometimes I'll go with his best pitch even if it goes against the report. Say I'm catching and the scouting report tells me that this guy is a good fastball hitter—but my pitcher has a *really* good fastball. I can't just throw that out the window. I still have to rely on my pitcher's strengths. This hitter may have hit seven other guys' fastball, but that doesn't mean he can hit my guy's. If a hitter definitely has a strength, then I'll try to avoid pitching to that strength. But if I have to make a call that goes against the scouting report, I'll do it.

Using the Bench and the Bullpen

A manager will usually want to start his best players whenever he can and use the reserves to pinch hit late in a game. We've already talked a bit about what a manager has to consider when he brings one of these bench players into the game.

Because there's no free substitution in baseball (meaning that, unlike in basketball or football, a player can't return once he is removed from the game), the moves that a manager makes with his bench and his bullpen—and when he makes them—are crucial. You only have so many bullets in the chamber, so to speak, and you have to fire them at the right time.

Most managers consult a notebook of statistics, highlighting favorable and unfavorable matchups, to help them decide who to put in and when. Head-to-head stats (pitcher versus hitter) are the most valuable numbers for a manager. Also useful are charts that tell a manager where a batter is most likely to hit the ball; these help a manager set his defense and determine how to pitch a particular hitter.

But managers can't rely solely on stats and charts. Some skippers, such as Bruce Bochy of the San Diego Padres, watch a lot of videotape. Bochy's theory is that a hitter could be 4-for-10 against a particular pitcher, but three of those hits could've been bloop singles. Another hitter could be 1-for-10 against a pitcher, but he may have hit three balls to the warning track.

A manager also has to go by what he sees, and not be afraid to make a gut decision that goes against the book. This line of thinking applies especially to pitching changes: The manager's assessment of how well the guy on the mound is throwing is a crucial decision-making factor.

Here's an example: In a 1995 American League Championship Series game, Cleveland Indians manager Mike Hargrove brought in lefty reliever Paul Assenmacher to face the left-handed Ken Griffey Jr. Assenmacher struck out Griffey, and Hargrove liked the way he was throwing, so he kept him in the game to face righty Jay Buhner, even though right-hander Eric Plunk was ready to come in. Assenmacher struck out Buhner as well, and the Indians went on to win the game.

Every once in awhile a player who doesn't normally get a start will be inserted into the starting lineup. The reason is simple. Not only does it give a regular a day of rest, it keeps a bench player on his toes. A sub might go a week or so without pinch hitting, so his manager will want to keep him from getting stale. There's more to using the bench than getting the right hitter to the plate in the right situation.

Dealing with Players

Sometimes a manager goes by the unwritten book. Sometimes he goes by stats. And sometimes he goes by his gut feeling, by intuition. I think a manager can make a difference in about seven or eight games a year, and it's up to the players to make the difference in the rest of them.

It's not always easy to deal with today's players—some of whom make 10 or 20 times what their manager pulls in. But a manager can't get anywhere without the respect of his players. Some skippers are known as *players' managers,* meaning they try to be one of the guys. A lot of times this leads to problems because a manager has to exude a certain amount of authority, and if he's too friendly with his players it undermines that authority.

On the other hand, if a manager is too aloof he won't last long either. Players often don't perform well playing for someone they don't like or don't respect. So a manager must perform a delicate balancing act. He has to relate to his players and get along with them while not letting them forget that he's the boss. Current Yankees manager Joe Torre does an exceptional job of this.

Talkin' Baseball

"The secret of managing is to keep the guys who hate you away from the guys who are undecided."

—Hall of Fame manager Casey Stengel

Dealing with the Media

Baseball lends itself to second-guessing, so it's inevitable that a manager will get taken to task for a failed move every once in a while. Getting ripped in the newspaper isn't fun, but managers can't afford to hold grudges with the press. The media can do a lot to shape the public's perception of a team and a manager, so it's in a manager's best interest to be media savvy.

Sometimes managers use the media to explain a decision, defuse a controversy, or put a certain spin on an event. So the relationship between the writers (who need information from the manager to do their job well) and the manager can be mutually beneficial. Most successful managers have at least decent professional relationships with the writers who cover their teams.

As Tommy Lasorda can tell you, being a big-league manager means having a mike in your face all the time.

Extra Innings

Television commentators spend a lot of their time publicly second-guessing managers. Sometimes when I'm watching a game I feel like saying to the broadcaster, "Hey, if you're so smart let's see you do better." Well, in 1997, one announcer did. Larry Dierker retired as a player in 1977, and spent 18 years as a broadcaster for the Houston Astros. Before the '97 season, Houston hired Dierker as manager, even though he had no managerial experience. Dierker led the Astros to the playoffs in each of his first two seasons, and was named the National League Manager of the Year in 1998. The American League Manager of the Year that season was the Yankees' Joe Torre—another former broadcaster.

Johnny's Best Managers

Now that we've looked at what makes a good manager, let's look at some of the guys who have had what it takes. The two greatest of all time were probably **Connie Mack** and **John McGraw**, who rank first and second, respectively, on the career list for managerial victories. Born Cornelius McGillicuddy, Mack, known as the Tall Tactician, managed the Pittsburgh Pirates from 1894 to '96, and then moved to Philadelphia, where he managed the Athletics for the next *50 years*. That's one record that'll never be broken. McGraw, whose nickname was "Little Napoleon," managed in the major leagues for 33 years, 30 of them with the New York Giants (1902–32).

Connie Mack (left) and John McGraw, the two greatest managers in baseball history, have 86 seasons, 6,616 wins, 17 pennants, and eight world championships between them.

I played most of my career with the Reds under the great **Sparky Anderson**. Sparky listened to his players, and when it came to strategy, he was always two or three innings ahead of the game. Sparky took the Reds to the World Series four times, won it twice, and won another championship with the Detroit Tigers in 1984.

Casey Stengel, best known for managing the Yankees in the 1950s—he won 10 pennants and seven World Series with New York from 1949 to '60—was the first manager I was exposed to, watching games on TV. I think Sparky and Casey were together in another life. Neither one spoke like a Berlitz graduate, but they were really smart baseball men who came up with some great quips. They loved the game— baseball was their life—and I admired that.

I loved **Leo Durocher,** who managed the Brooklyn Dodgers, the New York Giants, the Cubs, and the Astros over a career of 24 years. Leo went all out—his most famous line was "Nice guys finish last." But the guy was a winner, plain and simple, and a straight-shooter: You knew where you stood with him.

Walter Alston, who managed the Brooklyn/Los Angeles Dodgers for many years, was always in total control of his team, as was **Gil Hodges,** who managed the Washington Senators and New York Mets in the 1960s and early '70s. Both of those men were soft-spoken but effective leaders who took their clubs to world championships. I remember the emotional style of longtime Baltimore Orioles manager **Earl Weaver,** who won six division titles, four American League pennants, and one World Series. For years guys were in his face—and he in theirs—but they played hard every day for him. They were out there giving it everything they had every day.

I also like the current Yankees manager, **Joe Torre.** He has a very low-key style, but it's perfect for his veteran ballclub. His team plays hard for him every day, and you can tell they respect him. **Gene Mauch,** who managed the Philadelphia Phillies, Montreal Expos, Minnesota Twins, and California Angels, is the opposite of Torre. He's much more intense—he hollered a lot—but he was always one of my favorites. He really wanted to win—it was a total obsession. I don't think he's ever really gotten his due, and he probably won't be in the Hall of Fame, but I always liked him.

Now that we've covered the offensive side of the game—technique, execution, and strategy—we'll take a look in the next chapter at the players who have done the most damage in baseball history, at the plate and on the basepaths.

The Least You Need to Know

➤ Today's managers have loads of information at their fingertips, which can be both a blessing and a curse.

➤ It's more important for a manager to be well-respected by his players than to be considered one of the guys.

➤ Good playing skills don't necessarily translate to good managing skills.

➤ A staff of coaches, each of whom focuses on one aspect of the game, assists the manager, and in recent years the degree of specialization has increased.

Chapter 20

Johnny's Greatest Hits (of Yesterday and Today)

In This Chapter

➤ Johnny's all-time lineup

➤ The greatest pure hitters

➤ The most productive under pressure

➤ The best on the basepaths

Baseball fans love a good argument.

They used to argue over who was the best center fielder in New York—Mickey Mantle, Willie Mays, or Duke Snider. Today they argue over who's the best player in the game—Mark McGwire or Sammy Sosa or Ken Griffey Jr. or Barry Bonds.

And they argue about who would make their all-time lineup. Just in the outfield alone, how do you choose among Babe Ruth and Ty Cobb and Ted Williams and Hank Aaron and Willie Mays and Mickey Mantle?

Maybe you'll think I'm taking the easy way out, but in this chapter, when I name my all-time lineup, I think it's fair to consider only those I played against. In doing that, I'm going to have to leave out the great old-time players like Babe Ruth and Lou Gehrig and Ty Cobb and Rogers Hornsby. You can argue that that's unfair, and I'll understand, because Babe Ruth *is* baseball. It also hurts me to leave out Gehrig at first base. I read books about him when I was a kid. He and Mantle were my idols growing up. The reason I played hurt so much is that I admired Mickey and Lou for their skill and dedication to go out there and break records and play every day, even when they were hurting.

I played only in spring training against Mickey, but I have to put my idol on my all-time offense. And I didn't play against Ted Williams, but I was old enough to see him play, and I would be remiss if I didn't include probably the greatest hitter of all time.

Even when I narrow it down like that, I can't include some great players. There are only so many slots in the batting order! I leave out Henry Aaron, who has more career home runs than anyone in history. And I have to leave out Pete Rose, who has more career hits than anyone in history. Pete was my teammate, the greatest lead-off hitter, and the most versatile player in baseball, but there just wasn't room for him in my lineup.

Sorry, Charlie Hustle. Sorry, Sultan of Swat and the Iron Horse. Oh, Henry, what can I say?

Johnny's All-Time Lineup

Willie McCovey is the first baseman on my all-time offensive lineup. He's the only guy against whom I never could call a pitch I thought would get him out. Willie was the most intimidating left-handed batter in the National League when I played. The big, menacing slugger bashed 521 home runs, leading the league three times in round-trippers and twice in runs batted in. He was the 1969 Most Valuable Player and a 1986 Hall of Fame inductee.

Talkin' Baseball

"The trouble with baseball is that by the time you learn how to play it, you can't play it any more."

—Frank Howard

Joe Morgan is my second baseman. Joe was only five foot seven and 150 pounds, but he was a *five-tool player*. He could hit for average, hit for power, steal bases, field, and throw. He's the only second baseman ever to win consecutive MVP awards (in 1975 and '76). He was a Gold Glove fielder and ranks in the top 10 in history in both walks and steals. Joe's in the Hall of Fame, too.

Talkin' Baseball

"You've got to remember—I'm 73."

—Ty Cobb, explaining in 1960 why he thought he'd hit only .300 against modern-day pitching

At shortstop, I think most people would go for defense and think of either Ozzie Smith or the guy I played with for so long, Dave Concepcion. But most people forget about Ernie Banks hitting 47 home runs as a shortstop. So I've got to go with the offense and take Ernie at short. Ernie hit 512 home runs in his Hall of Fame career. He was MVP twice and led the league in homers and RBIs twice. Mr. Cub played more games at first base, but his greatest years were at shortstop.

My third baseman is Mike Schmidt. Good hands, great power, good RBI man. Schmitty was probably the best all-around third baseman ever. A first-ballot Hall of Famer, he led the league in homers eight times, slugging percentage five times, and RBIs four times. He hit 548 home runs and won 11 Gold Gloves.

My outfield consists of Mantle, Mays, and Williams, three more Hall of Famers. The Mick hit .298 with 536 career homers, and his numbers would have been even more astronomical if not for bad knees. Before his legs gave out, the Commerce Comet was one of the fastest players in the game. He scored more runs than he drove in, a rarity among sluggers. He was a three-time MVP and led the league in home runs four times, RBIs once, and batting average once.

Catching On

A **five-tool player** is one who can hit for average, hit for power, run, throw, and field.

If you said Mike Schmidt was the greatest all-around third baseman in baseball history, you wouldn't get many arguments.

Willie was the most versatile of all outfielders. The Say Hey Kid still ranks third in career home runs with 660 and finished with a .302 career average. He led the league in homers four times and won the 1954 batting championship and MVP trophy. Probably the best fielding center fielder ever, he won 12 straight Gold Gloves and was named to 20 straight All-Star teams.

Willie Mays would be a great guy to have in your lineup: You could play him anywhere in the outfield, put him anywhere in the order, and he would win games for you with his bat, his glove, and his feet.

Ted lost nearly five years of his career to military service in World War II and Korea and still hit 521 home runs while averaging .344, only once hitting less than .316. He had as many nicknames as home run titles—the Kid, the Splendid Splinter, the Thumper, and Teddy Ballgame. Ted probably worked harder at, and knew more about, hitting than any man who ever lived. He was the last man to hit over .400 (.406) in 1941—one of only five who've done it this century. He won six batting titles and four RBI titles, and he would have won more than two MVP awards if not for a sour relationship with the voters, the media, who jobbed him when he won Triple Crowns in 1942 and 1947. (Remember, you win a Triple Crown if you lead your league in the big three categories: batting average, home runs, and RBIs.)

Talkin' Baseball

"All I want out of life is that when I walk down the street, folks will say, 'There goes the greatest hitter who ever lived.'"

—Ted Williams

My best-hitting pitcher would be Warren Spahn. He'd probably be my left-handed pitcher, too. Warren won 363 games, lost only 245, and had 63 shutouts. He hit only .194 for his career, but he was no automatic out. He hit 35 home runs and one season hit .333.

The Kid, the Splendid Splinter, the Thumper, Teddy Ballgame—by any name, Ted Williams was probably the greatest hitter to ever play the game.

As much as I'd like to bat in this powerful lineup, I'm going to go with Hall of Famer Roy Campanella at catcher. Roy started in the Negro leagues in 1938, nine years before the major leagues were integrated. He joined the Brooklyn Dodgers in 1948, where for nine seasons he worked 100 or more games behind the plate, as well as 32 World Series games. He won the National League MVP Award three times, caught three no-hitters, led the league in putouts six times, and gunned down two out of every three would-be basestealers. He also hit more than 20 home runs in all but three seasons; in 1953 he hit 41 and set a big-league record for catchers, and led the league with 142 RBIs. After the 1957 season, just before the Dodgers moved to Los Angeles, Roy was paralyzed in a car accident and his career was over. He was elected to the Hall of Fame in 1969, and passed away in 1993.

We didn't use the designated hitter in my day, and the league I played in still doesn't, but if you want to include a DH and an active player, who better than Mark McGwire? Nobody ever hit more than 61 home runs in a season until Big Mac came along and smacked an unbelievable 70. Never say never, but Big Mac and Ken Griffey Jr. might be the only

Talkin' Baseball

"Mickey Mantle can hit just as good right-handed as he can left-handed. He's just naturally amphibious."

—Mantle's Yankee teammate Yogi Berra

guys with a chance ever to break that record. And Big Mac is the only player ever to hit 50 homers in three straight seasons, so he's no one-year wonder.

With this order, I'd probably lead off with Joe Morgan and bat Willie Mays second. But Mays could do everything, so you could put him anywhere. I'd probably bat Ted Williams third, Mick fourth, Willie McCovey fifth, Campy sixth, Schmitty seventh, Banks eighth. If you want to include a DH, slide Big Mac into the fourth or fifth spot and slide everyone else down a spot. I'd use Mickey in center field. Willie could play anywhere, so I'd put him in left, and Williams in right.

Johnny's All-Time Lineup

Spot	Player, Position	Best-Known Team(s)
1	Joe Morgan, 2B	Reds
2	Willie Mays, LF	Giants
3	Ted Williams, RF	Red Sox
4	Mickey Mantle, CF	Yankees
5	Mark McGwire, DH	Athletics/Cardinals
6	Willie McCovey, 1B	Giants
7	Roy Campanella, C	Dodgers
8	Mike Schmidt, 3B	Phillies
9	Ernie Banks, SS	Cubs
Pitcher	Warren Spahn	Braves

The Best Pure Hitters

When I think of pure hitters, I think of guys with great swings and high batting averages.

Talkin' Baseball

"At my age I'm just happy to be named the Greatest Living Anything."

—Joe DiMaggio in 1969, when told he was selected Baseball's Greatest Living Player

Ted Williams and Joe DiMaggio were pure hitters—and two of the best in history. Among the thirtysomething active players, Tony Gwynn, who hit an amazing .394 in 1994, and Paul Molitor, who led the AL in hits twice and runs three times in the early '90s, are pure hitters. And we see that with young Nomar Garciaparra now. He has that short, quick swing and a very small stride. The longer you wait to see the ball, obviously, the better chance you have of identifying the pitch. The guys who can wait and wait for the pitch—and then be quick enough to pounce on it—are more likely to hit for a high average.

In the old days, even the contact hitters used big-barreled bats. They choked up four or five inches and just punched short hits. They called it the deadball era, but the way they hit, it didn't really matter whether the ball was live or dead. They weren't going to hit a lot of home runs with that style. It was embarrassing in those days to strike out, so they constantly worried about contact, and they got a big bat that would last them all season if possible. I talked to Bill Terry, the last National League player to hit .400 (way back in 1930), and I think he broke only two bats in an entire season. And the second bat broke during an exhibition series down in Cuba. They didn't have many opportunities to get bats with really good wood, so when they had one, they really protected it.

Portraits of two of the game's best pure hitters: Tony Gwynn (left) and Paul Molitor.

Tony Gwynn helped change the outlook of hitters by going to such a short, light bat. All his batting titles show bat speed and bat control are more important than a thick, heavy bat. And even though Tony is mostly a singles and doubles hitter, he showed the sluggers how important bat speed was. I think that's why we see so many home runs today. Because the bats are so light, hitters are able to create terrific bat speed and still be able to wait longer before swinging.

Think Joe DiMaggio knew what to do with a bat in his hands? He compiled a career batting average of .325 and hit safely in a record 56 consecutive games in 1941.

The Best Clutch Hitters

Just as batting average is a good barometer of pure hitters, you can always find the best clutch hitters among the RBI leaders—guys like my old teammate on the Big Red Machine, Tony Perez, who drove in 90 or more runs for 11 straight years.

Batting average isn't a good indicator of a clutch hitter. One guy can hit .270 and be a great clutch hitter and another guy can hit .300 but be lousy in the clutch. The difference in average is three hits every 100 at bats, which is pretty insignificant, especially if the extra three hits are singles with nobody on. But if you dig deeper, you might find that .270 hitter is hitting .330 or .340 with men on base. When a clutch hitter comes up with men on base, his concentration level peaks. He thrives on those situations. He awaits them with glee, not fear of failure. As an opponent, you just dreaded seeing him come to the plate with the game on the line. You could almost bet on him to come through.

Extra Innings

Ten players have ended a World Series game with a home run, but only two—Bill Mazeroski and Joe Carter—have ended the entire Series with a homer. The following table shows the complete list.

Players Who Have Ended World Series Games with Home Runs

Player, Team	Year	Opponent	Game	Inning	Final
Tommy Henrich, Yankees	1949	Dodgers	1	9	1–0
Dusty Rhodes, Giants	1954	Indians	1	10	5–2
Eddie Mathews, Braves	1957	Yankees	4	10	7–5
Bill Mazeroski, Pirates	1960	Yankees	7*	9	10–9
Mickey Mantle, Yankees	1964	Cardinals	3	9	2–1
Carlton Fisk, Red Sox	1975	Red Sox	6	12	7–6
Kirk Gibson, Dodgers	1988	Athletics	1	9	5–4
Mark McGwire, Athletics	1988	Dodgers	3	9	2–1
Kirby Puckett, Twins	1991	Braves	6	11	4–3
Joe Carter, Blue Jays	1993	Phillies	6*	9	8–6

* Final game of Series

Earlier, I mentioned how Tom Seaver would pitch around one or two dangerous hitters to get to a guy he could get out. When the game's on the line, you don't want to see a clutch hitter up there. You don't want to let him beat you.

Clutch hitters take great pride at driving in runs and delivering in the big games. The guys with the big RBI totals are usually blessed with great leadoff men and second hitters who set the table and give them lots of opportunities to drive in runs. Reggie Jackson didn't have those great No. 1 and No. 2 hitters, so he didn't set any RBI records, but when the playoffs and World Series arrived, Reggie arrived.

Reggie's nickname was Mr. October (because that's when the playoffs and World Series take place). He thrived for the show and he loved it. He wanted to stand in the spotlight, and his intensity level rose to the occasion. And that's what creates great clutch hitters. When they have a chance and they know everybody's watching, they relish that opportunity. That's exactly what they play for.

Talkin' Baseball

"He hits the ball so hard, the guy on deck can score."

—Mike Stanley on slugger Mo Vaughn

275

Reggie Jackson, a.k.a. Mr. October, is one of only two men to hit three home runs in one World Series game. (Babe Ruth, who did it twice, is the other.)

The Best Basestealers

Maury Wills reminded teams that they could win with more than just home runs. Stealing bases had become a forgotten strategy until he came along and reinvented the art. He broke Ty Cobb's single-season record with 104 steals in 1962, so dominating games that he was voted MVP ahead of the great Willie Mays. The Dodgers were pitching-oriented and didn't have much offense, but Maury stole games for them with his daring feet.

Lou Brock followed in Maury's disruptive footsteps. He led the National League in steals eight times, and his 118 thefts in 1974 broke Maury's record and remains the NL standard. Lou led the Cardinals to three World Series, winning two, while batting .391, then a record for anyone who played in two or more World Series.

Davey Lopes came along right behind Wills in Los Angeles. He had great speed like Wills did and he read pitchers, and I'm sure part of that came from the Dodgers' organization, where players were always well-schooled on the fundamentals of baserunning and stealing.

Warning Track

Too many announcers and fans get caught up in statistics. It's one thing to play fantasy baseball; it's another to become obsessed with stats and focus on numbers as opposed to the pure joy of baseball. It's like the great sportswriter Jimmy Cannon wrote many years ago: "Baseball isn't statistics. Baseball is Joe DiMaggio rounding second."

And now we have Rickey Henderson, the most prolific thief for a season or a career. Rickey led the majors again with 66 steals in 1998, a few months before he turned 40 years old. Incredible!

The Smartest Baserunners

Pete Rose didn't have the great speed of Wills, Brock, Lopes, or Henderson, but he was as good as there was going from first to third. And that's a big part of being a good baserunner: knowing when you can take the extra base, being alert, doing the little things.

Joe Morgan didn't have the stolen base totals of Wills, Brock, Lopes, or Henderson, but he could steal a base whenever we needed it. Joe had very fragile legs, and the Big Red Machine had so much offensive firepower, he didn't need to steal often. Don't look just at stolen base records. Some guys never lead the league, but they know when to steal. In the late innings, when everybody knows you need a run, they get a walk or single and then they steal second, and they're hardly ever thrown out. The great baserunners don't take you out of innings by running into outs. They *make* big innings.

The Least You Need to Know

➤ Johnny's all-time lineup features an outfield of Mickey Mantle, Willie Mays, and Ted Williams.

➤ Tony Gwynn, one of the purest hitters baseball has ever seen, helped change the game with his emphasis on smaller bats and more bat speed.

➤ Tony Perez and Reggie Jackson were two of the best clutch hitters of Johnny's era.

➤ Maury Wills, Lou Brock, Davey Lopes, and Rickey Henderson are Johnny's top basestealers, and teammates Pete Rose and Joe Morgan were as good as they come on the basepaths.

Part 5

Take Me Out to the Ballgame: A Fan's Guide

This part of the book is about being a fan. First, you'll learn about the business of baseball, and how the market in which a team plays can ultimately bless or curse that team. We'll talk about following the game in person or via TV, radio, print media, or on-line services. I'll give you the lowdown on what to look for when you're out at the ballpark. We'll also take a look at the sport from Little League on up through college and the minor leagues.

Finally, one of baseball's biggest fans—yours truly—will offer a few suggestions for improving the game. There's not a whole lot wrong with it, but even the nicest antiques benefit from a little polish now and then.

Chapter 21

Baseball Means Business

In This Chapter

➤ Who needs Monty Hall? Let's make a deal!

➤ Why major leaguers love capitalism

➤ Is anyone worth $10 million a year?

➤ How baseball almost struck out

Let's do a little math, shall we? The 30 major league teams spent a total of $1,265,108,468 on player salaries in 1998. That's 1.2 *billion* dollars, or the approximate gross national product of Albania. Then consider all the baseball-related merchandise sold around the world. Factor in the sale of TV and radio rights, as well as the money spent on tickets, and it's obvious that a whole lot of money is changing hands in baseball.

Baseball is our national pastime, but it's also a big-money enterprise. Kids play it for fun, but when grown-ups play it, the stakes are substantial. In this chapter, we're going to examine the business of baseball. So grab your calculators and your accounting textbooks, and let's take a look.

Extra Innings

The first professional team was the 1869 Cincinnati Red Stockings. Two years later, the first professional league, the National Association, was formed. A century later I began my career with that same Red Stockings franchise (known by then simply as the Reds).

Want to Buy a Team?

More and more, baseball teams are being gobbled up by big conglomerates. For instance, in 1998 the Fox Corporation (owned by Rupert Murdoch) bought the Los Angeles Dodgers from the O'Malley family, who had owned them for as long as anyone can remember, for more than $300 million. We've entered the era of corporate ownership, which has its pluses and minuses.

Corporations have other sources of income, so they are less likely to have cash-flow problems than a team whose owner is mainly a baseball man. This lends some stability to the game. For the most part, the only teams that threaten to move these days are independently owned. But there was always something nice about knowing your owner as a person, as opposed to a faceless corporation. Even though some owners, like the New York Yankees' George Steinbrenner, can be meddlesome, you know that they're always looking out for the best interests of their team. When a baseball team is part of a corporation, you never know how much time and interest is being devoted to it. With big businesses, it always seems to be about the bottom line.

Talkin' Baseball

"When I played in Brooklyn, I could go to the ballpark for a nickel carfare. But now I live in Pasadena, and it costs me $15 or $16 to take a cab to Glendale. If I was a young man, I'd study to become a cab driver."

—Hall of Fame manager Casey Stengel

And when corporate people hire accountants and bean counters to try to run a ballclub, they sometimes lose sight of talent and other issues with regard to a particular player, and try to do it too much by numbers. Maybe they don't realize that a guy is past his prime, or that he's always hurt.

Extra Innings

The Toronto Giants? It almost happened. In 1976 a Toronto-based group was close to buying the San Francisco Giants and moving the team to Ontario. But at the last minute San Francisco officials rallied to keep the team. The proposed 1976 Toronto Giants logo is on display at the Canadian Baseball Hall of Fame and Museum in St. Mary's, Ontario.

Regardless of what you think of his methods, you have to admit that Yankees principal owner George Steinbrenner has been pretty successful at putting a competitive team on the field in his 25 years in New York.

The General Manager and the Front Office

Since owners are businessmen, they can't be expected to run their team's day-to-day operations. For that, they have a *front office*. In addition to various presidents and vice presidents who oversee the business side of things, the front office is comprised of a few baseball people who make the key personnel decisions.

The *general manager,* or *GM,* is responsible for trading players, signing free agents, and overseeing the drafting of amateur players. Some GMs are former players, while some have worked their way up through the front office without ever playing. The GM has plenty of people to consult with before making any move. He'll talk with the manager and coaching staff, ask scouts about players he might be interested in trading for, and he'll consult with the minor league personnel department to determine which prospects might be expendable and which ones have a future in the organization.

Talkin' Baseball

"In baseball, just about everybody gives up on just about everybody. Every player has nine lives. Almost nobody makes it, or at least makes it big, where he started."

—Writer Thomas Boswell

Let's Make a Deal

If a team has a need at one position and a surplus at another, the logical thing to do is take what it has extra of and swap it to someone else for what they need. Trades aren't that simple, though. A GM has to consider a variety of other factors. For instance, he has to consider the long-term consequences of the deal. He might have three third basemen, but if two of them are 35 years old and the other is 22, trading the younger one might be a bad idea.

Then there's the financial aspects of the deal. Some trades appear to be quite lopsided when you consider only the talent of the players involved. But a player's value on the open market depends on his contract as much as his abilities. A player who hits .275 with 20 homers and makes $750,000 will be worth a lot more than a player who hits .285 with 25 homers and makes $11 million, because the first guy is going to give you much better value.

Extra Innings

According to unofficial sources, just prior to the start of the 1977 season, the Toronto Blue Jays turned down a trade that would've sent pitcher Bill Singer to the Yankees for little-used lefty Ron Guidry. But because Singer was on the cover of the Jays' 1977 media guide, club officials felt it would be embarrassing, so they nixed the deal. Singer won two games for the Jays and retired after the 1977 season, while Guidry went on to win 170 games for the Yanks and was a Cy Young winner in '78.

Then there are the "salary dumps." Sometimes a team will find itself in financial straits and begin unloading any player with a big contract for younger, cheaper players and/or minor league prospects. The idea is that by the time the prospects mature, the team will be in better shape financially. It's an unpopular route to take. After they won the World Series in 1997, the Florida Marlins dumped $33 million worth of player salaries. In 1998, the reigning "world champions" had the worst record in the major leagues, but their payroll was only $19 million and they had a handful of prospects who made their future look a little brighter.

Still, what the Marlins did, essentially buying themselves a championship team and then just as quickly selling it off, wasn't a great thing for baseball. First, the Marlins reinforced the notion that the team that spends the most money wins. Then they pulled the rug out from under everyone: Fans want to see a championship club defending its title, not conducting a fire sale because it can't afford to make ends meet.

Extra Innings

On August 4, 1982, Joel Youngblood became the first player to play for two different major league teams in two different cities on the same day. He was in Chicago playing for the Mets when he found out he had been traded to the Montreal Expos. So he hopped on a plane and flew to Philadelphia, where he joined his new teammates that night and appeared in a game against the Phillies.

Free Agency: Anything but Free

When a player's contract with a team expires, he can become a *free agent* if he has enough major league service time (about four years). He can then offer his services up to the highest bidder.

When I started my career, every player's contract contained something called the *reserve clause,* which meant that the club reserved the right to your services every year. That meant it was entirely up to the club to either play you, cut you, or trade you—you had no say in the matter. The teams in the leagues honored each other's contracts, so a player was literally owned by a team. He couldn't offer his services to the highest bidder on the free market, he had little leverage to negotiate a higher salary, and if his team traded him, he had no choice but to go. Of course, he was free to not play professional baseball, but if he wanted a career in the majors, he had to accept that he was team property.

Because it kept salaries down and profits high, the reserve clause suited the owners, and although player groups organized to fight it periodically, the Supreme Court continued to uphold it until the 1970s, when it was overturned, allowing players to become "free agents" after their sixth season. Since then, salaries have gone through the roof. After I won my second MVP award in 1972, I was making $40,000 a year. If I were able to shop my services around in today's market, those two MVP trophies would probably get me about $12 million a year. It's amazing what a little competition will do for a player's value.

The following table provides a look at how much major league salaries have escalated in the past 10 years, thanks to free agency. Each player listed was the highest-paid player in baseball when he signed his contract.

Recent Record-Setting Major League Player Salaries

Date	Player	Team	Avg. Annual Salary
Dec. 12, 1998	Kevin Brown	Los Angeles Dodgers	$15 million
Nov. 25, 1998	Mo Vaughn	Anaheim Angels	$13,333,333
Oct. 26, 1998	Mike Piazza	New York Mets	$13 million
Dec. 12, 1997	Pedro Martinez	Boston	$12.5 million
Aug. 10, 1997	Greg Maddux	Atlanta	$11.5 million
Feb. 20, 1997	Barry Bonds	San Francisco	$11.45 million
Nov. 19, 1996	Albert Belle	Chicago White Sox	$11 million
Jan. 31, 1996	Ken Griffey, Jr.	Seattle	$8.5 million
Dec. 8, 1992	Barry Bonds	San Francisco	$7,291,666
March 2, 1992	Ryne Sandberg	Chicago Cubs	$7.1 million
Dec. 2, 1991	Bobby Bonilla	New York Mets	$5.8 million
Feb. 8, 1991	Roger Clemens	Boston	$5,380,250
June 27, 1990	Jose Canseco	Oakland	$4.7 million
April 9, 1990	Don Mattingly	New York Yankees	$3.86 million
Jan. 22, 1990	Will Clark	San Francisco	$3.75 million
Jan. 17, 1990	Dave Stewart	Oakland	$3.55 million
Dec. 11, 1989	Mark Davis	Kansas City	$3.25 million
Dec. 1, 1989	Mark Langston	California	$3.25 million
Nov. 28, 1989	Rickey Henderson	Oakland	$3 million
Nov. 22, 1989	Kirby Puckett	Minnesota	$3 million
Nov. 17, 1989	Bret Saberhagen	Kansas City	$2,966,667
Feb. 16, 1989	Orel Herhiser	Los Angeles	$2,633,333
Feb. 15, 1989	Roger Clemens	Boston	$2.5 million

As free-agent salaries have risen, so has the impact of player agents. It was a snowball effect: When salaries started going up in the 1970s, would-be baseball agents took notice. (Back when the average player salary was $15,000, an agent's cut wasn't worth much.) Then, as agents got more involved, they were able to jack salaries up even more. With the gains made on the labor front in the '70s (free agency, salary arbitration) it became more important for players to have a good agent, because they had more options and the potential to negotiate more lucrative deals.

The most powerful baseball player agent today is Scott Boras. His impact can be quantified thusly: One of his clients, Yankees center fielder Bernie Williams, who is a fine player but has never hit 30 homers or driven in more than 102 runs and is 30 years old, recently signed a seven-year, $87.5 million contract. Boras also brokered Kevin Brown's record-shattering seven-year, $105-million deal with the Dodgers last winter.

Talkin' Baseball

"Ninety percent I'll spend on good times, women, and Irish whiskey. The other 10 percent I'll probably waste."

—Philadelphia Phillies pitcher Tug McGraw in 1975, when asked how he intended to spend his $75,000 salary

The Amateur Draft

Since 1965, American amateur players have been subject to the major league amateur draft. Players can be drafted when they finish high school. If they choose to go to college, they can't be drafted until they finish their junior season at that level. A player can only sign with the team that drafts him, which doesn't give him much bargaining power. But unless he's a college senior, he always has the option of going back to school, at which point he goes back into the draft pool the following year and can try his luck again.

Extra Innings

When I was a rookie, I earned the major league minimum salary, which was $7,500 a year. In 1998, the minimum annual pay for a major league player was $170,000.

The selection order for the amateur draft goes in reverse order of a team's standing from the previous season, and the two leagues alternate picks. That is, the American League team with the worst won-lost record picks first in odd-numbered years (and subsequent AL teams have the third selection, fifth selection, and so on), and the NL team with the worst record picks first in even-numbered years.

In the past couple of years, kids in the draft have been signing deals worth upwards of $2 million before they ever play their first professional game. That's a lot of money for an unproven player, and veteran players sometimes resent these big-money kids.

From the Bench

Teams that can't afford lavish excursions into foreign countries would like to see a global draft, which would subject all amateur players to the draft. But it's very unlikely that the rich teams would want to give up their competitive advantage in Latin America.

Other Ways to Acquire Players

Players who are not from the United States are not subject to the draft, and as a result, they are considered free agents from the day they turn 16. Major league teams are free to swoop in and woo them by offering any amount of money they see fit.

This is an area that really separates the haves from the have-nots. Teams with a lot of money can spend it scouting Latin American countries for talent and signing the players. Some teams even set up "academies" in Central and South America. Young kids go to school at the academies, where they also learn how to play baseball, allowing teams to make inroads into the local talent pool.

Growing Talent: The Importance of a Farm System

Very few players make the jump right from college or high school to the majors. It almost always takes at least a couple of years of seasoning in the minor leagues. Each major league team has several *minor league affiliates,* which are subsidized by the big-league team. Some organizations spend more than others on minor league instruction. Branch Rickey, best known as the executive who broke major league baseball's color barrier by signing Jackie Robinson, is also credited with pioneering the concept of the minor league "farm" system as manager of the St. Louis Cardinals.

If you ask me, this is one of the most important places to spend money. Acquiring players via free agency is incredibly expensive. If you can develop your own players, it's not only cheaper in the long run, but it also builds loyalty and establishes a sense of continuity. Both of these are vital in developing good team chemistry. We'll talk more about the minor leagues in the next chapter.

Branch Rickey began developing the now-universal concept of a farm system about 80 years ago with the St. Louis Cardinals organization.

Small Markets vs. Big Markets

These days a lot is made of the disparity in the major leagues between small-market teams and big-market teams. To a certain extent, the size of a market does determine the team's financial fortunes. The New York Yankees benefit from the fact that there are eight million people in the city and several million more in the suburbs, so they have a huge fan base. They are also able to sell their local television rights for a handsome sum because the potential audience is so big.

A team like the Montreal Expos, on the other hand, is stuck in a small city that's not in a traditional baseball area. So the fan base that they have to draw from is small. As a result, the Expos don't have the cash flow the Yankees do, and it traps them in a downward spiral. They don't have enough money to pay good players, so they don't draw many fans, which hurts their bankroll even more. Why don't they move? Good question—and one a lot of baseball fans are asking.

Not all teams in small markets fare poorly, though. The city of Cleveland isn't huge by major league standards, but the Indians have benefited from playing in Jacobs Field, a new, "old-style" stadium that's an attraction in and of itself. And just like the Expos' failures perpetuated themselves, so it goes with the Indians' successes. The more fans show up, the more money the team has to spend on players to guarantee the team will continue to be successful and be a hot ticket. The Indians entered the

1999 season with a streak of 292 consecutive home sellouts—and counting.

Cleveland's success has helped give birth to a new trend: teams threatening to move unless their city builds them a new stadium. A recent example is the San Diego Padres, who felt that they needed a new ballpark, and intimated that they would be forced to pull up stakes if they didn't get one. A referendum to build a new park with tax dollars was put on the ballot for public voting in November 1998—a few days after the Padres lost the World Series. The team even posted signs on the outfield fences, encouraging fans to vote for the stadium funding, which ultimately passed.

The Twins are also currently threatening to leave Minnesota unless they get a new ballpark. This seems to be a new, cyclical trend: As technology improves and new ballpark amenities are unveiled, a team begins to consider its stadium outdated. The team then says something like, "We can't compete unless we have the revenue a new, state-of-the-art facility would produce," and they find another city to woo them, then use that as leverage to get their new park. The thing here is that someone's stadium is always going to obsolete—the Metrodome is less than 20 years old. When does it stop?

Baseball's biggest problem right now is figuring out how to make the sport more competitive for the small-market teams, because without money, winning isn't a realistic possibility. All eight teams that made the playoffs in 1998 were in the top 12 in terms of money spent on salaries.

One attempted solution implemented in the 1990s was a *luxury tax* system, which basically means that teams whose payrolls exceed a certain amount must pay a "tax," or an extra percentage, of that excess amount. Only the five teams with highest payrolls are taxed, at a rate of 35 percent, and the threshold is the average of the fifth- and sixth-highest payrolls. So once six teams have high payrolls, the threshold becomes so high that the taxes are not really significant. As the following table shows, only two teams paid more than $685,000 in luxury tax payments in 1998. (Note: Because a different formula is used for computing payrolls for luxury tax purposes, the team payroll order in this table varies from that of the table that follows.)

1998 Luxury Tax Payments

Team	Tax Payment
Baltimore	$3,138,621
Boston	$2,184,734
New York Yankees	$684,390
Atlanta	$495,625
Los Angeles	$49,593

A team's luxury tax payments go to the commissioner's office, and the money goes toward helping teams with lower payrolls and revenue levels. (Most of it goes into what's called the profit-sharing pool.) The idea was that the luxury tax would act as a deterrent to teams to spend big bucks, but it hasn't seemed to have had much of an impact so far.

The following table offers a look at the player salaries paid by each major league team in 1998, and how each team fared on the field. Notice how, for the most part, the more money a team spent, the more games it won—well, except for the Orioles.

1998 Major League Team Payrolls

Team	Payroll	Wins	Losses	Pct.
Baltimore	$73,995,921	79	83	.488
New York Yankees*	$73,813,698	125	50	.714
Texas*	$62,155,368	88	74	.543
Atlanta*	$61,740,254	106	56	.654
Los Angeles	$60,731,667	83	79	.512
Boston*	$59,347,000	92	70	.568
New York Mets	$58,660,665	88	74	.543
Cleveland*	$56,643,441	89	73	.549
Anaheim	$54,189,000	85	77	.525
San Diego*	$52,996,166	98	64	.605
Chicago Cubs*	$50,686,000	90	73	.552
Houston*	$48,294,000	102	60	.630
San Francisco	$47,914,715	89	74	.546
Colorado	$47,884,648	77	85	.475
St. Louis	$47,608,948	83	79	.512
Seattle	$44,735,014	76	85	.472
Chicago White Sox	$37,830,000	80	82	.494
Toronto	$37,268,500	88	74	.543
Milwaukee	$36,854,036	74	88	.457
Kansas City	$35,610,000	72	89	.447
Arizona	$32,814,500	65	97	.401
Philadelphia	$29,922,500	75	87	.463
Tampa Bay	$27,620,000	63	99	.389
Detroit	$23,318,980	65	97	.401
Minnesota	$22,027,500	70	92	.432
Cincinnati	$20,707,333	77	85	.475
Florida	$19,141,000	54	108	.333
Oakland	$18,585,114	74	88	.457
Pittsburgh	$13,695,000	69	93	.426
Montreal	$8,317,500	65	97	.401

Playoff team

You might ask, Doesn't the commissioner, the major leagues' highest authority, have the power to solve these problems? Well, no one is exactly sure what commissioner Bud Selig's powers are, because he's still pretty new on the job. But generally speaking, commissioners in recent years have been operating more and more under the aegis of the owners. After all, the owners hire him and pay his salary.

Extra Innings

On July 20, 1858, the first admission was charged for a baseball game, between all-star teams from New York and Brooklyn, at Long Island's Fashion Race Course. The price was 50 cents.

The first commissioner, Kennesaw Mountain Landis, ruled the game with a stern hand. He did what he thought was in the best interests of the game. His successor, Happy Chandler, tried to do the same, and the owners sacked him. In recent years, Fay Vincent was also run off for not being the owners' puppet. The problem is that the owners select the commissioner, but the public expects—and demands—that the commissioner appear to be neutral and that he act with the best interests of the game, not the owners, at heart. As a result, somebody is always going to be unhappy.

Also, remember that before he was commissioner, Bud Selig was an owner. Players weren't too crazy about that, and neither were a lot of people in the media. As for the question of power, Selig has the authority to suspend players and such, but his most important responsibility is keeping an eye on the big picture: keeping all 30 franchises healthy. With the current big market/small market disparity, that's no easy task.

Why Those Outlandish Player Salaries Aren't So Outlandish

I'm certainly no economist. But as *Sports Illustrated* writer Mark Bechtel, who was an economics major in college, has said, it's a fundamental economic principle that no team could survive if it was paying more than it could afford. The teams are making a profit, or they wouldn't survive. So as absurd as the notion sounds that a man should make $12 million a year to play baseball, the fact is that these guys are actually *earning* that money. The owners are obviously still making money, so the players deserve their share—after all, who are the fans paying to see?

Of course, if fans got so fed up with salaries that they refused to pay the ever-escalating ticket prices, the days of the $12 million player would be history. But that's the thing about baseball: No matter how much tickets cost, it seems that fans will pay for them. It's literally the price fans pay for enjoying baseball as much as they do.

Back when I was playing, money wasn't necessarily the object. You wanted to play in the major leagues, and you wanted to get the pension, because the pension probably meant more money than you were going to make in your playing career. So you wanted to get four years in so you'd qualify for that.

The pension system began in 1947, with players making contributions that were matched by the owners. In 1967, Marvin Miller, the head of the players association, got the owners to kick in $4.5 million annually, and the fund has grown steadily ever since. As it has grown, the amount of service time necessary to be vested has shrunk from five years to one day. (Obviously, the more service time a player has, the more he's vested.) As it stands now, a player with five years of major league service gets a $25,200 annuity at age 55. The top pension annuity is $112,221, for 10-year vets at age 62.

> **Talkin' Baseball**
>
> *"He wants Texas back."*
>
> —Los Angeles Dodgers manager Tommy Lasorda, when asked about Mexican-born pitching sensation Fernando Valenzuela's demands during his 1981 contract negotiations

The Perils of Salary Arbitration

One of the stranger things in baseball these days is *salary arbitration*. If a team can't reach an agreement with a veteran player, it can offer him binding arbitration. The team and the player each submit a salary figure and then they argue their case in front of an arbitrator, who then chooses one of the two numbers. There's no middle ground; the arbitrator has to pick one dollar figure or the other.

I've never really understood why a team would want to go to arbitration. To win the case, they have to convince the arbitrator that the player is not worth what he's asking for. And to do this they must, in effect, question his value to the team—while the guy is sitting right there in the room! I know it's business, but I just don't see how this can be a healthy solution. I guess that's why most arbitration cases are settled before they ever get that far.

The players won the right to salary arbitration following a 13-day strike in 1972. In the first arbitration case, before the 1974 season, Minnesota pitcher Dick Woodson won a $30,000 salary over the Twins' offer of $23,000.

Arbitration has become an important route to better money for younger players who don't yet qualify for free agency. As with free agency, a player's contract has to be up in order for him to be eligible. For example, Derek Jeter is eligible, but the Yankees are broaching the idea of a long-term contract, which would avoid arbitration. To be eligible for arbitration, a player generally must have three years of service time, but some players with less than three are eligible under certain circumstances. If a player has three years of service time but isn't yet eligible for free agency (that comes after six years), then either side can call for arbitration without the other's consent; because the player can't become a free agent, he has no other options. If a player is eligible for free agency and his team offers him arbitration, he can either agree to go to arbitration or opt to become a free agent.

The Post-Season Payoff

When I was making $40,000 a year, the prospect of winning the World Series was doubly exciting. Not only did it mean I'd be a part of history, it meant that I'd get a share of the post-season pot. Players are entitled to a certain amount of the post-season revenue. The money then gets divided up into shares, based on a vote of the players. The farther a team advances in the post-season, the bigger their shares are. The players vote to determine who gets a share, a half-share, or a quarter-share. Then the total pot is divided on that basis. So if the total pot was $10 million and there were 50 full shares, each full share would be worth $200,000.

In 1998, a full share for the World Series champion Yankees was worth a record $312,137.33. For players making $8 million that might not be a lot of money, but three Yankees—infielder Homer Bush, catcher Jorge Posada, and pitcher Ramiro Mendoza—earned more from their Series share than they did from their 1998 salary. So there's more at stake in the post-season than just pride.

Strikes, Lockouts, and Other Public Relations Nightmares

Baseball had its first players' strike in 1972. Since then, it seems like every time the collective bargaining agreement—which is the working labor agreement between the owners and players—expires, there's been a work stoppage. (Even the umpires have gone on strike!) The worst came in 1994, when the World Series was canceled because of a *lockout,* which is sort of like a strike by management.

The issues in work stoppages almost always deal with free agency. The players association (or the players union) feels that major league players should be given the utmost freedom in shopping their services, but the owners don't want to see this happen for two reasons. First, they fear that it will upset the competitive balance. Free agents only sign with the teams that can afford them, so the rich would just get richer. Second, and more importantly, the more a free-agency system resembles a free marketplace, the more money players can command. And that costs the owners a lot of money.

The issues are pretty complex, but this much, as we've discussed before, is clear: Work stoppages are very bad for the game. After the 1994 World Series was canceled, many fans finally got fed up and when play resumed, they stayed away from the ballparks in droves. It took several years for the players and owners to win the fans back. Hopefully they all learned their lesson and the situation won't repeat itself.

294

The Least You Need to Know

➤ Players are traded for a variety of reasons, many of which are financial.

➤ Since the advent of free agency, major league player salaries have skyrocketed.

➤ It's crucial for a major league team to be able to draft and sign good young players and develop them in the minor leagues.

➤ The economic inequalities between major league teams remain a threat to the pastime's well-being.

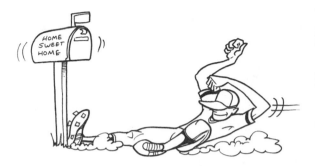

Chapter 22

Bringing Baseball Home

In This Chapter

➤ Radio's revolution

➤ TV's evolution

➤ Radio's re-creation

➤ TV's transformation

In these days of TVs, PCs, VCRs, satellite dishes, superstations, and Internet broadcasts, it seems downright prehistoric to even imagine baseball without radio and television.

But for baseball's first half-century, if you wanted to know what was happening in a game, you had to go to the ballpark. Or, if it were a big game, maybe the local telegraph office would post tickertape with inning-by-inning scores taped to their windows, or the newspaper would issue several editions with updated scores. Scoreboards were also sometimes erected in public areas, to keep fans apprised of the inning-by-inning developments in an important game.

But, as we'll see in this chapter, radio and television have both been very good for baseball, and vice versa.

Baseball Writers: The Media's First Bridge to the Fans

Baseball writing dates back to the mid-1800s. Henry Chadwick, the game's first editor and one of its first writers, began covering baseball in 1858. Known as the Father of Baseball and the Dean of Baseball Writers, Chadwick worked for many New York-area newspapers and publications, including nearly 50 years on the editorial staff of the Brooklyn *Eagle* and 27 years as the editor of the *Spalding Official Baseball Guide*. Chadwick also originated the system of scoring a game, devised the first box score, and compiled the first baseball rule book.

Extra Innings

To find the man known as the Dean of Baseball Writers, you might be surprised to find out that you have to go back more than 100 years. Henry Chadwick, who was the first baseball editor (with the New York *Clipper*) and one of the game's first writers, worked for many New York-area newspapers and publications, including nearly 50 years on the editorial staff of the Brooklyn *Eagle* and 27 years as the editor of the *Spalding Official Baseball Guide*. Known also as the Father of Baseball, Chadwick originated the system of scoring a game and compiled the first baseball rule book. He was inducted into the Baseball Hall of Fame in 1938.

But just as baseball—and the nation—experienced a boom in the 1920s, so did the baseball-writing profession. Among the legendary writers from that period:

➤ **Ford Frick** of the New York *Journal*, who was Babe Ruth's ghostwriter and later National League president and baseball commissioner

➤ **Ring Lardner**, the great writer of vivid, amusing baseball short stories, who had an unmatched capacity to capture the players' lingo

➤ **Fred Leib**, who covered the game in New York for more than 60 years; the colorful Damon Runyon of the New York *American*

➤ The legendary **Grantland Rice**, whose stories brimmed with literary references

➤ **Shirley Povich**, who covered baseball for the *Washington Post* for more than 50 years.

Talkin' Baseball

"Hello, Byron Saam, this is everybody speaking."

—Philadelphia broadcaster Byron Saam

This was the golden age of baseball writing. And the print media was one of the first ways in which the game's profitability was realized. But the '20s also marked the end of the print forum's media monopoly: It was the decade in which baseball would first be broadcast over the airwaves.

Radio Days: Baseball, B.T. (Before Television)

Baseball and radio took huge leaps forward on August 5, 1921, when Harold Arlin broadcast the first game from Forbes Field on Pittsburgh's KDKA, the nation's first radio station, using "wireless telegraphy" and a converted telephone as his microphone. Not even the radio pioneers had a clue what they had wrought, Arlin told Curt Smith in *Voices of the Game,* Smith's seminal book on baseball broadcasting.

"Sometimes the transmitter worked and sometimes it didn't. Sometimes the crowd noise would drown us out and sometimes it wouldn't. And quite frankly, we didn't know what the reaction would be—whether we'd be talking into a total vacuum or whether somebody would actually hear us," Arlin said.

"Our guys at KDKA didn't even think that baseball would last on radio. I did it sort of as a one-shot project.... No one had the foggiest idea, the slightest hint of an inkling, that what we'd started would take off like it did."

But two months to the day later, the first World Series broadcast occurred. Newspaper columnist Grantland Rice described the action over the phone to KDKA, while two Eastern stations re-created the scene. A newspaper reporter relayed the news to the radio stations, where Tommy Cowan repeated the essentials to his audience, blindly making up details and sound effects as he went along, without the benefit of statistics, media guides, scorecards, or any other reference material.

Extra Innings

Graham McNamee, a stage actor and singer, was the nation's first big-time baseball announcer. Working from a seat in the stands, he broadcast a dozen World Series beginning in 1923. The first ex-athlete to announce games, former Cleveland outfielder Jack Graney became the voice of the Indians in 1932. Other early players-turned-announcers included Walter Johnson, Lew Fonseca, Charlie Grimm, Rogers Hornsby, Frank Frisch, and Harry Heilmann. Hall of Fame pitcher Dizzy Dean became beloved for his quirky enthusiasm and reviled for the way he mangled the language.

By the following year, an estimated five million people listened to the World Series, even though only about three million radios could be found in America—which hints at just how popular the broadcasts were. Baseball on radio was such a novelty that retail radio stores would station a loudspeaker on the sidewalk and play-by-play would boom into the street, enticing fans to buy this space-aged invention.

Hall of Fame announcer Ernie Harwell remembers sharing earphones with his older brother, who moved a little piece of wire called a cat whisker over a dab of mercury to pull in a faraway broadcast of the 1926 World Series on his crystal set. When he couldn't join his brother, Harwell wrote in his book, *The Babe Signed My Shoe,* "I would walk through the neighborhood until I heard the baseball broadcast coming through a window. Then I would camp under that window as long as I could without arousing the suspicions of the household."

The dapper Graham McNamee, in his familiar vantage point for calling the World Series.

Back in those days, stations didn't have to pay the teams for the rights to broadcast their games, and by the mid-1920s, five stations were using their own announcers to broadcast Chicago Cubs games. Still, many teams feared broadcasts would deter fans from attending games—why pay to go to the ballpark when you could hear it for free?—so they banned broadcasts. In fact, from 1934 to '38, all three New York teams had a signed pact prohibiting radio broadcasts of their home games.

But when Larry MacPhail—the same man who in Cincinnati had pioneered night baseball in 1935 and who hired Red Barber to call Reds games on radio—was hired to run the Dodgers in 1938, he quickly put an end to that. "[The club owners] did not realize at the time the beneficial effect of radio," said Barber, whom MacPhail brought with him to Brooklyn, "that it would be making families of fans. MacPhail broke that with his broadcasting in Brooklyn in '39 and from then on there's been no question. Radio, television, more fans, more money."

By the 1930s, Americans owned 18 million radios, and gradually, like MacPhail, teams realized that radio actually boosted fan interest, as well as offering both rights fees and free advertising. By the end of World War II, every game of every team was being broadcast by at least one station. Still, half the broadcasts, like that first World Series call, were re-creations of the game—making them, in some respects, about as phony as pro wrestling is today.

Talkin' Baseball

"The Washington Senators and the New York Giants must have played a doubleheader this afternoon—the game I saw and the game Graham McNamee announced."

—Legendary baseball writer Ring Lardner, after listening to McNamee call the 1924 World Series

The Clever Art of Re-Creations

It seems quaint now, and it makes the fans seem incredibly naive and gullible, but the broadcasts of all road games in those early days were fakes. Radio stations thought phone line charges and travel expenses were too high, so they didn't send their announcing crews when teams went on the road.

Instead, the broadcasters stayed home and relied on Western Union. A telegraph operator in the ballpark would relay a concise recap of each at-bat via Morse code, and a telegraph operator at the opposite end would translate the dots and dashes into a code that the announcers had learned to decipher. They would see something like, "Ruth up...B1H (ball one high)...S1L (strike one low)...single...line drive to right field."

The operator delivered the code to Jack Graney in a Cleveland auto showroom. He delivered it to Arch McDonald, the "Rembrandt of the Re-Creation," in a Washington, D.C., drugstore basement. He delivered Cubs play-by-play to "Dutch" Reagan at WHO in Des Moines, Iowa. You might have heard of Dutch. He followed the Cubs to spring training on Catalina Island, and a friend suggested as long as he was that close to Hollywood, he ought to take a screen test. Thus was launched the acting and (later political) career of Ronald Reagan.

A lot of these broadcasters had to be real actors. Some, like Red Barber, let the audience hear the telegraph pounding out the dots and dashes. But most tried to deceive listeners into thinking they were at the ballpark. They used a variety of props. They tapped a hollow block of wood with a stick or pencil to mimic the sound of a batter connecting with a pitch. They played tape recordings of fans cheering, raising or lowering the volume based on the situation. They used sound effects of vendors, of umpires, of baseball chatter, of fans screaming at the umps and at bonehead plays. McDonald hit a gong once for a single, four times for a homer.

McDonald always stayed about an inning behind in case there was a transmission problem. Others tried to keep it as "live" as possible, and if news were slow to arrive—for instance, it was common for the wire to go dead—they made up fairy tales until the problems were fixed. Maybe they'd have one batter foul off 15 straight pitches. Or they'd have a storm blow in and delay the game. Whatever worked.

One time the St. Louis Cardinals' Dizzy Dean was pitching against the Cubs when the wire went dead in Des Moines. So Reagan stalled by telling his listeners about how Dizzy kept rubbing his hands on the resin bag and shaking off signals, and still the wire didn't come back. Finally, he said Dizzy threw a pitch and Billy Jurges fouled it off behind third base, and he described in great detail how two kids got into a fight over the ball. And then he made up a story about Jurges fouling off another that was just a foot wide of being a home run. Finally, after he had Jurges at the plate for about seven minutes, he got the note from the telegraph operator:

Jurges had popped out on the first pitch.

"But maybe I shouldn't tell that story," he recalled years later, when he was known not as Dutch but as Mr. President. "People are suspicious enough of those in politics."

A Brief History of Televised Baseball, 1939–99

The first live radio broadcast of a road baseball game didn't occur until 1946, when the Yankees gave up re-creations. Still, Liberty Broadcasting did a "Game of the Day" almost entirely with re-creations until the majors banned it in 1952. All major league teams gave up on re-creations by the early '50s, but the practice lingered on for years in the minors. The majors had to get rid of re-creations because the public was catching on—and so was television.

The first televised baseball game—the first televised sporting event of *any* kind—occurred on May 17, 1939, when W2XBS, an experimental NBC-TV station, televised the second game of a doubleheader between Princeton and Columbia at New York City's Baker Field.

The first primitive major league telecast occurred on August 26, 1939, with Red Barber announcing a Brooklyn Dodgers-Cincinnati Reds game from Brooklyn's Ebbets Field. Two cameras covered the action for W2XBS. The telecast, to fewer than 400 TV sets, featured uneven sound and a flickering picture that captured the shape of the players but couldn't pick up the ball too well. The *New York Times* reported that "television-set owners as far away as fifty miles viewed the action and heard the roar of the crowd," and "at times it was possible to catch a fleeting glimpse of the ball as it sped from the pitcher's hand toward home plate."

Not until 1947 was the World Series televised, through joint CBS, NBC, and DuMont network links. An estimated three million fans watched the telecast, but radio remained king. The first national baseball telecast was the final National League playoff game on October 3, 1951, which featured Bobby Thomson's famous "shot heard 'round the world."

Red Barber had the first television call of a baseball game, in 1939.

Baseball on TV took off when ABC began to air "The Game of the Week" in 1953. CBS took over in 1955 and expanded its popularity and monopoly. "The Game of the Week" was the only national game that fans could see on TV.

By 1956, 75 percent of homes in the U.S. had at least one television set, and baseball executives feared for the medium's impact on attendance and revenues. "Radio created a desire to see something," said longtime Brooklyn Dodgers president-general manager Branch Rickey, then the chairman of the board of directors for the Pittsburgh Pirates. "Television is giving it to them. Once a television set has broken them of the ballpark habit, a great many fans will never acquire it."

But baseball's presence on television nonetheless increased by leaps and bounds. By the mid-1980s, the cable superstations were reaching 66 million homes and showing more than 500 games a year. A decade later, cable outlets and satellite dishes bring an endless array of games to millions of homes.

Television has emerged as *the* dominant medium for fans. More fans watch games on TV than in person. They can see dozens of games each week on cable, and many more if they have a satellite dish. My buddy bought a dish for his father and they bought the baseball package, and they can watch just about every game in the country. It's wonderful.

Talkin' Baseball

"I know what the word media means. It's plural for mediocre."

—Minor league manager Rocky Bridges

303

Even with just cable, I can flip between two or three games at the same time and catch most of the action just by watching ESPN, CNN/SI, CNN, the superstations, the major networks, and the local stations. Television has sure come a long way.

And now if you move and you can't pick up your favorite team's broadcast over the radio, you can tune into it on the Internet. You can find pitch-by-pitch updates of every game on websites such as ESPN and CBS Sportsline (see Appendix C for details). We've come full circle, in a high-tech sort of way, since the days of the scoreboards posted at the town square and the Western Union office.

Yogi Berra once said, "You can observe a lot just by watching." You can learn a lot, too, by watching baseball games on TV. A lot of good commentators can explain the game. It's like having your own tutor. And, of course, reading this book should do a lot for your knowledge of the game, too.

Let's say you read about the slider here. Next, watch for it on TV. Now, go out to the ballpark and see it. You're learning how to follow and be a part of the game. When you go out to the park, you know what to look for, what to anticipate.

Extra Innings

Many catch phrases of the great baseball announcers have become part of the American language. Mel Allen coined "Going, going, gone!" and "How about that!" Bob Prince first used "We had 'em alllll the way!" and "Kiss it good-bye!" and "How sweet it is!" (The Gunner said Jackie Gleason stole that latter trademark and made it his own.) Red Barber called arguments "rhubarbs," exclaimed "Oh, doctor!" "Hold the phone!" or "The fat's in the fire!" at critical moments in games, and the Southerner drawled to his "Nooo Yahk" audiences (first the Dodgers, then the Yankees) about players "tearin' up the pea patch" and "walkin' in tall cotton." Arch McDonald described runners on base as "ducks on the pond," said a pitch down the middle came "right down Broadway," and greeted a Washington Senators home run with, "There she goes, Mrs. Murphy!"

Mel Allen was the long-time voice of the Yankees and This Week in Baseball.

Where the Games Are

ABC followed up the success of "Monday Night Football" with "Monday Night Base-ball" in 1976, but prime-time baseball has never caught on like its gridiron counter-part, though various networks have experimented with weekly games over the past two decades. The over-the-air networks rarely show baseball in prime time except for the All-Star Game and post-season games.

Fox broadcasts a "Game of the Week" every Satur-day afternoon, and also owns the rights to the 1999 All-Star Game, the 2000 World Series, and some of the Division Series and League Championship Series in 1999 and 2000. NBC will broadcast the 1999 World Series, the 2000 All-Star Game, and parts of the post-season in 1999 and 2000. ESPN broadcasts a single game on Sunday nights and a doubleheader every Wednesday night, and will share the Division Series from 1999 through 2002. Fox SportsNet and its string of regional outlets will cover hundreds of games, and every team has deals with one or more local TV stations to show many of their games.

Talkin' Baseball

"Never was a sport more ideally suited to television than baseball. It's all there in front of you. It's theater, really. The star in the spotlight on the mound, the supporting cast fanned out around him, the mathematical precision of the game moving with the kind of inevitability of Greek tragedy. With the Greek chorus in the bleachers!"

—Vin Scully

Every team has a local radio deal. Nationally, ESPN Radio owns the rights to a "Game of the Week," Sunday night baseball, the All-Star Game, and all postseason games.

Worthwhile Baseball Shows on TV

The majors unveiled the syndicated weekly series, *This Week in Baseball*, in 1977, and it was the highest-rated sport-highlight show for years. But it has lost some of its luster now because it's not as up-to-date as the plethora of sports shows that air today. You can see those highlights on ESPN and the local news five or 10 times before they air on *This Week in Baseball*, which these days is often relegated to weekend mornings, rain delays, and filler after short games.

Now, before games are even over, I'm seeing replays of guys making diving catches and hitting home runs and everything else. You can't beat the thrice-nightly editions of ESPN's *SportsCenter* for sports news and highlights. Currently, my favorite baseball show is *Baseball Tonight*, which airs several times a day during the season on ESPN.

Extra Innings

Ralph Kiner has entertained more baseball fans as a New York Mets broadcaster than he did as a slugger—and he was a Hall of Fame home run hitter. Ralph is famous for his malaprops, like the time he said Jeff Bagwell "was hit 13 times by pitchers' pitches." As opposed to what—catcher's pitches?

Or the time he said Joe Robbie Stadium was the future home of "the new expansion Dolphins"—when the Miami Dolphins had been playing football for two decades, and the new baseball team was the Florida Marlins.

Longtime San Diego Padres broadcaster Jerry Coleman once said a runner "slides into second with a standup double," and a reliever "is throwing up in the bullpen." Harry Caray once announced that Cubs pitcher Chuck McElroy had hit a single, a double, and a triple this year, and "If he gets a homer, he could be hitting for the scale." Uh, that's the cycle, Harry.

How TV Coverage Has Improved

You only needed two fingers to count the number of cameras at that initial baseball telecast in 1939. Today for a big game, you'd need all your fingers and toes to count them all. I don't know that we'll ever get a perfect camera angle for every close play, but they've come close to it. The directors do a tremendous job on the technical side of television. You get to see so many replays from so many angles. You get to see bang-bang plays in slow and super-slow motion. You get to see pitches from overhead, from center field, and even from atop the catcher's mask.

You get to hear managers and coaches hooked up with microphones during the games. And you get so many graphics and stats. You get graphics with scouting reports on every pitcher's best and worst pitches, on every hitter's hot and cold zones. On most networks, you get to see a little box giving the score, the pitch count, the number of outs, and even a little diamond highlighting runners on base. As it did in football, Fox has come up with a lot of these innovations and really pushed the envelope in technical improvements.

Today's telecasts can give you every statistic that's ever been invented, and they've probably invented a few new ones, but announcers can get carried away with statistics. Too many broadcasters use stats as crutches when they should be setting scenes and telling stories. I don't want 100,000 statistics when I watch a game. Let me enjoy the game for just a little bit. Give me a chance to sit back and savor it.

Talkin' Baseball

"You just have to watch your language. You have to turn your four-letter words into five letters."

—Former outfielder Glenn Wilson, on the fine art of broadcasting

The Job of a Broadcaster

There are two main roles in the broadcast booth. The *play-by-play man* simply tells you what's going on—he gives you the facts. The *analyst,* or *color commentator* (and sometimes there are two of them doing a game), takes it one step further and explains things for you: Why did they do that, and what might they do next? Play-by-play men are often guys like NBC's Bob Costas and Fox's Jack Buck, career broadcasters. Analysts are often former players and managers, such as NBC's and ESPN's Joe Morgan and Fox's Tim McCarver.

Today's broadcasters are armed with plenty of information: the team media relations departments provide daily press notes and statistics, and there are also statistical services, such as the Elias Sports Bureau, that provide even more in-depth data. Many networks also employ their own researchers and statisticians. But the best broadcasters are those who do their own digging—by talking to players, managers, and coaches in the clubhouse and around the batting cage, and acquiring their own inside slant.

Some team broadcasters are employees of the club (and may also travel with the team), so it's difficult for them to be openly critical about their team. Some broadcasters for club affiliates also tend to be "homers," which means they're rooting a bit while they're doing the game. Harry Caray was certainly something of a homer, but I know Chicago Cubs fans didn't mind that a bit. National broadcasters like Bob Costas and Joe Morgan have to be completely impartial, though.

I was a color commentator for CBS Radio for nine years, and I also worked on national telecasts for ABC and did Reds games locally. I loved it. Unfortunately, I just couldn't commit to that many games, especially all those games on the road. I didn't want to work every weekend. I do a lot of speaking engagements, and I share parenting of my son. I did the playoffs and World Series for CBS, but when they wanted to increase my regular-season workload from 10 to 18 games, I decided I couldn't sacrifice that much time away from my family.

I don't know how Joe Morgan does it, especially now, when it seems like he's on every network. To get on a red-eye flight and travel across country, and then go back two days later for another game—that's a commitment you have to totally focus on, and I just wasn't in a position to do that. Fans might think, "Oh, man, I'd love to travel like that and go to all those games. It'd be great!" But traveling gets old after 10 or 20 summers, and calling a game is harder than it sounds, even though the best announcers make it look easy.

Catching On

On a TV or radio broadcast, the **play-by-play man** gives you the "who," the "what", and the "where." The **analyst**, or **color commentator** provides the "how" and the "why."

There have been few better baseball play-by-play men than the Dodgers' Vin Scully, shown here in the Ebbets Field press box.

Johnny's Picks: The Best Behind the Mike

The best radio play-by-play men help you draw pictures in your mind, let you envision the ambiance and the grace, and don't scream their heads off over every play. TV play-by-play men usually talk a lot less, since the viewers can see the play for themselves and don't need as much description.

The best analysts, whether on radio or TV, explain and educate fans but don't talk down to them. They give you a little credit for understanding the game. I want to be entertained. I don't want the analyst to make me feel like I don't understand what's going on. Sometimes an analyst comes off sounding like, "I know the game, and you have to listen to me, because I know everything." That drives me up the wall—I have to turn the sound down.

I think **Joe Morgan** does an outstanding job as an analyst on NBC and ESPN, and **Bob Brenly** of Fox has really come along well. ESPN's **Buck Martinez** does a really good job, too. These guys explain things clearly and provide valuable insight and analysis without being condescending or pedantic.

The best play-by-play men? When I worked with **Vin Scully**, the longtime Dodgers and national play-by-play man, he was so good it was scary. I played baseball forever, and I can take in the whole field and understand the game and its nuances, but he knew *everything*. He anticipated things so well, I swear there were times that I thought Vinny had already seen the game and was doing a replay. He was that good. It was a joy the way he unfolded the game in front of you. I also worked with veteran St. Louis Cardinals broadcaster **Jack Buck**, who was great, and longtime Detroit Tigers broadcaster **Ernie Harwell** is in that class, too.

Extra Innings

Before they became TV and radio celebrities, Dan Rather was once a public-address announcer for the Houston Astros and Rush Limbaugh was a runner for Detroit Tigers broadcaster Ernie Harwell.

For 60 years, **Harry Caray** took his love of baseball to the ballpark. Harry started with the Cardinals, then moved to Chicago and the White Sox, and, finally, the Cubs. Yes, he'd be out in left field sometimes—you'd find yourself saying, "What the hell are you talking about, Harry?" But then there'd be a late-inning base hit, the runner would score, and Harry'd be shouting, *"Cubs win! Cubs win! Holy cow!"* He wasn't just a broadcaster doing his job. He was a fan who happened to broadcast the games. His tradition of singing "Take Me Out to the Ballgame"—which he actually started doing in Comiskey Park, when he worked for the White Sox—was a classic.

And now you've got some wonderful, talented young people carrying on the tradition of their fathers. You've got Jack Buck's son, Joe, on Fox. And there's Tom Brenneman, son of Marty, the longtime voice of the Reds. Fox also has Chip Caray, son of TBS's Skip and grandson of the late, great Cubs broadcaster Harry.

Talkin' Baseball

"Well, folks, that's the greatest opening in the history of television, bar none."

—Al Michaels, after an earthquake disrupted ABC's pregame show before Game 3 of the 1989 World Series

I think NBC's **Bob Costas** used to want to show how much he knew, but now he just shows how much he loves and appreciates the game, and he's become a tremendous broadcaster. **Al Michaels**, who used to call Reds games years ago, doesn't do much baseball anymore, but he's great when he does. He's always at the top of his game. Most of today's announcers are. To the others: Do me a favor. Let the game unfold. Tell me when you're giving a good, educated guess. Don't act like you know all the answers. Tell me when a player makes a heck of a play, or when he lets the ball play him, or when he's the victim of a bad hop. Give me the best possible camera angle you can. Make the game real, not a stage play. Treat the game with the love, respect, and appreciation it deserves.

Harry Caray always seemed like he was having a good time when he called a game—and if you were listening to him, you probably were, too.

The Least You Need to Know

➤ The first baseball radio broadcast occurred in 1921.

➤ For about 30 years, road baseball games were re-created on radio with the help of telegraphs, props, and fertile imaginations.

➤ The first baseball TV broadcast was in 1939, but the World Series didn't become a TV staple until 1947.

➤ You can watch hundreds of games if you have cable TV and even more if you have satellite TV.

➤ Play-by-play men Vin Scully and Bob Costas and analysts Joe Morgan, Bob Brenly, and Buck Martinez are some of the best in the business today.

Chapter 23

Everybody Grab a Bat

In This Chapter

➤ A game for all ages

➤ The road to the majors: college versus the minor leagues

➤ International baseball—it's not just our pastime anymore

➤ Why Little League is no small matter

If there's one truth in this sport, it's this: It's never too early to get your kids involved in baseball—and it's never too late to pick up the game as an adult. I started playing with my older brothers when I was six, so by the time I got to the majors at age 19, I'd already been playing for 13 years. Developing skills early is crucial for anyone who aspires to make it all the way to the big leagues.

So far in this book we've concentrated on the major leagues. In this chapter we'll look at various levels of non-big league baseball, from youth leagues to adult leagues, at which people can play and appreciate the game.

The Minor Leagues

Just after World War II, minor league baseball was among the most popular sports in the country. In 1949, nearly 42 million fans attended minor league games, a number that has dropped significantly over the years because of the growing popularity and accessibility of the major league game. It's easier than it used to be to hop in the car and visit a big-league ballpark—or stay home and watch the game on TV. But if you want to experience high-quality baseball with a grassroots feel—and pay a lot less for a ticket—there's no better place to go than to a minor league game.

The concept of a minor league farm system goes back to the early 1920s. Branch Rickey, a front-office executive of the St. Louis Cardinals, came up with the idea. Rickey reasoned that it was easier for a major league team to grow its own players than to bid against other clubs for amateur talent or buy established players from other teams, so he created a system of developing young prospects. Players could be nurtured, and their skills sharpened, as they worked their way up through the system. The same sort of framework is in place for every major league team today. A young player will usually start at the Rookie level, and then, if he continues to develop and improve, progress to Class A, Double A, Triple A, and then on to the majors.

Talkin' Baseball

"It's supposed to be hard. If it wasn't hard, everybody would do it. The hard is what makes it great."

—Jimmy Dugan (Tom Hanks) in the movie *A League of Their Own*

Not many players make it all the way to the major leagues, though: Fewer than 3 percent of all minor leaguers make it to the big leagues. The minors serve not only to give players a chance to refine their skills and mature personally, but the leagues also provide a weeding-out process. It's a Darwinian struggle. Only the strongest survive to see the bright lights of a major league playing field, but the rest of them at least enjoy a few more years playing the game they love.

Besides their primary function as a proving ground for young talent, the minor leagues also serve as a place for big-league veterans to get in an extra year or two while waiting for that one last shot at the majors, and as a training ground for future big-league managers.

Talkin' Baseball

"You've got a hundred more young kids than you have a place for on your club. Every one of 'em has had a goin' away party. They been given the shaving kit and the fifty dollars. They kissed everybody and said, 'See you in the majors in two years.' You see these poor kids who shouldn't even be there in the first place."

—Hall of Fame manager Earl Weaver, on the minor leagues

Minor leaguers are playing for the love of the game—and for a shot at future stardom—but certainly not for the glamour and money. To keep costs down, and because the teams in each league are generally concentrated in a particular geographic region, minor league teams usually travel by bus. The average salary for Triple A players is about $2,000 a month; at Double A it's about $1,600 a month; and at Class A it's about $1,200 a month. (Minor league players are not represented by the major league players union.) The season is a little shorter than 162-game major league schedule, but not much: Triple A and Double A teams play about 145 games a year, and Class A teams play about 130.

College Baseball

On July 1, 1859, Amherst defeated Williams College 73–32 at Pittsfield, Massachusetts, in the first college baseball game. In the late 19th century, it was considered a novelty for professional players to have attended college. That began to change in the 1910s when the Philadelphia Athletics signed five players straight out of college, and by 1927, one third of all the starters in the majors had played at least some college ball.

But college-experienced players dropped off dramatically in '30s for two primary reasons: The Depression made college unaffordable for most, and a vast minor league system was just beginning to emerge, offering players a chance to earn money straight out of high school. By the 1960s, there were still only 20-25 former college players among the 600 major leaguers. This figure has increased steadily through the '90s, as shown by the ratio of high school to college players in the amateur draft each year. In 1975, for example, 16 high schoolers and eight collegians were drafted in the first round. By 1985 those numbers had changed to nine and 17, respectively.

Extra Innings

In December 1998, the NCAA Division I committee ruled that, beginning with the 1999 NCAA playoffs, aluminum bats must be thinner and lighter, to make aluminum bats more like wooden bats. Aluminum bat heads won't be thicker than $2^5/_8$ inches, and the bats' overall weight will be decreased. But the committee didn't limit "exit velocity," how fast balls can fly off the bats, mainly out of concern that there wouldn't be enough bats for the 1999 season. Other divisions decided that the speed should not exceed 93 mph—20 mph slower than previously produced by some aluminum bats. The NCAA considers those speeds dangerous, especially to pitchers; its executive committee will study the issue. Another concern was that aluminum bats have caused a vast increase in home runs: The 1998 College World Series championship game, in which USC beat Arizona State 21–14, lasted four hours as the teams combined for nine home runs and 39 hits.

Today, more than two-thirds of major leaguers have some sort of college experience under their belt. As that number indicates, the college route now is just as viable as the minor league route for getting to the big leagues.

There are five basic differences between the college game and the pro game. In college baseball:

➤ There are no roll blocks allowed while sliding into a base.

➤ Tobacco products (i.e., chewing tobacco) aren't allowed on the field.

➤ Double ear flaps on batting helmets are required.

➤ The balk rule is relaxed, meaning that the pitcher need not step toward the base while throwing.

➤ Most significantly, aluminum bats are used.

The Road to the Big Leagues: College vs. the Minors

As in any sport, success in baseball ultimately depends on hard work over a long period of time to cultivate and develop natural talent. In baseball, that means joining an organized league at an early age and allowing skilled coaches to guide a player's development. By the time a player reaches high school, the star-caliber guys usually have emerged. While there always will be rare examples of players who were cut from their high school baseball team and went on to star in the major leagues, the stark reality is that mediocre players in their late teens rarely have a shot at the bigs.

The traditional post–high school route was for the best players to be drafted by a major league team and be assigned to a minor league ballclub for an extended apprenticeship. Such players would be promoted up through the ranks on their merit until they reached the big leagues.

In recent years an alternative path has emerged. The quality of baseball now played at major colleges is the equal to that played in the low minor leagues, and major league scouts keep an eye on talent on the college level. Players drafted out of college typically are assigned to the minor leagues, but the apprenticeship is shortened.

Current top college baseball powers include: LSU (the 1998 College World Series winner), Wichita State, Arizona, Oklahoma State, Stanford, Miami, USC, Pepperdine, UC-Fulton, and Texas.

Players who have always dreamed of making the big leagues and yet weren't drafted by a major league organization out of high school or college still have one last chance to turn the heads of pro scouts. Major league teams host periodic tryout sessions for aspiring ballplayers. It's a long shot, but players who shine might earn an opportunity. Such sessions are scheduled periodically and are publicized through the local media.

Independent Leagues

The independent leagues are the fringes of professional baseball. The teams are made up mostly of players who have spent some time in the minor leagues. Most players have been released, or were never considered good enough to sign in the first place. It's the place for dreamers, hangers-on, and guys looking to muster one last hurrah.

But many players have used the independent leagues as a place to display their talents to the scouts before moving on to the affiliated minor leagues.

What's the difference between *affiliated teams* and *independent teams*? An affiliated team is a member of the National Association of Professional Baseball Leagues (NAPBL) and is a part of the development system for Major League Baseball. Those teams, which are also designated Class A, Double A, or Triple A, are registered trademarks of Minor League Baseball. The classification indicates the level of play. Players climb the ladder through the minor league system, moving up toward Triple-A as they improve. An established major leaguer will also sometimes put in a minor league stint when he's rehabbing an injury.

Independent professional baseball is a bit different. Generally established as business ventures only, these teams and leagues may have a loose, unofficial relationship with Major League Baseball, and many players have moved from the independent ranks to minor league as well as major league ball.

Catching On

An **affiliated** team is one that is a member of the National Association of Professional Baseball Leagues (NAPBL) and is a part of the development system for Major League Baseball. An **independent** team or league may have a loose, unofficial relationship with Major League Baseball, but they're in business for themselves.

Extra Innings

In 1941 Joe DiMaggio hit in 56 consecutive games and Ted Williams hit .406, both outstanding feats. But Cleveland Indians outfielder Jeff Heath had more hits (199) than either player, hitting .340 with 123 RBIs. The Canadian-born (Fort William, Thunder Bay) Heath played for the Indians, Washington Senators, St. Louis Browns, and Boston Braves during his 14-year major league career, finishing with a career average of .293.

The World's Game: International Competition

Though baseball is the quintessential American game, in many respects it's also the world's game. Today baseball is played in every corner of the globe. If you want evidence of the game's growing world-wide popularity, all you have to do is scroll the rosters of a few major league and minor league teams to see the myriad countries that players list as their home: everywhere from Latin America to Japan to Australia.

The major leagues' best-known import in 1998 was Orlando "El Duque" Hernandez of Cuba, who helped the New York Yankees win the World Series.

The International League, baseball's first minor league, was formed in 1877. Three years earlier, the Boston Red Stockings and Philadelphia Athletics had conducted the major leagues' first foreign tour. This tour planted the seeds of the sport all around the world, but nowhere did the game take root quite like it did in Japan, where today the most popular sport is *beisboru*.

The first Japanese professional baseball team, the Nihon Undo Kyokai, debuted in 1920. The first pro league in Japan began play in 1936. In the last 20 years, the quality of Japanese baseball has improved dramatically. While a team of the best major leaguers would probably beat a team full of Japanese all-stars four out of five times, Japan has produced several major league–caliber players in the last few years, such as pitchers Hideo Nomo (currently of the New York Mets) and Hideki Irabu (currently of the Yankees).

Extra Innings

Who is baseball's all-time home run king? Technically speaking, it's not Hank Aaron, who only leads the *U.S.* major leagues. Sadaharu Oh, who hit 868 homers in his 22-year career with the Japanese League's Yomiuri Giants of Tokyo, is really the champ. (Appropriately, "Oh" in Japanese means "king.") Oh, whose 55 homers in 1964 set the Japanese single-season record, developed his left-handed stroke by swinging a samurai sword until he could cut a straw doll in half with one slice. His most memorable cut came on September 3, 1977, when he when he hit #756 into the right field bleachers of Tokyo's Koraku-en Stadium, passing Henry Aaron as the world's all-time home run leader. Oh retired in 1980 and became the Giants' manager four years later, guiding the team to a Japan Series appearance in '87, He resigned after five seasons; following a stint as a television analyst, he returned to the dugout in '95 to manage the Fukuoka Daiei Hawks.

Finding the Right Level

Baseball enthusiasts of all ages and skill levels have numerous opportunities in cities across the United States to join a league suited to their development and skill level. Each league typically has variations on certain baseball rules, but the basics remain the same.

As both parent and child search for a league that suits the player's level, it's important to keep these factors in mind:

➤ **Skill level**   Will teammates be similar in age and talent?

➤ **Proximity**   Are the league's baseball diamonds within a short drive or walk?

➤ **Cost**   Does the league fee include uniforms, caps, and umpires' fees, or could hidden costs mount up?

➤ **Coaching**   Is personal attention available, or will flaws in fundamentals at the plate or on the field go unnoticed?

Talkin' Baseball

"A ballplayer's got to be kept hungry to become a big leaguer. That's why no boy from a rich family ever made the big leagues."

—Hall of Famer Joe DiMaggio

➤ **Facilities** Are the fields maintained well, or will rocks and broken glass on the infield spoil the fun and increase risk of injury?

➤ **Equipment** Does the league supply catcher's equipment, uniforms, and bats, or do players have to provide them?

➤ **Philosophy** Is the goal simply to win, or can players have fun and improve their game as well?

➤ **Progression** Does the league structure allow players to hone their skills and move up to a higher level?

Extra Innings

Also known as the Latin American World Series, the Caribbean World Series was first held in 1949 with Cuba, Puerto Rico, Panama, and Venezuela as the participating countries. Over the years, the Caribbean World Series, which is now held as a winter event among the major Latin American leagues, has attracted some of the top major league players of Hispanic descent. Recently, big leaguers such as the Alomar brothers (Sandy and Roberto), Sammy Sosa, and Carlos Baerga have participated in the Series, which is one of the biggest sporting events in Latin America each year.

Tryouts are common in almost all leagues, though in youth leagues such an audition is typically designed to screen players for placement in the appropriate skill level and to provide for parity among the teams, rather than to exclude any players from participating.

Youth Leagues

Youth baseball leagues are organized by schools, municipalities, park districts, churches, civic organizations, and non-profit groups chartered exclusively for that purpose. They typically are organized by geographic area or town.

The largest organized youth sports program in the world is Little League Baseball, which has about three million participants on 190,000 teams in more than 80 countries, including 2.5 million players in all 50 states. Little League has become the model for many other youth baseball leagues since it was founded in 1939 in Williamsport,

Pennsylvania. The league features divisions separated by age for players between the ages of 8 and 18. Prospective players can call (717) 326-1921 for information about the nearest Little League affiliated league.

Every August in Williamsport (population 32,400), one of the most thrilling events in baseball takes place: the Little League World Series. The journey to Williamsport begins each year on June 15 for the three million or so Little Leaguers who play in countries all over the world, from the Dominican Republic to Taiwan to the U.S. Each local Little League city selects its 14-player tournament team to represent the town in the tournament. Over the next two months, more than 7,400 teams play in district, state, and regional competitions. According to the folks in Little League, there are as many tournament games played in these two months as there are in six full seasons at the major league level.

The Little League World Series was first played in 1939 with three teams, and since 1947 has featured eight teams, but in 2001 the field will expand to 16. A new multimillion-dollar stadium is also planned, replacing the existing 40-year-old stadium and doubling the seating capacity to 10,000.

Extra Innings

Over the years, many well-known names have played in the Little League World Series, including former National League MVPs Dale Murphy and Mike Schmidt, legendary pitchers Jim Palmer and Nolan Ryan, NASA astronaut Story Musgrave, and former senator Bill Bradley, to name a few.

Other leagues designed for youths include the Bronco League (ages 11-12), Pony League (ages 13-14), Babe Ruth League (ages 13-15), and Colt League (ages 15-16). Teenagers under the age of 18 are eligible to play American Legion Baseball.

Adult and Semipro Leagues

Like youth leagues, leagues for adults come in all types. There are company-organized leagues, park leagues, and municipal leagues. There also are leagues geared toward either younger players or older players, while other leagues have non-traditional rules that require lob pitching or some other unusual constraint.

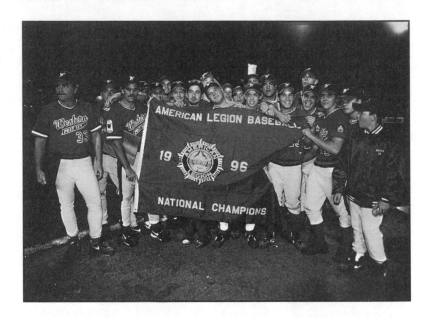

The thrill of victory, as displayed by the 1996 American Legion Baseball national champs.

To find out what's in your area, would-be players should call local municipal and park recreation departments. Like youth leagues, some adult baseball leagues are organized by churches or other non-profit groups, so it might be necessary to scout area parks to discover the caliber and type of leagues available.

Higher quality baseball is played in semipro leagues. Typically such leagues are geared to former high school and college athletes who are very skilled. One of the largest national semipro leagues is sponsored by the 60-year-old National Baseball Congress. The group has 250 affiliated teams across the country and conducts district, state, regional, and national championship tournaments.

Talkin' Baseball

"There is no logical reason why girls shouldn't play baseball. It's not that tough. Not as tough as radio and TV announcers make it out to be .... Some can play better than a lot of guys who've been on that field .... Baseball is not a game of strength; hitting is not strength."

—Hank Aaron

Women's Baseball

Preparing for the possibility that the major leagues would shut down during World War II, Chicago Cubs owner Philip K. Wrigley planned to form a women's softball league that would play in major league ballparks. When the big leagues stayed in business, Wrigley went with a scaled-down version of his plan, switching to baseball and forming a four-team league with clubs in Kenosha, Wisconsin (Belles); Racine, Wisconsin (Belles); Rockford, Illinois (Peaches); and South Bend, Indiana (Blue Sox).

The All-American Girls Professional Baseball League, the first organized women's baseball league, debuted in 1943 with underhand pitching and a 12-inch ball. Within a few years the league switched to overhand pitching and a smaller ball, and increased the distance between the bases from 65 feet to 72 feet. The league, which was the subject of the 1992 movie *A League of Their Own*, peaked in 1948 with 10 teams and total attendance of close to one million. It folded in 1954.

An all-women's baseball league wasn't established again until 1987, when Darlene Mehrer founded the American Women's Baseball Association in Glenview, IL. The league adopted a few rule changes, such as a 50-foot pitching distance and 80 feet between the bases. It lasted only a few years.

Though there currently aren't any operational professional leagues for women to shoot for, there's no denying that baseball remains a popular sport among women of all ages. Today, for example, there are about 8,000 girls playing Little League baseball alone.

In recent years there has also been a growth in women's baseball leagues at the amateur and semipro level, especially in the larger metropolitan areas. Potential players should check with their local parks system for information on such leagues in their area.

Extra Innings

In 1994, an all-women's baseball team named the Colorado Silver Bullets was formed to play games against men's minor league teams. In their first game, on May 8, 1994, the Silver Bullets, who were led by first baseman Julie Croteau, lost 19-0 to a group of Northern League all-stars. Two weeks later, the Silver Bullets announced they would play no more games against male professionals. The team, which was financed by Coors Brewery and featured Hall of Fame pitcher Phil Niekro as manager, notched its first win two weeks later, beating a 35-and-over men's amateur team in St. Paul, Minn. For their first season, the club drew more than 300,000 fans and compiled a record of 6-37. The team disbanded after the 1997 season when Coors decided to cut funding.

A League of Your Own

One of the enduring American rituals is sandlot baseball, where a group of neighborhood kids form two baseball teams and square off in a dusty lot for bragging rights. The rules are casual but the rivalry is intense. To combine the appeal of the do-it-yourself approach of sandlot baseball with the structure of a league, pioneer players sometimes band together to form their own league. It's a lot of hard work, but the rewards of creating a new tradition are obvious.

The short-lived Colorado Silver Bullets gave female stars such as first baseman Julie Croteau a chance to play pro ball.

Here's a checklist of what to think about when forming a league:

➤ **Mission**   It's important to put in writing why a new league is being created. What are the guidelines for players? What are the league rules? Just putting the league's mission and plan in writing clarifies planning. And it's crucial to know whether all of the league organizers are of like mind on crucial issues to avoid later problems.

➤ **Players**   Generally it's a good idea to gear a league to a certain caliber of player, whether beginning, experienced, or advanced. Naturally there will be variations in talent, but if players of a certain skill and/or age level are not recruited up front, there's the danger of having wide variations in play, resulting in frustration for participants. Recruit players from existing leagues, among a circle of friends, or through newspaper advertising.

League founders can schedule a general tryout and draft attended by the coaches from the various teams, or the league can put the responsibility of player recruitment on the coaches of each of the teams. The former can ensure some uniformity of talent on each team, while the latter can decentralize the process.

➤ **Umpires**   The quality of umpires can make or break a league. The more ambitious league founders will want to recruit and train their own umpires, but simply starting up a league can be overwhelming. Instead, it's recommended to contact the National Association of Umpires at (316) 267-3372, or a similar group, to obtain a list of certified umpires in the area. Also check with existing leagues in the area to recruit officials.

➤ **Fields**   The search for a baseball diamond requires a league organizer to pound the pavement in search of existing fields at public parks. The recommended approach is to limit the search to a certain geographic area and to scout out locations, rather than contacting park districts and municipalities to discuss facilities sight unseen. Since it is likely that there are existing leagues in the area, many choice times and dates may already be taken. Organizers should be realistic about the options in the league's first season.

It's essential to include among the league organizers an attorney to ensure that any contracts to rent baseball fields are legally binding and protect the league's interests. That means building in rain-makeup days and adequate dates for playoffs.

➤ **Insurance**   The possibility of injuries to players or damage to property is very real. And a lawsuit can be a fatal blow to a young league. Insurance coverage, therefore, should be in place before the first pitch is thrown. Organizers will be wise to scout out existing leagues and inquire about their insurance coverage. Insurance should be considered when a field is rented, since public bodies often have coverage in place only for existing leagues. Here again, an attorney is a crucial part of the league formation committee.

➤ **Fees**   Only when rental of fields, cost of umpires, and insurance coverage are firmed up should players' fees be set. It's at this point that league organizers should consider whether it's important to require uniforms and other hallmarks of established leagues. Or is cost containment important until a league is firmly established?

Talkin' Baseball

"Well, this year I'm told the team did well because one pitcher had a fine curve ball. I understand that a curve ball is thrown with a deliberate attempt to deceive. Surely that is not an ability we should want to foster at Harvard."

—Charles William Eliot, Harvard president from 1869 to 1909, on why he wanted to drop baseball at the university

The Least You Need to Know

➤ It's never too early—or too late—to get involved in organized baseball.

➤ Little League Baseball, which has about three million participants in more than 80 countries, is the largest organized youth sports program in the world.

➤ The two most common ways for a player to reach the major leagues are to play college ball and then get drafted, or to go straight from high school into a team's minor league system.

➤ Baseball is played all over the world, and though the best ball is played in the U.S., the quality of players around the world has improved immensely in the last 20 years.

Chapter 24

Be a Superfan

In This Chapter

➤ The fundamentals of fandom

➤ It ain't rocket science: how to calculate stats

➤ Covering the baseball beat: where to go for information

➤ Why pay to go when you can watch on TV for free?

Before I ever stepped onto a major league field, I was a fan—a rabid fan. My favorite player was Mickey Mantle, and I tried to emulate everything he did: How he walked, how he talked, how he held the bat, how he ran to first base. I studied him as hard as any subject in school, and in doing so I learned the fundamentals of the game.

But you don't have to be a baseball zealot to be involved with the sport. You can watch games on television. You can read about baseball in the newspaper and in magazines. You can follow it on the Internet. You can debate it on the radio. And, of course, you can go sit in the stands and watch a game unfold right in front of you. But no matter what your level of involvement is, always remember this: Have fun. It's a game, so treat it as such.

How to Read a Box Score

As a fan, one of the most basic things you need to know how to do is read a *box score,* a chart that provides a concise statistical summary of a baseball game. During the baseball season, you'll find box scores every day in the sports section of your newspaper. To someone who doesn't follow the game, a box score can look like inscrutable hieroglyphics. But once you break it down and get an understanding of all the symbols and numbers, reading a box score becomes as easy—and as entertaining—as reading the comics.

A sample box score is shown on the next page. The format here is an *extended box score*, the one used by most newspapers today (though you'll notice slight variations in style and content from paper to paper). "Extended" basically means that it includes a few more bells and whistles than your basic box score, such as strikeouts and walks for batters, pitch counts for pitchers, and updated batting averages and ERAs for all the players who appeared in the game. As we break down the components of the box score, we'll refer to different parts of the box shown in the figure.

Talkin' Baseball

"Open up a ballplayer's head and you know what you'd find? A lot of little broads and a jazz band."

—Former manager Mayo Smith

Catching On

A **box score** is a chart that provides a concise statistical summary of a baseball game.

The first thing to look at in a box score is, of course, the final score, which usually appears at the top. In our example, the New York Yankees have defeated the Tampa Bay Devil Rays 8–3. You can tell the game was played in New York, because the first thing you see is a list of Tampa Bay batters. In almost all cases in statistics, and especially in a box score, the visiting team is listed first—because they bat first.

A series of abbreviations serve as the column headings. Going from left to right, the abbreviations go as follows: AB (for at-bats), R (for runs scored), H (for hits), BI (or RBI, for runs batted in); BB (for bases on balls, or number walks), SO (for strikeouts), and Avg. (for the player's cumulative season batting average after the game).

The first player listed is Winn, the Devil Rays' leadoff hitter. (Box scores usually use only a player's last name, unless there are more than one player with the same last name.) The letters "cf" follow Winn's name, meaning he played center field. (The following table lists the abbreviations used for all the positions.)

Common Abbreviations for Positions

Abbreviation	Position
p	pitcher
c	catcher
1b	first baseman
2b	second baseman
3b	third baseman
ss	shortstop
lf	left fielder
cf	center fielder
rf	right fielder
dh	designated hitter
ph	pinch-hitter
pr	pinch-runner

YANKEES 8, DEVIL RAYS 3

Tampa Bay	AB	R	H	BI	BB	SO	Avg.
Winn cf	5	0	1	0	0	2	.278
QMcCracken lf	3	0	0	0	0	0	.292
Robinson lf	2	0	0	0	0	1	.000
BSmith 3b	4	0	1	0	0	2	.276
McGriff 1b	3	1	3	0	0	0	.284
SMcClain pr-1b	1	1	0	0	0	0	.100
Trammell dh	4	1	1	0	0	0	.286
MKelly rf	1	0	0	1	1	0	.240
RButler rf	2	0	1	2	0	0	.226
Ledesma ss	4	0	2	0	0	1	.324
Cairo 2b	4	0	0	0	0	0	.268
Difelice c	4	0	2	0	0	0	.230
Totals	**37**	**3**	**11**	**3**	**1**	**6**	

NY Yankees	AB	R	H	BI	BB	SO	Avg.
Knoblauch 2b	1	1	0	0	2	0	.265
Bush 2b	1	1	1	0	0	0	.380
Jeter ss	3	1	1	0	0	1	.324
O'Neill rf	2	0	1	1	0	0	.317
Curtis lf-cf	1	1	1	1	1	0	.243
BWilliams cf	2	1	2	1	0	0	.339
b-Ledee ph-lf	1	0	0	0	0	0	.241
LarsAnderson 1b	2	0	0	0	0	1	.381
Sojo 1b	2	1	1	1	0	0	.231
Strawberry dh	2	0	2	0	0	0	.247
a-KipHesse ph-dh	1	1	0	0	1	0	.291
Spencer lf-rf	4	1	1	4	0	1	.373
JPosada c	3	0	0	0	0	2	.268
Brosius 3b	3	0	0	0	0	0	.300
Lowell 3b	1	0	0	0	0	0	.267
Totals	**29**	**8**	**10**	**8**	**4**	**5**	

Tampa Bay	0 0 0	1 0 2	0 0 0 — 3	11	1
NY Yankees	0 0 2	0 5 1	0 0 x — 8	10	0

a-walked for Strawberry in the 5th; b-pinch-hit for Williams in the 7th.

E—Ledesma (16). **LOB**—Tampa Bay 18, New York 10. **2B**—McGriff (33, Bruske), Strawberry (11, Rekar), Trammell (18, Irabu). **3B**—BWilliams (5, Rekar). **HR**—Spencer (10, 5th inning off ALopez, 3 on, 2 out). **RBIs**—MKelly (33), RButler 2 (20), O'Neill (116), BWilliams (97), Sojo (14), Spencer 4 (27), Curtis (56). **SB**—Knoblauch (31, 2nd base off Yan/Difelice). **CS**—Winn (12, 2nd base by Bruske/J Posada), Curtis (5, 2nd base by A Lopez/Difelice). **S**—Jeter. **SF**—BWilliams. **GIDP**—Brosius. **2-out RBIs**—RButler 2, Sojo, Spencer 4, Curtis. **Runners left in scoring position, 2 out**—Difelice 2, Robinson 1, JPosada 2. **Picked off**—Knoblauch (2nd base, Yan). **DP**—Tampa Bay 1.

A sample box score.

To the right of Winn's name are a series of numbers, which are called his *line*—his statistics from the game. He had five at-bats, scored no runs, had one hit, had no runs batted in, and struck out twice. So right away we know that Winn didn't have a particularly good game.

The team's number-two hitter to start the game was Q. McCracken. Looking at his numbers you can tell that he went hitless in three at-bats. Below McCracken is Robinson, who also played left field. The fact that he's listed below McCracken and played the same position tells us that he replaced McCracken at some point in the game. Substitutes are always listed below the player whose spot in the batting order they took. (Some newspapers, such as *USA Today,* will slightly indent the names of substitutes in the box score to make them more noticeable.)

Now look three spots below Robinson and you'll see S. McClain, who also played the same position as the player above him. Behind McClain's name, however, is "pr-1b." This indicates that McClain first entered the game as a pinch-runner, replacing McGriff, and then stayed in the game as the first baseman. Many box scores include a footnote that tells you how a pinch-hitter performed; the Yankees' Ledee is an example of that in our sample box. At the bottom of the list of Tampa Bay's hitters is a line that gives the team's totals in all the categories.

Still going down the box score, the next section is dedicated to giving the same information for the Yankees. Below that, you'll see the *line score,* which is the inning-by-inning account of how many runs were scored. The run, hit, and error totals for each team are listed in the last three columns.

Below that is a section that gives the particulars of the teams' and individuals' batting and baserunning performance. (See the following table for a complete list of statistical abbreviations. Note: Many of these abbreviations are used in box scores; you'll see others in team statistical summaries and the like.)

Common Abbreviations for Statistics

Abbreviation	Statistic
Offensive Statistics	
G	Games
AB	At-bats
H	Hits
2B	Doubles
3B	Triples
HR	Home runs
TB	Total bases
R	Runs scored
RBI or BI	Runs batted in
BB or TBB	Total bases on balls (or walks)
IBB	Intentional bases on balls (or walks)

Abbreviation	Statistic
SO or K's	Strikeouts
LOB	Runners left on base
HBP	Times hit by pitch
S or SH	Sacrifice hits
SF	Sacrifice flies
SB	Stolen bases
CS	Times caught stealing
SB%	Stolen base percentage
GIDP or GDP	Times grounded into double play
Avg. or BA	Batting average
OBP	On-base percentage
SLG	Slugging percentage
PA	Plate appearances

Pitching Statistics

G	Games pitched
GS	Games started
CG	Complete games
GF	Games finished
IP	Innings pitched
H	Hits allowed
R	Runs allowed
ER	Earned runs allowed
HR	Home runs allowed
SH	Sacrifice hits allowed
SF	Sacrifice flies allowed
HBP or HB	Hit batsmen
BB or TBB	Total bases on balls issued
IBB	Intentional bases on ball issued
SO or K's	Strikeouts
WP	Wild pitches
IR	Inherited runners
IRS	Inherited runners who scored
QS	Quality starts
Bk	Balks
W	Wins
L	Losses
Pct.	Winning percentage
ShO	Shutouts
S or SV	Saves
ERA	Earned run average
Avg., Opp. BA, or BAA	Batting average allowed
NP	Number of pitches thrown

Defensive Statistics

G	Number of games at position
GS	Number of starts

continues

continued

Abbreviation	Statistic
PO	Putouts
A	Assists
E	Errors
DP	Double plays turned
PB	Passed ball
FA OR FP	Fielding average or fielding percentage
Other Abbreviations	
T	Time (length) of game
A	Attendance

The next section of the box score is devoted to summarizing each team's pitching performance for the game. By referring to the abbreviation table, you can examine how each pitcher performed in our sample game. R. White of Tampa Bay, who gave up two runs in two-thirds of an inning and has (L, 2–6) next to his name, took the loss, dropping his record for the season to 2–6. Bruske, the starting pitcher for the Yankees, won the game (hence the W), for his first win of the season.

The final section of the box score provides some additional stats on pitchers, and lets you know who the umpires were, the time of the game, the attendance, and the weather and wind conditions.

Extra Innings

The first box score, a summary of New York's 37–19 win over Brooklyn, appeared in the October 25, 1845, edition of the *New York Herald*. The brainchild of editor/writer Henry Chadwick, the first box score wasn't nearly as detailed as those that you see in newspapers today: It listed only the number of outs made and runs scored by each batter.

How to Score a Game

Keeping a baseball *scorecard* is an easy and fun way to keep a concise record of each game. For players coming up through the ranks in a school or recreational league, the scorecard is an efficient way to evaluate each player's performance. For fans watching a game at any level, keeping score is also a good way to "stay in the game," really concentrate on it, and perhaps end up with a treasured souvenir of a no-hitter, perfect game, or other memorable performance.

There is no "standard" method for scoring a baseball game; if 10 avid fans scored the same game and compared their scorecards, they'd all have their own unique symbols and shorthand. The method described here uses the basic principles and will produce a detailed account of a game. The important thing in scoring a game is to use a style that is comfortable and comprehensible, first and foremost, to the person scoring.

Catching On

A **scorecard** is a sheet of paper or cardboard, usually included in a program and sold separately at the ballpark, on which fans can record the batter-by-batter progress of a game. The tradition dates back to the 1880s.

The following figure shows a partially completed scorecard. Like any scorecard, it uses a certain set of symbols to track each player's progress around the bases. One way to do this is to make the box in the row next to each player's name and in the appropriate inning column into a diamond.

Tampa Bay	IP	H	R	ER	BB	SO	NP	ERA
Rekar	2	2	0	0	0	0	30	4.98
RWhite (L, 2-6)	2/3	2	2	2	1	0	18	3.80
Duvall	1/3	1	0	0	0	1	11	6.75
Yan	1 2/3	2	3	3	2	3	38	3.86
Aldred	0	0	1	1	1	0	10	3.73
ALopez	1 1/3	3	2	2	0	0	20	2.60
RTatis	1	0	0	0	0	0	11	13.89
DSpringer	1	0	0	0	0	1	10	5.45
NY Yankees	**IP**	**H**	**R**	**ER**	**BB**	**SO**	**NP**	**ERA**
Bruske (W, 1-0)	5	4	1	1	1	2	71	3.00
Irabu (S, 1)	4	7	2	2	0	4	92	4.06

Duvall pitched to 1 batter in the 4th; Aldred pitched to 1 batter in the 5th.

IBB—off Yan (KipHesse). **HBP**—by Rekar (Posada). **WP**—Yan.
PB—Difelice. **Umpires**—HP, Zitzewitz; 1B, Vinyon; 2B, Tongen, 3B, Husemoller.

T—2:53. **A**—49,608. **Weather**—82 degrees, partly cloudy. **Wind**—12 mph, left to right.

A sample scorecard.

One line, drawn from the center of the bottom of the box ("home plate") to the middle of the right side ("first base"), indicates that the hitter reached first base safely. A second line drawn to the top of the box means the runner reached second, and so forth. For a runner who scores, the diamond is completed and often colored in.

Talkin' Baseball

"Any person claiming to be a baseball fan who does not also claim to have invented the quickest, simplest, and most complete method of keeping score probably is a fraud."

—*Washington Post* columnist Thomas Boswell

Various symbols and abbreviations are used to indicate how each runner reached base and how he moved to subsequent bases. And often numbers are written near each base to indicate the position in the batting order of the hitter who was at the plate when that runner advanced to that base.

Universal to all scoring methods is the numbering system for the defensive positions. That way, by simply writing a number or two on your scorecard, you can indicate in a small amount of space what transpired on a given play. The following table lists the number assigned to each position on the field.

Numbers Assigned to Defensive Positions

Position	Number
Pitcher	1
Catcher	2
First base	3
Second base	4
Third base	5
Shortstop	6
Left field	7
Center field	8
Right field	9

The other essential component of a scorecard is a system of symbols or abbreviations, which will likely vary a bit depending on who's doing the scoring. The next table lists some common scoring symbols.

Common Scoring Symbols

Symbol	Stands For
1B	Single
2B	Double
3B	Triple

Symbol	Stands For
HR	Home run
BB	Base on balls (or walk)
IW	Intentional walk
E	Error
HP	Hit by pitch
K	Strikeout (swinging)
Backwards "K"	Strikeout (looking)
WP	Wild pitch
PB	Passed ball
BK	Balk
L	Line drive
B	Bunt
FC	Fielder's choice
F	Flyout
FO	Foul out
DP	Double play
SH	Sacrifice hit
SF	Sacrifice fly
SB	Stolen base
CS	Caught stealing
PO	Picked off
PH	Pinch hitter
PR	Pinch runner

By consulting the two tables, you can interpret the sample scorecard like this:

In the first inning, Rose singled and stole second while Griffey was batting. Griffey grounded out to the second baseman for the first out of the inning (outs can be tallied with a circled numeral), with Rose moving to third on the play. Morgan struck out swinging. Bench homered (hey, it's my sample, right?), driving in two runs (runs batted in can be tallied with dots in the corner of the appropriate box). Perez flew out to center field to end the inning. (Two runs and two hits are tallied at the bottom of the scorecard.)

To open the second inning, Foster walked. Concepcion reached first and Foster second on an error by the shortstop. With Geronimo hitting, both runners moved up one base on a wild pitch. Geronimo then struck out looking. Driessen, pinch-hitting for Gullett, hit a sacrifice fly to left, driving in Foster. Rose lined out to first to end the inning, stranding Concepcion on second. (One run and no hits.)

Many scorecards, like our sample, have space to record each pitcher's stats, as well as extra-base hits, time of the game, attendance, and other extras.

How to Read the Standings

Once you have a team to root for, you'll want to track their progress in the won-lost column, which is really the most important statistic there is. The best way to do that is by checking the *standings,* which is a listing of the teams in each division, ranked according to who has the best record, or *winning percentage.* The next figure shows what the standings for the National League West might look like.

When reading the standings in the newspaper or online, the most important figure to look at is the *Games Behind* column (under the heading GB). That column tells you how many games behind (or ahead) your team is with respect to the division leader, as well as all the other teams in the division. This is the universal method used to track a team—that's why you hear fans or sportscasters say something like, "They trail by eight games," or "their lead is five-and-a-half games." (Read on to see what they mean by a half-game.)

Sample division standings.

NATIONAL LEAGUE WEST				
TEAM	**W**	**L**	**Pct.**	**GB**
San Diego	98	64	.605	—
San Francisco	89	74	.546	9 1/2
Los Angeles	83	79	.512	15
Colorado	77	85	.475	21
Arizona	65	97	.401	33

To figure out how many games your team is behind the division leader, add the difference between the two teams' win totals and the difference between the loss totals, and divide by two. Let me give you an example: In the standings in the figure, San Diego's record is 98–64 and San Francisco's is 89–74. The difference in the win column is 9 games (98 minus 89); in the loss column it's 10 games (74 minus 64). Nine plus 10 equals 19, divide that by two and you get $9^1/_2$, which is how many games San Francisco trails San Diego by. (Of course, you don't have to do the math: It's right there in the GB column. But that's where the number comes from.)

The Magic Number

Around late summer, you may have heard people talking about a baseball team's *magic number.* There's no wizardry involved: A team's magic number is simply the number of wins and/or the number of losses from its closest competitor that it needs to clinch a playoff spot. Let me give you an example: Let's say the Reds are in first place by 12 games over the Astros, with 20 games remaining for each team. The Reds' magic number to clinch the division title would be nine—meaning that any combination of Reds' wins and Astros' losses that adds up to nine would clinch the crown for the Reds. Say the Reds won five games in a row and the Astros lost four games in a row—then the Reds would lead by 16½ games with 16 games to go for Houston and 15 left for Cincinnati, and the race would be over.

A Guide to Some Basic Stats

When I was playing, I couldn't quote my statistics for you. I knew what I was hitting that year, but I wasn't real sure about my lifetime statistics; it wasn't something I kept totaled up. There was always another pitcher to catch, and there was always another pitch to call.

But for fans, and anyone who follows the game, statistics are the lifeblood of baseball. So here's a quick lesson in baseball math (there are also more stats explained in Appendix A):

➤ **Winning percentage, or win-loss percentage** For either a team or an individual pitcher, divide the number of wins by the number of games played (the sum of the W and L columns).

➤ **Batting average** The most common barometer of a hitter's performance is derived by simply dividing hits by at-bats. An at-bat is an official time up at the plate for a hitter. A batter who walks, sacrifices, hits a sacrifice fly, or is hit by a pitch is not charged with an at-bat.

➤ **Earned run average** To compute ERA, multiply earned runs allowed times nine (because ERA is the number of earned runs that pitcher allows per nine innings) and divide by the number of innings actually pitched. Here's an example: Say a pitcher has allowed 20 earned runs in 60 innings. Multiply 20 times nine and you get 180. Divide by 60 and you get an ERA of 3.00.

➤ **Runs batted in** RBIs are a good way to measure how productive a player is at the plate. A hitter earns a *ribbie* when he drives in a run via a hit, walk, sacrifice (fly or bunt), fielder's choice, or hit batsmen, or on an error when the official scorer rules that the run would've scored anyway.

Warning Track

Say a starting pitcher opens the seventh inning by giving up a hit and a walk, and he's replaced without getting an out. The two men on base are called *inherited runners,* and they're charged against the record of the starting pitcher, not the reliever. If the reliever doesn't allow anyone to score, the starter's ERA is unaffected. But if the reliever allows those runners to score, the runs would count against the starter. The reliever could give up a couple of hits, but if none of the men who he put on base score, his ERA for the inning is 0.00. It's not exactly fair, is it? The reliever can do a bad job and his ERA won't necessarily reflect it. Thus, an ERA of 3.00 is a lot more impressive for a starter than a reliever, and ERA is a significant—but not necessarily completely accurate—gauge of a pitcher's ability.

➤ **Fielding percentage**   If you want to know how good a particular player is in the field, this is the statistic to examine. To compute fielding percentage, add putouts plus assists and divide that figure by the total chances, or putouts plus assists plus errors.

➤ **Saves**   A relief pitcher can earn a save when, entering a game with his team in the lead, he finishes the game (but not to be the winning pitcher) and he meets one of the three following conditions:

1. He has a lead of no more than three runs and he has the opportunity to pitch at least one inning,

2. He enters the game with the potential tying run either on base, at bat, or on deck,

3. He pitches three or more innings regardless of the size of the lead and the official scorer credits him with a save.

If the reliever comes through, and finishes the game, he gets the save. A relief pitcher is charged with a *blown save* if he enters a game in a save situation and loses the lead.

➤ **On-base percentage**   This statistic is the most important one for a leadoff hitter, because it measures how often he gets on base. To compute on-base percentage, add hits plus walks plus times hit by pitch and divide that figure by the sum of at-bats, walks, times hit by pitch, and sacrifice flies.

➤ **Total bases**   To compute a hitter's total bases, add his hits, plus his doubles, plus twice his number of triples, plus three times his number of home runs.

➤ **Slugging percentage**   A statistic used to measure overall offensive performance, one that's especially important for power hitters. To compute a player's slugging percentage, divide his total bases by his at-bats.

Talkin' Baseball

"About this autograph business. Once someone in Washington sent up a picture to me and I wrote, 'Do good in school.' I look up, this guy is 78 years old."

—Casey Stengel

Talkin' Baseball

"Fans are the only ones who really care. There are no free-agent fans. There are no fans who say, 'Get me out of here. I want to play for a winner.'"

—Writer Dick Young

The Best on the Internet

If you like surfing the Net and want to learn about baseball, you're in luck. Hundreds of sites deal with baseball in some fashion (many of which are listed in Appendix C), but here are the five that I think are the best:

➤ **www.fastball.com**   This site keeps you up to date with news throughout the entire world of baseball (major leagues, minor leagues, and other leagues). Fastball offers interesting features and insider information and provides detailed statistics for all major and minor league teams.

➤ **www.totalbaseball.com**   The neatest feature of this site is the "totalcast," which gives real-time pitch-by-pitch accounts of games as they unfold. Every ball in play is charted according to its location on the field and every pitch is illustrated as to where it did or didn't cross home plate.

➤ **www.cnnsi.com**   The best feature on this site, which is jointly maintained by CNN and *Sports Illustrated*, is the section that gives historical statistical profiles for every player who has ever played. CNNSI also provides a free fantasy game.

➤ **www.majorleaguebaseball.com**   The official site of Major League Baseball offers links to all the official team pages and information about buying tickets at every big league ballpark.

➤ **www.espn.com**   This site offers up-to-the-minute box scores, insider information from ESPN reporters, and longer features.

Peerless Periodicals

Baseball's growing popularity has increased interest in the newspapers and magazines that cover the game. These periodicals that are the best in the biz today as far as covering baseball:

➤ *USA Today*   This national newspaper gives daily reports on every team and provides readers with the most comprehensive lineup of box scores and statistics available in print. Even if you're just a casual fan, you ought to include *USA Today* in your daily diet of reading.

➤ *Baseball America*   A respected bi-weekly publication, *Baseball America* excels in its coverage of entire organizations, specifically how it reports on player development. This magazine is a must-read for the serious fan.

➤ *USA Today Baseball Weekly*   An offshoot of *USA Today*, *Baseball Weekly* provides weekly team reports, statistics, and interesting features and columns on the previous week in baseball.

➤ *Sports Illustrated*   If you want to know about the personal lives of those in baseball, there's no better place to turn than *SI*. The magazine also provides readers with a notes section each week that gives the inside dish on what's really going on, but *SI's* hallmark has always been its profiles and features.

➤ *The Sporting News*   *The Sporting News* covers all mainstream sports, but provides a substantial amount of baseball coverage in each issue. With correspondents in each major league city, there are always nuggets of inside information within the magazine's pages.

At the Old Ballyard

Watch a game on television and you don't have to pay for your seat, your peanuts, or your Crackerjacks. You don't have to fight traffic or crowds. You get to sit in your easy chair and see the controversial instant replays.

But to really experience and enjoy a game, nothing beats going out to the ballpark. When you watch on television, you're limited to what the directors and cameramen want to show you, but at the ballpark, you can focus on more than just the pitcher-hitter confrontation. You can watch the whole field. You can go over strategy in your mind, then watch it unfold, how everything comes together as the ball leaves the bat and all the fielders move. It's the next-best thing to being on the field itself. Here's some information that will hopefully make your next trip to the ballpark more enjoyable.

Old Stadiums vs. New Stadiums

When I broke in with the Reds, we played at Crosley Field, which was built way back in 1911. It was one of a generation of ballparks built in the early part of the century. Other parks of that era included Fenway Park in Boston (built in 1912), Shibe Park in Philadelphia (1909), New York's Polo Grounds (1911), Chicago's Wrigley Field (1914) and Comiskey Park (1910), Forbes Field in Pittsburgh (1909), and Ebbets Field in Brooklyn (1913).

Those stadiums were each truly unique. Most of them were crammed in between already existing streets, so they were asymmetrical and have some odd measurements. Fenway has a 37-foot high wall in left field called "The Green Monster." The center field fence in the Polo Grounds was 483 feet from home plate, but the fence in right was only 257 feet away. Shibe Park had a corrugated iron fence in right field, and balls would fly off it at crazy angles. Crosley Field had a 58-foot high scoreboard in play in left-centerfield.

Unfortunately, these old parks eventually became outdated. They tended to be small and cramped, with a lot of seats obstructed by poles and pillars. As construction techniques improved, teams began building new stadiums that would seat more fans and feature more amenities, such as skyboxes and restaurants. Also, because the population had begun moving away from the cities and using cars as their primary transportation, new stadiums weren't built right in the cities, but in the suburbs.

It's really a shame that most of these old ballparks are gone. A few, like Wrigley, Fenway, and Tiger Stadium in Detroit, are still in use, but their days seem to be numbered. Tiger Stadium will be gone by 2000, and there's a lot of talk about replacing Fenway as well. I guess that's the price of progress. A lot of history was made in those old buildings, and their quirks and charms made them pretty endearing. But I understand how fans would want to see a game in more luxurious surroundings, and more seats and corporate suites bring in more profits for the owners.

Extra Innings

Opened in 1914 for the Federal League's Chicago Whales (and originally known as Weegham Park), Wrigley Field is one of the major leagues' oldest and most charming ballparks. It was the last to add lights for night games—not until 1988. Its ivy-covered outfield wall—the brainchild of owner Bill Veeck in 1937—is an instantly recognizable sight. The Wrigley scoreboard is one of the few in the majors still operated by hand, and after each game, a blue flag with a white *W* flies from the centerfield flag pole to signal a Cub win, while a white flag with a blue *L* means a Cub loss.

During the late 1960s and early '70s, several old ballparks were replaced by so-called "cookie-cutter parks," such as Riverfront in Cincinnati, Veterans Stadium in Philly, and Three Rivers Stadium in Pittsburgh. They were called that because they were virtually identical and very generic-looking. They were built to house both football and baseball teams, so they had to be big enough to fit a 120-yard football field. As a result, a lot of seats are far away from the baseball action. Another drawback of these stadiums is that they use artificial turf, which has never been popular with traditionalist baseball fans. It's not a lot of fun playing on the fake grass either, because your knees take a brutal pounding. One thing people don't realize about artificial turf is that it's not very soft, and it's laid right on top of concrete, which means it's tough on your legs.

In the early '90s, though, a revolution took place. Baltimore decided to replace aging, cavernous Memorial Stadium. Instead of going the cookie-cutter route, the Orioles built a baseball-only facility near Baltimore's inner harbor. The park had the aesthetic qualities of an old-time park, but it also had all the amenities such parks lacked. The stadium, called Oriole Park at Camden Yards, became an attraction in and of itself. Not only did it do wonders for the Orioles' attendance, but it also revitalized the surrounding neighborhood.

A few years later, Cleveland followed suit, replacing dreary Municipal Stadium with Jacobs Field. "The Jake" has sold out every game for more than three years now, which has a lot to do with the Indians' recent success. Because fans were coming out to the new park and companies were paying top dollar for

Talkin' Baseball

"There is still nothing in life as constant and as changing at the same time as an afternoon at the ballpark."

—Talk-show host Larry King

luxury suites, the team's cash flow improved, allowing it to spend more money on quality players. It's no coincidence that the Indians have won their division every year since Jacobs Field opened, or that, like Baltimore, downtown Cleveland has made a remarkable comeback.

The main entrance to Wrigley Field, at the corner of Clark and Addison streets, where the words "National League Champions" haven't appeared since 1945.

Where to Sit at a Game

As a fan, I like any park with seats that let me get close to the field. Of course, as a retired catcher, I prefer seats down low, right behind home plate, where I get the best view of the pitches and how the catcher is handling them. That's not always easy for me, however, because a lot of fans don't let me watch the game: I spend two or three hours signing autographs! I truly enjoy meeting people—especially baseball fans—but sometimes sitting in the stands gets to be too much of a hassle, so I often sit in a luxury box.

If you can't get choice seats behind home plate, don't give up. There's a lot to be said for sitting in the upper deck. You can't hear the players' chatter or see their facial expressions up close, but you get a much better sense of the big picture. What you lose in not seeing the action up close, you gain in being able to see more things at once.

If you do end up in the upper deck, try to sit just off to one side of home plate. You'll get a bird's-eye view of the infield, and you'll be in prime foul-ball territory. Here's a tip: Check out the lineups ahead of time. If there are a lot of right-handed hitters, sit on the first-base side. If there are a lot of lefties, sit off to the third-base side. Most foul pops come on pitches where the hitter swings late, so you'll increase your chances of snaring a souvenir if you play the percentages and position yourself on the opposite field side of as many hitters as you can.

If you have to sit in the outfield, try not to sit too low. There's not as much to be gained from sitting near the field when you're 400 feet from the plate. Move back a few rows so you can get a clearer view of the infield. Also, try to sit toward center field. The worst seats are generally in the corners, because in many parks you have to crane your neck to see the action.

Keep in mind, however, that, especially in the newer parks, so much thought was given to the layout of the field and seats that there really aren't many bad seats. Try moving around. Don't sit in the same place every time. You know what they say: Variety is the spice of life.

Catching On

The **bleachers** are the cheapest seats in the ballpark, usually bench seating behind the outfield wall. The denizens of those seats sometimes earn nicknames, like the Bleacher Bums of Chicago's Wrigley Field, and the Bleacher Creatures of Yankee Stadium.

What to Watch—and When

If you can, get there early and see batting practice. (Mark McGwire's BP sessions have almost become more popular than the games!) Pregame warm-ups usually start about two-and-a-half hours before the game, but some parks don't open that early. So it's best to call ahead and find out what time the gates open, and then be there as close to that time as you can. Watch how certain guys swing the bat. Watch how the hands move. Watch the timing of the feet. Then stick around and watch infield practice. See how the catcher throws. See how everything is synchronized.

Once you're settled in, you need to know what to look for. When you're sitting at home, the TV camera stays focused on the ball, but there's so much more to see at the ballpark. When the hitter comes to bat, watch the infielders and outfielders shift into

position. If the left fielder moves toward the line against a left-handed hitter, it means they expect him to go the other way. But what if the left fielder moves and the right fielder stays in his position? You might think, "Why wouldn't he move over, too?" Well, the hitter might have a tendency to pull an off-speed pitch but go the other way on hard stuff.

Watch the catcher after he calls the pitch. Does he tip his hand by moving early? Does he shift inside or scoot to the outside edge to try to set up the target? Watch the stolen-base threat leading off at first base. Watch the runner go, then quickly look

Talkin' Baseball

"I could never play in New York. The first time I came into a game there, I got in the bullpen car and they told me to lock the doors."

—Pitcher Mike Flanagan

back to the catcher. Watch his timing and how he gets the ball out of the glove to throw down to second base.

Check out where the infielders position themselves. Are they at double-play depth? Is the infield in? Watch how situations dictate their moves. Who covers second on a hit-and-run? Watch a ball hit into the gap in the outfield and how the outfielders coordinate who picks it up. Watch where the relay man is and whether he cuts off the ball or lets it go through. Watch the center fielder play captain, making the call on who handles
fly balls.

Watch the coordination of the second baseman or the shortstop turning the double play. Sometimes the announcers just say, "It's a ground ball and he should turn the double play," and we gloss over the grace of all they do. The second baseman is Baryshnikov at the ballet. The catcher is a stone wall blocking home plate. Study and appreciate Derek Jeter playing shortstop. Or Ken Griffey Jr. chasing down a fly ball. Or Robbie Alomar turning the double play. Or Ken Caminiti's arm. Or Pudge Rodriguez behind the plate. There's a theater out there. Don't just wait for the pitcher to put the ball back in play.

The Least You Need to Know

➤ Reading a box score and keeping a scorecard are two simple ways to get involved with baseball.

➤ Calculating basic baseball statistics doesn't require an advanced degree in mathematics.

➤ If you want information on your favorite team or player, you can find it in newspapers and magazines, on the internet, and on the radio.

➤ The best way to enjoy a baseball game is to savor all the intricacies of the ballpark.

Chapter 25

Baseball's Future: Gazing into the Crystal Ball

In This Chapter

➤ Why baseball's future looks bright

➤ Winning back old fans and discovering new ones

➤ Improving the game, on and off the field

➤ The most promising stars of today and tomorrow

Mark McGwire, Sammy Sosa, and the greats of '98 got people talking about baseball's comeback. Me, I never thought baseball had a big problem to begin with, and I never thought baseball had gone away. I think there are a lot of people who have always loved the game, and some who just don't like it. To each his own!

A Homer-Happy '98: Increasing the Fan Base

The home run race of 1998 did bring back some old fans and generate new ones. It was terrific—the excitement revitalized the game and the fans. We all got caught up in it, watching the sports shows and checking the paper to see if Mark or Sammy had hit another home run and if they were still on pace to surpass Babe Ruth's mark of 60 home runs and Roger Maris's record 61. Mark and Sammy generated fans not only by hitting home runs but by carrying themselves so well. They showed so much respect for the Babe and for Roger and his family. Mark showed so much love for his son and for Sammy, and Sammy was always applauding Mark and thanking his mom, and it was great.

Fans turned off by the strikes and the money talk and the bickering came back. People who had been indifferent to the game suddenly were saying, "Wow, did you see that?"

or, "I never followed baseball, but I started watching that race this year and it was really good." They were talking about baseball, not about presidential sex scandals and stock market crashes and all the other problems in the world. Suddenly, people were interested, asking me all sorts of questions. After all the bashing baseball has taken, I was happy to see people finally talking about the positive side of the game I love. A team might not be in the playoffs or the World Series, or even a pennant race, and yet people came to the park, and every time Mark or Sammy stepped out of the dugout, people who had never experienced the excitement of baseball were wrapped up in the anticipation and suspense that are so much a part of it.

The 1998 season featured an exciting—and classy— show by Mark McGwire (left, hitting home run number 70) and Sammy Sosa (clubbing No. 62).

The playoffs brought more excitement, starting with the one-game showdown between Sammy Sosa's Cubs and the San Francisco Giants for the National League wild card spot. Even though the World Series was a four-game sweep, we could celebrate the New York Yankees winning a record 125 games and argue about their place in history alongside my Big Red Machine, the Yankees' old "Murderers' Row" teams, and all the other great teams of the past century.

It was great fun, and I think some of those fans are here to stay. Some will be happy to grab part of history and move on to the next must-see event, but some who had never experienced baseball have found they liked it, and they'll be back for more.

Talkin' Baseball

"More than any other American sport, baseball creates the magnetic, addictive illusion that it can almost be understood."

—Writer Thomas Boswell

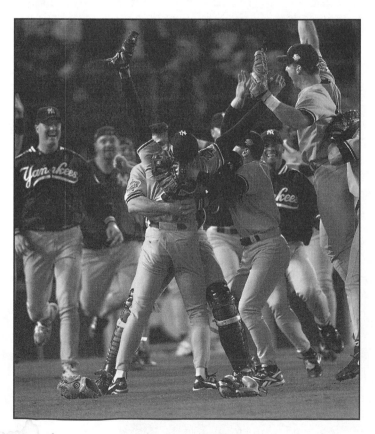

After sweeping the San Diego Padres in the World Series, the 1998 Yankees celebrated a truly historic season.

Looking Ahead

In 1998, when baseball added two expansion teams and moved the Milwaukee Brewers from the American to the National League (to keep an even number of teams in each league for scheduling purposes), it wound up with 14 teams in the AL and 16 in the NL. I think that's only temporary, and soon you'll see two more teams added to the AL so we can have 32 teams, 16 in each league. Then I don't think you'll see expansion again for awhile.

Despite baseball's popularity in Mexico, Japan, and Latin America, I don't see another expansion team being added outside the United States. I think the costs and time involved in international travel would be too difficult to coordinate. But I do think we'll see a continuing influx of international players. The talent coming from the Latin countries and from around the world allows us to expand without diluting the product too much. Their skills are tremendous—look at the incredible number of Latin players at the 1998 All-Star Game—and they raise the talent level. The 1998 Most Valuable Player voting resulted in the first time two Latin players (Sammy Sosa of the Chicago Cubs and Juan Gonzalez of the Texas Rangers) won the honor in their respective leagues.

I know some people complain about the shortage of good players, how guys who should be in the minors are forced to play in the majors before they're ready, but they've been saying that ever since there were 16 teams. You can never fill every team with All-Stars—you'll always have .220 hitters, and pitchers with losing records.

From the Bench

Babe Ruth's record of 60 home runs stood for 34 years, and Roger Maris's mark of 61 lasted another 37. Mark McGwire blasted the record into the stratosphere with 70 in 1998. Can anyone top that? It's unlikely, but if anybody has the potential to break it, it's Ken Griffey Jr.—probably as gifted an athlete as there's ever been in baseball. Mark McGwire himself just might do it again, too. He's already proven the impossible is possible.

Talkin' Baseball

"You can't sit on a lead and run a few plays into the line and just kill the clock. You've got to throw the ball over the plate and give the other man his chance. That's why baseball is the greatest game of them all."

—Hall of Fame manager Earl Weaver

Improving the Game off the Field

There are some serious problems I'd like to see corrected before the majors add any new teams. The words "competitive imbalance" are starting to get tossed around a lot: Teams with lucrative stadiums and/or big television deals can afford big payrolls, and small-market teams can't afford to compete. Rich teams that are smart enough can buy themselves pennants, and poor teams struggle to play .500 ball no matter how smart they are. The New York Yankees, Atlanta Braves, and Cleveland Indians dominate, while teams like the Kansas City Royals, Montreal Expos, and Pittsburgh Pirates struggle to hang on, unable to keep their best players once they become free agents, and unable to draw fans to the ballpark once they lose their best players.

Of the 13 teams with payrolls above $48 million last season, only the Baltimore Orioles finished with a losing record. Of the 17 teams with payrolls under $48 million, only the St. Louis Cardinals and Toronto Blue Jays had winning records. Commissioner Bud Selig has said that this disparity is the biggest problem facing baseball today. Is there a solution? Do you put every team with a payroll under $30 million in one league and every team over it in another? Probably not. Who wants to see inferior talent? How do you still have a true World Series? But salaries and ticket prices continue to escalate, and the owners have to do something.

Before free agency, the owners had all the leverage, and the players were victimized by the reserve clause. Owners were able to keep salaries down because their monopoly gave them the power to control the players' market. Now the players have more leverage—and are profiting from it—and they're understandably reluctant to give that up. So the owners come back to the fans: How many does the team have, and how much are they willing to pay for a ticket? (Teams profit from lucrative broadcast rights, but these are also based on fan numbers.)

I think the owners have to be smart enough to rein themselves in, not to overbid on players and create an imbalance. The rich owners don't want to share revenue with the small-market clubs (as is done in the National Football League), but I think they have to, for the good of the game. If they run a few franchises out of business, it does nobody any good. I'd like to see some sort of a salary cap with bonuses tied to performance, but the players union will probably never let that happen. Neither side is solely to blame—it's just a problematic situation that has evolved, and the responsibility for finding a solution rests on both sides: players and owners. How baseball adjusts will dictate the future.

Talkin' Baseball

"These days baseball is different. You come to spring training, you get your legs ready, your arms loose, your agents ready, your lawyer lined up."

—Former slugger Dave Winfield

Improving the Game on the Field

The designated hitter would have been great for a guy like me when I needed a day off, and it could have lengthened my career after I was too beat up to catch every day—but I don't like the rule. I hope the American League gets rid of it and the National League never adds it. It diminishes strategy: American League managers never have to consider the strategic component of pinch hitting for a pitcher.

Talkin' Baseball

"The most difficult thing that American League managers have to do is maintain straight faces while addressing each other as 'Sparky' and 'Stump.'"

—Sports Illustrated writer Steve Rushin

Baseball is supposed to be a thinking game for managers and fans alike, and the American League lost an element of that when it adopted the DH rule. Plus, I think a major leaguer should have to handle all aspects of the game, and not be one-dimensional.

And I think baseball should quit wasting time while a pitcher lobs four balls outside for an intentional walk. Let the pitcher or manager signal for an intentional walk and immediately send the hitter to first base. Put him on and let's get on with the game.

I'd also like to see the first base bag moved outside the foul line. Right now it's just inside (left of) the line, but a runner coming down to first base is supposed to run *outside* (to the right of) the line. No hitter ever comes out of the batter's box outside the foul line, so he has to circle back outside the line, run to first, then come back inside to touch first. (A play involved this call in the 1998 American League Championship Series between the Yankees and Indians—see Chapter 9 on umpires.)

Catching On

The **baseline** is defined by the area three feet on either side of an imaginary, direct line connecting the bases.

Between every other base on the field there's a *baseline,* an imaginary, six-foot-wide path that leads straight from one base to the next. If a runner runs out of the baseline to try to avoid a tag, he's called out. Anywhere else on the field except first base, the baseline extends three feet on either side of the base, and that line shouldn't change. There should be the same planes all over the field.

Improving the Players

I give talks all across the country, often addressing the issue of how people can be the best they can be. I talk about a little formula I've devised called the Vowels of Success, which I think applies to major league baseball players as well.

A is for attitude, accountability, achievement, and adaptability to every pitch, to every field, to every town.

E is for the effort and the excellence that you must maintain for yourself and the standards you must set. And employability. Would you hire yourself?

I is for the individual. You put eight All-Stars out on the field and you've got a world-class team, because individually they distinguish themselves with their gloves and their bats. Individually you have to take the responsibility to do your job every time you walk out there.

O is the opportunity. Everyone should be given the opportunity to take advantage of their abilities.

U is for using the instructions you receive, and using your talents. Use other people's knowledge. When I came up through the major leagues, Deron Johnson would say, "Hey kid, you know this pitcher?" I'd say, "No." And he'd say, "Well, he's going to throw you such and such. He's got a good curve ball and he's got a little slider." The first day I walked onto Crosley Field, Deron said, "Hey, kid, this guy has a slider. He's going to try to throw it to you." Use the knowledge that all these people have. Take advantage of what they've experienced.

U also stands for you. You are important. Don't base your happiness on what others think of you. Don't expect them to always clap, and don't get down on yourself if they boo. Don't judge yourself based on their response.

Tomorrow's Stars: Coming Soon to a Ballpark Near You

A thousand guys have been labeled "The Next Mickey Mantle," but of course there was only one Mick. So even the best scouts are wise not to offer any money-back guarantees. I'm not saying these guys are the next anybody, but I do think that, barring injury, these 10 minor league phenoms have very bright futures in the majors:

➤ **Eric Chavez**, Oakland Athletics third baseman Just 20 years old, and in just his second pro season, Eric hit 33 homers and drove in 126 runs in 135 games split between Double A and Triple A. *Baseball America's* Minor League Player of the Year, the left-handed slugger is Oakland's likely third baseman on Opening Day '99.

➤ **Gabe Kapler**, Detroit Tigers outfielder Kapler set league records for RBIs (146), doubles (47), and extra-base hits (81) in the Double A Southern League, and will probably open the '99 season in Triple A.

➤ **Ruben Mateo**, Texas Rangers rightfielder Mateo is a five-tool player: He can hit for average, hit for power, run, throw, and catch fly balls. But a broken bone slowed him last year, and he probably won't be a Ranger until the year 2000.

➤ **Rick Ankiel**, St. Louis Cardinals pitcher The best pitching prospect down on the farm, this lefty led the minors with 222 strikeouts in just 161 innings. He showed great control (50 walks) for a 19-year-old and wiped out lefties, who hit just .191 against him as he went 12–6 with a 2.63 ERA in Class A ball. Give him another year or two before he makes it big.

➤ **Pat Burrell**, Philadelphia Phillies first baseman Can this guy hit? Well, his nickname is Pat the Bat. In 37 games at Class A, the University of Miami product hit .303 with 7 homers, 7 doubles, 30 RBIs, and 29 runs scored.

➤ **George Lombard**, Atlanta Braves outfielder The former running back is blessed with great tools but still has a lot to learn about baseball. He didn't set the world on fire in his first four years at the Rookie and Class A levels, but in 1998 he made the jump to Double A and hit .301 with 20 homers, 23 doubles, 60 RBIs, 75 runs scored, and 31 stolen bases in 112 games.

➤ **Bruce Chen**, Atlanta Braves pitcher   Signed as a 16-year-old, this Panamanian lefty was 15–8 with a 3.09 ERA in Double A and Triple A in 1998 before spending September in the bigs. With Denny Neagle having been traded in the off-season, the Braves may turn Bruce loose in the rotation. Otherwise he'll probably spend '99 in the Atlanta bullpen.

➤ **Russell Branyan**, Cleveland Indians third baseman   An all-or-nothing free swinger, Branyan has blasted 119 minor league homers in five years from the Rookie to Double A levels, but he's whiffed 558 times in 428 games over that span. His .294 average at Double A Akron was a career high and helped him earn a stint with the Indians in '98.

➤ **Calvin Pickering**, Baltimore first baseman   A massive 6'3" and 275 pounds, Pickering led the Double A Eastern League with 31 home runs and 114 RBIs while hitting .309.

➤ **Alex Escobar**, New York Mets outfielder   Another five-tool player, this 19-year-old Venezuelan hit .310 with 27 homers, 91 RBIs, and 49 stolen bases in just 416 at bats in Class A in '98.

Extra Innings

On Sunday, Sept. 21, 1998, Baltimore Orioles third baseman Cal Ripken Jr. did something he hadn't done in more than 16 years: He sat out a ballgame. Ripken said he was comfortable with his decision to end his record streak of 2,632 consecutive games, which began in the second game of a May 29, 1982, doubleheader. "It's my choice," he said. "I don't want to manage that any more." Thus was cemented an Iron Man standard that will almost certainly never be broken.

Today's Brightest Young Stars

While waiting for the stars of tomorrow to arrive, you can catch plenty of rising stars now. We have some of the greatest young players I've ever seen, and they give baseball a chance for a great future.

Everyone talks about Mark McGwire hitting 70 home runs, but Sammy Sosa had 66, Ken Griffey Jr., 56, and Greg Vaughn, 50. Thirteen guys hit 40 or more home runs. We built ballparks for home runs, guys are hitting 'em, and fans are loving 'em.

Ken Griffey Jr., one of baseball's biggest stars, hit 56 home runs in both the 1997 and '98 seasons.

McGwire and Vaughn are thirtysomething, but there are so many good players out there in their mid-20s and early 30s. Mo Vaughn is 31, Sosa and Houston's Jeff Bagwell are 30, Griffey and Texas' Juan Gonzalez are 29. You can go down the list of cities and pick out at least one star in almost every town, stars you'd pay money to see play.

And have we ever been blessed with so many great young shortstops who can hit? Alex Rodriguez of the Seattle Mariners became just the third player ever to join the 40-40 club—42 homers, 46 steals— at age 23. Nomar Garciaparra of the Boston Red Sox hit .323 with 35 homers, 122 RBIs, 80 extra-base hits, and 111 runs at age 25. He's tremendous to watch, another MVP candidate. Derek Jeter hit .324, led the American League in runs with 127, stole 30 bases, hit 19 homers, committed just nine errors and helped the Yankees win their second World Series in three years—all at age 24.

Talkin' Baseball

"The one constant through all the years... has been baseball. Baseball has marked the time. This field, this game, is a part of our past.... It reminds us of all that once was good, and that could be good again."

—Terence Mann (James Earl Jones) in the movie *Field of Dreams*

Chipper Jones hit 34 home runs for Atlanta, and he's going to get bigger and stronger because he's still young. Another terrific young third baseman is Philadelphia's Scott Rolen. You've got great 1998 rookies like Cubs pitcher Kerry Wood and Athletics outfielder Ben Grieve. You've got slugging outfielders like Vladimir Guerrero in Montreal and Manny Ramirez in Cleveland.

With guys who are so talented, so graceful, and so much stronger than players of my era, the future of baseball is in very, very good shape.

The Least You Need to Know

➤ Mark McGwire, Sammy Sosa, and the record-setting New York Yankees got more people talking baseball in 1998, but the game never really went away.

➤ If major league teams shared revenues more equitably and based pay more on performance, the game would be even better.

➤ The American League should eliminate the designated hitter rule. (At least that's one fan's opinion!)

➤ The major leagues are full of promising young players, particularly at shortstop, and future stars, currently in the minor leagues, will soon establish themselves in the big leagues.

Johnny's Glossary of Diamond Dialogue

ace   See *starting rotation*.

advance scouts   Scouts who watch a team's upcoming opponents and prepare reports on what to expect, such as hitting and pitching tendencies of certain players. These reports come in especially handy if the opposing team features a new player, such as a pitcher who has just come into the league and whom no one on the scout's team has faced before.

ahead/behind in count   When a hitter or pitcher has the advantage in terms of balls and strikes, he is said to be ahead in the count; a hitter is ahead when the count is 1–0, 2–0, 3–0, 2–1, or 3–1, and behind if the count is 0–1, 0–2, 1–2, or 2–2; the opposite applies for pitchers.

alley   See *gap*.

All-Star Game   Major League Baseball's mid-season (early to mid-July) showcase, featuring a team of National League stars against the American League's best. Fans can pick up ballots at any professional ballpark and vote for one player at each position (except pitcher). And these days, you can actually vote online. The votes are tallied up, with the top vote-getters winning the opportunity to start the All-Star Game. The reserves and pitchers are then selected by each team's respective manager, who must make sure that each team has at least one representative.

American League (AL)   One of the two leagues, along with the National League, that comprise the major leagues. The *AL* was formed in 1901, and currently consists of 14 teams in three divisions: East, Central, and West.

analyst   One of the two main roles in the broadcast booth. The analyst, or *color commentator* (and sometimes there are two of these doing a game), explains things for you: Why did they do that, and what might they do next? He gives you the "how" and the "why." Analysts are often former players and managers, such as NBC and ESPN's Joe Morgan and Fox's Tim McCarver.

appeal play   A team can appeal a call—or the lack of a call—and ask for a correct ruling in a few specific instances. See Chapter 8 for details.

around the horn   Infielders throw the ball around the horn—from first to second or short and then to third—after an out when there's no one on base, and at the end of their warm-ups between innings.

assist   A player's throw to a teammate that results in a putout.

at-bat   An official time up at the plate for a hitter. A batter who walks, sacrifices, hits a sacrifice fly, or is hit by a pitch is not charged with an at-bat.

away   Another way of saying *outside*. A pitcher who's working a hitter away is throwing him a lot of outside pitches.

backdoor   A *backdoor breaking ball* starts far outside and breaks toward the batter for a called strike on the outside part of the plate.

backstop   The wall or fence behind home plate. Also another name for the catcher.

back to the box   A ball that's hit back to the box is a shot right back toward the pitcher.

back up   To position oneself behind the defensive player who's fielding a ball or receiving a throw, in the event that the ball gets by the other player or the throw is errant. For example, in many routine ground ball situations, the catcher backs up the play at first base.

bad-ball hitter   One who often gets hits on pitches that are out of the strike zone. Yogi Berra was a bad-ball hitter.

bad hop   When a infield grounder takes an unexpected bounce—say it hits a pebble and caroms off the shortstop's glove—it's said to have taken a bad hop.

bag   See *base.*

balk   An illegal movement by a pitcher that results in all baserunners being allowed to advance one base. What's legal and what isn't? Even the most dedicated fans can't recite all 13 ways that a pitcher can commit a balk. There are some very gray areas here, and just how strictly they're enforced varies from game to game and umpire to umpire.

ball   A pitch that the batter takes and that's judged by the home plate umpire to have been outside of the strike zone.

Baltimore chop   A batted ball that hits the ground near home plate and bounces high enough in the air to allow the runner to beat the throw to first base. The term dates back to the 1890s, when the National League's Baltimore Orioles, led by players such as John McGraw and Willie Keeler, would try to purposely chop down on the ball to produce such hits.

bang-bang play   A play in which the ball and the runner arrive at virtually the same time. A fast runner who hits a ground ball might be thrown out at first—or just beat the throw—on a bang-bang play.

base   One of four 15-inch square canvas bags that form a diamond in the infield. The four bases, a.k.a. *bags* or *sacks,* (first base, second base, third base, and home base—a five-sided rubber plate set in the ground, commonly known as *home plate*) are 90 feet apart.

baseball   A major league baseball must weigh between five and five-and-a-quarter ounces, and its circumference must be between nine and nine-and-a-quarter inches. In recent years, as sluggers have hit more and more home runs, there has been much speculation that baseballs have become livelier. However, no scientific evidence has been offered that the ball is *juiced.*

base hit   A single.

baseline   The baselines are defined by the area three feet on either side of an imaginary, direct line connecting the bases.

base on balls   A batter draws a *base on balls,* a *walk,* or a *free pass,* and is thus entitled to first base, when he accumulates four balls in his time at bat.

baserunner   An offensive player who has reached base safely. There are seven ways to become a baserunner, or runner; see Chapter 18 for the complete list.

bases loaded   Runners on first, second, and third base.

basket catch   A catch made on a fly ball with the glove at about waist level, with the palm facing up. Willie Mays made the basket catch famous.

bat   *Bats* come in all weights and sizes, but they do have one thing in common: They're all made of wood. In most cases, the wood is white ash from the forests of New York or Pennsylvania. So long as the bat is round, not more than 42 inches long and not more than $2^3/4$ inches in diameter, it's legal for use in major league play.

bat around   To send 10 players up to the plate in one inning; that is, everyone in the batting order has gotten up to hit, and you're back to the guy who led off the inning.

bat boy   A boy who's in charge of picking up and storing the players' bats during the game, supplying the home plate umpire with fresh baseballs, and myriad other duties around the dugout and clubhouse. Bat boys wear a uniform just like the players. Today there are bat girls, too.

bat speed   How fast a batter's swing is through the hitting zone—a crucial component to hitting. The batter's dominant hand, which is on top, generates the bat speed.

batter   The player on the offensive team who is at the plate, taking his turn at bat. Means the same as *hitter.*

batter's box   The area on either side of home plate (defined with white chalk lines in the dirt) within which the hitter must stand during his time at bat.

battery   The pitcher and catcher.

batting average   A statistic derived by dividing hits by at bats; the most common barometer of a hitter's performance.

batting cage   A fenced-in enclosure in which players practice their hitting.

batting glove   Many hitters wear batting gloves, made of soft leather, to keep their hands from becoming blistered. Some players like the feel of the bat in their bare hands.

batting helmet   Required protective headgear for hitters: a hard plastic helmet with padding inside. They come with or without ear flaps, and if a player has a facial injury he needs to protect, the batting helmet can be outfitted with a faceguard. In fact, faceguards are required at many levels of amateur ball.

batting order   The order in which the players on a team must come to bat. If a player bats out of turn, deliberately or otherwise, he's called out—provided that the other team recognizes the transgression and appeals to the umpire immediately after the player's at bat. The only way a batting order, which is also called a *lineup,* can be changed is by the use of a pinch-hitter. Once a player has been substituted for, he's out of the game and is not allowed to return.

batting practice (BP)   Pregame ritual in which players work on their hitting. The players take batting practice in groups, usually of four or five, with a batting practice pitcher or coach *laying the ball in there.* When a player's group isn't hitting, he'll stand out in the field and shag balls.

BBWAA   Commonly used acronym for the *Baseball Writers Association of America,* which votes on most of the major leagues' major individual awards.

beanball   A pitch that hits a batter. It used to be part of the game; now, baseball tries to protect the hitter more, and the umpire has the discretion to eject a pitcher if he thinks he threw at a batter intentionally.

bench   Where the players sit (in the dugout) when they're not in the game. The term also refers collectively to a team's *reserve,* or *bench players,* as in, The Braves have a good bench.

bench jockey   A guy who shouts derisive comments, or *rides* the opposing team or the umpires, from his seat on the bench. Bench jockeying is a lost art in the major leagues.

bender   A curveball.

bequeathed runner(s)   In statistical parlance, any runner(s) on base when a pitcher leaves a game are considered bequeathed by the departing pitcher.

big market   These days a lot is made of the disparity in the major leagues between *big-market teams* and *small-market teams.* Big market is a buzzword for rich (think New York Yankees). Small market means poor (think Montreal Expos).

bird dog   A part-time scout, usually assigned to a particular region.

357

the black   The outer edges of the plate or strike zone (so-called because of the black border around home plate). A pitcher who is said to be *painting the black* is masterfully working the corners, or edges of the strike zone.

Black Sox   Eight members of the 1919 Chicago White Sox who were banned from baseball for conspiring with gamblers to throw the World Series.

bleachers   The cheapest seats in the ballpark, usually bench seating behind the outfield wall. The denizens of those seats sometimes earn nicknames, like the *Bleacher Bums* of Chicago's Wrigley Field and the *Bleacher Creatures* of Yankee Stadium.

bleeder   A weak hit; either a slow ground ball that just gets through the infield or a pop-up that barely drops in.

block the plate   When one of his teammates is trying to gun down a runner at home plate, a good catcher wants to make it difficult for the runner to touch home plate, and then tag him out. So most catchers try to prevent runs by blocking the plate.

bloop/blooper   A ball that's hit weakly and falls in *no man's land,* between the infielders and outfielders; also called a *dying quail, flare, looper, Texas Leaguer, or wounded duck.*

blown save   A relief pitcher is charged with a blown save—that is, he *blows a save*—if he enters a game in a save situation and loses the lead.

bonehead play   A stupid mental error.

the book   Baseball has been played for more than 100 years, so no matter how bizarre a situation a manager finds himself in, chances are dozens of other managers have been in the exact same position. And the more basic scenarios are played out so frequently that for most situations there is a generally accepted strategy to be used. A manager who applies that generally accepted strategy is said to be managing by the book. The book is unwritten, but every manager knows it. See Chapter 19 for more on the book.

boot   To make an error, as in, "The shortstop booted a ground ball."

bottom of the inning   The half of the inning in which the home team is up to bat and the visiting team is in the field.

bottom of the order   The lower portion of the batting order, generally from the sixth or seventh spot down through the ninth spot.

box score   A chart that provides a concise statistical summary of a baseball game. You'll find box scores in the sports section of your newspaper—and on-line—every day during the baseball season.

breaking pitch/breaking ball   A pitched ball that has movement, or *breaks,* as it nears home plate; for example, a curveball or a slider.

break up the double play   The objective of a runner who's on first base when there's a ground ball hit to an infielder. Runners with good speed obviously have a better chance to break up the double play, but there's more to it than just speed. There's aggressiveness and attitude. As soon as contact is made and the ball is on the ground, you have to charge toward second. You have to find the infielder who's taking the relay and slide as hard as you can toward him, try to run into part of his legs with yours, and try to get him off-balance so he can't throw to first base at all, or at least can't get anything on the throw.

bring the infield in   In a close game with the bases loaded or a runner on third, the manager sometimes will bring the infield in. The idea is that by having all the infielders move in, closer to home plate, they can get to a ground ball quickly and throw home to prevent the tying or winning run from scoring. But this can be risky, because a ground ball is more likely to get past the infielders for a single.

brushback pitch   Brushback or purpose pitches are thrown high and tight, often tight enough to clobber a batter, to make him a little scared and a lot less aggressive.

bullpen   An area, usually behind the outfield fence or outside the foul lines behind first and third base, where relief pitchers reside during the game and warm up in preparation to enter the game. The term is also used to refer collectively to a team's corps of relief pitchers, as in, "The Mets have really improved their bullpen (or pen)."

bunt   To hit the ball with the bat held virtually still, so that it rolls slowly on the infield; executed by a hitter trying to either move a runner over to the next base (*sacrifice bunt*) or to reach first base himself (*bunting for a hit*). Bunt is also a noun that describes the batted ball itself.

bush league   Another way of saying *minor league*. Something that lacks class is also sometimes called bush or bush league.

call   An umpire's ruling—ball or strike, safe or out, fair or foul—is his call.

called game   One in which, for any reason, the umpire-in-chief terminates play.

called strike   A pitch that the batter takes and that's judged by the home plate umpire to have passed through the strike zone.

call off   On a high fly ball, a fielder has to decide whether or not to call off the guy next to him. That's when you see a guy wave his arm and shout, "Mine!" or "I got it!" to let the players around him know that he'll take responsibility for catching the ball.

can of corn   A nice, easily catchable fly ball. The terms dates back to the turn of the century, when grocers would store canned goods on high shelves, where they could then be pushed off with a long stick, and fall into the grocer's hands below.

captain   Some managers officially appoint a player to serve as captain, while others simply let the player or players with the most pronounced leadership skills act as a de facto captain.

catch   The act of a fielder getting secure possession, in his glove or hand, of a ball in flight, and firmly holding it. If it's a nice play on a line drive it might be called a *stab*. A catch of a ground ball is sometimes called a *stop* or a *pickup*.

catcher   The defensive player who's positioned directly behind home plate, and who has myriad responsibilities; also called a *backstop* or a *receiver*. See Chapter 13 for details.

catcher's ERA   The earned run average of a team's pitchers when a particular catcher is behind the plate.

catcher's interference   See *defensive interference*.

caught stealing   The official designation for a runner who's thrown out on a stolen base attempt.

center fielder   The defensive player who's stationed in *center field*, or *center*, which is the middle part of the outfield, between left field and right field.

change speeds   To throw the ball at different velocities, or rates of speed, which is something all good pitchers do.

changeup   A slow pitch intended to put a hitter off-balance because it's delivered with the same motion as a fastball.

chase a pitch   To swing at a bad pitch that's out of reach and thus difficult for the batter to hit. As a catcher, if the batter is a dead low-ball hitter and I've got a low-ball pitcher, I may call for low-ball sinkers that are way down and out of the strike zone, hoping that he'll chase a pitch in the dirt.

cheat   Refers to how a defensive player will play a few steps, or *shade*, in a certain direction to gain an advantage. For example, with a man on first and fewer than two outs, the second baseman and shortstop often cheat toward the second base bag, trying to get in better position to turn a double play.

check swing   A hitter has to have the discipline to lay off pitches that are out of the strike zone or that give him trouble. Often, he can't make that decision until he has started his swing. Then he has to be quick enough and strong enough to stop, or check his swing (or *hold up*) before his wrists break, or the umpire will rule that he has gone around on his swing and charge him with a strike.

choke up   To hit by gripping the bat further up the *handle,* toward the *barrel* (the thickest part of the bat) and away from the *knob* at the other end. By choking up a hitter gets better bat control and a faster swing, but less power.

circus catch   A spectacular, acrobatic catch.

Class A   The third step down the minor league ladder, the Class A level includes Advanced A, Regular A (or Slow A), and Short-Season A.

cleanup hitter   The fourth hitter in the batting order, so-called because he often comes up with runners on base and is asked to "clean the bases" with a big hit. The cleanup hitter should be the team's best power hitter.

closed stance   A hitting position in which the front foot is closer to the inside line of the batter's box than the back foot. So a righty with a closed stance stands with his left (front) foot close to the plate and his right (back) side further away. A closed stance is more conducive to opposite-field hitting.

closer   The relief pitcher designated as the primary game-finisher. The closer therefore leads his team in saves.

clubbies   Short for clubhouse attendants.

clutch   A player who consistently comes through under pressure is said to be great *in the clutch,* or a *clutch player.*

coach   A staff of coaches assists the manager. Each coach focuses on one aspect of the game, and in recent years the degree of specialization has increased. The *first base* and *third base coaches* advise runners on the basepaths. The *pitching coach* works with the pitching staff on their mechanics as well as the mental aspect of the game. The *hitting instructor* works with the hitters during batting practice or in the batting cage. Most managers have a *bench coach,* whose primary function is to discuss strategic options during the course of the game. The *bullpen coach* oversees the pitchers as they warm up before entering the game.

comebacker   A batted ball that comes right back at the pitcher.

Comeback Player of the Year   The *Comeback Player of the Year* award, handed out by *The Sporting News,* goes to the player in each league who has best bounced back, from either an injury or just a bad season.

commissioner   The highest-ranking official in Major League Baseball. The current baseball commissioner is Allan "Bud" Selig.

complete game   A pitcher who starts and finishes an official game is credited with a complete game. He's also said to have *gone the distance* or *gone the route.*

control   Refers to how accurately a pitcher can throw the ball where he needs to, or how well he *hits his spots,* throwing the ball perfectly, with great *location,* right where you want it, the majority of the time.

corked bat   An illegal bat that has been hallowed out in the barrel and had cork placed inside; a corked bat is lighter and therefore provides better bat speed.

corner   The outside edges of the plate, or strike zone; so a pitch that's *on the outside corner* is just barely a strike. Corner also refers to first and third base, so the players who play those positions are called *cornermen.*

count   The number of balls and strikes on the batter at any given point in time, with balls listed first. Thus, a batter with a *count* of 2–0 (pronounced two-and-oh, or simply two-oh) has two balls and no strikes on him.

crooked number   A number greater than one.

cup of coffee   A short stay in the major leagues. A minor leaguer who's called up to the majors for a few games is said to be up for a cup of coffee.

curveball   A pitch thrown with spin that causes it to break, or curve, as it nears the plate. A right-hander's *curveball* breaks down and in to a right-handed hitter (which makes it tougher to hit) and away from a left-handed hitter (which means it may be breaking out over the plate, which isn't good for the pitcher). A left-hander's *curve* breaks the opposite way. That's why managers are always trying to create desired righty-lefty matchups—to improve their odds.

cutoff man   A key to playing well in the outfield is being able to *hit the cutoff man*. Before the ball is ever hit, the outfielder has to be thinking enough to know where he should be throwing, based on the number of outs and runners on base. The infielder who is serving as the cutoff man has to hustle out into the shallow outfield and get in good position to accept the *relay*.

cycle   See *hit for the cycle.*

Cy Young Award   The BBWAA votes to select the best pitcher in each league and awards him the Cy Young Award. It usually goes to a starting pitcher, but recently, as managers have begun to depend more and more on their bullpens, relievers have occasionally taken home the trophy. Appendix D lists all the Cy Young winners.

day game   Generally, any game that begins before 5 p.m.

dead ball   An umpire extends both arms skyward, with the palms facing forward, to signal for time, which means that it's a dead ball situation (or the ball is dead)—time is out.

decision   For a pitcher a decision is either a win or a loss.

deep   This word can mean a number of things. If a batter hit a *deep fly ball,* it means he hit it a long way (and, conversely, a ball that's hit to *shallow* left field is just barely past the infield). If a shortstop went *deep in the hole* to backhand a ball and throw a guy out, it means the shortstop went really far to his left. If a pitcher went *deep in the count* to a lot of hitters, it basically means he threw a lot of pitches.

defensive interference   Major league rules define defensive interference as "an act by a fielder which hinders or prevents a batter from hitting a pitch" (usually it's *catcher's interference*).

delayed steal   With runners on first and third, a team might try a delayed steal. The man on first takes off, hoping to entice the catcher to throw. Sometimes he'll even stop midway between the bases. The catcher has a quandary: Does he throw to second and risk letting the man on third score before the infielder can fire the ball back to the catcher? Does he hold onto the ball and risk letting a man reach scoring position without even trying to throw him out?

designated hitter (DH)   With the exception of the National League, essentially every baseball league, including the American League, allows the offensive team to use a designated hitter to hit in place of the weakest hitter in the lineup (i.e., the pitcher). During interleague play (including the World Series), the *DH* is used only in AL parks.

diamond   A baseball field, or specifically the infield, is called a diamond, because that's the shape formed by the four bases.

disabled list (DL)   When a player is injured and unable to play, he's taken off the active roster and placed on the disabled list.

Division Series   The best-of-five first-round playoff series in the major leagues. There are two Division Series in each league, with the division winner with the best record playing the wild-card winner, and the other two division winners playing each other. The winners then meet in the League Championship Series.

double   A two-base hit; also called a *two-bagger*.

Double A   The second-highest level of the minor leagues; current Double A leagues are the Eastern League, Southern League, and Texas League.

doubleheader   Two games played back-to-back in the same ballpark, between the same two teams. Also called a *twin bill*. A *twi-night doubleheader* is one that starts at twilight, or late afternoon. If one team wins both games (or *ends*) of a doubleheader, it's called a *sweep*. If each team wins one game, the doubleheader goes down as a *split*.

double play   A defense gets a double play when it records two outs on the same play. The most common double play occurs when a runner is on first base and the batter grounds the ball to the shortstop or third baseman, who flips the ball to the second baseman to *force out* the runner at second base, then fires to first base to *double up* the batter.

double-steal   Exactly what it sounds like: two runners trying to steal. If they're on first and second, the *trail runner* takes off as soon as he's sure the *lead runner* is going (and not just bluffing toward third), and the catcher has to decide where to throw. He can throw out only one, if that.

double-switch   A manager makes a double switch when he replaces two players at once. This is usually done when the manager wants to substitute for an ineffective pitcher who's scheduled to bat in the next half-inning.

down   Another way of saying *low*. For most pitchers to be effective, they have to keep the ball down, which means keep their pitches low in the strike zone.

drag bunt   An attempt to get a base hit via a bunt, usually to start a rally or break out of a slump. It's most often employed by speedsters, especially if they see the third baseman and/or first baseman playing fairly deep. Maury Wills of the Dodgers earned a lot of hits this way, but bunting for a hit seems to be a lost art these days.

ducks on the pond   Runners on base.

dugout   An enclosure on each side of the field (one for each team, usually along the baselines) where players sit while not on the field during a game.

earned run   Any run scored without the aid of an error or passed ball.

earned run average (ERA)   The average number of earned runs a pitcher allows per nine innings; the most common measure of a pitcher's effectiveness. To compute *ERA*, multiply the total number of earned runs by 9, then divide that figure by the total number of innings pitched.

error   A defensive miscue, as judged by the official scorer. If a defensive player botches— *boots, muffs*—a play that's considered routine—either by not fielding a ball cleanly or by throwing it errantly to his intended target—he's said to have committed an error. When a player has trouble picking up a ball they say he *can't find the handle*.

expansion team   A newly created team, or franchise. The major leagues added their first expansion teams in the early 1960s. The most recent additions are the Arizona Diamond-backs and Tampa Bay Devil Rays.

extra innings   If the two teams are tied at the end of nine innings, they go into extra innings. They play until an inning ends with one team having more runs than the other. As soon as the home team holds the lead in the bottom of an *extra inning*, the game is over.

fair territory   The area inside (and including) the foul lines. A batted ball that lands there is called a *fair ball*.

farm team   A minor league club that's affiliated with (and subsidized by) a major league club, for the purpose of developing young players. A team's network of minor league clubs is called a *farm system,* and the players for these teams are called *farmhands*.

fastball   The most common pitch, which moves straighter and faster than the others. There are two types of *fastballs:* the two-seam fastball and the four-seam fastball.

fielder's choice   A fielder's choice occurs when a defensive player fields a ground ball and tries to throw out a baserunner other than the batter. The batter is then said to have reached base on a *fielder's choice*.

fielding percentage   A statistic used to measure a player's defensive performance; to compute *fielding percentage,* add putouts plus assists and divide that figure by the total of putouts plus assists plus errors.

fireman   A team's top relief pitcher, or closer, is sometimes called a fireman, because he has to come in and "put out the fire," or bail his team out of a tight situation.

first base   The base located 90 feet from home plate, along the right field foul line. This is the base toward which a batter runs after he hits a ball.

first baseman   The defensive player who's positioned closest to first base.

five o'clock hitter   A player who's known for putting on a prodigious power display in batting practice and then having no success in the game—when it counts.

five-tool player   One who can hit, hit for power, run, throw, and field. Mickey Mantle and Willie Mays were exceptional *five-tool players.* Ken Griffey Jr. and Barry Bonds are great ones today.

flash a sign   A catcher will *flash a sign* to his pitcher to tell him which type of pitch he wants to be thrown next.

fly ball   A ball that's hit in the air. A fly ball that's caught is called a *flyout.*

force out/force play   A force play occurs when the ball is hit on the ground and a runner is required to go to the next base, but the ball gets there before he does. For example, if there's a runner on first and a grounder hit to the shortstop, who flips to the second baseman covering at second, the runner who was on first has been forced out.

forkball   A pitch thrown with the index and middle fingers spread widely apart; the movement is somewhat unpredictable but the pitch usually breaks downward.

foul line   One of two white chalk lines on the playing field that delineate between fair and foul territory.

foul off/foul away   To hit a ball into foul territory, as in, "The batter fouled off a two-strike pitch."

foul pole   One of two (usually yellow) vertical poles in the outfield (one in left field and one in right) that delineate between fair and foul territory. A ball that lands between the foul poles (or hits one of them) is fair (and good for a home run in most ballparks); a ball that falls outside the poles is foul.

foul territory   The area outside the foul lines; also called *foul ground.* A batted ball that lands there is called a *foul ball.*

foul tip   A pitch that's just nicked with the bat, causing it to deflect backwards, into the catcher's mitt. A batter is out if, with two strikes, his foul tip is caught by the catcher.

four-seam fastball   The basic pitch in baseball (also known as a basic fastball or simply a fastball) is called a four-seam fastball. The *four-seamer* is thrown with the index and middle finger across the wide part of the leather (the part of the ball that looks like a lightbulb), with the first finger joints over the seam. The pitcher's arm comes down on his follow-through, pulling down on the seams, and the rotation creates velocity.

free agent   When a player's contract with his team expires, he can become a free agent if he has enough major league service time (about four years). He can then offer his services up to the highest bidder. Free agency has produced incredible increases in ballplayers' salaries.

front office   The staff that runs a team's day-to-day operations. In addition to various presidents and vice presidents who oversee the business side, the front office is comprised of a few baseball men, most notably the general manager, who make the key personnel decisions.

frozen rope   A sharply hit line drive is called a frozen rope, or simply a rope.

full count   Three balls and two strikes.

full windup   The delivery usually used by a pitcher when there are no runners on base. A pitcher working from the windup brings his hands together, rocks sideways, brings his hands over or near his head, lifts his front leg, rocks backward, and then flings his arm forward while striding toward the plate to get his weight behind the pitch. He releases the ball with a snap of the wrist and makes a complete follow-through.

fungo   A fielding drill, usually performed in batting practice, in which a coach or player throws up a ball and hits ground balls and fly balls (or hits fungoes) to fielders with a fungo bat. The practice dates back to the 1860s.

fungo bat   A specially designed bat with a long, thin handle and a short, thick barrel, used for *fungo-hitting*.

fungo circles   The two circular areas outside the baselines on either side of home plate from which fungoes are hit.

gap   The area between the left fielder and the center fielder, and the area between the center fielder and right fielder; they're also called *alleys* or *power alleys*.

general manager (G.M.)   The person responsible for trading players, signing free agents, and overseeing the drafting of amateur players. The *G.M.* asks scouts for their opinion on players he might be interested in trading for, and he'll consult with the minor league personnel department to determine which prospects might be expendable and which ones have a future in the organization.

glove   The large leather hand covering, with a webbed pocket, that a fielder wears on the hand with which he catches the ball (as opposed to his *throwing hand*). All fielders wear gloves (which have a five-fingered design) except the catcher and first baseman, who wear *mitts* (which have more padding and, like mittens, don't have individual fingers). A player who's a good fielder is called a good *glove man*.

go-ahead run   The run, runner, or batter who, if he scores, will give his team the lead. A player who drives in a run that takes the lead is credited with a *go-ahead RBI* (this isn't an official statistic).

goat   A player who makes a crucial mistake is sometimes called the goat, or is said to *wear the goat horns*.

Gold Glove   Rawlings, a major manufacturer of baseball gloves, hands out a *Gold Glove* award for each season to the player at each position (three outfielders are chosen) deemed to be the best fielder in each league. The awards, which were first given out in 1957, are voted on by coaches and managers.

gopher ball   A pitch that the batter hits for home run.

go with the pitch   To hit an outside pitch to the opposite field, as opposed to pulling the ball; for example, a right-handed hitter goes with the pitch to right field.

grand slam   A home run with the bases loaded; also known as a *grand salami*.

Green Monster   The 37-foot high left field wall in Boston's Fenway Park. With balls bouncing off the Green Monster and the ballpark's scoreboard, and the funky angles in left field, an outfielder has to know how to play caroms off the wall. Red Sox Hall of Famers Ted Williams and Carl Yastrzemski threw out a lot of runners because they mastered the Monster.

groove   A pitcher who throws a pitch right down the middle of the plate is said to have *grooved one*. Also, a hitter who's on a hot streak is said to be *in a groove* or *in a good groove*.

ground ball/grounder   A batted ball that bounces on the ground. You also might hear the terms *bouncer, chopper, dribbler, hopper, nubber, roller, squibber, tapper* and *worm-burner*. A ground ball on which the batter is thrown out is called a *groundout*.

ground-rule double   A hit on which the ball becomes dead (usually by bouncing into the stands or being touched by a fan), resulting in the batter being held up at second.

guard the lines   In certain situations a manager will station his first and third basemen closer to the foul lines in hopes of flagging down hard-hit balls that could be doubles or triples if they get past the infield.

gun   A strong throwing arm.

half an inning   Three outs, or one team's turn at bat, constitutes half an inning.

Hall of Fame   The greatest honor that can be bestowed upon a professional baseball player is enshrinement into the Baseball Hall of Fame in Cooperstown, NY. As of 1998, just 237 men—former major league and Negro league players, managers, executives, pioneers, and umpires—have earned this honor. Members of the Hall of Fame are elected by the Baseball Writers Association of America and specially appointed committees, such as the Veterans Committee and the now-defunct Committee on the Negro Leagues. Appendix D lists all the members of the Hall of Fame.

handcuff   When a fielder has difficulty playing a ball that's hit right at him—such as a ground ball that takes a tough *in-between* hop—he's said to have been handcuffed by the ball.

hang a pitch   To throw a pitch, usually a curveball or breaking ball, that breaks high in the strike zone. A *hanging curve* usually ends up getting hit a long way.

heat   Another way of referring to a good fastball, as in, "He's really throwing heat." Other terms: *cheese, gas,* and *smoke.*

high-ball hitter   A batter who likes pitches that are up in the strike zone.

hill   The pitcher's mound.

hit   A ball hit into fair territory (including a home run), allowing the batter to reach base safely without the benefit of an error or a fielder's choice.

hit-and-run   An offensive strategy in which the runner on first base breaks for second and the batter swings at the pitch. The idea is that one of the middle infielders will vacate his position to cover second, and the hitter will hit the ball through that hole. On this play the manager is said to be *starting* the runner, or putting the runner *in motion.*

hit by pitch/hit batsmen   A hit batsmen, obviously, has been hit by a pitch and is entitled to take first base. (He's also said to have *taken one for the team.*)

hitch   A batter dropping his hands just before swinging. A *hitch in your swing* is usually a bad habit that throws off your timing at the plate.

hit for the cycle   To have a single, a double, a triple, and a home run in the same game.

hitter   See *batter.*

hitting zone   The area right out in front of home plate, where most good contact is made.

hold   A relief pitcher is credited with a hold any time he enters a game in a save situation, records at least one out, and leaves the game without having relinquished the lead; a pitcher who finishes a game cannot receive credit for a hold, nor can a pitcher earn a hold and a save (a hold isn't an official statistic).

hold a runner   When there's a runner on first base and the first baseman stands near the bag, waiting to take a pickoff throw from the pitcher, he's holding the runner, or holding the runner on. A base coach is also said to hold the runner when he instructs the runner not to try for the next base.

hole   The spaces between the first and second baseman, and the shortstop and third baseman, are called holes.

home plate   A five-sided slab of rubber set in the ground in between the two batters' boxes. The plate is where a hitter stands during his turn at bat, and a player must touch *home* in order to score a run; also called the *dish*.

home run   A four-base hit, which results in the batter and all baserunners scoring. A long home run is called a *tape-measure home run*. A home run that stays within the ballpark (say, a long fly ball that just rolls around, and the hitter races home before they can throw him out) is called an *inside-the-park home run*.

homestand   An extended stretch of games in your home ballpark.

hop   A bounce, as in, "a two-hopper to short."

hook   When a pitcher is taken out of a game, he's said to have been *given the hook. Hook* can also mean a curveball.

hook slide   A slide in which the runner goes wide of the base, *hooking* his foot around the bag, in order to elude a tag; also called a *fadeaway slide*.

hot corner   The third base position is called the hot corner, because of the number of hard-hit balls there. Sometimes you've got no chance at all, like when a left-handed pitcher throws a breaking ball and a right-handed power hitter smokes it down the left field line.

the House that Ruth Built   New York's Yankee Stadium. So named because the Yankees, who played in the Polo Grounds, were forced to build a larger stadium to accommodate the throngs that turned out to see Babe Ruth's prodigious feats in the early 1920s.

independent league/team   A non-affiliated minor league or team that may have a loose, unofficial relationship with Major League Baseball, but is in business for itself.

infield   The part of the playing field, enclosed by the foul lines, that extends from home plate to where the outfield begins. The term can also refer collectively to the four players who are stationed there, as in, "The Dodgers have a great defensive infield."

infielder   A defensive player who's stationed in the infield; the first baseman, second baseman, shortstop, and third baseman are all *infielders*.

infield fly rule   Baseball rules define an infield fly as "a fair fly ball (not including a line drive nor an attempted bunt) which can be caught by an infielder with ordinary effort, when first and second, or first, second, and third bases are occupied, before two are out." Invoked by the umpire under the appropriate conditions, the batter is automatically out—whether the ball is caught or not—but baserunners may advance at their own risk. The point of the rule is to prevent the defensive team from intentionally letting an easy pop-up drop to get an easy double-play (or triple-play).

infield hit/infield single   A base hit on which the batted ball stays within the infield, such as a bunt single. A player who really hustles to *beat out* an infield hit is said to have *legged out* a hit.

infield practice   Pregame ritual in which infielders work on their fielding by having a coach hit them ground balls. This practice is usually referred to simply as *taking infield*.

infield shift   Managers occasionally use the infield shift, or *the shift*, when a batter has a strong tendency to hit the ball to one side of the field or the other. If a right-handed batter comes up, and throughout the season he's tended to pull the ball, or hit it between second and third base, the manager of the defensive team might move his third baseman closer to the third base line (guarding the line), his shortstop into the hole between his normal position and third, and his second baseman behind second base or even a bit toward third. Three infielders are now on the left side of the infield. The outfielders often move a few steps left of their normal positions, too.

inherited runner(s)   In statistical parlance, any runner(s) on base when a relief pitcher enters a game are considered inherited by the incoming pitcher. If any of those runners scores, the runs are charged to the record of the pitcher against whom they reached base.

inning   A baseball game is divided into nine innings. In each inning, both teams get a turn at bat, which lasts until three outs are made. The visiting team bats first, in the top half of the inning. The home team bats last, in the bottom half of the inning. Each out is sometimes referred to as a third of an inning. So if a pitcher starts an inning and gets two batters out before leaving the game, he is said to have pitched two-thirds (2/3) of an inning.

inside   A pitch that's close to the hitter is said to be inside, or *tight*. A pitcher can *tie up* a hitter on a tough inside pitch.

inside-out swing   A swing from an open stance with the hands in close to his body, that usually results in the ball going to the opposite field.

intentional walk   A manager orders an intentional walk when he doesn't want to give a particular batter a chance to hit. The pitcher lobs four balls and the batter draws the automatic base on balls.

interference   Major league rules define several types of interference (see Chapter 8). All result in a dead ball situation.

jam   If a team (or a pitcher) is in a tough spot, say, bases loaded and no outs, they're said to be in a jam. Also, if a pitcher is throwing far inside to a hitter, or *in on the hands,* he's *jamming* him.

journeyman   A veteran player (and usually a pretty mediocre player) who has played for several teams and never seems to stay with one club for too long.

junkballer   A pitcher who throws a lot of slow breaking pitches, and no hard stuff.

K   Symbol for *strikeout*.

keystone combination   A team's second baseman and shortstop. Keystone refers to second base, because the two players that play nearest there are so important to a club.

kick   When an umpire botches a close call he's said to have kicked it.

knuckleball   A pitch thrown by gripping the ball with the thumb and tips (or fingernails) of the index and middle fingers and released so that the ball travels toward home plate with little or no rotation; the result is a pitch that moves unpredictably.

lead   Before each pitch, a baserunner *takes a lead,* trying to get as close to the next base as he can and still be able to get back before the pitcher can pick him off.

leadoff man   The first hitter in the batting order. He's usually a fast runner and a good contact hitter. He typically doesn't have much power, but his on-base percentage is high because he can hit singles and draw a lot of walks. Once on base, he should be a threat to steal.

lead runner   The runner who's furthest ahead on the basepaths. If there are men on first and second, the runner on second is the lead runner.

League Championship Series   The second round of the playoffs, a best-of-seven series pitting the winners of the two Division Series in each league. The winners of the *LCS* go on to the World Series.

left fielder   The defensive player who's stationed in left field, or left, which is the part of the outfield between center field and the left field line.

left-hander/lefty   A left-handed pitcher or hitter; a lefty pitcher is also called a *southpaw* or *portsider*.

left on base (LOB)   Any runners who are *stranded,* or still on base, at the end of the inning. A lot of men left on base means a lot of missed scoring opportunities.

lift   To remove from the game, as in, "He was lifted for a pinch-hitter."

line   The series of numbers that appear next to a player's name in the box score—his statistics from the game—are called his line. For a pitcher, these numbers would include innings pitched, hits and runs allowed, walks, and strikeouts.

line drive   A batted ball that's hit in the air, but hard, and on a level trajectory. You might also hear: *blue darter, bullet, liner, rope,* and *frozen rope.*

line score   The horizontally displayed, inning-by-inning account of how many runs were scored by each team in a game. The runs are then totaled up on the right, followed by the hit and error totals for each team.

lineup   See *batting order.*

lineup card   Before each game, the managers of each team fill out a batting order form that the league provides, called a lineup card. Each manager makes three copies of the card: One goes to the opposing manager, one goes to the home plate umpire, and the manager who filled the card out keeps a copy.

live ball   Refers to when time is in and the ball is in play.

load the bases   To put runners on first, second, and third base at the same time.

location   Usually refers to where a pitcher's pitches are going—one of the key measures of whether or not a guy is throwing effectively.

lockout   A work stoppage, sort of like a strike by management. A 1994 lockout caused the unprecedented cancellation of the World Series.

long reliever   A pitcher who's used to pitch several innings (usually three or more). A *long man* is often used to replace a starting pitcher who's struggling early in a game.

loss   The pitcher who allows the run(s) that caused his team to lose a game is charged with the loss. A starting pitcher takes the loss when he leaves a game in which his team is behind and never comes back. (If his club does come back to tie or take the lead, the starter avoids the loss and is therefore said to be *off the hook.*) A relief pitcher is charged with a loss if he enters a tie game, or comes in with a lead, and *blows the lead,* allowing the run(s) that put the opposing team ahead for good.

low-ball hitter   A batter who likes pitches that are down in the strike zone.

luxury tax   The luxury tax is an attempt at resolving the economic and competitive disparity between major league teams that was implemented in the 1990s. It basically means that teams whose payrolls exceed a certain amount must pay a "tax," or an extra percentage, of that excess amount.

magic number   The number of wins and/or the number of losses from its closest competitor that a team needs to clinch a playoff spot.

major leagues   There are two major leagues: the American League and the National League.

Major League Baseball (MLB)   The official name of the organization that governs play in the major leagues.

Major League Baseball Players Association   The labor union for players in the major leagues.

manager   The manager, or *skipper,* runs a baseball team on the field. He makes out a lineup each day, deciding what position each player will take on defense and the batting order. He makes all personnel decisions during the game, and usually consults with the general manager regarding transactions such as trades and free-agent signings.

Manager of the Year   The BBWAA votes on the top skipper in each league. The Manager of the Year Award usually goes to the manager of a team that performed significantly better than expected.

meat of the order   Generally refers to the third, fourth, and fifth hitters in the batting order, who are a team's best power hitters; also called *the heart of the order.*

middle infielder   The second baseman or shortstop. The best such pairings, also called *double-play combinations,* feature telepathic precision borne of years of practice, communication, and study.

middle reliever   A relief pitcher who enters the game in the *middle innings*, usually around the fifth or sixth.

minor leagues   A professional league that features players who are trying to work their way up to the major leagues. It almost always takes at least a couple of years of seasoning in the minor leagues. Each major league team has several minor league *affiliates,* which are subsidized by the big-league team. See *affiliated league/team* and *independent league/team.*

mitt   See *glove.*

mop-up man   A pitcher who's called upon to come in when his team is losing by a lopsided score.

Most Valuable Player (MVP):   Each league has its Most Valuable Player chosen by a vote of the members of the Baseball Writers Association of America (BBWAA). Usually, the award is won by the position player, or every-day player, (though a few pitchers have won it) deemed to have made the most significant contribution to his team. The *MVP* is really the most prestigious award a player can win for a season. There are also MVP awards given each year for the All-Star Game, League Championship Series, and World Series. Appendix D provides a complete list of all the MVP winners.

movement   When someone says a pitch *moves* or has great movement, they mean the ball is slicing, or *breaking,* inside or outside, rising or sinking. A pitcher wants a ball that doesn't hang but continues to break, continues to bite and rotate down or away from the normal pattern of flight.

Murderers' Row   The powerful lineup of the 1927 New York Yankees, which featured Babe Ruth, Lou Gehrig, Earle Combs, Tony Lazzeri, Bob Meusel, and Mark Koenig, and is widely considered to be the best of all time.

National Anthem   A pregame ritual in the major leagues is the playing and/or singing of "The Star Spangled Banner." Became popular at ballparks during World War I; in the seventh-inning stretch during the first game of the 1918 World Series between the Cubs and the Red Sox, the band struck up the song and the whole crowd joined in.

National League (NL)   One of the two leagues, along with the American League, that comprise the major leagues. The National League, which has been in existence since 1876, is the older of the two, and is therefore sometimes referred to as the *Senior Circuit.* The *NL* currently consists of 16 teams in three divisions: East, Central, and West.

Negro leagues   A catch-all term used to refer to the leagues for black players, most of which existed in the early to mid-1900s, before black players were permitted in the major leagues. The two major Negro leagues were the Negro American League and the Negro National League.

nightcap   The second game of a doubleheader.

night game   Generally, any game that begins after 5 p.m.

no decision   When a starting pitcher is credited with neither a win nor a loss, he is said to have gotten a no decision.

no-hitter   A complete-game victory in which a pitcher or pitchers allow(s) no hits to the opposing team (i.e., there may have been batters who reached base via a walk or an error).

obstruction   According to the rule book, obstruction is "the act of a fielder who, while not in possession of the ball and not [in the umpire's judgment] in the act of fielding the ball, impedes the progress of any runner."

offensive interference According to the rule book, offensive interference occurs when the team at bat "interferes with, obstructs, impedes, hinders or confuses any fielder attempting to make a play." If an umpire calls a baserunner out for interference, all other runners must return to the last base that they had legally touched at the time of the interference.

official scorer The scorekeeper/statistician of record for a game makes rulings such as whether a particular play is a hit or an error.

off-speed pitch See *changeup.*

on base Any batter(s) who have *reached base* safely are said to be on base (or *aboard).* Often they'll just say, "two *on,"* which is short for "two runners on base."

on-base percentage A statistic used to measure offensive performance; to compute on-base percentage, add hits plus walks plus times hit by pitch and divide that figure by the sum of at-bats, walks, times hit by pitch, and sacrifice flies.

on deck Next up for a turn at bat.

on-deck circle Either of two circular areas, one between each dugout and home plate, where the hitter who is next to bat waits.

on the fly A ball that's caught in the air (without having touched the ground) is said to have been caught on the fly.

open base A base that's unoccupied. This expression is most commonly used with respect to first base, when there's a runner on second (and perhaps on third).

Opening Day The first day of the regular season. Every winter, players and fans begin looking forward to *Opening Day.* It's the first sign that winter is over, a time when hope springs eternal in the breast of every fan. Every team starts the season with the same blank slate; for many teams, Opening Day is the only time they'll be tied for first place.

open stance A hitting position in which the front foot is further away from the inside line of the batter's box than the back foot. So a righty with an open stance stands with his right foot close to the plate and his left (front) side further away. This stance is more conducive to pull hitting.

opponent batting average A statistic used to measure a pitcher's performance; to compute opponent batting average, divide the number of hits allowed by this number: batters faced minus walks minus hit batsmen minus sacrifice hits minus sacrifice flies minus times reached on catcher's interference.

opposite field The side of the field opposite from the side of the plate on which the hitter stands; e.g., the right field side is the opposite field for a right-handed hitter.

out The defensive team needs to record three outs, or *retire* three offensive players, in each inning.

outfield The area of the playing field that's bordered by the back edge of the infield, the back fence or wall of the ballpark, and the foul lines. The term can also refer collectively to the three players who are stationed there, as in, "The Yankees have a great defensive outfield."

outfielder A defensive player who's stationed in the out field; the left fielder, center fielder, and right fielder are all outfielders.

out of play A foul ball that goes into the stands is said to be out of play.

out pitch A pitcher's most effective pitch, and therefore the one on which he gets most of his outs.

outside A pitch that's far away from the hitter is said to be outside, or *wide.*

palmball As the name suggests, the palmball is thrown by holding the ball tightly in the palm, with two fingers across the seam, so as to slow down the pitch's speed while maintaining a consistent delivery to a fastball.

passed ball   A pitch that, in the judgment of the official scorer, is catchable but is misplayed by the catcher and gets away from him, allowing the baserunner(s) to advance. Contrast with *wild pitch*.

payoff pitch   A pitch thrown when the batter has a full count.

peg   A throw.

pennant   Literally speaking, a pennant is a triangular flag, usually with a team name and colors. In the major leagues it's also used more figuratively to refer to a league championship. (For example, "The Giants win the *pennant*," means they've won the National League championship and will go on to the World Series.)

pennant race   A late-season, down-to-the-wire battle between two or more teams for a division title (or in the old days, a league title).

pepper   A drill, usually performed before a game, in which a batter chops the ball on the ground to other players standing in a semicircle around him who catch it and quickly flip it back to him.

perfect game   A no-hitter in which all batters are retired in order, without any reaching base.

pick it   Refers to a defensive player's fielding prowess; rough translation is "field the ball really well," as in, Brooks Robinson could really pick it.

pickoff   A play in which the pitcher or catcher throws to a fielder at a particular base who tags a baserunner out before the runner can return safely to that base. A pitcher often tries to pick off a runner before throwing a pitch.

pinch-hitter   A player whom a manager designates to bat in place of another player. The player who has been replaced cannot return to the game. In a key situation, a manager will call upon a good hitter to pinch hit for a pitcher or a weak hitter. And because he's usually up with men on base, a good pinch-hitter can really help his club.

pinch-runner   A player whom a manager designates to serve as a replacement baserunner for another player. The player who's replaced cannot return to the game.

pine tar   A sticky, blackish-brown substance that players rub on their bat handles (usually with a *pine tar rag* in the on-deck circle) to improve their grip on the bat.

pitch   When the pitcher throws the baseball to a batter at home plate, that's called a *pitch*, or a *delivery*, or an *offering*. It's also a verb: a player who *makes a pitch* is *pitching*.

pitch around   To pitch to a batter, but try not to give him any good pitches to hit. Say we're facing Willie McCovey, and I don't really believe that we can get him out. So I'll try to *pitch around* him and get to another hitter in their lineup that I'm pretty sure we can get out.

pitch count   The number of pitches that a pitcher has thrown in a game is his *pitch count*. Usually when a starting pitcher gets up over 100 pitches or so, the manager starts watching him more closely for signs of fatigue.

pitcher   The player who stands on the pitcher's mound, 60 feet, 6 inches from home plate, and whose job it is to pitch the ball.

pitcher of record   One of two pitchers in a game who's eligible to earn a decision. One is the *pitcher of record on the winning side,* and one is the *pitcher of record on the losing side*.

pitching change   When a manager replaces one pitcher with another, he's making a *pitching change*.

pitching rubber   A white, rectangular (24" x 6") slab of rubber set in the ground 18 inches behind the center of the pitcher's mound; in the major leagues the front edge of *the rubber* is 60 feet 6 inches from the back of home plate. In order to make a legal pitch, the pitcher's back foot must be touching the rubber; otherwise a balk is called.

pitchout   A pitch that's intentionally thrown wide of home plate, and out of the batter's reach, to give the catcher a better chance to throw out a runner attempting to steal. A *pitchout* is a gamble that can give a catcher a split-second advantage, and sometimes that's all you need. Of course, if the manager is wrong and the opposing runner doesn't take off, the pitch is a ball instead of a strike, and now the hitter and runner have the advantage.

plate appearance   Basically any instance in which a player comes up to hit. Any at bat, walk, time hit by pitch, sacrifice hit, sacrifice fly, or time reached on defensive interference counts as a *plate appearance.*

platoon   Managers sometimes *platoon* two players at one position, using the right-handed hitter against left-handed starting pitchers and the left-handed hitter against right-handed starters. Because more pitchers are right-handed, the lefty hitter gets a lot more at bats. As baseball has grown more specialized in recent years, managers have become more reliant on the *platoon system* at certain positions.

playable   A ball (usually a fly ball) that's hit either in fair territory or in the part of foul territory that's on the field (as opposed to in the stands) is said to be *playable,* or *in play.*

"Play ball"   What the home plate umpire shouts to signal the beginning of a game, or the resumption of play after a dead ball.

play-by-play man   One of the two main roles in the broadcast booth. The *play-by-play man* simply tells you what's going on—just basically gives you the facts, the "who," the "what", and the "where." Play-by-play men are often guys like NBC's Bob Costas and Fox's Jack Buck, career broadcasters.

players' manager   Some skippers are what's known as *players' managers,* meaning they try to be one of the guys. A lot of times this leads to problems because a manager has to exude a certain amount of authority, and if he's too friendly with his players it undermines that authority.

pocket   The portion of the glove that covers the palm of the fielder's hand. Players try to break their glove in by making the *pocket* deeper and rounder, making it easier to catch the ball.

pop up/pop fly   A high fly ball, which usually stays within the infield. A batter who hits one is said to have *popped up* (and if the ball's caught, to have *popped out*).

porch   Refers to the depth of the outfield in a particular ballpark. For example, the distance from home plate to the right field wall in Yankee Stadium is relatively short compared to other parks, so the Stadium is said to have a short *porch* in right.

position   Where a player is stationed on the field. There are nine defensive *positions* in baseball: pitcher, catcher, first base, second base, shortstop, third base, left field, center field, and right field; designated hitter is also technically considered a position, although the DH doesn't play in the field.

post-season   Refers collectively to the Division Series, League Championship Series, and World Series.

power   A player who can hit the ball a long way—and therefore hit a lot of home runs—is said to have good *power,* or to be a *power hitter.* A pitcher who throws the ball really hard—just tries to blow it by people—is called a *power pitcher.*

protection   A good hitter needs another good hitter behind him—someone who will strike some measure of fear in the other team's heart—for *protection.* For example, the fifth-place hitter has to be able to *protect* the fourth place-hitter, by making it tough for the opposition to pitch around the cleanup man.

protect the plate   If the pitcher is ahead of the hitter—say the count is no balls and two strikes, or one ball and two strikes—then the hitter has to *protect the plate,* or go on the *defensive* to prevent a strikeout. He can't afford to take a pitch that's close to the strike zone; he has to at least try to foul it off to stay alive.

protest   If he believes that an incorrect ruling was made, a manager may inform the head umpire that he is playing the game *under protest.* The case is then reviewed by the league office, which issues a decision. Protests are almost never upheld.

pull out   A right-handed hitter who *pulls out* is *opening his shoulder* toward third base. (A lefty *bails out* toward first base). When the shoulder opens, the hips open, the head goes up, and the hands come forward too soon, and the batter is hitting with his arms instead of his whole body.

pull the ball   To hit the ball to the side of the field that's on the same side of home plate as where the hitter stands; for example, a right-handed hitter *pulls the ball* to the left field side. A player who does a lot of *pull hitting* is called a *pull hitter.*

push bunt   A bunt on which the batter tries to *push* the ball between first and second for a base hit.

putout   The act of getting an offensive player out, or retiring him. A *putout* is credited to the defensive player who catches a fly ball, tags a player out, or touches a base to retire a player on a forceout. On a strikeout, the catcher gets the putout.

put the ball in play   To hit the ball into fair territory.

quality start   A start in which a pitcher works six or more innings while allowing three or fewer earned runs.

quick pitch   According to the rulebook, a *quick pitch* is an illegal pitch that occurs when the pitcher steps quickly onto the pitching rubber and, in the umpire's judgment, delivers the pitch "before the batter is reasonably set in the batter's box." With the bases empty, the penalty for a quick pitch is a ball awarded to the hitter; with runners on base, the penalty is a balk, meaning that all runners advance one base.

rainout   A game that's canceled because of rain.

range   The amount of area that a defensive player can safely cover; usually used with respect to an infielder. A big, slow guy usually doesn't have great *range.*

record   A team or a pitcher's *record* is their number of wins followed by their number of losses.

Regular A   Segment of Class A minor league ball featuring less experienced players than Advanced A; current *Regular A* leagues are the Midwest League and South Atlantic League (also known as the Sally League).

regular season   The 162-game schedule that all major league teams play (not including spring training, or exhibition, games or playoff games).

relay   A throw from one fielder to another, who then throws the ball to a third player. For example, say there's a runner on first, and the batter hits the ball off the wall in right field. The second baseman has to hustle into shallow right field to take the *relay* from the right fielder, and then whirl around and throw quickly and accurately to cut down the lead runner at the plate.

relief pitcher   A pitcher who enters the game after the starting pitcher; also called a *reliever.*

reserve clause   The means by which a major league team used to automatically retain a player's rights in perpetuity, even after his contract ran out. When I started my career in the late 1960s, the club just *reserved* your rights every year. So before each season, you'd sign a contract for the upcoming year, and after the season you'd do it all over again. The clause was challenged in court in the 1970s, and it was eventually overturned, paving the way for the free-agency system that exists today.

retired number   The uniform numbers once worn by great players of that team, and now, in honor of that player, no one on that club will ever wear that number again.

rhubarb An argument—and sometimes a fight—between teams, players, or one player or team and the umpires.

right fielder The defensive player who's stationed in *right field,* or *right,* which is the part of the outfield between center field and the right field line.

right-hander/righty A right-handed pitcher or hitter.

road trip An extended stretch of games away from home.

rookie A player with little or no major league experience.

rookie leagues The traditional entry level of minor league ball; current *Rookie leagues* are the Appalachian League and Pioneer League (Rookie Advanced leagues), and the Arizona League, Dominican Summer League, Gulf Coast League, and Venezuelan Summer League (Regular Rookie leagues).

Rookie of the Year: The *Rookie of the Year Award,* voted on by the BBWAA, goes to the best first-year player in each league, whether he's a pitcher or a hitter.

roster A major league team usually consists of 25 players. Those players constitute the team's active *roster.* On Sept. 1 teams are allowed to increase their roster to 40.

rotation play The most common way to defend the sacrifice bunt. On *the rotation play,* the first and third basemen charge toward the plate when the pitch is released, the second baseman heads to cover first base, and the shortstop to cover second or third, wherever the runner is headed. The pitcher and catcher also chase the bunt, but the man who gets there fastest and has the best throwing angle is the one who makes the play.

Rotisserie baseball *Rotisserie,* or *fantasy, baseball* provides fans with the opportunity to "manage" their own teams of major league players. "Owners" of each team in the league (there are normally 8-12 owners in each league) draft major league players onto their rosters before the season starts. The owners draft their players based on their statistics from the previous season and how well the owners think the players will perform in the upcoming season. The composite statistical performance of the players on each owner's team—in such categories as batting average, stolen bases, home runs, RBIs, wins, losses, ERA, and saves—determines the final standings of each team.

round When a runner runs past a base and takes a few steps, or *takes a turn* in the direction of the next base, he's *rounding* the base. A batter will usually *round* first base on a single, so that if there's a misplay he's in position to break for second. A batter also *rounds the bases* after hitting a home run.

roundhouse A *roundhouse* curveball is one with a really big break to it. Roger Clemens throws one.

rout A team that wins by a large margin is said to have won in a *rout,* or to have *routed* the opposition. Other terms: *blowout, laugher.*

rubber game The third game of a three-game series in which the two teams have split the first two.

run In baseball, you win when at game's end you've scored more *runs* than the other team. A run in baseball is like a point in football or basketball. A team scores a run when one of its players advances all the way around the bases, in order, from home plate to first base to second base to third base and then back to home.

run-and-hit A similar play to the hit-and-run, except that the batter isn't obligated to swing at the pitch unless it's a strike, nor is it as crucial for him to hit the ball through the vacated hole at second or short. If he doesn't swing, the play just becomes a straight steal attempt.

run batted in (RBI) A hitter earns a *run batted in* when he *drives in a run* via a hit, walk, sacrifice (fly or bunt), fielder's choice, or hit batsmen, or on an error when the official scorer rules that the run would've scored anyway. *RBIs,* or *ribbie,* are a good way to measure how productive a player is at the plate.

rundown A baserunner who gets caught between two bases—and two or more defensive players with the ball—is said to be caught in a *rundown.*

runner See *baserunner.*

run support If the number of runs scored by a pitcher's team while he is still in the game is high, then he's said to be getting good *run support.*

SABR Commonly used acronym for the *Society for American Baseball Research.*

sacrifice bunt A bunt on which the hitter is *giving himself up* as an out in order to advance a runner or runners one base. The *sacrifice bunt* (or *sac,* or *sacrifice hit*) is most often employed by pitchers and mediocre hitters, especially in close games where one run is significant.

sacrifice fly A fly ball on which the runner on third base is able to tag up and score. A *sacrifice fly* doesn't count as an at bat, so it doesn't affect a player's batting average, but the hitter is credited with an RBI.

safe The opposite of *out.* Any player who, in the umpire's judgment, reaches a base *safely,* is entitled to that base.

safety squeeze See *squeeze play/squeeze bunt.*

salary arbitration If a major league team can't reach an agreement with a veteran player, it can offer him binding *salary arbitration.* The team and the player each submit a salary figure, and they argue their case in front of an arbitrator, who then chooses one of the two numbers. There's no middle ground; the arbitrator has to pick one dollar figure or the other.

save A statistical reward for a relief pitcher who finishes a game and pitches effectively enough to preserve his team's lead; only one *save* can be awarded in a given game. A relief pitcher is credited with a save when he finishes a game won by his club and isn't credited with a victory and meets one of these conditions: 1) He enters the game with a lead of no more than three runs and pitches at least one inning, or 2) He pitches effectively for at least three innings, or 3) He enters the game, regardless of the count, with the potential tying run either on base, at bat, or on deck.

save situation A relief pitcher is in a *save situation* when, upon entering a game with his team in the lead, he has the opportunity to be the pitcher who finishes the game (but not to be the winning pitcher) and he meets any one of the three following conditions: 1) he has a lead of no more than three runs and he has the opportunity to pitch at least one inning, 2) he enters the game with the potential tying run either on base, at bat, or on deck, or 3) he pitches three or more innings regardless of the size of the lead and the official scorer credits him with a save.

scorecard A sheet of paper or cardboard, usually included in a program and sold separately at the ballpark, on which fans can record the batter-by-batter progress of a game. For fans watching a game at any level, *keeping score* is a good way to "stay in the game," and perhaps provide a treasured souvenir of a no-hitter, perfect game, or other memorable performance.

scoring position Either second or third base; a runner on one of these two bases is said to be in *scoring position* because there's a good chance that he'll score on a base hit.

scout An employee of a team whose occupation is studying and evaluating players' talents. A *scout's* main role is critiquing and grading potential prospects—young players whom the club is considering drafting or signing. But there are also advance scouts, who watch a team's upcoming opponents and prepare reports on what to expect.

screwball A pitch that breaks the opposite way as a curveball; for example, away from a right-handed batter when thrown by a left-handed pitcher. The grip is similar to that of the four-seam fastball, but the pitcher rotates his index finger in an inverted manner so that his hand actually points outward as he comes over the ball. The screwball breaks the opposite way of the curve.

second base   The base which is directly aligned with home plate and the pitcher's mound, in front of center field.

second baseman   The defensive player who's generally positioned halfway between first base and second base.

seeing-eye hit   A ground ball that's perfectly placed to sneak through a hole in the infield. Sometimes they say, "That ball had *eyes*."

serve one up   If a pitcher throws a pitch that's easily hittable, such as a fastball right *down the middle* of the plate, he's said to have *served one up*.

set position   The pitcher's stance during the momentary pause that must occur when he's working from the stretch. A pitcher in the *set position* stands with his back foot on the rubber, holding his hands together in front of his body, usually belt- or chest-high. The pitcher must come to a complete stop in the set position or a balk is called.

set up   It's important for a pitcher to *set up* hitters, to try to fool them about what pitch he's going to throw next. A pitcher wants a hitter to be expecting one pitch when he's actually getting another.

setup man   A relief pitcher who enters the game before the closer, ideally to preserve a lead and thus *"set up"* the closer for a possible save.

seventh-inning stretch   In the middle of the seventh inning (before the home team comes up to bat), all the fans stand up and stretch their legs, usually accompanied by the playing and singing of "Take Me Out to the Ball Game." Many historians believe that President Taft—at the same 1910 game that saw him throw out the first ball—inadvertently started the tradition when he stood up to stretch in the seventh inning. Assuming the president was getting up to leave, the fans also stood up, out of respect. But when they observed Taft stretching, they did the same—and continued to do so at subsequent games as the practice caught on.

shake off   If the pitcher wants to throw a different pitch than the one his catcher calls for, he'll *shake off* his catcher, usually by shaking his head as if to say, "no." And the catcher will keep flashing signs until they agree on the pitch selection.

shoestring catch   A lunging catch made when the ball is right about at the player's feet, usually after a long run. Speedy outfielders specialize in *shoestring grabs*.

Short-Season A   Segment of Class A minor league ball featuring a shorter season than Regular A; current *Short-Season A* leagues are the New York-Penn League and Northwest League.

shortstop   The defensive player who's generally positioned halfway between second base and third base; called *short* for short.

"the shot heard 'round the world"   Bobby Thomson's dramatic three-run, ninth-inning home run that lifted the New York Giants past the Brooklyn Dodgers in a 1951 National League pennant playoff. The Giants had come from $13^1/_2$ games back to force a tie.

The Show   The major leagues.

shutout   A game in which one team is held scoreless. A pitcher who pitches a complete game and allows no runs is credited with a *shutout*. Such a pitcher is said to have *shut out, blanked,* or *whitewashed* the opposition.

sign/signal   A strategic instruction, usually made with a gesture or hand *signal,* from a manager, coach, or player, to a player on the field. A catcher uses his fingers—one for a fastball, two for a curve, or whatever—to *put down the signs* for his pitcher, to tell him which type of pitch he wants to be thrown next.

Silver Slugger   *The Sporting News* hands out the *Silver Slugger* awards to the best hitter at each position in each league, based on a poll of coaches and managers. Like the Gold Gloves, three outfielders are selected.

single   A one-base hit.

sinker (sinkerball)   See *two-seam fastball*.

sit on a pitch   If a batter is anticipating or waiting for a fastball, he's said to be *sitting on* the fastball.

slide   To dive feet-first or head-first when approaching a base. The intention is to come to a stop quickly without losing contact with, *overrunning,* the bag, and also to perhaps avoid a tag.

slider   A pitch thrown with the velocity of fastball that breaks late, and in the opposite direction of a curveball. A left-hander's *slider* breaks down and in to right-handed hitters, and away from left-handed hitters. A right-hander's slider breaks the opposite way.

slugfest   A game in which both teams get a lot of hits and runs.

slugger   A hitter who specializes in the long ball. Babe Ruth is probably the greatest *slugger* of all time, and Mark McGwire is today's best.

slugging percentage   A statistic used to measure offensive performance; to compute a player's *slugging percentage,* divide his total bases by his at bats.

slump   A prolonged period of subpar hitting. "*Slumps* are like a soft bed: They're easy to get into and hard to get out of." Any bad habit can plunge you into a *batting slump*—but it can take a long time to pull yourself up.

small market   See *big market*.

snow cone   A catch made with the ball sticking out of the very tip of the glove is called a *snow cone* or an *ice cream cone*, because that's what it looks like.

solo home run   A homer with no one on base.

southpaw   A left-handed thrower.

spectator interference   According to the rule book, *spectator interference* occurs when a fan "reaches out of the stands, or goes on the field, and touches a live ball."

spitball   An illegal pitch that's just what it sounds like: the ball's doctored with a little saliva (or Vaseline, or the like) to make it break more sharply. Although he would never admit it, Hall of Famer Gaylord Perry got away with throwing *spitballs* all the time. A *spitter* moves so much that it's like trying to catch the wind.

split-fingered fastball   To throw the *split-fingered fastball,* the pitcher grips the ball by splitting his fingers as wide as he can across the outside part of the seam. The ball rests in a V between his index finger and his middle finger. It kind of slips out of his hand with a little more rotation than a knuckleball and a little less rotation than a fastball. It tends to sink and it can go in different directions depending on how much pressure is applied with the fingers and what angle the fingers are at when the ball is released.

Spring Training   Before each season, major league ballplayers spend five or six weeks—from mid-February until opening day in late March or early April—in *spring training,* a chance for established players to get back into regular-season shape, and an opportunity for young players to make an impression on the coaches. The teams that compete in spring training in Florida play in what is known, unofficially, as the *Grapefruit League*. The teams in Arizona play in the *Cactus League*.

squeeze play/squeeze bunt   A bunt attempt with a runner on third base. There are two versions of the *squeeze play*. The riskiest, but most exciting, is the *suicide squeeze,* in which the runner breaks for home on the pitch. The batter must make contact, even if the pitch is far out of the strike zone, because otherwise, his runner will likely be tagged out at the plate. And if the hitter pops the ball up, he's out and his runner is probably doubled up, too. That all-or-nothing risk element is why the play is called the suicide squeeze. The less-risky variation is the *safety squeeze,* in which the runner on third breaks only once the ball is bunted. That way he isn't hung out to dry if the bunt attempt fails—but the bunt had better be a good one because the runner is getting a later break from third.

standings A listing of the teams in each division, ranked according to who has the best record, or winning percentage. When reading the standings in the newspaper or on-line, the most important figure to look at is the *Games Behind* column (usually under the heading "GB"). The differential in that column tells you how many games behind (or ahead) your team is with respect to the division leader, as well as all the other teams in the division.

starting pitcher The pitcher who begins the game on the mound for his team is the *starter*.

starting rotation The four or five pitchers who regularly start games for a team make up what's called the *starting rotation,* or simply the *rotation.* Most teams today use a *five-man rotation.* A dominant number-one starter is called an *ace.*

stay alive A batter who has fouled off a two-strike pitch (and has thus prolonged his at bat) is said to have *stayed alive.*

steal A play in which a runner breaks for the next base (usually on the pitch), and gets there before the catcher can throw him out. If successful, a *stolen base attempt* results in a *stolen base.* On a *delayed steal,* the runner breaks either after the catcher has thrown the ball back to the pitcher, or while a play is being made on another baserunner.

steal signs Baseball teams are not above a little espionage, so players and coaches have to be careful of an opponent *stealing signs,* or breaking their code of signals. For instance, a runner on second has a good view of the catcher's signals, so the catcher will usually go to a different, more complex set of signs in that situation.

step in the bucket A hitter is said to *step in the bucket* when his front foot strides away from the pitch, toward the nearest baseline. This is also called *opening up* or *bailing out,* and it's a common mistake among timid hitters who are afraid of getting hit. They end up opening up their hip and shoulder and costing themselves power and the chance to drive an outside pitch.

stickball A variation of baseball in which players hit a rubber ball with a broomstick.

stolen base See *steal.*

strand a runner To leave a runner on base.

stretch Pitchers usually throw from what's called *the stretch,* as opposed to the full windup, when runners are on base. The stretch is a truncated version of the windup, used so that base runners don't have as much time to steal a base or take as big a lead. The leg kick isn't as high and the other motions are neither as deliberate nor as long.

stretch run The last few weeks of the season, often when playoff berths are decided; also called the *stretch drive.*

strike A batter is charged with a strike if he does one of the following: swings at a pitch and misses; takes a pitch that's judged by the home plate umpire to have passed through the strike zone; or fouls off a pitch. (However, a foul ball usually doesn't count as a third strike; for more on that, see Chapter 8.)

strike out A batter *strikes out* (and the pitcher records a *strikeout* (or a *K* or a *punchout*), when he accumulates three strikes in his time at bat.

strike out looking A batter is said to have *struck out looking* when his third strike is a called strike.

strike out swinging A batter is said to have *struck out swinging* when he swings and misses at a third strike.

strike out the side To strike out all three batters in an inning.

strike zone Major League Baseball's official rules define the strike zone as "that area over home plate the upper limit of which is a horizontal line at the midpoint between the top of the shoulders and the top of the uniform pants [often called *the letters,* because that's where the team name is written on most uniforms], and the lower level is a line at the hollow beneath the kneecap. The strike zone shall be determined from the batter's stance as the batter is prepared to swing at a pitched ball." That's what the rule says, but what major league umpires call a strike is often quite different. It varies from league to league and from umpire to umpire. Today's umpires have lowered the strike zone so that pitches not much higher than the waist are called balls and pitches as low as the bottom of the knee are called strikes.

stuff   Shorthand for quality, effective pitches. If someone says a guy has his *good stuff* today, they mean he has everything working well, his fastball is really buzzing and his breaking balls are moving well.

Subway Series   A World Series that pits two New York City teams against one another (such as the New York Yankees and Brooklyn Dodgers of old). Today, with the Dodgers and Giants having moved to California, the only possible such matchup would be Yankees-Mets.

suicide squeeze   See *squeeze play/squeeze bunt.*

sweep tag   I developed the *sweep tag* for catchers, reaching across my body to catch the ball on throws from right field, and then sweeping my glove back to the other side to tag out the runner.

sweet spot   The best place on the barrel of the bat to hit the ball well.

swing away   To take a full swing at a pitch.

swinging strike   A pitch at which the batter swings and misses.

switch hitter   A player who can hit from both sides of the plate—right-handed or left-handed—in an effort to gain an edge over whoever's pitching. He bats right-handed against left-handed pitchers and left-handed against right-handed pitchers. Mickey Mantle, Pete Rose, and Eddie Murray were all great *switch-hitters.*

tag (out)   Unless time is called, a baserunner is out if a fielder *tags,* or touches, him with the ball while the runner is not touching a base.

tag up   To advance to the next base after a fly ball is caught. To *tag up,* a runner must be in contact with the base until after the ball is caught and then run to the next base before the fielder there gets the ball and tags him out.

tailing fastball   A fastball that breaks slightly away from the batter as it crosses the plate.

take   To let a pitch go by without swinging; as in, "The batter *took* a pitch on the outside corner."

"Take Me Out to the Ball Game"   Baseball's most famous song, usually played during the seventh-inning stretch. It was written in 1908 by Jack Norworth (lyrics) and Albert von Tilzer (melody), neither of whom had ever been to a professional baseball game. See Chapter 3 for the lyrics.

Texas League single   A little looper that just clears the infield, falling in front of the outfielders for a base hit. As the story goes, during the late 1800s, cowboys wore their six-shooter pistols when they went to watch a Texas League (minor league) ballgame. One cowboy whipped out his revolver and angrily shot at an untimely pop fly as it was sailing through the air. Fearing for their lives, none of the players moved to field the ball, which fell in for a hit. So from then on, pop-ups that dropped in for base hits were called *Texas League singles,* or *Texas Leaguers.*

third base The base located 90 feet from home plate, along the left field foul line.

third baseman   The defensive player who's positioned closest to third base.

third of an inning   In terms of a pitcher's statistics, one out constitutes a *third of an inning.*

throw out   Umpires have the right—and they're not afraid to use it—to *throw out,* or *eject,* a player, coach, or manager for arguing a call too vehemently, using profanity, pushing the ump, spitting—you name it. Once you're *thrown out of the game,* or given the *heave-ho,* you have to leave the field and the dugout area.

throw out the first ball   A long-standing baseball tradition is the *ceremonial first pitch,* which dates back to the game's early days. It's simply a way of kicking off the game with little extra ceremony, having an honored guest toss the ball (either from the pitcher's mound or from the stands) to a player from the home team (usually a catcher).

time   How you say "timeout" in baseball. But it's not enough for a player, coach, or manager to ask for *time*—an umpire must grant it.

top of the inning   The half of the inning in which the visiting team is up to bat and the home team is in the field.

top of the order   Generally refers to the first three hitters in the batting order.

total bases   To compute a hitter's *total bases,* add his hits, plus his doubles, plus twice his number of triples, plus three times his number of home runs.

triple   A three-base hit; also called a *three-bagger.*

Triple A   The highest level of the minor leagues; current *Triple A* leagues are the International League, Mexican League, and Pacific Coast League.

triple crown   The mythical honor awarded to a player who leads his league in home runs, runs batted in, and batting average.

triple play   A rarity that occurs when three outs are made on the same play. An *unassisted triple play* is one in which all three outs are made by the same defensive player.

turn two   To pull off a double play.

twin killing   A double play.

two-seam fastball   In the old days, they called this pitch a *sinker,* or *sinkerball.* Now they call it a *two-seam fastball.* Whatever you call it, if you watch this pitch on its path from the pitcher's hand to home plate, it drops, sinks, or dives more than a basic fastball. The *two-seamer* is thrown with the fingers between the narrowest part of the seams, where they come closest together. A pitcher can force the ball to sink more by putting a little bit more pressure on the inside finger, the index finger. The more pressure he puts on it, the air currents hit those seams in a different fashion, and the more it sinks.

umpire   *Umpires,* or *umps* for short, make the calls and enforce the rules on the field. They're an indispensable part of the game. Umpires work in crews of four. One crew member is assigned to home plate (called the *home plate umpire,* or simply the *plate umpire;* he's the only one that wears a mask) and one to each of the other three bases; collectively, the *first base umpire, second base umpire,* and *third base umpire* are called the *base umpires* or *field umpires.* The umpires rotate positions for each game. Each crew has a *crew chief,* or umpire-in-chief, who has sole authority to forfeit a game and final say on any controversies.

umpire's box   The *umpire's box* is directly behind home plate. This is the area in which the home plate umpire stands—or, more accurately, squats—behind the catcher to call balls and strikes.

umpire's interference   According to the rule book, *umpire's interference* occurs "when an umpire hinders, impedes, or prevents a catcher's throw attempting to prevent a stolen base, or when a fair ball touches an umpire on fair territory before passing a fielder."

Uncle Charlie   See *curveball.*

unearned run   Any run scored with the aid of an error or catcher's interference.

up   Another way of saying *high.* For many pitchers, if they're getting the ball *up*—which means their pitches are high in the strike zone—they're in trouble.

up the middle   A ball that goes between the second baseman and shortstop is said to have gone *up the middle.* There's also an old baseball adage that a team builds a good defense *up the middle*—meaning at catcher, shortstop, second base, and center field—because that's where most balls are hit.

utilityman/utility player   A player who can play several positions. A lot of defensive specialists make their living not just on their good gloves, but on their versatility.

walk   See *base on balls*.

warning track   A swath of dirt, about six feet wide, at the base of the outfield wall. The *warning track* gets its name because it serves as a warning to outfielders that the wall is approaching. On a deep fly, for example, an outfielder will have his eyes on the ball as he runs toward the wall. The change in surface underfoot tells him that he's approaching the wall.

waste pitch   One that's way out of the strike zone. Sometimes if a pitcher is ahead of a hitter 0–2, he'll *waste a pitch,* just to see if the guy will chase it and strike out.

wheelhouse   A pitch that's tailor-made for a batter to hit—usually a nice high one—is said to be *in his wheelhouse.*

wheels   A player with good speed is said to have *wheels,* or *good wheels.*

whiff   A strikeout.

whiffle ball   A variation of baseball in which a plastic ball and bat are used.

wild   A pitcher with control problems—meaning he can't get the ball over the plate—is called *wild.*

wild pitch   A pitch which, in the judgment of the official scorer, is thrown errantly by the pitcher, eluding the catcher and allowing the baserunner(s) to advance.

win   A starting pitcher is credited with a *win,* or a *victory,* if he throws at least five complete innings, at the end of which his team holds the lead, and his team remains in the lead the rest of the game. A relief pitcher earns a win if he enters a game with his team tied or behind, and he's still the pitcher of record when his club takes the lead for good. (The official scorer, however, has the authority to award the victory to a subsequent reliever if he feels that the reliever who would've gotten the win pitched ineffectively.)

windup   See *full windup.*

winning percentage   Wins divided by the sum of wins plus losses (or total decisions); sometimes called *win-loss percentage.*

World Series   Major League Baseball's October showcase. A best-of-seven series between the champions of the American and National leagues.

the yard   Short for *the ballyard,* slang for *the ballpark.*

Johnny's Baseball Who's Who: The Names You Need to Know

* Member of the Baseball Hall of Fame

Hank Aaron* Baseball's all-time home run king with 755 in his 23-year career as an outfielder in the 1950s, '60s and '70s, mostly with the Milwaukee and Atlanta Braves.

Jim Abbott Left-handed pitcher in the late 1980s and 1990s for the California Angels, New York Yankees, and Chicago White Sox, who was born without a right hand; pitched a no-hitter in 1993 for New York, and in 1998 made a successful comeback to the major leagues with Chicago after a nearly two-year hiatus.

Grover Cleveland Alexander* Outstanding pitcher of the 1910s and '20s for the Philadelphia Phillies, Chicago Cubs, and St. Louis Cardinals; National League's all-time leader in shutouts (90, including a single-season record 16 in 1916) and complete games (436), and tied with Christy Mathewson for first in victories with 373.

Mel Allen* "The Voice of the Yankees" worked as a broadcaster for New York from 1938 to '64, and then again on cable TV in the 1980s; the original host of the syndicated highlight show "This Week In Baseball."

Walter Alston* Soft-spoken manager of the Brooklyn/Los Angeles Dodgers for 23 years (1954–76); won seven pennants and four World Series.

Felipe Alou Montreal Expos manager, known for winning despite his financially strapped club's penchant for trading away talented players; he and his brothers, Matty and Jesus, played together in the same outfield for the San Francisco Giants in 1963; his son, Moises Alou, is a Houston Astros outfielder.

Sparky Anderson Big league manager for 26 years, the first nine for Cincinnati's "Big Red Machine" in the 1970s and the final 17 for the Detroit Tigers; known as "Captain Hook" for his quick and frequent pitching changes; won two World Series with Cincinnati and one with Detroit.

Roger Angell Superb baseball writer whose works include *The Summer Game, Five Seasons, Late Innings, Season Ticket,* and *Once More Around the Park.*

Cap Anson* First baseman and manager of the late 19th century, and first player to collect 3,000 hits in a career; said to be the man who originally established the major leagues' covert agreement to ban black players.

Luis Aparicio* Venezuelan shortstop for the Chicago White Sox and Baltimore Orioles in the 1950s and '60s; one of the first great major leaguers from Latin America.

Luke Appling*   A hypochondriac nicknamed "Old Aches and Pains" who also hit for a high average while playing sparkling shortstop for the Chicago White Sox from 1930 to 1950.

Richie Ashburn*   Outfielder in the 1950s and '60s, mainly for the Philadelphia Phillies, and two-time National League batting champ; also a popular broadcaster for the Phillies until his death in 1997.

Emmett Ashford   Became the first black umpire in the major leagues when he worked the Washington Senators' home opener in 1966; worked in the majors through 1970.

Dusty Baker   Outfielder, mostly with the Atlanta Braves and Los Angeles Dodgers, in the 1970s and '80s; with the 1993 San Francisco Giants, he established the major league record for most wins by a rookie manager (103).

Frank "Home Run" Baker*   Third baseman for the Philadelphia Athletics and New York Yankees in the first three decades of the 20th century; one of the game's first great power hitters.

Ernie Banks*   "Mr. Cub" was a shortstop and first baseman for the Chicago Cubs from 1953 to '71, hitting 512 home runs in his career.

Red Barber*   Folksy Hall of Fame broadcaster from 1934 to '66 for the Cincinnati Reds, Brooklyn Dodgers, and New York Yankees.

James "Cool Papa" Bell*   Negro leagues infielder and outfielder in the 1920s, '30s, and '40s; said to have been one of the fastest men ever to play the game.

Albert Belle   Outfielder for the Cleveland Indians, Chicago White Sox, and Baltimore Orioles who in 1995 became the only man in baseball history to hit 50 home runs and 50 doubles in a single season; notorious for his off-field troubles and adversarial relationship with the media.

Johnny Bench*   Catcher for the Cincinnati Reds' "Big Red Machine" of the 1970s; two-time National League MVP (1970 and '72), and second all-time (to Carlton Fisk) in home runs by a catcher (389).

Chris Berman   Sportscaster for ESPN, best known for his player nicknames or "Bermanisms"; play-by-play man and part-time host of *Baseball Tonight*.

Yogi Berra*   Catcher, mainly for the New York Yankees, in the 1950s and early 60's; managed from the '60s into the '80s; the man who first said, "It ain't over till it's over," and numerous other memorable lines.

Ron Blomberg   Became the first designated hitter in major league history when he batted for the New York Yankees on Opening Day in 1973.

Wade Boggs   Third baseman since 1982 for the Boston Red Sox, New York Yankees, and Tampa Bay Devil Rays, and one of the greatest contact hitters in history; has won five American League batting titles and had 200 or more hits in seven consecutive seasons (1983–89).

Barry Bonds   San Francisco Giants and former Pittsburgh Pirates outfielder; only man in history to hit 400 home runs and steal 400 bases in a career and one of the finest fielding left fielders in history; son of former major league outfielder Bobby Bonds and godson of Willie Mays.

Scott Boras   Baseball superagent famous for his tough negotiating style and his ability to get huge contracts for the players he represents; his clients include pitcher Kevin Brown and outfielders Bernie Williams and J.D. Drew.

Jim Bouton   Pitched for nine years in the major leagues (1962–70), with New York Yankees, Seattle Pilots, and Houston Astros; made a brief comeback with the Atlanta Braves in 1978 at age 39, starting five games; author of the controversial, tell-all book *Ball Four* in the early 1970s.

Bob Brenly   Game analyst for the Fox Network's baseball telecasts; catcher for the San Francisco Giants and Toronto Blue Jays from 1981 to '89.

Roger Bresnahan*   Versatile player in the early 1900s, mostly for the Baltimore Orioles, New York Giants, St. Louis Cardinals, and Chicago Cubs; started out as a pitcher, moved to the outfield, and then became one of the game's best all-around catchers; equipment pioneer who developed the first batting helmet and shin guards.

George Brett   A 12-time All-Star third baseman for the Kansas City Royals from 1973 to '93; only player to win a batting title in three different decades ('70s, '80s, '90s); a sure-fire Hall of Famer, eligible for election in 1999.

Lou Brock*   Outfielder for the Chicago Cubs and St. Louis Cardinals in the 1960s and '70s who stole a then-record 118 bases in 1974; the former career stolen base king now ranks second to Rickey Henderson with 938.

Kevin Brown   Sinkerballing right-hander, one of the toughest pitchers of the 1990s; led the Florida Marlins and San Diego Padres to the World Series in 1997 and '98; has also pitched for the Texas Rangers and Baltimore Orioles; after the 1998 season he became the first baseball player to break the $100 million barrier when he signed a $105 million, seven-year contract with the Los Angeles Dodgers; at $15 million a year, that contract also made him the game's highest-paid player on a per-season basis.

Mordecai "Three Finger" Brown*   One of the most effective pitchers in history despite a deformed right hand, the right-hander pitched mainly for the Chicago Cubs in the early 1900s; his 2.06 career ERA ranks third on the all-time list.

Bill Buckner   A career .289 hitter for five teams from 1969 to '90, but best known as the first baseman who let New York Mets outfielder Mookie Wilson's ground ball go through his legs to allow the winning run to score in the ninth inning of Game 6 of the 1986 World Series (the Mets went on to win the Series).

Dr. Gene Budig   President of the American League.

Roy Campanella*   Catcher in the Negro leagues and for the Brooklyn Dodgers whose career was cut short in 1958 after he was paralyzed in an auto accident.

Jose Canseco   Outfielder, designated hitter, and one of the original "Bash Brothers" (along with Mark McGwire) for the Oakland A's of the late 1980s and early '90s; the first player in major league history to hit 40 home runs and steal 40 bases in one season; has also played for the Texas Rangers, Boston Red Sox, and Toronto Blue Jays.

Chip Caray   Broadcaster for Fox Sports; grandson of Harry Caray and son of Skip Caray.

Harry Caray   Hall of Fame broadcaster for the St. Louis Cardinals, Chicago White Sox, and Chicago Cubs from the 1940s until his death in 1998; famous for leading the crowd in the singing of "Take Me Out to the Ballgame," for his hometown partisanship, and for his catchphrase, "Holy Cow!"

Skip Caray   Play-by-play man on TBS's coverage of Atlanta Braves games; son of Harry, father of Chip.

Rod Carew*   Second and first baseman for the Minnesota Twins and California Angels in the 1970s and '80s; named to 18 American League All-Star teams; won seven AL batting titles and had a career batting average of .328.

Steve Carlton*   With a deadly slider, "Lefty" won three Cy Young Awards as a pitcher in three decades, primarily for the St. Louis Cardinals and Philadelphia Phillies; ranks second all time to Nolan Ryan with 4,136 strikeouts.

Joe Carter   Slugging outfielder in the 1980s and '90s for several teams, most notably the Toronto Blue Jays, for whom he ended the '93 World Series for with a home run off Philadelphia Phillies reliever Mitch Williams in the bottom of the ninth inning of Game 6.

Alexander Cartwright* One of baseball's pioneers, instrumental in the organization, formulation, and establishment of rules for the sport; formed the first baseball club, the Knickerbocker Base Ball Club of New York, in 1845, and umpired the first game ever played, on June 19, 1846.

Henry Chadwick* Baseball's first editor and one of the game's first writers, worked for many New York-area newspapers and publications, including nearly 50 years on the editorial staff of the Brooklyn *Eagle* and 27 years as the editor of the *Spalding Official Baseball Guide;* known as the "Father of Baseball" and the "Dean of Baseball Writers;" originated the system of scoring a game, devised the first box score, and compiled the first baseball rule book.

Frank Chance* First baseman from 1898 to 1914, mostly for the Chicago Cubs, with whom he played on four pennant-winners; part of the famed double play combination of "Tinker to Evers to Chance."

A.B. "Happy" Chandler* Baseball commissioner from April 24, 1945, to July 15, 1951.

Ray Chapman The only player ever killed in a major league game, the Cleveland Indians shortstop died after being hit by a fastball from New York Yankees right-hander Carl Mays on August 16, 1920.

Jack Chesbro* Pitcher, mostly for the New York Highlanders (who became the Yankees) and Pittsburgh Pirates, who won a big league record 41 games for New York in 1904.

Oscar Charleston* Outfielder in the 1920s through the '40s in the Negro leagues; considered among the best fielders, hitters, and baserunners in the history of the game.

Roger Clemens "The Rocket" is the major leagues' only five-time Cy Young Award-winning pitcher, for the Boston Red Sox and Toronto Blue Jays; he also shares the single-game record for strikeouts with 20.

Roberto Clemente* Puerto Rican-born outfielder for the Pittsburgh Pirates from 1955 to '72; four-time National League batting champion; collected his 3,000th career hit three months before his untimely death in a plane crash on New Year's Eve, 1972.

Ty Cobb* Center fielder and major league leader in career batting average (.367), mainly with the Detroit Tigers; all-time hit leader until 1985, when his record of 4,191 was broken by Pete Rose; member of the Hall of Fame's first class in 1936; "the Georgia Peach" was one of the most competitive players ever to take the field.

Mickey Cochrane* Catcher in the 1920s and '30s for the Philadelphia Athletics and Detroit Tigers; batted .300 or better nine times and ended his career with a .320 average.

Leonard Coleman Jr. President of the National League.

Eddie Collins* Second baseman for the Philadelphia Athletics and Chicago White Sox from 1906 to '30; played more games at the position than anyone else in history.

Earle Combs* Center fielder on the New York Yankees in the 1920s and '30s, prior to the arrival of Joe DiMaggio.

Charles Comiskey* Player and manager in the 1880s and '90s and the original owner of the Chicago White Sox.

Dave Concepcion Shortstop for the "Big Red Machine" of the 1970s and an eight-time All-Star; the first infielder to take advantage of artificial turf by bouncing his throws to first for better accuracy.

David Cone Right-handed pitcher who has established a reputation as a gutty competitor, winning 168 games from 1986 through 1998 for the New York Mets, Toronto Blue Jays, Kansas City Royals, and, most recently, the New York Yankees.

Jocko Conlan* Former player and National League umpire from 1941 to '64.

Bob Costas NBC play-by-play man and studio host whose specialty is baseball; named Sportscaster of the Year seven times and has won 11 Emmy Awards for sportscasting.

Robert Creamer   Noted baseball author whose works include *Babe: The Legend Comes to Life, Stengel: His Life and Times,* and *Baseball in '41.*

Joe Cronin*   Shortstop, mostly for the Washington Senators and Boston Red Sox from the 1920s to the mid-1940s; went on to become a manager, team official, and American League president.

Dizzy Dean*   Four-time 20-game winner for the St. Louis Cardinals in the 1930s; known for his colorful personality and his southern drawl, with which he later charmed fans as a broadcaster.

Bucky Dent   Light-hitting shortstop for four teams of the 1970s and '80s; hit a memorable three-run home run to help the New York Yankees beat the Boston Red Sox in a 1978 American League playoff game, and was named MVP of the '78 World Series.

Bill Dickey*   Catcher for the New York Yankees in the 1920s and '30s; hit .300 or better 11 times and finished with a lifetime average of .313.

Joe DiMaggio*   Center fielder for the New York Yankees from the mid-1930s until the early 1950s; one of the greatest players in the history of baseball; "the Yankee Clipper" holds the major league record for most consecutive games with a hit (56 in 1941).

Larry Doby*   The former Negro leagues star became the American League's first black player when he debuted as a second baseman with the Cleveland Indians in 1947; hit 20 or more home runs in eight consecutive seasons (1949–56) and twice led the AL in homers ('52 and '54).

Abner Doubleday   Army captain who served in the Mexican and U.S. civil wars and who, as legend has it, introduced the game of baseball in Cooperstown, N.Y., in 1839; this legend is now widely believed to be false.

Don Drysdale*   Dominating right-handed pitcher for the Los Angeles Dodgers in the 1950s and '60s; known for brushing back opposing batters and for pitching a then-record 58 consecutive scoreless innings in 1968.

Leo Durocher*   "The Lip" was a feisty manager from 1939 until '72 for the Brooklyn Dodgers, New York Giants, Chicago Cubs, and Houston Astros; guided the '54 Giants to the world championship; credited with saying, "Nice guys finish last."

Dennis Eckersley   Has pitched in more games than anyone in major league history; began his career as a starter and won 20 games for the Boston Red Sox in 1978, then switched to the bullpen in 1987 with the Oakland A's; ranks third in career saves with 390.

General William Eckert   Baseball commissioner from Nov. 17, 1965, to Dec. 20, 1968.

Johnny Evers*   Second baseman in the early 1900s, mostly for the Chicago Cubs, with whom he played on three pennant-winners, and the Boston Braves, with whom he won one; part of Chicago's famed double-play combination of "Tinker to Evers to Chance."

Donald Fehr   Executive director and general counsel of the Major League Baseball Players Association since 1984.

Bob Feller*   Best known for his blazing fastball which led to three no-hitters and 12 one-hitters in his 18-year career for the Cleveland Indians; decorated serviceman in World War II.

Mark Fidrych   Quirky right-hander for the Detroit Tigers in the 1970s; known for talking to the baseball, smoothing out the dirt on the mound on his hands and knees, and refusing to pitch a ball that had been struck for a hit; won the 1976 American League Rookie of the Year Award, but his career was cut short due to arm trouble.

Rollie Fingers*   One of the greatest relief pitchers of the 1970s and '80s, the handle bar-mustachioed Fingers is best known as the closer for the Oakland A's and Milwaukee Brewers.

Charlie Finley   Flamboyant owner of the A's from 1961 to '80; moved the team from Kansas City to Oakland in 1968; a proponent of such innovations as an orange baseball, his A's made three straight World Series appearances in the mid-'70's, but he had traded or sold the team's stars by the late '70s.

Carlton Fisk   "Pudge," an 11-time All-Star catcher in the 1970s and 80s, played for both the Boston Red Sox and Chicago White Sox; his most memorable moment was a game-winning home run in the bottom of the 12th in Game 6 of the 1975 World Series; certain Hall of Famer, eligible in 1999.

Curt Flood   Outfielder, primarily for the St. Louis Cardinals in the 1960s, who challenged major league baseball's reserve clause all the way to the Supreme Court; although he lost his case and never played again, he helped open the door for the advent of free agency.

Whitey Ford*   Left-handed pitcher for the great New York Yankee teams of the 1950s and '60s; holds the record with 10 career World Series victories.

Rube Foster*   Pitcher at the turn of the century and organizer of the Negro National League; known as "The Father of Black Baseball."

Jimmie Foxx*   First baseman and prolific home run hitter; "Double X" hit 30 or more homers in 12 straight seasons for the Philadelphia Athletics and Boston Red Sox (1929–40).

Ford Frick*   Baseball commissioner from Sept. 20, 1951, to Nov. 16, 1965.

Frankie Frisch*   "The Fordham Flash" was a second baseman for the St. Louis Cardinals' "Gas House Gang" and New York Giants in the 1920s and '30s.

Eddie Gaedel   Three-foot, seven-inch midget sent up to bat for the St. Louis Browns by owner Bill Veeck in 1951; he walked in his only plate appearance.

Peter Gammons   *Boston Globe* baseball writer who was voted the National Sportswriter of the Year for 1989, '90, and '93; serves as a studio analyst for ESPN and also does regular reports during the baseball season for ESPN's *SportsCenter*.

Joe Garagiola   Catcher from 1946 to '54 for the St. Louis Cardinals, Chicago Cubs, and Pittsburgh Pirates who became an author and announcer after his playing career; has also served as host of NBC's *Today Show*; president of the Baseball Assistance Team (BAT), which aids former major leaguers who need financial help.

Nomar Garciaparra   One of the finest young shortstops in baseball, along with Alex Rodriguez and Derek Jeter; 1997 American League Rookie of the Year for the Boston Red Sox.

Lou Gehrig*   Played in a then-record 2,130 consecutive games as a first baseman and captain for the New York Yankees; teamed with Babe Ruth to form the most productive hitting tandem in baseball history; career ended prematurely when he was diagnosed in 1939 with ALS, a rare disease now known as Lou Gehrig's Disease.

A. Bartlett (Bart) Giamatti   Former president of Yale University, served as baseball commissioner from April 1, 1989, until his death on Sept. 1, 1989; banned Pete Rose from baseball for gambling on the sport.

Bob Gibson*   National League MVP in 1968 after posting a minuscule 1.12 ERA in more than 300 innings of work for the St. Louis Cardinals; two-time Cy Young Award winner; hard-throwing, intimidating style, always willing to knock down opposing hitters if necessary.

Josh Gibson*   Power-hitting catcher who may have hit as many as 900 home runs in the Negro leagues; never got a chance to play in the majors due to the color barrier and died three months before Jackie Robinson's 1947 Brooklyn Dodgers debut.

Tom Glavine   Great left-hander for the Atlanta Braves; one of the club's big three pitchers, along with Greg Maddux and John Smoltz; won the 1991 National League Cy Young Award.

Juan Gonzalez   One of the most dangerous right-handed hitters of the 1990s, the Texas Rangers' outfielder drove in 432 runs from 1996 to 1998.

Dwight "Doc" Gooden   Cleveland Indians right-hander began his career as a hard thrower with a wicked curveball for the New York Mets; in 1985, "Dr. K" was 24–4 with a 1.53 ERA and won the Cy Young Award; his career turned sour due to a substance abuse problem, but in 1996 he made a comeback and threw a no-hitter for the New York Yankees.

Hank Greenberg*   Slugging first baseman in the 1930s and '40s for the Detroit Tigers; two-time American League MVP, ended his career with 331 home runs; missed more than four years due to service in the Army during World War II.

Ken Griffey Jr.   Center fielder for the Seattle Mariners and son of former major league outfielder Ken Griffey Sr.; played alongside his dad in 1990 and '91 for the Mariners, making them the majors' first such father-son combo; hit 56 home runs in both '97 and '98; he and Mark McGwire are the only players in history to hit that many homers in consecutive seasons.

Clark Griffith*   Spent seven decades in baseball as a pitcher, manager, and owner of the Washington Senators.

Burleigh Grimes*   The last legal spitball pitcher in the big leagues, mainly for the Brooklyn Dodgers; won 20 games five times in his career, from 1916 to '34.

Lefty Grove*   Won 300 games and had a winning percentage of .680 for the Philadelphia Athletics and Boston Red Sox of the mid-1920s to early '40s.

Tony Gwynn   San Diego Padres outfielder since 1982; possesses one of the most technically perfect swings in baseball; sure-fire Hall of Famer has led the National League in hitting eight times, tying a record held by Honus Wagner, and has hit .300 or better in 16 straight seasons (1983–98); also one of the best defensive right fielders in the game.

Gabby Hartnett*   Catcher from 1922 to '41, mostly for the Chicago Cubs, for whom he played on four pennant-winners; his "homer in the gloamin'" at Wrigley Field won a key late-season game and propelled Chicago to the '38 World Series.

Rickey Henderson   Star outfielder for the Oakland A's (a few times), New York Yankees, Toronto Blue Jays, San Diego Padres, and New York Mets; only man in major league history to steal 1,000 bases in a career, and the single-season record holder with 130.

Orel Hershiser   Right-hander set the record for consecutive scoreless innings with 59 for the Los Angeles Dodgers in 1988; that same year, he won the Cy Young Award and the League Championship Series and World Series MVP awards; has also pitched for the Cleveland Indians and San Francisco Giants.

Steve Hirdt   Executive vice president of the Elias Sports Bureau, the official statisticians for Major League Baseball.

Rogers Hornsby*   Second baseman, mainly for the St. Louis Cardinals and Chicago Cubs; holds the modern major league record for highest batting average in a season (.424 in 1924).

Carl Hubbell*   Pitcher and two-time National League MVP; "the Meal Ticket" was famous for his screwball and for striking out five future Hall of Famers—Babe Ruth, Lou Gehrig, Jimmie Foxx, Al Simmons, and Joe Cronin—in succession in the 1934 All-Star Game.

Jim "Catfish" Hunter*   Pitcher for the Kansas City/Oakland A's and New York Yankees; won 20 or more games five straight years (1971–75); in 1975, became the first big-money free agent ever signed (by New York).

Bo Jackson   Heisman Trophy-winning football player who played outfield for the Kansas City Royals, Chicago White Sox, and California Angels in the 1980s and early '90s; also played running back for the NFL's Oakland Raiders; a hip injury forced him to miss the 1992 season and after a comeback in '93, he retired from pro sports the next year.

389

Joe Jackson   Known as "Shoeless Joe"; one of the finest hitters in history, his .356 batting average ranks third all-time; banned from baseball for life for his involvement in the 1919 Black Sox gambling scandal (although he batted .375 and made no errors in that infamous World Series), he is therefore not eligible for the Hall of Fame.

Reggie Jackson*   "Mr. October" was a clutch-hitting outfielder for the Oakland A's, New York Yankees, and California Angels of the 1960s through the 1980s; the first player to stand at the plate and admire his home runs.

Bill James   One of the game's most astute statisticians and historians, his *Baseball Abstracts* are packed with great information and analysis.

Derek Jeter   Slick-fielding, solid-hitting shortstop has become baseball's late-'90s matinee idol with the New York Yankees.

Ban Johnson*   Founder and president of the American League from 1900 to '27.

Davey Johnson   Second baseman who, along with Hank Aaron and Darrell Evans with the Atlanta Braves in 1973, was part of the first trio of teammates to hit 40 or more home runs in a single season; after retiring as a player, he went on to manage the New York Mets, Cincinnati Reds, Baltimore Orioles, and Los Angeles Dodgers.

Randy Johnson   "The Big Unit" is the most menacing left-handed pitcher in baseball; tallest player in baseball history at 6'10"; since 1988 has pitched for the Montreal Expos, Seattle Mariners and Houston Astros; in 1998 signed with the Arizona Diamondbacks.

Walter Johnson*   From 1907 to '27, "the Big Train" won 417 games for the Washington Senators, including a major league-record 110 shutouts.

Addie Joss*   Pitched in the major leagues from 1902 to '10 for the Cleveland Indians; won 20 or more games four times; his career ERA of 1.88 is the second lowest of all time.

Jim Kaat   Left-handed pitcher in four different decades (1950s to '80s); holds the record for Gold Gloves by a pitcher with 16 straight for the Minnesota Twins, Chicago White Sox, and Philadelphia Phillies from 1962 to '77; currently a broadcaster for the New York Yankees.

Roger Kahn   Renowned baseball writer; author of *The Boys of Summer, A Season in the Sun,* and *The Seventh Game.*

Al Kaline*   Had 3,007 hits and started 10 All-Star Games as an outfielder for the Detroit Tigers in the 1950s, '60s, and '70s; elected to the Hall of Fame on the first ballot.

Wee Willie Keeler*   Turn-of-the-century infielder for the Baltimore Orioles and New York Highlanders; only 5'4", but was the consummate contact hitter; famous for saying, " I hit 'em where they ain't."

Harmon Killebrew*   Third and first baseman from the mid-1950s to the mid-'70s, mostly for the Washington Senators, which became the Minnesota Twins in 1961; hit more home runs than any other right-handed hitter in American League history and averaged a homer every 14.22 at bats, fourth best all time.

Ralph Kiner*   Slugger in the 1940s and '50s, mostly for the Pittsburgh Pirates; hit 369 home runs in just 1,472 at bats—only Babe Ruth and Mark McGwire have a more productive ratio; has been a New York Mets broadcaster since 1962.

Chuck Klein*   Outfielder who in 1933 had one of the finest seasons in history for the Philadelphia Phillies, winning the National League Triple Crown with 40 home runs, 170 RBIs, and a batting average of .386.

Sandy Koufax*   Probably the most dominant left-handed pitcher in history; led the National League in ERA five straight years (1962–66) for the Los Angeles Dodgers; National League MVP in 1963 and Cy Young Award winner in 1963, '65 and '66.

Bowie Kuhn   Baseball commissioner from Feb. 4, 1969, to September 30, 1984.

Napoleon "Nap" Lajoie* Second baseman from 1896 to 1916 for the Philadelphia Phillies and Athletics, and the Cleveland Naps (Indians); holds the American League record for highest single-season batting average (.426 in 1901).

Judge Kenesaw Mountain Landis* Baseball's first commissioner; served from Nov. 12, 1920, until his death on Nov. 25, 1944.

Ring Lardner Legendary writer of vivid, amusing baseball short stories, with an unmatched capacity to capture the players' lingo; his most popular collection is called *You Know Me, Al.*

Don Larsen Journeyman pitcher who, with the New York Yankees, threw the only postseason perfect game in big-league history on October 8, 1956, to beat the Brooklyn Dodgers in Game 5 of the World Series.

Tony La Russa Innovative manager from 1979 to the present of the Chicago White Sox, Oakland A's, and St. Louis Cardinals; in 1998, La Russa experimented with batting his pitchers eighth instead of in the traditional ninth spot.

Tommy Lasorda* Longtime manager of the Los Angeles Dodgers; won two World Series in 21 seasons with L.A.; was a longtime Dodger farmhand as a left-handed pitcher.

Tony Lazzeri* "Poosh 'Em Up" was the power-hitting second baseman for the New York Yankees' Murderers' Row teams of the 1920s and '30s.

Buck Leonard* First baseman who, along with Josh Gibson, formed the most feared 1–2 combination in the Negro leagues with the Homestead Grays of the 1930s and '40s.

Jim Leyland Manager for the great, young Pittsburgh Pirates teams of the 1980s; managed the Florida Marlins to a world championship in 1997, but the Marlins, like Leyland's champs in Pittsburgh, sold off their star players for economic reasons, and in 1998 became the first team to go from World Series winners to the worst record in baseball in one year; left Florida after the '98 season to manage the Colorado Rockies.

Ernie Lombardi* Slow-footed, but a career .306 hitter as a catcher, mainly for the Cincinnati Reds of the 1930s and '40s.

Al Lopez* Great-fielding and durable catcher for the Brooklyn Dodgers, Milwaukee Braves, Pittsburgh Pirates, and Cleveland Indians from 1928 to '47; led the Indians and White Sox to the World Series as a manager.

Steve Lyons Eccentric journeyman utility player in the 1980s and '90s, mainly for the Boston Red Sox and Chicago White Sox; "Psycho" is now a sportscaster for Fox Sports.

Connie Mack* Manager and owner of the Philadelphia Athletics for 50 years; big league catcher for 11 seasons; "the Tall Tactician" won a record 3,776 games in his managerial career, but also lost a record 4,025; born Cornelius McGillicuddy in 1862, he died in 1956 at age 93.

Larry MacPhail* Former front office executive for the Cincinnati Reds, Brooklyn Dodgers, and New York Yankees and one of baseball's greatest innovators; helped institute night baseball, radio and television coverage, and such traditions as old-timers day and season tickets.

Greg Maddux The dominant pitcher of the 1990s with the Chicago Cubs and Atlanta Braves; the only man to win four straight Cy Young Awards (1992–95); has teamed with John Smoltz and Tom Glavine in Atlanta to form one of the greatest starting pitching staffs in history.

Mickey Mantle* The greatest switch-hitter in history, hit 536 regular-season and 18 World Series home runs, many of them mammoth blasts, for the New York Yankees in the 1950s and '60s; one of the most popular players of all time, the center fielder's career was hampered by a series of leg injuries.

Juan Marichal* Native of the Dominican Republic is the second-winningest Latin American-born pitcher in history (behind Dennis Martinez); a nine-time All-Star who won 20 or more games in five of six years for the San Francisco Giants of the 1960s; known for a high leg kick in his right-handed delivery.

Roger Maris Two-time American League MVP was a right fielder for the New York Yankees, whose 61 home runs in 1961 broke Babe Ruth's 34-year-old record and lasted 37 years until passed by Mark McGwire (70) and Sammy Sosa (66) in 1998.

Mike Marshall Journeyman right-hander who made a single-season record 106 relief pitching appearances for the Los Angeles Dodgers in 1974.

Billy Martin Intense, argumentative, brawling player and manager from the 1950s to the '80s; on-again, off-again manager of the Yankees, who had an infamous feud in the late 1970s with Reggie Jackson and George Steinbrenner; also managed the Minnesota Twins, Oakland A's, and Texas Rangers.

Buck Martinez Catcher in the major leagues from 1969 to '86, compiling a .225 career batting average, with the Kansas City Royals, Milwaukee Brewers, and Toronto Blue Jays; serves as analyst on ESPN's national baseball telecasts.

Dennis Martinez In 1998, "El Presidente" became the winningest Latin American–born pitcher in major league history; pitched for 22 years from 1976 through 1998, primarily for the Baltimore Orioles, Montreal Expos, and Cleveland Indians; threw a perfect game for Montreal in 1991. He retired from playing in February 1999.

Pedro Martinez Boston Red Sox right-hander has command of four pitches: a riding fastball, a sharp curve, a wicked slider, and a nasty cutter; 1997 National League Cy Young Award winner with the Montreal Expos; brother Ramon has pitched for the Los Angeles Dodgers since 1988.

Eddie Mathews* Third baseman, mostly for the Milwaukee Braves of the 1950s and '60s, Mathews hit 30 or more home runs nine times.

Christy Mathewson* Won 20 or more games 12 times, and his 373 career victories ties him with Grover Cleveland Alexander for the National League record; played nearly all of his career (1900–16) with the New York Giants; "Big Six" pitched three shutouts in six days in the 1905 World Series; a member of the first class inducted into the Hall of Fame in 1936.

Willie Mays* Center fielder, mainly for the New York and San Francisco Giants in the 1950s and '60s; Mays combined speed, power, and fielding prowess like few other players; hit 660 career home runs, third all-time; known for his underhanded "basket catches."

Bill Mazeroski Pittsburgh Pirates' slick-fielding second baseman who ended Game 7 of the 1960 World Series with a home run, giving Pittsburgh a four-games-to-three win over the New York Yankees.

Joe McCarthy* The most successful manager in baseball history with a winning percentage of .615 between 1926 and 1950 with the Chicago Cubs, New York Yankees (16 years), and Boston Red Sox; his seven world championships are tied with fellow Yankee manager Casey Stengel for the most ever.

Tim McCarver Catcher from 1959 to 1980, mostly for the St. Louis Cardinals and Philadelphia Phillies; MVP of the 1964 World Series with the Cardinals; became a broadcaster after his retirement and currently works for Fox Sports.

Willie McCovey* Stretch was National League Rookie of the Year in 1959 and NL MVP in 1969 as a slugging first baseman for the San Francisco Giants.

John McGraw* Manager of the Baltimore Orioles and New York Giants from 1899 to 1932; won 2,763 games as a skipper and is widely considered the best manager of all time

Mark McGwire   St. Louis Cardinals' first baseman hit 70 home runs in 1998, breaking the single-season mark of 61 set by Roger Maris in 1961; "Big Mac" has the best ratio of home runs to at-bats of any hitter in history; played for the Oakland A's from 1986 to '97.

Denny McLain   The last pitcher to win 30 games in a season (31–6 for the Detroit Tigers in 1968); but since his retirement in 1972 he has been convicted of an assortment of felonies and has been in and out of prison.

Graham McNamee   Stage actor and singer who became the nation's first big-time baseball announcer; called a dozen World Series beginning in 1923.

Joe Medwick*   "Ducky" was a nine-time All-Star outfielder for the St. Louis Cardinals, Brooklyn Dodgers, and New York Giants; won the National League triple crown in 1937.

Fred Merkle   First baseman from 1907 to '26; as a Giant rookie in 1908, his infamous baserunning blunder, known as "Merkle's Boner"—he failed to touch second base after Al Bridwell's apparent game-winning single—cost New York a victory (and ultimately the National League pennant) in a crucial late-season game against the Chicago Cubs.

Jon Miller   Longtime play-by-play announcer for the Baltimore Orioles, San Francisco Giants, and ESPN.

Marvin Miller   Executive director of the Players Association from 1966 to '84; his extensive contributions include the advent of free agency and the establishment of a pension fund.

Johnny Mize*   The Big Cat hit three home runs in one game six times as a burly first baseman for the St. Louis Cardinals, New York Giants, and New York Yankees in the 1930s, '40s, and '50s.

Paul Molitor   Versatile infielder and outfielder for 21 seasons with the Milwaukee Brewers, Toronto Blue Jays, and Minnesota Twins; with one of the purest swings ever, he had 3,319 career hits at the end of the '98 season.

Joe Morgan*   Power-hitting second baseman and two-time National League MVP; the man who made Cincinnati's Big Red Machine of the 1970s go; now a television analyst for NBC and ESPN.

Manny Mota   Outfielder, mainly for the Pittsburgh Pirates and Los Angeles Dodgers of the 1960s and '70s; all-time leader with 150 pinch hits.

Rupert Murdoch   Controversial media mogul is chairman of Newscorp and the head of Fox; purchased the Los Angeles Dodgers from the O'Malley family in 1998.

Dale Murphy   All-Star outfielder, mostly for the Atlanta Braves in the 1970s and '80s; won the National League MVP award in 1982 and 1983 and hit 20 or more home runs 12 times; eligible for Hall of Fame election in 1999.

Eddie Murray   Slugging first baseman, primarily for the Baltimore Orioles; finished his career in 1996 with 501 home runs, second only to Mickey Mantle among switch-hitters.

Stan Musial*   Stan the Man was a three-time National League MVP as an outfielder for the St. Louis Cardinals from the early 1940s through the early '60s; batted .300 or better 17 times, a modern record, and finished with a .331 career average and 475 home runs.

Hal Newhouser*   Pitcher in the 1940s and early '50s, mostly with the Detroit Tigers; won back-to-back American League MVP Awards in 1944 and '45.

Phil Niekro*   Known for his knuckleball, Niekro was a right-hander primarily in the 1960s and '70s for the Atlanta Braves; later became the manager of the Silver Bullets women's baseball team.

Dan Okrent   Accomplished baseball writer whose works include *Baseball Anecdotes, Nine Innings,* and *The Ultimate Baseball Book.*

393

Mel Ott* New York Giants right fielder from the 1920s to the '40s; won the single-season home run title six times; first National League player to hit 500 career home runs.

Satchel Paige* Pitched in five decades, from the 1920s to the '60s, mostly in the Negro leagues; made a big splash in 1948 as an aging rookie for the Cleveland Indians; his most awesome display came in 1930, when he struck out 22 hitters in a nine-inning exhibition game against major leaguers; oft-quoted line was, "Don't look back. Something might be gaining on you."

Jim Palmer* Won 268 games and three Cy Young Awards for the Baltimore Orioles in the 1960s and '70s; in 3,948 career innings the right-hander never gave up a grand slam.

Tony Perez First baseman for Cincinnati's "Big Red Machine" of the 1970s; had six seasons with 100 or more RBIs; also played for the Montreal Expos, Philadelphia Phillies, and Boston Red Sox in a career that lasted from 1964 to '86.

Mike Piazza One of the best-hitting catchers in history, Piazza played for the Los Angeles Dodgers from 1992 to '98, when he was traded to the Florida Marlins in one of the biggest swaps ever; Florida then dealt him to the New York Mets, with whom he signed a contract worth a record $91 million.

Gaylord Perry* Right-handed pitcher who won 314 games for eight different teams from 1962 until '83; won the Cy Young Award in both leagues; best remembered for reputedly loading up his pitches with illegal substances such as Vasoline.

Richie Phillips General counsel of the Major League Baseball Umpires Association.

Kirby Puckett Center fielder and most popular player in Minnesota Twins history; played from 1984 to '95, when he was forced to retire due to vision problems; eligible for Hall of Fame election in 2001.

Jerry Reinsdorf Real-estate magnate who, along with Eddie Einhorn, purchased the Chicago White Sox from Bill Veeck in 1981; instrumental in the ouster of commissioner Fay Vincent in 1992; also owns the Chicago Bulls, and it was his decision that allowed Michael Jordan a stint as a minor league ballplayer during Jordan's brief NBA retirement in the mid-1990s.

Pee Wee Reese* Shortstop and captain of the great Brooklyn Dodger teams of the 1940s and '50s.

Branch Rickey* General manager for the St. Louis Browns, St. Louis Cardinals, Brooklyn Dodgers, and Pittsburgh Pirates; the man who signed Jackie Robinson, the major leagues' first black player in the 20th century, for the Dodgers; in the 1920s with the Cardinals, he created the first minor league system.

Cal Ripken Jr. Shortstop and third baseman for the Baltimore Orioles from 1982 to the present; baseball's "Iron Man" holds the major league record with 2,632 consecutive games played.

Lawrence S. Ritter Acclaimed baseball writer whose works include *The Glory of Their Times, The Babe,* and *The Story of Baseball.*

Phil Rizzuto* The Scooter was a shortstop for the New York Yankees in the 1940s and '50s; after his retirement he became a popular broadcaster for the club.

Brooks Robinson* Undoubtedly the greatest fielding third baseman of all time; won the Gold Glove for the Baltimore Orioles every season from 1960 to '75.

Frank Robinson* Outfielder, mainly for the Cincinnati Reds and Baltimore Orioles, whose career spanned from 1956 until '76; the only man to win the MVP Award in both leagues; in 1975 he became the first black manager in the majors when he became player-manager of the Cleveland Indians.

Jackie Robinson* Became the century's first black player in the major leagues when he debuted as a second baseman for the Brooklyn Dodgers in 1947; won that season's Rookie of the Year Award and was voted National League MVP in 1949; endured many trying times in his days in the majors with an intense competitive spirit and dignified restraint.

Alex Rodriguez   Power-hitting shortstop of the Seattle Mariners; only infielder to ever have 40 stolen bases and 40 home runs in a single season.

Ivan Rodriguez   "Pudge" (nicknamed after his childhood idol, Carlton Fisk) is one of the finest defensive catchers in history; his strong arm and quick release make running on his team, the Texas Rangers, a risky proposition.

Pete Rose   Baseball's all-time leader with 4,256 hits and 3,562 games played for the Cincinnati Reds, Philadelphia Phillies, and Montreal Expos; hit in 44 consecutive games in 1978, a modern National League record; banned from baseball in 1989 (and thus barred from the Hall of Fame) by commissioner Bart Giamatti for betting on baseball.

Amos Rusie*   Three-time 30-game winner for the New York Giants in the late 1800s; set single-season major league record for starts (52), innings (482), and complete games (50) in 1893.

George Herman "Babe" Ruth*   Outfielder and pitcher, mainly for the New York Yankees and Boston Red Sox in the 1910s, '20s, and '30s; the most prolific power hitter in baseball history; upon his retirement in 1935, he held records for most home runs in a season (60 in 1927) and in a career (714).

Nolan Ryan   Right-handed pitcher for the New York Mets, California Angels, Houston Astros, and Texas Rangers; possessed one of the game's best fastballs; pitched a record seven no-hitters and is baseball's all-time strikeout leader with 5,714 in his 27-year career; eligible for Hall of Fame election in 1999.

David Sabino   Writer-reporter and statistical guru for *Sports Illustrated*; specializes in baseball stats and history.

Deion Sanders   Outfielder who played pro baseball and football in the same year during the late 1980s and early '90s for the Atlanta Braves and Atlanta Falcons; "Neon" Deion, who has also played for the Yankees and Reds, is one of the greatest cornerbacks in NFL history.

Marge Schott   Controversial owner of the Cincinnati Reds; became infamous for repeated insensitive remarks, mostly about her staff, discriminatory hiring practices, and racial slurs; part of her daily routine was to let her St. Bernard, Schottzie, on the field during pregame warmups; banned from baseball and was ordered to sell her controlling interest in the club.

Mike Schmidt*   Third baseman for the Philadelphia Phillies in the 1970s and '80s; arguably the greatest player ever at his position; hit 536 home runs, the most ever by a third baseman.

Vin Scully   Longtime Dodgers broadcaster; began his career in the 1950s as Red Barber's partner in Brooklyn, and is the current play-by-play man for Los Angeles.

Tom Seaver*   Three-time National League Cy Young Award winner and leader of the 1969 Miracle Mets; "Tom Terrific" struck out 200 or more batters in a record nine straight seasons and won 311 games for the New York Mets, Cincinnati Reds, Chicago White Sox, and Boston Red Sox from 1967 to '86.

Allan "Bud" Selig   Owner of the Milwaukee Brewers from the mid-1970s until he became baseball's commissioner in 1998.

Al Simmons*   A .334 lifetime hitter and one of the best defensive left fielders ever; played mainly for the Philadelphia Athletics from the 1920s to the '40s.

Ken Singleton   Switch-hitting outfielder and designated hitter for the New York Mets, Montreal Expos, and Baltimore Orioles from 1970 to '84; now a broadcaster for Major League Baseball International and the New York Yankees.

George Sisler*   A .304 career hitter in 15 seasons with the St. Louis Browns, Washington Senators, and Boston Braves; holds the major league record with 257 hits in 1920.

Lee Smith   The all-time leader in saves with 478; right-hander began his career in 1980 with the Chicago Cubs and pitched for eight different big-league teams in his 18-year career.

Ozzie Smith   Probably the finest-fielding shortstop in history, with 13 Gold Gloves; the Wizard of Oz played for the San Diego Padres and St. Louis Cardinals from the late 1970s to the mid-'90s; eligible for Hall of Fame election in 2002.

John Smoltz   Hard-throwing Atlanta Braves right-hander is one of the most reliable big-game pitchers in history; has more post-season wins than any pitcher; 1996 National League Cy Young Award winner.

Duke Snider*   Great center fielder, mostly for the Brooklyn/Los Angeles Dodgers from the 1940s to the '60s; an eight-time All-Star; hit 40 or more home runs in four straight seasons (1953–56).

Sammy Sosa   Former shoeshine boy in his native Dominican Republic has become one of the best players in baseball; right fielder hit 66 home runs in 1998 for the Chicago Cubs, finishing second to Mark McGwire in the chase for the single-season record; has also played for the Texas Rangers and Chicago White Sox.

Warren Spahn*   The winningest left-handed pitcher in major league history with 363 victories, most of them for the Boston/Milwaukee Braves in the 1940s, '50s, and '60s; also one of the best-hitting pitchers of all time.

Al Spalding*   Won 252 games in seven seasons in the 1870s; founder of the sporting goods company that bears his name.

Tris Speaker*   Probably the finest-fielding center fielder of baseball's first century, he used to begin moving with the pitch; during his 22-year career with the Boston Red Sox, Cleveland Indians, Washington Senators, and Philadelphia Athletics, he batted a whopping .345 and hit .300 or better 18 times.

Willie Stargell*   "Pops" was an outfielder and first baseman for the Pittsburgh Pirates from 1962 to '82; the left-handed-hitting slugger belted 475 career homers for the Bucs.

George Steinbrenner   Controversial managing general partner of the New York Yankees since the mid-1970s; "the Boss" is best-known for his frequent firings of managers and for his free-spending on expensive free agents; the Yankees have won four World Series under his ownership.

Casey Stengel*   Great player in the 1910s and '20s became one of the best managers in baseball history; "the Old Perfesser" took the New York Yankees to 10 World Series in 12 seasons from 1949 to '60; went on to become the first manager of the New York Mets in 1962; that year his record was 40–120, the worst of all time.

Don Sutton*   Right-handed pitcher, primarily for the Los Angeles Dodgers, who won 324 games in his 23-year career (1966–88); currently a broadcaster on TBS for Atlanta Braves telecasts.

Bobby Thigpen   Reliever who saved a single-season record 57 games for the Chicago White Sox in 1990.

Bobby Thomson   Outfielder and third baseman in the late 1940s and 1950s, mostly with the New York Giants, Milwaukee Braves, and Chicago Cubs; his three-run home run in a 1951 National League playoff game off the Brooklyn Dodgers' Ralph Branca, known as "the shot heard 'round the world," won the pennant for the Giants.

Jim Thorpe   Regarded by many as the greatest athlete ever; an Olympian and a pro football player as well as an outfielder for the New York Giants, Boston Braves, and Chicago Cubs from 1913 to '19.

Joe Tinker*   Shortstop from 1902 to '16, mostly for the Chicago Cubs, with whom he played on four pennant-winners; part of the famed double-play combination of "Tinker to Evers to Chance."

Joe Torre   All-Star catcher and third baseman for the Milwaukee/Atlanta Braves, St. Louis Cardinals, and New York Mets from 1960 to '77; since '77 he has managed the Mets, Braves, Cardinals, and (currently) New York Yankees, with whom he has won two world championships ('96 and '98); his '98 team won an American League-record 114 regular-season games.

Pie Traynor*   The first third baseman ever elected to the Hall of Fame played for the Pittsburgh Pirates from 1920 to '37; batted .320 in his career; was a broadcaster for 33 years after he retired.

Peter Ueberroth   Baseball commissioner from Oct. 1, 1984, to March 31, 1989; prior to that he was the head of the Los Angeles Olympic Organizing Committee.

Bob Uecker   "Mr. Baseball" was a backup catcher in the 1960s with the Milwaukee/Atlanta Braves, St. Louis Cardinals, and Philadelphia Phillies; later became a radio and television broadcaster and a comic actor with a starring role in the TV show "Mr. Belvedere."

Fernando Valenzuela   Stout, screwball-throwing left-hander, primarily for the Los Angeles Dodgers, the Mexico native was named National League Rookie of the Year in 1981; "Fernandomania" swept through L.A. during his decade with the team.

Johnny Vander Meer   Southpaw in the late 1930s and '40s, mostly for the Cincinnati Reds; only pitcher ever to throw back-to-back no-hitters; did so with the Reds in 1938 against the Boston Braves (June 11) and Brooklyn Dodgers (June 15).

Mo Vaughn   Left-handed-hitting first baseman for the Boston Red Sox from 1991 to '98; hit at least .300 with 35 or more home runs in every season from 1995 to '98; signed as a free agent with the Anaheim Angels after the '98 season.

Bill Veeck*   Former owner of the Cleveland Indians, St. Louis Browns, and Chicago White Sox, and the P.T. Barnum of baseball;. the son of the Chicago Cubs' president, he began his baseball career as a vendor and stockboy; famous for his bizarre promotions and stunts.

Tom Verducci   Senior writer who covers baseball for *Sports Illustrated*.

Francis "Fay" Vincent   Baseball commissioner from Sept. 2, 1989, to Sept. 13, 1992.

Rube Waddell*   Turn-of-the-century left-hander who led the American League in strikeouts for six consecutive years with the Philadelphia Athletics.

Honus Wagner*   "The Flying Dutchman" led the National League in batting average eight times and hit .300 or better 17 times as a shortstop, mostly for the Pittsburgh Pirates in the 1900s and '10s; he is featured on the most valuable baseball card in history and was a member of the Hall of Fame's inaugural class.

Ed Walsh*   His 1.82 career ERA is the lowest of all time; one of only two pitchers (along with Jack Chesbro) to win 40 games in a season (40 in 1908 for the Chicago White Sox).

Earl Weaver*   Fiery manager who won four American League pennants in 17 seasons (1968–86) with the Baltimore Orioles.

David Wells   Burly pitcher in the late 1980s and '90s for the Toronto Blue Jays, Detroit Tigers, Cincinnati Reds, Baltimore Orioles, and New York Yankees; a Babe Ruth fanatic, he pitched a perfect game and was the ALCS MVP for the Yankees in 1998.

Hoyt Wilhelm*   A knuckleballer who pitched in 1,074 games, second most in history; hit a home run in his first at-bat in the majors for the New York Giants in 1952, and never hit another; first relief pitcher to be inducted into the Hall of Fame; all-time leader in relief wins with 124.

Bernie Williams   Center fielder for the New York Yankees; in 1998 he became the only player to ever win a batting title, a Gold Glove, and the World Series in the same season.

Ted Williams* Probably the best hitter in baseball history; "the Splendid Splinter" is the last player to hit .400 in the big leagues (he led the major leagues with a .406 average in 1941); played left field for the Boston Red Sox from 1939 to '60, with two stints in the military in World War II and the Korean War; homered in his final at bat in the majors in 1960.

Hack Wilson* Chicago Cubs slugger who set the National League single-season record with 190 RBIs in 1930; held the NL record for home runs in a season (56) for 68 years until it was broken by Mark McGwire and Sammy Sosa in 1998.

Dave Winfield Excellent fielder with a great arm, he played all three outfield positions from 1973 to '95, mostly for the San Diego Padres and New York Yankees; remembered for the record-breaking 10-year, $25 million contract he signed with Yankees in 1981; was drafted in three professional sports (baseball, football, basketball); eligible for Hall of Fame election in 2001.

Early Wynn* Won 300 games in a 22-year career for the Washington Senators, Cleveland Indians, and Chicago White Sox; became the oldest pitcher to win the Cy Young Award when he took home the prize at age 39 in 1959.

Carl Yastrzemski* Outfielder for the Boston Red Sox, "Yaz" had 3,419 career hits and was the last player to win baseball's triple crown, in 1967.

Cy Young* The man whom baseball's premier pitching award is named after is both the winningest (511) and losingest (316) pitcher in major league history; pitched from 1890 to 1911 for the Cleveland Spiders, St. Louis Cardinals, Boston Red Sox, Cleveland Indians, and Boston Braves.

Robin Yount Shortstop and outfielder for the Milwaukee Brewers from 1974 to '93; just the third player in history to win an MVP award at two different positions; eligible for Hall of Fame election in 1999.

Baseball in Print, at the Movies, and on the Web

Johnny's Baseball Library

Babe, Robert Creamer   In this acclaimed biography of Babe Ruth, Creamer reveals the man behind the legend. *Sports Illustrated* called it "the best biography ever written about an American sports figure."

Ball Four, Jim Bouton   A pitcher's diary of the season in which he tried to pitch his way back from oblivion on the strength of his knuckleball. One of the funniest, most revealing insider's takes on baseball life in the early 1970s.

Bang the Drum Slowly, Mark Harris   Harris's most acclaimed novel is the tale of the relationship between a star pitcher and his terminally ill catcher. Jeff Silverman of Amazon.com wrote, "Harris's story—funny, bittersweet, and affecting—is, in the end, a haunting meditation on life, death, friendship, and loyalty. A brilliant study of human nature, passionately felt and beautifully crafted … enduring literature."

Baseball America: The Heroes of the Game and the Times of Their Glory, Donald Honig   A dazzling volume featuring interviews with players from all eras, and showing how such legends as Babe Ruth, Ty Cobb, Dizzy Dean, and Ted Williams reflected America's changing society.

Baseball Anecdotes, Dan Okrent and Steve Wulf   This national bestseller is a rousing tribute to the exhilarating triumphs, heartbreaking losses, awe-inspiring feats, and amusing blunders that are part of baseball's great tradition, from its earliest times to the present.

The Baseball Encyclopedia, edited by Joseph L. Reichler   An indispensable resource volume that includes year-by-year recaps, all-time leaders, and career statistics for every player who ever appeared in a major league game. The definitive source for baseball information.

Baseball: An Illustrated History, Geoffrey C. Ward and Ken Burns   The companion volume to Burns' magnificent PBS television series, featuring essays by Thomas Boswell, Robert Creamer, Bill James, Dan Okrent, and George Will, as well as more than 500 photographs, many of them in color.

Baseball's Greatest Quotations, Paul Dickson   Featuring more than 5,000 quotations, from Estella Aaron (Hank's mom) to former pitcher Sam Zoldack, this book, from the author of the equally valuable *Dickson Baseball Dictionary*, is the Bartlett's of baseball.

The Bill James Historical Baseball Abstract, Bill James   Here James, one of the games most astute statisticians and historians, applies his analysis to a decade-by-decade study of the game's history. Rich with great anecdotes and information.

The Boys of Summer, Roger Kahn   The personal story of the remarkable Brooklyn Dodgers of the 1950s, featuring Jackie Robinson, Pee Wee Reese, Roy Campanella, and Leo Durocher. "This isn't a book; it's a love affair between a man, his team, and an era," said *The Christian Science Monitor.*

The Bronx Zoo, Sparky Lyle and Peter Goldenbock   An absolutely hilarious diary of the 1978 season through the eyes of Lyle, the Cy Young Award-winning relief pitcher of the New York Yankees.

Fathers Playing Catch With Sons, Donald Hall   Said Hall, "Half of my poet friends think I am insane to waste my time writing about sports and to loiter in the company of professional athletes. The other half would murder to take my place." Either way, devotees of both sports and words should simply sit back and enjoy Hall's graceful writing.

The Fireside Books of Baseball, edited by Charles Einstein   A difficult-to-find (but well worth the effort) three-volume collection of baseball fiction and non-fiction anthologies.

The Great American Novel, Philip Roth   This wickedly satiric novel tells the story of the Ruppert Mundys, the only homeless baseball team in history.

The Glory of Their Times, Lawrence S. Ritter   The first—and still the best—book to feature extensive interviews with old-time players. Dan Okrent wrote that the ex-players' "memories are as compelling as Ritter's superb interviewing technique."

The Kid from Tomkinsville, John R. Tunis   This is just one of several of Tunis's outstanding baseball novels for children.

Men at Work, George Will   The Pulitzer Prize-winning political commentator and long-time baseball fanatic breaks down the game into essential tasks: hitting, fielding, pitching, and managing. By analyzing the way Tony Gwynn, Cal Ripken Jr., Orel Hershiser, and Tony La Russa approach their jobs, Will finds striking similarities in intelligence, dedication, drive, and desire.

Nine Innings, Dan Okrent   Using one day in baseball—a June 10, 1982, game between the Milwaukee Brewers and Baltimore Orioles—Okrent explains the important facets of the game that may go unnoticed by the uninitiated fan, such as catcher's signals, pitching physiology, and owners' balance sheets.

Shoeless Joe, W.P. Kinsella   The inspiration for the movie *Field of Dreams*, in which former Black Sox star Joe Jackson returns to play baseball in an Iowa cornfield. A mystical, magical novel.

The Southpaw, Mark Harris   Some, including noted baseball writer Dan Okrent, have called this novel superior to Harris' highly praised *Bang the Drum Slowly*. Okrent went so far as to call it "the best baseball novel I've got in my collection of over 200."

The Summer Game, Roger Angell   These superb writings, which first appeared in *The New Yorker*, encompass 10 years of profound change in the history of our national pastime.

Total Baseball, edited by Pete Palmer and John Thorn   A fantastic encyclopedic resource for the game's statistics and history, featuring more than two dozen essays by noted baseball writers, historians, and researchers.

The Ultimate Baseball Book, Dan Okrent   A classic baseball book with a lineup of essayists that includes Red Smith, Robert Creamer, Wilfred Sheed, and Tom Wicker. This coffee-table volume separates the game's rich history into decades and includes 850 photographs.

Underworld, Don DeLillo   Not really a baseball book per se, but a recurring, central element of this highly acclaimed Cold War novel is the ball that Bobby Thomson hit out of the Polo Grounds to win the 1951 National League playoff.

You Know Me, Al, Ring Lardner   A collection of very vivid—and very amusing—baseball stories from a writer with an unmatched capacity to capture the players' lingo.

Selected Bibliography

Bakalar, Nick. *The Baseball Fan's Companion.* Macmillan General Reference, 1996.

Burke, Larry. *The Baseball Chronicles: A Decade-by-Decade History of the All-American Pastime.* Smithmark, 1996.

Cherry, Jack. *All Star Quotes.* All Star Books, 1988.

Creamer, Robert. *Stengel: His Life and Times.* University of Nebraska Press, 1996.

Dickson, Paul. *Baseball's Greatest Quotations.* HarperCollins Publishers, 1991.

Ercolano, Patrick. *Fungoes, Floaters and Fork Balls: A Colorful Baseball Dictionary.* Prentice-Hall, Inc., 1987.

Garber, Angus G. *Inside Baseball.* Friedman/Fairfax Publishers, 1994.

Green, Lee. *Sportswit.* Fawcett Crest Books, 1984.

Halberstam, David. *Summer of '49.* Avon, 1997.

　　　 October 1964. Fawcett Books, 1995.

Harwell, Ernie. *The Babe Signed My Shoe.* Diamond Communications, 1994.

Koppett, Leonard. *Koppett's Concise History of Major League Baseball.* Temple University Press, 1998.

MacFarlane, Paul, ed. *The Sporting News Hall of Fame Fact Book.* The Sporting News Publishing Company, 1983.

McCarver, Tim. *Tim McCarver's Baseball for Brain Surgeons & Other Fans.* Villard Books, 1998.

Neft, David S., and Cohen, Richard M. *The Sports Encyclopedia: Baseball.* St. Martin's Press, 1994.

Okkonen, Marc. *Baseball Uniforms of the 20th Century: The Official Major League Baseball Guide.* Sterling Publishing Co., Inc., 1993.

Reidenbaugh, Lowell. *Take Me Out to the Ball Park.* The Sporting News Publishing Company, 1988.

Simpson, Allen, ed. *Baseball America's 1998 Directory.* Baseball America, 1998.

Johnny's Favorite Baseball Movies

Angels in the Outfield (1951), Paul Douglas and Janet Leigh   This original version of the story of angels coming to the aid of a bungling baseball team (here it's the Pittsburgh Pirates) is vastly superior to the 1994 remake.

The Bad News Bears (1976), Walter Matthau and Tatum O'Neal   A clever comedy about a beer-guzzling former minor leaguer (Matthau) pressed into service as coach of a hopeless Little League team whose fortunes change once a girl pitcher (O'Neal) arrives on the scene.

Bang the Drum Slowly (1973), Michael Moriarty and Robert De Niro   In the highly emotional screen version of Mark Harris's novel, Moriarty plays the pitcher and De Niro the slow-witted, terminally ill catcher.

Bull Durham (1988), Kevin Costner, Susan Sarandon, and Tim Robbins   Costner plays Crash Davis, a catcher who's brought in to tutor Nuke LaLoosh (Robbins), a young fireballer "with a million-dollar arm, but a five-cent head." My first full season in the minor leagues was spent in the Carolina League, with the Peninsula Grays of Newport News and Hampton, Va., and the last game I played at the Class A level was in Durham, N.C., the hometown of the team in the movie. There are definitely characters out there like the players in the film. There are guys in Class A ball who are 25, 26 years old, who dreamed of playing in the major leagues, and they're either on their way down or it's their last stop. For a guy

401

down there who'd been to "the Show," he'd had his cup of coffee, and he probably had no chance of getting back. But he'd stay in it for the love of the game—one more chance, maybe one more hit, one more pitch that'll get him to the major leagues again.

Cobb (1994), Tommy Lee Jones and Robert Wuhl   Jones has the title role in the true story of cantankerous Ty Cobb's relationship with sportswriter Al Stump (Wuhl), who is hired to write Cobb's biography.

Damn Yankees (1958), Tab Hunter and Gwen Verdon   The movie version of the long-running Broadway show in which a middle-aged Washington Senators fan sells his soul to the devilish Mr. Applegate and is transformed into Joe Hardy, a star who will take the lowly Senators to the top.

Eight Men Out (1988), John Cusack, David Strathairn, and D.B. Sweeney   A well-acted and convincing depiction of the 1919 Chicago Black Sox scandal, in which eight players conspired with gamblers to throw the World Series.

Fear Strikes Out (1957), Anthony Perkins   The real-life story of Jimmy Piersall, a promising young player who suffers a nervous breakdown but eventually returns to the major leagues.

Field of Dreams (1989), Kevin Costner, Amy Madigan, and James Earl Jones   Based on W.P. Kinsella's novel *Shoeless Joe*, this is the story of an Iowa farmer (Costner) who follows the instructions of a mysterious voice—"If you build it, they will come"—to construct a baseball diamond in his cornfield. Once the field is ready, the ghost of Joe Jackson returns to play there, as well as other former major leaguers. This movie really hit home for me because of the reunion of Costner's character with his father. That was me playing catch with my dad at the end of the film. Any baseball player would give anything to be able to come back and get on the field again—to smell the grass, to smell the locker room, to hear the other players, and to get the feel once again of all those things. It was a fraternity and an individual sport combined. The team worked together and was one, but individually you had to perform.

It Happens Every Spring (1949), Ray Milland, Jean Peters, and Paul Douglas   Milland plays a chemistry professor who creates a substance that makes anything to which it is applied magically avoid wood. He thus becomes an unhittable pitcher by dabbing his concoction on baseballs.

The Jackie Robinson Story (1950), Jackie Robinson and Ruby Dee   Robinson does a commendable acting job in the film that depicts his trials as the man who broke major league baseball's color barrier.

Kill the Umpire (1950), William Bendix   Bendix, who in 1948 had the title role in *The Babe Ruth Story* (widely considered the worst baseball movie of all time), fares much better here as a rabid fan and former player who's forced to become an umpire.

A League of Their Own (1992), Tom Hanks, Geena Davis, and Lori Petty   An immensely entertaining and vivid recreation of the first season of the All-American Girls Professional Baseball League, a women's professional league formed during World War II.

The Natural (1984), Robert Redford   Based on the Bernard Malamud novel of the same name (although there are significant differences), this is the story of Roy Hobs, a young pitching phenom who is shot and nearly killed by a mysterious woman in black. Hobs returns 16 years later as a middle-aged rookie with a bat named Wonderboy and a flair for the dramatic.

The Pride of the Yankees (1942), Gary Cooper and Teresa Wright   The sad story of Lou Gehrig, who died of amyotrophic lateral sclerosis at age 37, is really more of a love story than a baseball movie. Cooper and Wright turn in solid performances.

Rhubarb (1951), Ray Milland and Jan Sterling   A charming comedy/fantasy about a cat who inherits the Brooklyn baseball team.

Rookie of the Year (1993), Thomas Ian Nicholas, Gary Busey, and Albert Hall   A fractured arm results in a magical transformation that enables a young boy to throw a baseball 100 miles an hour, which makes him a hero for his beloved, hapless Chicago Cubs.

The Sandlot (1993), Tom Guiry, Mike Vitar, and Patrick Renna   A touching, well-played reminiscence about a group of kids playing sandlot baseball in 1962.

Take Me Out to the Ball Game (1949), Gene Kelly, Frank Sinatra, and Esther Williams   One of the best-known baseball musicals features Kelly, Sinatra, and Jules Munshin as a musical diamond trio.

The Winning Team (1952), Ronald Reagan and Doris Day   The future president portrays Grover Cleveland Alexander from his rise to big-league stardom to his post-retirement struggles with alcohol abuse to his subsequent recovery.

Periodicals

Baseball America
P.O. Box 2089
Durham, NC 27702
(919) 682-9635

Baseball Digest
990 Grove Street
Evanston, IL 60201-4370
(847) 491-6440

ESPN Magazine
19 E. 34th Street
New York, NY 10016
(212) 515-1000
(212) 515-1290 (fax)

Newsweek
251 W. 57th Street
New York, NY 11019-6999
(212) 445-4000
(212) 445-5068 (fax)

Sport Magazine
110 Fifth Avenue
4th Floor
New York, NY 10011
(212) 886-3600
(212) 886-2812 (fax)

Sporting Goods Business
One Penn Plaza
New York, NY 10119-0004
(212) 615-2633
(212) 279-4454 (fax)

The Sporting News
10176 Corporate Square Drive
Suite 200
St. Louis, MO 63132
(314) 997-7111
(314) 997-0765 (fax)

Sports Illustrated
Time & Life Building
Rockefeller Center
New York, NY 10020-1393
(212) 522-1212

Sports Illustrated for Kids
Time & Life Building
Rockefeller Center
New York, NY 10020-1393
(212) 522-1212

Sportstyle
7 W. 34th Street
New York, NY 10001
(212) 630-3735
(212) 630-3726 (fax)

Team Licensing Business
3300 N. Central Avenue
Suite 2400
Phoenix, AZ 85012
(602) 990-1101
(602) 990-0819 (fax)

Time Magazine
Time & Life Building
Rockefeller Center
New York, NY 10020-1393
(212) 522-1212

Total Baseball
445 Park Avenue
19th Floor
New York, NY 10022
(212) 319-6611
(212) 319-3820 (fax)

USA Today
1000 Wilson Boulevard
Arlington, VA 22229
(703) 276-3400
(703) 558-3988 (fax)

USA Today Baseball Weekly
1000 Wilson Boulevard
21st Floor
Arlington, VA 22229
(703) 558-5630
(703) 558-4678 (fax)

Johnny's Favorite Baseball Web Sites

http://www.majorleaguebaseball.com/   Major League Baseball's official site, with links to team and player information as well as a library of lifetime statistical leaders.

http://www.minorleaguebaseball.com/   Minor League Baseball's official site, with links to team and player information.

http://www.fastball.com/   Team and player information for the majors and minors, including feature stories, stats, links, and scores.

http://www.bigleaguers.com/   Players' site aimed toward younger fans, with stats and bio information of most big league players and lots of baseball-related activities.

http://www.sabr.org/   Society for American Baseball Research's official site, with links to member sites and original baseball research.

http://www.baseballhalloffame.org/   Official site of the Baseball Hall of Fame in Cooperstown, N.Y., featuring news and information about the museum.

http://www.baseball-links.com/   John Skilton's Baseball Links, featuring more than 4,000 links for nearly all imaginable baseball-related topics, everything from the majors to the youth leagues.

http://www.ncaa.org/stats/baseball.cgi   Provides official NCAA baseball statistics.

http://www.totalbaseball.com/   Features lots of historical and contemporary baseball information.

http://www.baseball-links.com/internat.shtml   International baseball links to sites in more than 30 countries around the world.

http://www.ballparks.com/baseball/index.htm   Information and photos for major league ballparks of the past, present, and future.

http://www.fansonly.com/channels/news/sports/baseball/index.html   News and links to official college baseball team pages.

http://www.baseball-links.com/realaud.shtml   Visitors can listen to live radio broadcasts of major league, minor league, and college baseball games over the Internet.

http://www.baseball.ca   Baseball Canada's official website.

http://www.baseball.smallworld.com/   A free fantasy baseball site where fans can create their own division, draft their team, and buy and sell players.

News Organization Web Sites

Baseball America:
http://www.fanlink.com/ba/
CBS Sportsline:
http://www.cbs.sportsline.com/mlb/index.html
CNN/SI:
http://www.cnnsi.com/baseball/
ESPN:
http://espn.sportszone.com/mlb/
Fox Sports:
http://www.foxsports.com/baseball/
MSNBC:
http://www.msnbc.com/news/mlb_front.asp
The Sporting News:
http://www.sportingnews.com/baseball/
USA Today:
http://www.usatoday.com/sports/mlb.htm
USA Today Baseball Weekly:
http://www.usatoday.com/bbwfront.htm
Yahoo:
http://baseball.yahoo.com/mlb/

The Major League Honor Roll

Hall of Fame Members

The Baseball Hall of Fame was founded in 1936. The Hall of Fame's charter members were Ty Cobb, Walter Johnson, Christy Mathewson, Babe Ruth, and Honus Wagner. Except for Mathewson, all were present when the National Baseball Hall of Fame was established in Cooperstown, N.Y., on June 12, 1939, as were Grover Cleveland Alexander, Eddie Collins, Napoleon Lajoie, Tris Speaker, and Cy Young.

Players	Career	Inducted
Henry Aaron, outfield	1954–76	1982
Grover Alexander, pitcher	1911–30	1938
Cap Anson, first base	1876–97	1939
Luis Aparicio, shortstop	1956–73	1984
Luke Appling, shortstop	1930–50	1964
Richie Ashburn, outfield	1948–62	1995
Earl Averill, outfield	1921–41	1975
Home Run Baker, third base	1908–22	1955
Dave Bancroft, shortstop	1915–30	1971
Ernie Banks, shortstop	1953–71	1977
Jake Beckley, first base	1888–1907	1971
Cool Papa Bell, outfield	Negro leagues	1974
Johnny Bench, catcher	1967–83	1989
Chief Bender, pitcher	1903–25	1953
Yogi Berra, catcher	1946–65	1972
Jim Bottomley, first base	1922–37	1974
Lou Boudreau, shortstop	1938–52	1970
Roger Bresnahan, catcher	1897–1915	1945
Lou Brock, outfield	1961–79	1985
Dan Brouthers, first base	1879–1904	1945
Three Finger Brown, pitcher	1903–16	1949
Jim Bunning, pitcher	1955–71	1996

continues

continued

Players	Career	Inducted
Jesse Burkett, outfield	1890–1905	1946
Roy Campanella, catcher	1948–57	1969
Rod Carew, second base	1967–85	1991
Max Carey, outfield	1910–29	1961
Steve Carlton, pitcher	1965–88	1994
Frank Chance, first base	1898–1914	1946
Oscar Charleston, outfield	Negro leagues	1976
Jack Chesbro, pitcher	1899–1909	1946
Fred Clarke, outfield	1894–1915	1945
John Clarkson, pitcher	1882–94	1963
Roberto Clemente, outfield	1955–72	1973
Ty Cobb, outfield	1905–28	1936
Mickey Cochrane, catcher	1925–37	1947
Eddie Collins, second base	1906–30	1939
Jimmy Collins, third base	1895–1908	1945
Earle Combs, outfield	1924–35	1970
Roger Connor, first base	1880–97	1976
Stan Coveleski, pitcher	1912–28	1969
Sam Crawford, outfield	1899–1917	1957
Joe Cronin, shortstop	1926–45	1956
Candy Cummings, pitcher	1872–77	1939
Kiki Cuyler, outfield	1921–38	1968
Ray Dandridge, third base	Negro leagues	1987
George Davis, shortstop	1890–1909	1998
Leon Day, pitcher/outfield	Negro leagues	1995
Dizzy Dean, pitcher	1930–47	1953
Ed Delahanty, outfield	1888–1903	1945
Bill Dickey, catcher	1928–46	1954
Martin Dihigo, pitcher	Negro leagues	1977
Joe DiMaggio, outfield	1936–51	1955
Larry Doby, outfield	1947–59	1998
Bobby Doerr, second base	1937–51	1986
Don Drysdale, pitcher	1956–69	1984
Hugh Duffy, outfield	1888–1906	1945
Johnny Evers, second base	1902–29	1939
Buck Ewing, catcher	1880–97	1946
Red Faber, pitcher	1914–33	1964
Bob Feller, pitcher	1936–56	1962
Rick Ferrell, catcher	1929–47	1984
Rollie Fingers, pitcher	1968–85	1992

Players	Career	Inducted
Elmer Flick, outfield	1898–1910	1963
Whitey Ford, pitcher	1950–67	1974
Bill Foster, pitcher	Negro leagues	1996
Nellie Fox, second base	1947–65	1997
Jimmie Foxx, first base	1925–45	1951
Frankie Frisch, second base	1919–37	1947
Pud Galvin, pitcher	1879–92	1965
Lou Gehrig, first base	1923–39	1939
Charlie Gehringer, second base	1924–42	1949
Bob Gibson, pitcher	1959–75	1981
Josh Gibson, catcher	Negro leagues	1972
Lefty Gomez, pitcher	1930–43	1972
Goose Goslin, outfield	1921–38	1968
Hank Greenberg, first base	1930–47	1956
Burleigh Grimes, pitcher	1916–34	1964
Lefty Grove, pitcher	1925–41	1947
Chick Hafey, outfield	1924–37	1971
Jesse Haines, pitcher	1918–37	1970
Billy Hamilton, outfield	1888–1901	1961
Gabby Hartnett, catcher	1922–41	1955
Harry Heilmann, outfield	1914–32	1952
Billy Herman, second base	1931–47	1975
Harry Hooper, outfield	1909–25	1971
Rogers Hornsby, second base	1915–37	1942
Waite Hoyt, pitcher	1918–38	1969
Carl Hubbell, pitcher	1928–43	1947
Catfish Hunter, pitcher	1965–79	1987
Monte Irvin, outfield	1949–56	1973
Reggie Jackson, outfield	1967–87	1993
Travis Jackson, shortstop	1922–36	1982
Ferguson Jenkins, pitcher	1965–83	1991
Hugie Jennings, shortstop	1891–1918	1945
Judy Johnson, third base	Negro leagues	1975
Walter Johnson, pitcher	1907–27	1936
Addie Joss, pitcher	1902–10	1978
Al Kaline, outfield	1953–74	1980
Tim Keefe, pitcher	1880–93	1964
Willie Keeler, outfield	1892–1910	1939
George Kell, third base	1943–57	1983
Joe Kelley, outfield	1891–1908	1971

continues

continued

Players	Career	Inducted
George Kelly, first base	1915–32	1973
King Kelly, outfield	1878–93	1945
Harmon Killebrew, first base	1954–75	1984
Ralph Kiner, outfield	1946–55	1975
Chuck Klein, outfield	1928–44	1980
Sandy Koufax, pitcher	1955–66	1972
Nap Lajoie, second base	1896–1916	1937
Tony Lazzeri, second base	1926–39	1991
Bob Lemon, pitcher	1941–58	1976
Buck Leonard, first base	Negro leagues	1972
Fred Lindstrom, third base	1924–36	1976
John Henry Lloyd, shortstop	Negro leagues	1977
Ernie Lombardi, catcher	1931–47	1986
Ted Lyons, pitcher	1923–46	1955
Mickey Mantle, outfield	1951–68	1974
Heinie Manush, outfield	1923–39	1964
Rabbit Maranville, shortstop	1912–35	1954
Juan Marichal, pitcher	1960–75	1983
Rube Marquard, pitcher	1908–25	1971
Eddie Mathews, third base	1952–68	1978
Christy Mathewson, pitcher	1900–16	1936
Willie Mays, outfield	1951–73	1979
Tommy McCarthy, outfield	1884–96	1946
Willie McCovey, first base	1959–80	1986
Joe McGinnity, pitcher	1899–1908	1946
Joe Medwick, outfield	1932–48	1968
Johnny Mize, first base	1936–53	1981
Joe Morgan, second base	1963–84	1990
Stan Musial, outfield	1941–63	1969
Hal Newhouser, pitcher	1939–55	1992
Kid Nichols, pitcher	1890–1906	1949
Phil Niekro, pitcher	1964–87	1997
Jim O'Rourke, outfield	1876–1904	1945
Mel Ott, outfield	1926–47	1951
Satchel Paige, pitcher	1948–65	1971
Jim Palmer, pitcher	1965–84	1990
Herb Pennock, pitcher	1912–34	1948
Gaylord Perry, pitcher	1962–83	1991
Eddie Plank, pitcher	1901–17	1946
Hoss Radbourn, pitcher	1880–91	1939

Players	Career	Inducted
Pee Wee Reese, shortstop	1940–58	1984
Sam Rice, outfield	1915–35	1963
Eppa Rixey, pitcher	1912–33	1963
Phil Rizzuto, shortstop	1941–56	1994
Robin Roberts, pitcher	1948–66	1976
Brooks Robinson, third base	1955–77	1983
Frank Robinson, outfield	1956–76	1982
Jackie Robinson, second base	1947–56	1962
Joe Rogan, pitcher/outfield	Negro leagues	1998
Ed Roush, pitcher	1913–31	1962
Red Ruffing, pitcher	1924–47	1967
Amos Rusie, pitcher	1889–1901	1977
Babe Ruth, outfield	1914–35	1936
Ray Schalk, catcher	1912–29	1955
Mike Schmidt, third base	1972–89	1995
Red Schoendienst, second base	1945–63	1989
Tom Seaver, pitcher	1967–86	1992
Joe Sewell, shortstop	1920–33	1977
Al Simmons, outfield	1924–44	1953
George Sisler, first base	1915–30	1939
Enos Slaughter, outfield	1938–59	1985
Duke Snider, outfield	1947–64	1980
Warren Spahn, pitcher	1942–65	1973
Al Spalding, pitcher	1871–78	1939
Tris Speaker, outfield	1907–28	1937
Willie Stargell, outfield	1962–82	1988
Don Sutton, pitcher	1966–88	1998
Bill Terry, first base	1923–36	1954
Sam Thompson, outfield	1885–1906	1974
Joe Tinker, shortstop	1902–16	1946
Pie Traynor, third base	1920–37	1948
Dazzy Vance, pitcher	1915–35	1955
Arky Vaughan, shortstop	1932–48	1985
Rube Waddell, pitcher	1897–1910	1946
Honus Wagner, shortstop	1897–1917	1936
Bobby Wallace, shortstop	1894–1918	1953
Ed Walsh, pitcher	1904–17	1946
Lloyd Waner, outfield	1927–45	1967
Paul Waner, outfield	1926–45	1953
Monte Ward, shortstop	1887–94	1964

continues

continued

Players	Career	Inducted
Mickey Welch, pitcher	1880–92	1973
Willie Wells, shortstop	Negro leagues	1997
Zack Wheat, outfield	1909–27	1959
Hoyt Wilhelm, pitcher	1952–72	1985
Billy Williams, outfield	1959–76	1987
Ted Williams, outfield	1939–60	1966
Vic Willis, pitcher	1898–1910	1995
Hack Wilson, outfield	1923–34	1979
Early Wynn, pitcher	1939–63	1972
Carl Yastrzemski, outfield	1961–83	1989
Cy Young, pitcher	1890–1911	1937
Ross Youngs, outfield	1917–26	1972

Managers	Career	Inducted
Walter Alston	1954–76	1983
Leo Durocher	1939–73	1994
Ned Hanlon	1889–1907	1996
Bucky Harris	1924–56	1975
Miller Huggins	1913–29	1964
Tommy Lasorda	1976–96	1997
Al Lopez	1951–69	1977
Connie Mack	1894–1950	1937
Joe McCarthy	1926–50	1957
John McGraw	1899–1932	1937
Bill McKechnie	1915–46	1962
Wilbert Robinson	1902–31	1945
Casey Stengel	1934–65	1966
Earl Weaver	1968–86	1996
Harry Wright	1876–93	1953

Pioneers/Executives	Role	Inducted
Ed Barrow	Manager/executive	1953
Morgan Bulkeley	Executive	1937
Alexander Cartwright	Executive	1938
Henry Chadwick	Writer/statistican	1938
Happy Chandler	Commissioner/executive	1982
Charles Comiskey	Player/executive	1939
Rube Foster	Player/executive	1981
Ford Frick	Commissioner/executive	1970

Pioneers/Executives	Role	Inducted
Warren Giles	Executive	1979
Clark Griffith	Player/manager/executive	1946
Will Harridge	Executive	1972
William Hulbert	Executive	1995
Ban Johnson	Executive	1937
Kenesaw Mountain Landis	Commissioner	1944
Larry MacPhail	Executive	1978
Lee MacPhail	Executive	1998
Branch Rickey	Manager/executive	1967
Bill Veeck	Executive	1991
George Weiss	Executive	1971
George Wright	Manager/executive	1937
Tom Yawkey	Executive	1980

Umpires	Year Inducted
Al Barlick	1989
Jocko Conlan	1974
Tom Connolly	1953
Billy Evans	1973
Cal Hubbard	1976
William Klem	1953
Bill McGowan	1992

Most Valuable Player Award Winners

Since 1931, the Baseball Writers Association of America (BBWAA) has voted to select the most valuable player in each league. From 1922 to '28 in the American League and from 1924 to '29 in the National League, the MVP was named by a special committee in each league. From 1911 to 1914 the Chalmers Motor Company presented an automobile to the outstanding player in each league (as selected by a committee of baseball writers).

National League

1998	Sammy Sosa, Chicago		1989	Kevin Mitchell, San Francisco
1997	Larry Walker, Colorado		1988	Kirk Gibson, Los Angeles
1996	Ken Caminiti, San Diego		1987	Andre Dawson, Chicago
1995	Barry Larkin, Cincinnati		1986	Mike Schmidt, Philadelphia
1994	Jeff Bagwell, Houston		1985	Willie McGee, St. Louis
1993	Barry Bonds, San Francisco		1984	Ryne Sandberg, Chicago
1992	Barry Bonds, Pittsburgh		1983	Dale Murphy, Atlanta
1991	Terry Pendleton, Atlanta		1982	Dale Murphy, Atlanta
1990	Barry Bonds, Pittsburgh		1981	Mike Schmidt, Philadelphia
			1980	Mike Schmidt, Philadelphia

411

1979	Willie Stargell, Pittsburgh (co-winner)	1948	Stan Musial, St. Louis
	Keith Hernandez, St. Louis (co-winner)	1947	Bob Elliot, Boston
1978	Dave Parker, Pittsburgh	1946	Stan Musial, St. Louis
1977	George Foster, Cincinnati	1945	Phil Cavarretta, Chicago
1976	Joe Morgan, Cincinnati	1944	Marty Marion, St. Louis
1975	Joe Morgan, Cincinnati	1943	Stan Musial, St. Louis
1974	Steve Garvey, Los Angeles	1942	Mort Cooper, St. Louis
1973	Pete Rose, Cincinnati	1941	Dolf Camilli, Brooklyn
1972	Johnny Bench, Cincinnati	1940	Frank McCormick, Cincinnati
1971	Joe Torre, St. Louis	1939	Bucky Walters, Cincinnati
1970	Johnny Bench, Cincinnati	1938	Ernie Lombardi, Cincinnati
1969	Willie McCovey, San Francisco	1937	Joe Medwick, St. Louis
1968	Bob Gibson, St. Louis	1936	Carl Hubbell, New York
1967	Orlando Cepeda, St. Louis	1935	Gabby Harnett, Chicago
1966	Roberto Clemente, Pittsburgh	1934	Dizzy Dean, St. Louis
1965	Willie Mays, San Francisco	1933	Carl Hubbell, New York
1964	Ken Boyer, St. Louis	1932	Chuck Klein, Philadelphia
1963	Sandy Koufax, Los Angeles	1931	Frankie Frisch, St. Louis
1962	Maury Wills, Los Angeles	1930	*No award given*
1961	Frank Robinson, Cincinnati	1929	Rogers Hornsby, Chicago*
1960	Dick Groat, Pittsburgh	1928	Jim Bottomley, St. Louis*
1959	Ernie Banks, Chicago	1927	Paul Waner, Pittsburgh*
1958	Ernie Banks, Chicago	1926	Bob O'Farrell, St. Louis*
1957	Hank Aaron, Milwaukee	1925	Rogers Hornsby, St. Louis*
1956	Don Newcombe, Brooklyn	1924	Dazzy Vance, Brooklyn*
1955	Roy Campanella, Brooklyn	*(No award given from 1915 to 1923.)*	
1954	Willie Mays, New York	1914	Johnny Evers, Boston**
1953	Roy Campanella, Brooklyn	1913	Jake Daubert, Brooklyn**
1952	Hank Sauer, Chicago	1912	Larry Doyle, New York**
1951	Roy Campanella, Brooklyn	1911	Frank Schulte, Chicago**
1950	Jim Konstanty, Philadelphia		
1949	Jackie Robinson, Brooklyn		

* League selection
** Chalmers Award winner

American League

1998	Juan Gonzalez, Texas	1982	Robin Yount, Milwaukee
1997	Ken Griffey Jr., Seattle	1981	Rollie Fingers, Milwaukee
1996	Juan Gonzalez, Texas	1980	George Brett, Kansas City
1995	Mo Vaughn, Boston	1979	Don Baylor, California
1994	Frank Thomas, Chicago	1978	Jim Rice, Boston
1993	Frank Thomas, Chicago	1977	Rod Carew, Minnesota
1992	Dennis Eckersley, Oakland	1976	Thurman Munson, New York
1991	Cal Ripken Jr., Baltimore	1975	Fred Lynn, Boston
1990	Rickey Henderson, Oakland	1974	Jeff Burroughs, Texas
1989	Robin Yount, Milwaukee	1973	Reggie Jackson, Oakland
1988	Jose Canseco, Oakland	1972	Dick Allen, Chicago
1987	George Bell, Toronto	1971	Vida Blue, Oakland
1986	Roger Clemens, Boston	1970	Boog Powell, Baltimore
1985	Don Mattingly, New York	1969	Harmon Killebrew, Minnesota
1984	Willie Hernandez, Detroit	1968	Denny McLain, Detroit
1983	Cal Ripken Jr., Baltimore	1967	Carl Yastrzemski, Boston

1966	Frank Robinson, Baltimore	1940	Hank Greenberg, Detroit
1965	Zoilo Versalles, Minnesota	1939	Joe DiMaggio, New York
1964	Brooks Robinson, Baltimore	1938	Jimmie Foxx, Philadelphia
1963	Elston Howard, New York	1937	Charlie Gehringer, Detroit
1962	Mickey Mantle, New York	1936	Lou Gehrig, New York
1961	Roger Maris, New York	1935	Hank Greenberg, Detroit
1960	Roger Maris, New York	1934	Mickey Cochrane, Detroit
1959	Nellie Fox, Chicago	1933	Jimmie Foxx, Philadelphia
1958	Jackie Jensen, Boston	1932	Jimmie Foxx, Philadelphia
1957	Mickey Mantle, New York	1931	Lefty Grove, Philadelphia
1956	Mickey Mantle, New York	1930	*No award given*
1955	Yogi Berra, New York	1929	*No award given*
1954	Yogi Berra, New York	1928	Mickey Cochrane, Philadelphia*
1953	Al Rosen, Cleveland	1927	Lou Gehrig, New York*
1952	Bobby Shantz, Philadelphia	1926	George Burns, Cleveland*
1951	Yogi Berra, New York	1925	Roger Peckinpaugh, Washington*
1950	Phil Rizzuto, New York		
1949	Ted Williams, Boston	1924	Walter Johnson, Washington*
1948	Lou Boudreau, Cleveland	1923	Babe Ruth, New York*
1947	Joe DiMaggio, New York	1922	George Sisler, St. Louis*
1946	Ted Williams, Boston	*(No award given from 1915 to 1921.)*	
1945	Hal Newhouser, Detroit	1914	Eddie Collins, Philadelphia**
1944	Hal Newhouser, Detroit	1913	Walter Johnson, Washington**
1943	Spud Chandler, New York	1912	Tris Speaker, Cleveland**
1942	Joe Gordon, New York	1911	Ty Cobb, Detroit**
1941	Joe DiMaggio, New York		

* *League selection*
** *Chalmers Award winner*

Cy Young Award Winners

From 1956 to '66, the BBWAA presented the Cy Young Award to the best pitcher in the major leagues. Beginning in 1967, a Cy Young winner was named in each league.

National League

1998	Tom Glavine, Atlanta	1982	Steve Carlton, Philadelphia
1997	Pedro Martinez, Montreal	1981	Fernando Valenzuela, Los Angeles
1996	John Smoltz, Atlanta	1980	Steve Carlton, Philadelphia
1995	Greg Maddux, Atlanta	1979	Bruce Sutter, Chicago
1994	Greg Maddux, Atlanta	1978	Gaylord Perry, San Diego
1993	Greg Maddux, Atlanta	1977	Steve Carlton, Philadelphia
1992	Greg Maddux, Chicago	1976	Randy Jones, San Diego
1991	Tom Glavine, Atlanta	1975	Tom Seaver, New York
1990	Doug Drabek, Pittsburgh	1974	Mike Marshall, Los Angeles
1989	Mark Davis, San Diego	1973	Tom Seaver, New York
1988	Orel Hershiser, Los Angeles	1972	Steve Carlton, Philadelphia
1987	Steve Bedrosian, Philadelphia	1971	Ferguson Jenkins, Chicago
1986	Mike Scott, Houston	1970	Bob Gibson, St. Louis
1985	Dwight Gooden, New York	1969	Tom Seaver, New York
1984	Rick Sutcliffe, Chicago	1968	Bob Gibson, St. Louis
1983	John Denny, Philadelphia	1967	Mike McCormick, San Francisco

413

American League

1998	Roger Clemens, Toronto	1981	Rollie Fingers, Milwaukee
1997	Roger Clemens, Toronto	1980	Steve Stone, Baltimore
1996	Pat Hentgen, Toronto	1979	Mike Flanagan, Baltimore
1995	Randy Johnson, Seattle	1978	Ron Guidry, New York
1994	David Cone, Kansas City	1977	Sparky Lyle, New York
1993	Jack McDowell, Chicago	1976	Jim Palmer, Baltimore
1992	Dennis Eckersley, Oakland	1975	Jim Palmer, Baltimore
1991	Roger Clemens, Boston	1974	Jim Hunter, Oakland
1990	Bob Welch, Oakland	1973	Jim Palmer, Baltimore
1989	Bret Saberhagen, Kansas City	1972	Gaylord Perry, Cleveland
1988	Frank Viola, Minnesota	1971	Vida Blue, Oakland
1987	Roger Clemens, Boston	1970	Jim Perry, Minnesota
1986	Roger Clemens, Boston	1969	Mike Cuellar, Baltimore (co-winner)
1985	Bret Saberhagen, Kansas City		Denny McLain, Detroit (co-winner)
1984	Willie Hernandez, Detroit	1968	Denny McLain, Detroit
1983	LaMarr Hoyt, Chicago	1967	Jim Lonborg, Boston
1982	Pete Vukovich, Milwaukee		

Major Leagues

1966	Sandy Koufax, Los Angeles	1960	Vernon Law, Pittsburgh
1965	Sandy Koufax, Los Angeles	1959	Early Wynn, Chicago (AL)
1964	Dean Chance, Los Angeles	1958	Bob Turley, New York (AL)
1963	Sandy Koufax, Los Angeles	1957	Warren Spahn, Milwaukee
1962	Don Drysdale, Los Angeles	1956	Don Newcombe, Brooklyn
1961	Whitey Ford, New York (AL)		

Rookie of the Year Award Winners

Since 1947, the BBWAA has presented the Rookie of the Year Award. One major league winner was named in each of the first two years, and separate awards in each league have been given since 1949.

National League

1998	Kerry Wood, Chicago	1984	Dwight Gooden, New York
1997	Scott Rolen, Philadelphia	1983	Darryl Strawberry, New York
1996	Todd Hollandsworth, Los Angeles	1982	Steve Sax, Los Angeles
1995	Hideo Nomo, Los Angeles	1981	Fernando Valenzuela, Los Angeles
1994	Raul Mondesi, Los Angeles	1980	Steve Howe, Los Angeles
1993	Mike Piazza, Los Angeles	1979	Rick Sutcliffe, Los Angeles
1992	Eric Karros, Los Angeles	1978	Bob Horner, Atlanta
1991	Jeff Bagwell, Houston	1977	Andre Dawson, Montreal
1990	David Justice, Atlanta	1976	Butch Metzger, San Diego (co-winner)
1989	Jerome Walton, Chicago		Pat Zachry, Cincinnati (co-winner)
1988	Chris Sabo, Cincinnati	1975	John Montefusco, San Francisco
1987	Benito Santiago, San Diego	1974	Bake McBride, St. Louis
1986	Todd Worrell, St. Louis	1973	Gary Matthews, San Francisco
1985	Vince Coleman, St. Louis	1972	Jon Matlack, New York

1971   Earl Williams, Atlanta
1970   Carl Morton, Montreal
1969   Ted Sizemore, Los Angeles
1968   Johnny Bench, Cincinnati
1967   Tom Seaver, New York
1966   Tommy Helms, Cincinnati
1965   Jim Lefebvre, Los Angeles
1964   Dick Allen, Philadelphia
1963   Pete Rose, Cincinnati
1962   Ken Hubbs, Chicago
1961   Billy Williams, Chicago
1960   Frank Howard, Los Angeles

1959   Willie McCovey, San Francisco
1958   Orlando Cepeda, San Francisco
1957   Jack Sanford, Philadelphia
1956   Frank Robinson, Cincinnati
1955   Bill Virdon, St. Louis
1954   Wally Moon, St. Louis
1953   Junior Gilliam, Brooklyn
1952   Joe Black, Chicago
1951   Willie Mays, New York
1950   Sam Jethroe, Boston
1949   Don Newcombe, Brooklyn

American League

1998   Ben Grieve, Oakland
1997   Nomar Garciaparra, Boston
1996   Derek Jeter, New York
1995   Marty Cordova, Minnesota
1994   Bob Hamelin, Kansas City
1993   Tim Salmon, California
1992   Pat Listach, Milwaukee
1991   Chuck Knoblauch, Minnesota
1990   Sandy Alomar Jr., Cleveland
1989   Gregg Olson, Baltimore
1988   Walt Weiss, Oakland
1987   Mark McGwire, Oakland
1986   Jose Canseco, Oakland
1985   Ozzie Guillen, Chicago
1984   Alvin Davis, Seattle
1983   Ron Kittle, Chicago
1982   Cal Ripken Jr., Baltimore
1981   Dave Righetti, New York
1980   Joe Charboneau, Cleveland
1979   Alfredo Griffin, Toronto (co-winner)
       John Castino, Minnesota (co-winner)
1978   Lou Whitaker, Detroit
1977   Eddie Murray, Baltimore
1976   Mark Fidrych, Detroit
1975   Fred Lynn, Boston

1974   Mike Hargrove, Texas
1973   Al Bumbry, Baltimore
1972   Carlton Fisk, Boston
1971   Chris Chambliss, Cleveland
1970   Thurman Munson, New York
1969   Lou Piniella, Kansas City
1968   Stan Bahnsen, New York
1967   Rod Carew, Minnesota
1966   Tommie Agee, Chicago
1965   Curt Blefary, Baltimore
1964   Tony Oliva, Minnesota
1963   Gary Peters, Chicago
1962   Tom Tresh, New York
1961   Don Schwall, Boston
1960   Ron Hansen, Baltimore
1959   Bob Allison, Washington
1958   Albie Pearson, Washington
1957   Tony Kubek, New York
1956   Luis Aparicio, Chicago
1955   Herb Score, Cleveland
1954   Bob Grim, New York
1953   Harvey Kuenn, Detroit
1952   Harry Byrd, Philadelphia
1951   Gil McDougald, New York
1950   Walt Dropo, Boston
1949   Roy Sievers, St. Louis

Major Leagues

1948   Alvin Dark, Boston (NL)
1947   Jackie Robinson, Brooklyn

All-Star Game Results

The National League leads the all-time series 40–28–1. There were two All-Star Games played annually from 1959 to '62.

Year	Winner, Score	Site
1998	AL, 13–8	Coors Field, Denver
1997	AL, 3–1	Jacobs Field, Cleveland
1996	NL, 6–0	Veterans Stadium, Philadelphia
1995	NL, 3–2	The Ballpark at Arlington, Tex.
1994	NL, 8–7 (10 inn.)	Three Rivers Stadium, Pittsburgh
1993	AL, 9–3	Camden Yards, Baltimore
1992	AL, 13–6	Jack Murphy Stadium, San Diego
1991	AL, 4–2	SkyDome, Toronto
1990	AL, 2–0	Wrigley Field, Chicago
1989	AL, 5–3	Anaheim Stadium, Anaheim
1988	AL, 2–1	Riverfront Stadium, Cincinnati
1987	NL, 2–0 (13 inn.)	Oakland Coliseum, Oakland
1986	AL, 3–2	Astrodome, Houston
1985	NL, 6–1	Metrodome, Minnesota
1984	NL, 3–1	Candlestick Park, San Francisco
1983	AL, 13–3	Comiskey Park, Chicago
1982	NL, 4–1	Olympic Stadium, Montreal
1981	NL, 5–4	Municipal Stadium, Cleveland
1980	NL, 4–2	Dodger Stadium, Los Angeles
1979	NL, 7–6	Kingdome, Seattle
1978	NL, 7–3	Jack Murphy Stadium, San Diego
1977	NL, 7–5	Yankee Stadium, New York
1976	NL, 7–1	Veterans Stadium, Philadelphia
1975	NL, 6–3	County Stadium, Milwaukee
1974	NL, 7–2	Three Rivers Stadium, Pittsburgh
1973	NL, 7–1	Royals Stadium, Kansas City
1972	NL, 4–3 (10 inn.)	Atlanta Fulton County Stadium
1971	AL, 6–4	Tiger Stadium, Detroit
1970	NL, 5–4 (12 inn.)	Riverfront Coliseum, Cincinnati
1969	NL, 9–3	RFK Stadium, Washington, D.C.
1968	NL, 1–0	Astrodome, Houston
1967	NL, 2–1 (15 inn.)	Anaheim Stadium, Anaheim
1966	NL, 2–1 (10 inn.)	Busch Stadium, St. Louis
1965	NL, 6–5	Metropolitan Stadium, Bloomington
1964	NL, 7–4	Shea Stadium, New York
1963	NL, 5–3	Municipal Stadium, Cleveland
1962	NL, 3–1	D.C. Stadium, Washington, D.C.
1962	AL, 9–4	Wrigley Field, Chicago
1961	1–1, rain (9 inn.)	Fenway Park, Boston
1961	NL, 5–4 (10 inn.)	Candlestick Park, San Francisco

Year	Winner, Score	Site
1960	NL, 6–0	Yankee Stadium, New York
1960	NL, 5–3	Municipal Stadium, Kansas City
1959	AL, 5–3	Memorial Stadium, Los Angeles
1959	NL, 5–4	Forbes Field, Pittsburgh
1958	AL, 4–3	Memorial Stadium, Baltimore
1957	AL, 6–5	Sportsman's Park, St. Louis
1956	NL, 7–3	Griffith Stadium, Washington, D.C.
1955	NL, 6–5 (12 inn.)	Milwaukee Stadium, Milwaukee
1954	AL, 11–9	Municipal Stadium, Cleveland
1953	NL, 5–1	Crosley Field, Cincinnati
1952	NL, 3–2	Shibe Park, Philadelphia
1951	NL, 8–3	Briggs Stadium, Detroit
1950	NL, 4–3 (14 inn.)	Comiskey Park, Chicago
1949	AL, 11–7	Ebbets Field, Brooklyn
1948	AL, 5–2	Sportsman's Park, St. Louis
1947	AL, 2–1	Wrigley Field, Chicago
1946	AL, 12–0	Fenway Park, Boston
1945	*No All-Star Game (World War II)*	
1944	NL, 7–1	Forbes Field, Pittsburgh
1943	AL, 5–3	Shibe Park, Philadelphia
1942	AL, 3–1	Polo Grounds, New York
1941	AL, 7–5	Briggs Stadium, Detroit
1940	NL, 4–0	Sportsman's Park, St. Louis
1939	AL, 3–1	Yankee Stadium, New York
1938	NL, 4–1	Crosley Field, Cincinnati
1937	AL, 8–3	Griffith Stadium, Washington, D.C.
1936	NL, 4–3	Braves Stadium, Boston
1935	AL, 4–1	Municipal Stadium, Cleveland
1934	AL, 9–7	Polo Grounds, New York
1933	AL, 4–2	Comiskey Park, Chicago

All-Star Game MVPs

1998 Roberto Alomar, Baltimore
1997 Sandy Alomar Jr., Cleveland
1996 Mike Piazza, Los Angeles
1995 Jeff Conine, Florida
1994 Fred McGriff, Atlanta
1993 Kirby Puckett, Minnesota
1992 Ken Griffey Jr., Seattle
1991 Cal Ripken Jr., Baltimore

1990 Julio Franco, Texas
1989 Bo Jackson, Kansas City
1988 Terry Steinbach, Oakland
1987 Tim Raines, Montreal
1986 Roger Clemens, Boston
1985 Lamarr Hoyt, San Diego
1984 Gary Carter, Montreal
1983 Fred Lynn, California

417

1982 Dave Concepcion, Cincinnati	1959 Yogi Berra, New York (AL)
1981 Gary Carter, Montreal	(second game)
1980 Ken Griffey Sr., Cincinnati	1959 Don Drysdale (first game)
1979 Dave Parker, Pittsburgh	1958 Billy O'Dell, Baltimore
1978 Steve Garvey, Los Angeles	1957 Minnie Minoso, Chicago (AL)
1977 Don Sutton, Los Angeles	1956 Ken Boyer, St. Louis
1976 George Foster, Cincinnati	1955 Stan Musial, St. Louis
1975 Bill Madlock, Chicago (NL) (co-winner)	1954 Al Rosen, Cleveland
Jon Matlack, New York (NL) (co-winner)	1953 Pee Wee Reese, Brooklyn
1974 Steve Garvey, Los Angeles	1952 Hank Sauer, Chicago (NL)
1973 Bobby Bonds, San Francisco	1951 Bob Elliott, Boston (NL)
1972 Joe Morgan, Cincinnati	1950 Red Schoendienst, St. Louis (NL)
1971 Frank Robinson, Baltimore	1949 Joe DiMaggio, New York (AL)
1970 Carl Yastrzemski, Boston	1948 Vic Raschi, New York (AL)
1969 Willie McCovey, San Francisco	1947 Stan Spence, Washington
1968 Willie Mays, San Francisco	1946 Ted Williams, Boston (AL)
1967 Tony Perez, Cincinnati	1945 *No All-Star Game (World War II)*
1966 Brooks Robinson, Baltimore	1944 Rip Sewell, Pittsburgh
1965 Juan Marichal, San Francisco	1943 Bobby Doerr, Boston (AL)
1964 Johnny Callison, Philadelphia	1942 Rudy York, Detroit
1963 Willie Mays, San Francisco	1941 Ted Williams, Boston (AL)
1962 Leon Wagner, Los Angeles (AL)	1940 Max West, Boston (NL)
(second game)	1939 Bob Feller, Cleveland
1962 Maury Wills, Los Angeles (NL)	1938 Johnny Vander Meer, Cincinnati
(first game)	1937 Lou Gehrig, New York (AL)
1961 Jim Bunning, Detroit (second game)	1936 Lon Warnek, Pittsburgh
1961 Roberto Clemente, Pittsburgh	1935 Jimmie Foxx, Philadelphia (AL)
(first game)	1934 Earl Averill, Cleveland
1960 Willie Mays, San Francisco (both games)	1933 Babe Ruth, New York (AL)

Division Champions and Wild Cards

National League

Year	East	Central	West	Wild Card
1998	Atlanta	Houston	San Diego	Chicago
1997	Atlanta	Houston	San Francisco	Florida
1996	Atlanta	St. Louis	San Diego	Los Angeles
1995	Atlanta	Cincinnati	Los Angeles	Colorado
1994	*Playoffs cancelled due to players' strike*			

Year	East	West
1993	Philadelphia	Atlanta
1992	Pittsburgh	Atlanta
1991	Pittsburgh	Atlanta
1990	Pittsburgh	Cincinnati

Year	East	West
1989	Chicago	San Francisco
1988	New York	Los Angeles
1987	St. Louis	San Francisco
1986	New York	Houston
1985	St. Louis	Los Angeles
1984	Chicago	San Diego
1983	Philadelphia	Los Angeles
1982	St. Louis	Atlanta
1981*	Montreal/Philadelphia	Los Angeles/Houston
1980	Philadelphia	Houston
1979	Pittsburgh	Cincinnati
1978	Philadelphia	Los Angeles
1977	Philadelphia	Los Angeles
1976	Philadelphia	Cincinnati
1975	Pittsburgh	Cincinnati
1974	Pittsburgh	Los Angeles
1973	New York	Cincinnati
1972	Pittsburgh	Cincinnati
1971	Pittsburgh	San Francisco
1970	Pittsburgh	Cincinnati
1969	New York	Atlanta

* Split season due to players' strike

American League

Year	East	Central	West	Wild Card
1998	New York	Cleveland	Texas	Boston
1997	Baltimore	Cleveland	Seattle	New York
1996	New York	Cleveland	Texas	Baltimore
1995	Boston	Cleveland	Seattle	New York
1994	*Playoffs cancelled due to players' strike*			

Year	East	West
1993	Toronto	Chicago
1992	Toronto	Oakland
1991	Toronto	Minnesota
1990	Boston	Oakland

continues

continued

Year	East	West
1989	Toronto	Oakland
1988	Boston	Oakland
1987	Detroit	Minnesota
1986	Boston	California
1985	Toronto	Kansas City
1984	Detroit	Kansas City
1983	Baltimore	Chicago
1982	Milwaukee	California
1981*	New York/Milwaukee	Oakland/Kansas City
1980	New York	Kansas City
1979	Baltimore	California
1978	New York	Kansas City
1977	New York	Kansas City
1976	New York	Kansas City
1975	Boston	Oakland
1974	Baltimore	Oakland
1973	Baltimore	Oakland
1972	Detroit	Oakland
1971	Baltimore	Oakland
1970	Baltimore	Minnesota
1969	Baltimore	Minnesota

* Split season due to players' strike

League Championship Series Results and MVPs

League Championship Series have been played since 1969, and LCS MVP awards have been presented since 1977 in the National League and 1980 in the American League. Games won by each team are shown; the LCS began as a best-of-five series and was expanded to best-of-seven in 1985.

National League Championship Series Results and MVPs

1998	San Diego 4, Atlanta 2	Sterling Hitchcock
1997	Florida 4, Atlanta 2	Livan Hernandez
1996	Atlanta 4, St. Louis 3	Javier Lopez
1995	Atlanta 4, Cincinnati 0	Mike Devereaux
1994	*No Series (players' strike)*	
1993	Philadelphia 4, Atlanta 2	Curt Schilling
1992	Atlanta 4, Pittsburgh 3	John Smoltz

1991	Atlanta 4, Pittsburgh 3	Steve Avery
1990	Cincinnati 4, Pittsburgh 2	Rob Dibble, Randy Myers
1989	San Francisco 4, Chicago 1	Will Clark
1988	Los Angeles 4, New York 3	Orel Hershiser
1987	St. Louis 4, San Francisco 3	Jeffrey Leonard
1986	New York 4, Houston 2	Mike Scott
1985	St. Louis 4, Los Angeles 2	Ozzie Smith
1984	San Diego 3, Chicago 2	Steve Garvey
1983	Philadelphia 3, Los Angeles 1	Gary Matthews
1982	St. Louis 3, Atlanta 0	Darrell Porter
1981	Los Angeles 3, Montreal 2	Burt Hooton
1980	Philadelphia 3, Houston 2	Manny Trillo
1979	Pittsburgh 3, Cincinnati 0	Willie Stargell
1978	Los Angeles 3, Philadelphia 1	Steve Garvey
1977	Los Angeles 3, Philadelphia 1	Dusty Baker
1976	Cincinnati 3, Philadelphia 0	
1975	Cincinnati 3, Pittsburgh 0	
1974	Los Angeles 3, Pittsburgh 1	
1973	New York 3, Cincinnati 2	
1972	Cincinnati 3, Pittsburgh 2	
1971	Pittsburgh 3, San Francisco 1	
1970	Cincinnati 3, Pittsburgh 0	
1969	New York 3, Atlanta 0	

American League Championship Series Results and MVPs

1998	New York 4, Cleveland 2	David Wells
1997	Cleveland 4, Baltimore 2	Marquis Grissom
1996	New York 4, Baltimore 1	Bernie Williams
1995	Cleveland 4, Seattle 2	Orel Hershiser
1994	*No Series (players' strike)*	
1993	Toronto 4, Chicago 2	Dave Stewart
1992	Toronto 4, Oakland 2	Roberto Alomar
1991	Minnesota 4, Toronto 1	Kirby Puckett
1990	Oakland 4, Boston 0	Dave Stewart
1989	Oakland 4, Toronto 1	Rickey Henderson
1988	Oakland 4, Boston 0	Dennis Eckersley
1987	Minnesota 4, Detroit 1	Gary Gaetti
1986	Boston 4, California 3	Marty Barrett
1985	Kansas City 4, Toronto 3	George Brett
1984	Detroit 3, Kansas City 0	Kirk Gibson

continues

1983	Baltimore 3, Chicago 1	Mike Boddicker
1982	Milwaukee 3, California 2	Fred Lynn
1981	New York 3, Oakland 0	Graig Nettles
1980	Kansas City 3, New York 0	Frank White
1979	Baltimore 3, California 1	
1978	New York 3, Kansas City 1	
1977	New York 3, Kansas City 2	
1976	New York 3, Kansas City 2	
1975	Boston 3, Oakland 0	
1974	Oakland 3, Baltimore 1	
1973	Oakland 3, Baltimore 2	
1972	Oakland 3, Detroit 2	
1971	Baltimore 3, Oakland 0	
1970	Baltimore 3, Minnesota 0	
1969	Baltimore 3, Minnesota 0	

World Series Results and MVPs

Each team is listed with the number of Series games it won. World Series Most Valuable Player Awards have been presented since 1955.

1998	New York 4, San Diego 0	Scott Brosius
1997	Florida 4, Cleveland 3	Livan Hernandez
1996	New York 4, Atlanta 2	John Wetteland
1995	Atlanta 4, Cleveland 2	Tom Glavine
1994	*No series (players' strike)*	
1993	Toronto 4, Philadelphia 2	Paul Molitor
1992	Toronto 4, Atlanta 2	Pat Borders
1991	Minnesota 4, Atlanta 3	Jack Morris
1990	Cincinnati 4, Oakland 0	Jose Rijo
1989	Oakland 4, San Francisco 0	Dave Stewart
1988	Los Angeles 4, Oakland 1	Orel Hershiser
1987	Minnesota 4, St. Louis 3	Frank Viola
1986	New York 4, Boston 3	Ray Knight
1985	Kansas City 4, St. Louis 3	Bret Saberhagen
1984	Detroit 4, San Diego 1	Alan Trammell
1983	Baltimore 4, Philadelphia 1	Rick Dempsey
1982	St. Louis 4, Milwaukee 3	Darrell Porter
1981	Los Angeles 4, New York 2	Ron Cey Pedro Guerrero Steve Yeager (co-winners)
1980	Philadelphia 4, Kansas City 2	Mike Schmidt
1979	Pittsburgh 4, Baltimore 3	Willie Stargell

1978	New York 4, Los Angeles 2	Bucky Dent
1977	New York 4, Los Angeles 2	Reggie Jackson
1976	Cincinnati 4, New York 0	Johnny Bench
1975	Cincinnati 4, Boston 3	Pete Rose
1974	Oakland 4, Los Angeles 1	Rollie Fingers
1973	Oakland 4, New York 3	Reggie Jackson
1972	Oakland 4, Cincinnati 3	Gene Tenace
1971	Pittsburgh 4, Baltimore 3	Roberto Clemente
1970	Baltimore 4, Cincinnati 1	Brooks Robinson
1969	New York 4, Baltimore 1	Donn Clendenon
1968	Detroit 4, St. Louis 3	Mickey Lolich
1967	St. Louis 4, Boston 3	Bob Gibson
1966	Baltimore 4, Los Angeles 0	Frank Robinson
1965	Los Angeles 4, Minnesota 3	Sandy Koufax
1964	St. Louis 4, New York 3	Bob Gibson
1963	Los Angeles 4, New York 0	Sandy Koufax
1962	New York 4, San Francisco 3	Ralph Terry
1961	New York 4, Cincinnati 1	Whitey Ford
1960	Pittsburgh 4, New York 3	Bobby Richardson
1959	Los Angeles 4, Chicago 2	Larry Sherry
1958	New York 4, Milwaukee 3	Bob Turley
1957	Milwaukee 4, New York 3	Lew Burdette
1956	New York 4, Brooklyn 3	Don Larsen
1955	Brooklyn 4, New York 3	Johnny Podres
1954	New York 4, Cleveland 0	
1953	New York 4, Brooklyn 2	
1952	New York 4, Brooklyn 3	
1951	New York (AL) 4, New York 2	
1950	New York 4, Philadelphia 0	
1949	New York 4, Brooklyn 1	
1948	Cleveland 4, Boston 2	
1947	New York 4, Brooklyn 3	
1946	St. Louis (NL) 4, Boston 3	
1945	Detroit 4, Chicago 3	
1944	St. Louis (NL) 4, St. Louis 3	
1943	New York (AL) 4, St. Louis 1	
1942	St. Louis (AL) 4, New York 1	
1941	New York 4, Brooklyn 1	
1940	Cincinnati 4, Detroit 3	
1939	New York 4, Cincinnati 0	
1938	New York (AL) 4, Chicago 0	

continues

1937	New York (AL) 4, New York 1
1936	New York (AL) 4, New York 2
1935	Detroit 4, Chicago 2
1934	St. Louis 4, Detroit 0
1933	New York 4, Washington 1
1932	New York (AL) 4, Chicago 0
1931	St. Louis (NL) 4, Philadelphia 3
1930	Philadelphia (AL) 4, St. Louis 2
1929	Philadelphia (AL) 4, Chicago 1
1928	New York 4, St. Louis 0
1927	New York 4, Pittsburgh 0
1926	St. Louis (NL) 4, New York 3
1925	Pittsburgh 4, Washington 3
1924	Washington 4, New York 3
1923	New York (AL) 4, New York 2
1922	New York (NL) 4, New York 0
1921	New York (NL) 5, New York 3
1920	Cleveland 5, Brooklyn 2
1919	Cincinnati 5, Chicago 3
1918	Boston (AL) 4, Chicago 2
1917	Chicago (AL) 4, New York 2
1916	Boston 4, Brooklyn 1
1915	Boston (AL) 4, Philadelphia 1
1914	Boston (NL) 4, Philadelphia 0
1913	Philadelphia (AL) 4, New York 1
1912	Boston (AL) 4, New York 3
1911	Philadelphia (AL) 4, New York 2
1910	Philadelphia (AL) 4, Chicago 1
1909	Pittsburgh 4, Detroit 3
1908	Chicago 4, Detroit 1
1907	Chicago 4, Detroit 0
1906	Chicago (AL) 4, Chicago 2
1905	New York (NL) 4, Philadelphia 1
1904	No Series (NL Giants declined to participate)
1903	Boston 5, Pittsburgh 3

The Major League Record Book

Career Batting Leaders

Games

1.	Pete Rose	3,562
2.	Carl Yastrzemski	3,308
3.	Hank Aaron	3,298
4.	Ty Cobb	3,034
5.	Stan Musial	3,026
6.	Eddie Murray	3,026
7.	Willie Mays	2,992
8.	Dave Winfield	2,973
9.	Rusty Staub	2,951
10.	Brooks Robinson	2,896

Consecutive Games

1.	Cal Ripken Jr.	2,632
2.	Lou Gehrig	2,130
3.	Everett Scott	1,307
4.	Steve Garvey	1,207
5.	Billy Williams	1,117
6.	Joe Sewell	1,103
7.	Stan Musial	895
8.	Eddie Yost	829
9.	Gus Suhr	822
10.	Nellie Fox	798

Consecutive-Game Hitting Streaks

1.	Joe DiMaggio, 1941	56
2.	Willie Keeler, 1897	44
2.	Pete Rose, 1978	44
4.	Bill Dahlen, 1894	42
5.	George Sisler, 1922	41
6.	Ty Cobb, 1911	40
7.	Paul Molitor, 1987	39
8.	Tommy Holmes, 1945	37
9.	Billy Hamilton, 1894	36
10.	Fred Clarke, 1895	35
10.	Ty Cobb, 1917	35

At Bats

1.	Pete Rose	14,053
2.	Hank Aaron	12,364
3.	Carl Yastrzemski	11,988
4.	Ty Cobb	11,429
5.	Eddie Murray	11,336
6.	Robin Yount	11,008
7.	Dave Winfield	11,003
8.	Stan Musial	10,972
9.	Willie Mays	10,881
10.	Paul Molitor	10,835

Runs

1.	Ty Cobb	2,245
2.	Babe Ruth	2,174
2.	Hank Aaron	2,174
4.	Pete Rose	2,165
5.	Willie Mays	2,062
6.	Rickey Henderson	2,014
7.	Stan Musial	1,949
8.	Lou Gehrig	1,888
9.	Tris Speaker	1,881
10.	Mel Ott	1,859

Batting Average
(minimum 4,000 at bats)

1.	Ty Cobb	.367
2.	Rogers Hornsby	.358
3.	Joe Jackson	.356
4.	Pete Browning	.354
5.	Dan Brouthers	.349
6.	Ed Delahanty	.346
7.	Willie Keeler	.345
8.	Tris Speaker	.345
9.	Ted Williams	.344
10.	Billy Hamilton	.344

Hits

1.	Pete Rose	4,256
2.	Ty Cobb	4,191
3.	Hank Aaron	3,771
4.	Stan Musial	3,630
5.	Tris Speaker	3,515
6.	Honus Wagner	3,430
7.	Carl Yastrzemski	3,419
8.	Paul Molitor	3,319
9.	Eddie Collins	3,309
10.	Willie Mays	3,283

Singles

1.	Pete Rose	3,215
2.	Ty Cobb	3,052
3.	Eddie Collins	2,639
4.	Willie Keeler	2,534
5.	Honus Wagner	2,426
6.	Rod Carew	2,404
7.	Tris Speaker	2,383
8.	Paul Molitor	2,366
9.	Nap Lajoie	2,345
10.	Cap Anson	2,330

Doubles

1.	Tris Speaker	793
2.	Pete Rose	746
3.	Stan Musial	725
4.	Ty Cobb	724
5.	George Brett	665
6.	Napoleon Lajoie	652
7.	Honus Wagner	651
8.	Carl Yastrzemski	646
9.	Hank Aaron	624
10.	Paul Waner	605
10.	Paul Molitor	605

Triples

1.	Sam Crawford	312
2.	Ty Cobb	298
3.	Honus Wagner	252
4.	Jake Beckley	246
5.	Roger Connor	227
6.	Tris Speaker	222
7.	Fred Clarke	219
8.	Dan Brouthers	212
9.	Paul Waner	191
10.	Joe Kelley	189

Home Runs

1.	Hank Aaron	755
2.	Babe Ruth	714
3.	Willie Mays	660
4.	Frank Robinson	586
5.	Harmon Killebrew	573
6.	Reggie Jackson	563
7.	Mike Schmidt	548
8.	Mickey Mantle	536
9.	Jimmie Foxx	534
10.	Ted Williams	521
10.	Willie McCovey	521

Runs Batted In

1.	Hank Aaron	2,297
2.	Babe Ruth	2,204
3.	Lou Gehrig	1,990
4.	Ty Cobb	1,960
5.	Stan Musial	1,951
6.	Jimmie Foxx	1,921
7.	Eddie Murray	1,916
8.	Willie Mays	1,903
9.	Mel Ott	1,861
10.	Carl Yastrzemski	1,844

Slugging Percentage
(minimum 4,000 total bases)

1.	Babe Ruth	.690
2.	Ted Williams	.634
3.	Lou Gehrig	.632
4.	Jimmie Foxx	.609
5.	Rogers Hornsby	.577
6.	Stan Musial	.559
7.	Willie Mays	.557
7.	Mickey Mantle	.557
9.	Hank Aaron	.555
10.	Frank Robinson	.537

Stolen Bases

1.	Rickey Henderson	1,297
2.	Lou Brock	938
3.	Billy Hamilton	937
4.	Ty Cobb	892
5.	Tim Raines	803
6.	Arlie Latham	791
7.	Vince Coleman	752
8.	Harry Stovey	744
9.	Eddie Collins	743
10.	Max Carey	738

Strikeouts

1.	Reggie Jackson	2,597
2.	Willie Stargell	1,936
3.	Mike Schmidt	1,883
4.	Tony Perez	1,867
5.	Dave Kingman	1,816
6.	Bobby Bonds	1,757
7.	Dale Murphy	1,748
8.	Lou Brock	1,730
9.	Mickey Mantle	1,710
10.	Harmon Killebrew	1,699

Walks

1.	Babe Ruth	2,056
2.	Ted Williams	2,019
3.	Rickey Henderson	1,890
4.	Joe Morgan	1,865
5.	Carl Yastrzemski	1,845
6.	Mickey Mantle	1,734
7.	Mel Ott	1,708
8.	Eddie Yost	1,614
9.	Darrell Evans	1,605
10.	Stan Musial	1,599

Grand Slams

1.	Lou Gehrig	23
2.	Eddie Murray	19
3.	Willie McCovey	18
4.	Jimmie Foxx	17
4.	Ted Williams	17
6.	Babe Ruth	16
6.	Hank Aaron	16
6.	Dave Kingman	16
9.	Gil Hodges	14
10.	Joe DiMaggio	13
10.	Ralph Kiner	13
10.	George Foster	13

Pinch Hits

1.	Manny Mota	150
2.	Smokey Burgess	145
3.	Greg Gross	143
4.	Jose Morales	123
5.	Jerry Lynch	116
6.	Red Lucas	114
7.	Steve Braun	113
8.	Denny Walling	108
9.	Terry Crowley	108
10.	Gates Brown	107

Pinch Hit Home Runs

1.	Cliff Johnson	20
2.	Jerry Lynch	18
3.	Gates Brown	16
3.	Smokey Burgess	16
3.	Willie McCovey	16
6.	George Crowe	14
7.	Joe Adcock	12
7.	Bob Cerv	12
7.	Jose Morales	12
7.	Graig Nettles	12

Career Pitching Leaders

Games

1.	Dennis Eckersley	1,071
2.	Hoyt Wilhelm	1,070
3.	Kent Tekulve	1,050
5.	Jesse Orosco	1,025
4.	Lee Smith	1,022
6.	Goose Gossage	1,002
7.	Lindy McDaniel	987
8.	Rollie Fingers	944
9.	Gene Garber	931
10.	Cy Young	906

Wins

1.	Cy Young	511
2.	Walter Johnson	416
3.	Christy Mathewson	373
3.	Grover Alexander	373
5.	Warren Spahn	363
6.	Pud Galvin	361
6.	Kid Nichols	361
8.	Tim Keefe	342
9.	Steve Carlton	329
10.	John Clarkson	327

Losses

1.	Cy Young	313
2.	Pud Galvin	309
3.	Nolan Ryan	292
4.	Walter Johnson	279
5.	Phil Niekro	274
6.	Gaylord Perry	265
7.	Don Sutton	256
8.	Jack Powell	254
9.	Eppa Rixley	251
10.	Bert Blyleven	250

Starts

1.	Cy Young	818
2.	Nolan Ryan	773
3.	Don Sutton	756
4.	Phil Niekro	716
5.	Steve Carlton	709
6.	Tommy John	700
7.	Gaylord Perry	690
8.	Bert Blyleven	685
9.	Pud Galvin	682
10.	Walter Johnson	666

Innings Pitched

1.	Cy Young	7,377
2.	Pud Galvin	5,959
3.	Walter Johnson	5,923
4.	Phil Niekro	5,403
5.	Nolan Ryan	5,387
6.	Gaylord Perry	5,352
7.	Don Sutton	5,281
8.	Warren Spahn	5,246
9.	Steve Carlton	5,216
10.	Grover Alexander	5,188

Complete Games

1.	Cy Young	751
2.	Pud Galvin	641
3.	Tim Keefe	554
4.	Walter Johnson	531
4.	Kid Nichols	531
6.	Mickey Welch	525
7.	John Clarkson	487
8.	Hoss Radbourn	479
9.	Tony Mullane	464
10.	Jim McCormick	462

Shutouts

1.	Walter Johnson	110
2.	Grover Alexander	90
3.	Christy Mathewson	83
4.	Cy Young	76
5.	Eddie Plank	64
6.	Warren Spahn	63
7.	Tom Seaver	61
7.	Nolan Ryan	61
9.	Bert Blyleven	60
10.	Ed Walsh	58
10.	Don Sutton	58

Earned Run Average
(minimum 1,500 innings pitched)

1.	Ed Walsh	1.82
2.	Addie Joss	1.88
3.	Mordecai Brown	2.06
4.	Monte Ward	2.10
5.	Christy Mathewson	2.13
6.	Rube Waddell	2.16
7.	Walter Johnson	2.17
8.	Orval Overall	2.24
9.	Tommy Bond	2.25
10.	Will White	2.28

Strikeouts

1.	Nolan Ryan	5,714
2.	Steve Carlton	4,136
3.	Bert Blyleven	3,701
4.	Tom Seaver	3,640
5.	Don Sutton	3,574
6.	Gaylord Perry	3,534
7.	Walter Johnson	3,508
8.	Phil Niekro	3,342
9.	Ferguson Jenkins	3,192
10.	Roger Clemens	3,153

Walks

1.	Nolan Ryan	2,795
2.	Steve Carlton	1,833
3.	Phil Niekro	1,809
4.	Early Wynn	1,775
5.	Bob Feller	1,764
6.	Bobo Newsome	1,732
7.	Charlie Hough	1,665
8.	Amos Rusie	1,637
9.	Gus Weyhing	1,569
10.	Red Ruffing	1,541

Relief Wins
1. Hoyt Wilhelm   124
2. Lindy McDaniel   119
3. Goose Gossage   108
4. Rollie Fingers   107
5. Sparky Lyle   99
6. Roy Face   96
7. Gene Garber   94
7. Kent Tekulve   94
9. Mike Marshall   92
10. Don McMahon   90

Saves
1. Lee Smith   478
2. John Franco   397
3. Dennis Eckersley   390
4. Jeff Reardon   367
5. Randy Myers   347
6. Rollie Fingers   341
7. Tom Henke   311
8. Goose Gossage   310
9. Bruce Sutter   300
10. Jeff Montgomery   292

Single-Season Batting Leaders

At-Bats
1. Willie Wilson, 1980   705
2. Juan Samuel, 1984   701
3. Dave Cash, 1975   699
4. Matty Alou, 1969   698
5. Woody Jensen, 1936   696
6. Maury Wills, 1962   695
6. Omar Moreno, 1979   695
7. Bobby Richardson, 1962   692
8. Kirby Puckett, 1985   691
9. Lou Brock, 1967   689
9. Sandy Alomar, 1971   689

Runs
1. Billy Hamilton, 1894   196
2. Tom Brown, 1891   177
2. Babe Ruth, 1921   177
4. Tip O'Neill, 1887   167
4. Lou Gehrig, 1936   167
6. Billy Hamilton, 1895   166
7. Willie Keeler, 1894   165
7. Joe Kelley, 1894   165
9. Arlie Latham, 1887   163
9. Babe Ruth, 1928   163
9. Lou Gehrig, 1931   163

Batting Average
1. Hugh Duffy, 1894   .438
2. Tip O'Neill, 1887   .435
3. Ross Barnes, 1876   .429
4. Willie Keeler, 1897   .424
5. Rogers Hornsby, 1924   .424
6. Nap Lajoie, 1901   .422
7. George Sisler, 1922   .420
8. Ty Cobb, 1911   .420
9. Tuck Turner, 1894   .416
10. Fred Dunlap, 1894   .412

Hits
1. George Sisler, 1920   257
2. Lefty O'Doul, 1929   254
2. Bill Terry, 1930   254
4. Al Simmons, 1925   253
5. Rogers Hornsby, 1922   250
5. Chuck Klein, 1930   250
7. Ty Cobb, 1911   248
8. George Sisler, 1922   246
9. Heinie Manush, 1928   241
9. Babe Herman, 1930   241

Doubles
1. Earl Webb, 1931   67
2. George Burns, 1926   64
2. Joe Medwick, 1936   64
4. Hank Greenberg, 1934   63
5. Paul Waner, 1932   62
6. Charlie Gehringer, 1936   60
7. Tris Speaker, 1923   59
7. Chuck Klein, 1930   59
9. Billy Herman, 1935   57
9. Billy Herman, 1936   57

Triples
1. Owen Wilson, 1912   36
2. Dave Orr, 1886   31
2. Heinie Reitz, 1894   31
4. Perry Werden, 1893   29
5. Harry Davis, 1897   28
6. George Davis, 1893   27
6. Sam Thompson, 1894   27
6. Jimmy Williams, 1899   27
9. Long John Reilly, 1890   26
9. George Treadway, 1894   26
9. Joe Jackson, 1912   26
9. Sam Crawford, 1914   26
9. Kiki Cuyler, 1925   26

429

Home Runs

1. Mark McGwire, 1998	70
2. Sammy Sosa, 1998	66
3. Roger Maris, 1961	61
4. Babe Ruth, 1927	60
5. Babe Ruth, 1921	59
6. Jimmie Foxx, 1932	58
6. Hank Greenberg, 1938	58
6. Mark McGwire, 1997	58
9. Hack Wilson, 1930	56
9. Ken Griffey Jr., 1997	56
9. Ken Griffey Jr., 1998	56

RBIs

1. Hack Wilson, 1930	190
2. Lou Gehrig, 1931	184
3. Hank Greenberg, 1937	183
4. Lou Gehrig, 1927	175
4. Jimmie Foxx, 1938	175
6. Lou Gehrig, 1930	174
7. Babe Ruth, 1921	171
8. Chuck Klein, 1930	170
8. Hank Greenberg, 1935	170
10. Jimmie Foxx, 1932	169

Slugging Percentage

1. Babe Ruth, 1920	.847
2. Babe Ruth, 1921	.846
3. Babe Ruth, 1927	.772
4. Lou Gehrig, 1927	.765
5. Rogers Hornsby, 1925	.764
6. Jimmie Foxx, 1932	.756
7. Mark McGwire, 1998	.752
8. Babe Ruth, 1924	.749
9. Babe Ruth, 1926	.739
10. Ted Williams, 1941	.735

Stolen Bases

1. Rickey Henderson, 1982	130
2. Lou Brock, 1974	118
3. Vince Coleman, 1985	110
4. Vince Coleman, 1987	109
5. Rickey Henderson, 1983	108
6. Vince Coleman, 1986	107
7. Maury Wills, 1962	104
8. Rickey Henderson, 1980	100
9. Ron LeFlore, 1980	97
10. Ty Cobb, 1915	96
10. Omar Moreno, 1980	96

Strikeouts

1. Bobby Bonds, 1970	189
2. Bobby Bonds, 1969	187
3. Rob Deer, 1987	186
4. Pete Incaviglia, 1986	185
5. Cecil Fielder, 1990	182
6. Mike Schmidt, 1975	180
7. Rob Deer, 1986	179
8. Dave Nicholson, 1963	175
8. Gorman Thomas, 1979	175
8. Jose Canseco, 1986	175
8. Rob Deer, 1991	175
8. Jay Buhner, 1997	175

Walks

1. Babe Ruth, 1923	170
2. Ted Williams, 1947	162
2. Ted Williams, 1949	162
2. Mark McGwire, 1998	162
5. Ted Williams, 1946	156
6. Eddie Yost, 1956	151
6. Barry Bonds, 1996	151
8. Eddie Joost, 1949	149
9. Babe Ruth, 1920	148
9. Eddie Stanky, 1945	148
9. Jimmy Wynn, 1969	148

Single-Season Pitching Leaders

Wins

1. Jack Chesbro, 1904 — 41
2. Ed Walsh, 1908 — 40
3. Christy Mathewson, 1908 — 37
4. Amos Rusie, 1894 — 36
4. Walter Johnson, 1913 — 36
6. Cy Young, 1895 — 35
6. Joe McGinnity, 1904 — 35
8. Frank Killen, 1893 — 34
8. Kid Nichols, 1893 — 34
8. Cy Young, 1893 — 34
8. Smokey Joe Wood, 1912 — 34

Losses

1. Red Donahue, 1897 — 33
2. Ted Breitenstein, 1895 — 30
2. Jim Hughey, 1899 — 30
4. Bill Hart, 1896 — 29
4. Jack Taylor, 1898 — 29
4. Vic Willis, 1905 — 29
7. Duke Esper, 1893 — 28
7. Still Bill Hill, 1896 — 28
9. Chick Fraser, 1896 — 27
9. Bill Hart, 1897 — 27
9. Willie Sudhoff, 1898 — 27
9. Bill Carrick, 1899 — 27
9. Dummy Taylor, 1901 — 27
9. George Bell, 1910 — 27
9. Paul Derringer, 1933 — 27

Starts

1. Amos Rusie, 1893 — 52
2. Jack Chesbro, 1904 — 51
2. Ted Breitenstein, 1894 — 50
2. Amos Rusie, 1894 — 50
2. Ted Breitenstein, 1895 — 50
2. Pink Hawley, 1895 — 50
2. Frank Killen, 1896 — 50
8. Ed Walsh, 1908 — 49
8. Wilbur Wood, 1972 — 49
10. Frank Killen, 1893 — 48
10. Jouett Meekin, 1894 — 48
10. Joe McGinnity, 1903 — 48
10. Wilbur Wood, 1973 — 48

Innings Pitched

1. Amos Rusie, 1893 — 482
2. Ed Walsh, 1908 — 464
3. Jack Chesbro, 1904 — 455
4. Ted Breitenstein, 1894 — 447
5. Amos Rusie, 1894 — 444
5. Pink Hawley, 1895 — 444
7. Joe McGinnity, 1903 — 434
8. Frank Killen, 1896 — 432
9. Ted Breitenstein, 1895 — 430
10. Kid Nichols, 1893 — 425

Complete Games

1. Amos Rusie, 1893 — 50
2. Jack Chesbro, 1904 — 48
3. Ted Breitenstein, 1894 — 46
3. Ted Breitenstein, 1895 — 46
5. Amos Rusie, 1894 — 45
5. Vic Willis, 1902 — 45
7. Cy Young, 1894 — 44
7. Pink Hawley, 1895 — 44
7. Frank Killen, 1896 — 44
7. Joe McGinnity, 1903 — 44

Shutouts

1. Grover Alexander, 1916 — 16
2. Jack Coombs, 1910 — 13
2. Bob Gibson, 1968 — 13
4. Christy Mathewson, 1908 — 12
4. Grover Alexander, 1915 — 12
6. Ed Walsh, 1908 — 11
6. Walter Johnson, 1913 — 11
6. Sandy Koufax, 1963 — 11
6. Dean Chance, 1964 — 11
10. *(12 pitchers tied for 10th)*

Earned Run Average

1. Dutch Leonard, 1914 — 1.01
2. Mordecai Brown, 1906 — 1.04
3. Walter Johnson, 1913 — 1.09
4. Bob Gibson, 1968 — 1.12
5. Christy Mathewson, 1909 — 1.14
6. Jack Pfiester, 1907 — 1.15
7. Addie Joss, 1908 — 1.16
8. Carl Lundgren, 1907 — 1.17
9. Grover Alexander, 1915 — 1.22
10. Cy Young, 1908 — 1.26

Strikeouts

1.	Nolan Ryan, 1973	383
2.	Sandy Koufax, 1965	382
3.	Nolan Ryan, 1974	367
4.	Rube Waddell, 1904	349
5.	Bob Feller, 1946	348
6.	Nolan Ryan, 1977	341
7.	Nolan Ryan, 1972	329
8.	Nolan Ryan, 1976	327
9.	Sam McDowell, 1965	325
10.	Curt Schilling, 1997	319

Walks

1.	Amos Rusie, 1893	218
2.	Cy Seymour, 1898	213
3.	Bob Feller, 1938	208
4.	Nolan Ryan, 1977	204
5.	Nolan Ryan, 1974	202
6.	Amos Rusie, 1894	200
7.	Bob Feller, 1941	194
8.	Bobo Newsom, 1938	192
9.	Ted Breitenstein, 1894	191
10.	Tony Mullane, 1893	189

Relief Appearances

1.	Mike Marshall, 1974	106
2.	Kent Tekulve, 1979	94
3.	Mike Marshall, 1973	92
4.	Kent Tekulve, 1978	91
5.	Wayne Granger, 1969	90
5.	Mike Marshall, 1979	90
5.	Kent Tekulve, 1987	90
8.	Mark Eichhorn, 1987	89
8.	Julian Tavarez, 1997	89
9.	Wilbur Wood, 1968	88
9.	Mike Myers, 1997	88
9.	Sean Runyan, 1998	88

Relief Wins

1.	Roy Face, 1959	18
2.	John Hiller, 1974	17
2.	Bill Campbell, 1976	17
4.	Jim Konstanty, 1950	16
4.	Ron Perranoski, 1963	16
4.	Dick Radatz, 1964	16
4.	Tom Johnson, 1977	16
8.	Mace Brown, 1938	15
8.	Hoyt Wilhelm, 1952	15
8.	Luis Arroyo, 1961	15
8.	Dick Radatz, 1963	15
8.	Eddie Fisher, 1965	15
8.	Mike Marshall, 1974	15
8.	Dale Murray, 1975	15

Saves

1.	Bobby Thigpen, 1990	57
2.	Randy Myers, 1993	53
2.	Trevor Hoffman, 1998	53
4.	Dennis Eckersley, 1992	51
4.	Rod Beck, 1998	51
6.	Dennis Eckersley, 1990	48
6.	Rod Beck, 1993	48
6.	Jeff Shaw, 1998	48
9.	Lee Smith, 1991	47
10.	Dave Righetti, 1986	46
10.	Bryan Harvey, 1991	46
10.	Jose Mesa, 1995	46
10.	Tom Gordon, 1998	46

Index

A

A League of Their Own, 322-323, 402
A.G. Spalding & Brothers, 100
Aaron, Hank, 48, 68, 225, 383
Abbattichio, Ed "Batty," 50
Abbott, Jim, 383
accredited umpire schools, 125-126
ace, 160
Adair, Jerry, 91
Addy, Bob, 252
adult baseball leagues, 321-322
advance scouts, 261-262
affiliated teams, 317
agents, 287
ahead in the count, 112
Alexander, Grover Cleveland, 48, 383
All-Star Game, 143-144
   Most Valuable Players (MVPs), 417-418
   yearly results, 415-417
All-American Girls Professional Baseball League, 322-323
Allen, Mel, 305, 383
Alomar, Sandy Jr., 178
Alou, Felipe, 383
Alston, Walter, 266, 383
aluminum bats, 89, 315
amateur draft, 287-288
American Association of Base Ball Clubs, 137
American League, 135
   Championship Series, 421-422
   Cy Young Award winners, 414
   Designated Hitter Rule, 237
   division champions, 419-420
   history of, 138
   Most Valuable Player (MVP) Award winners, 412-413
   Rookie of the Year Award winners, 415
   triple crown winners, 57
   wildcard winners, 419
American Legion Baseball, 321-322

American Women's Baseball Association, 323
analysts (broadcasters), 307-308
Anderson, Sparky, 259, 265, 383
Angell, Roger, 383
Ankiel, Rick, 351
Anson, Cap, 383
Aparicio, Luis, 383
appeals, 116-117
Appling, Luke, 384
arbitration, 293-294
arguments with umpires, 131-132
Arlin, Harold, 299
around the horn, 194
artificial turf, 81-82, 341
Ashburn, Richie, 384
Ashford, Emmett, 384
Aspromonte, Ken, 254
awards, 52-53
   Comeback Player of the Year, 53
   Cy Young, 52, 413-414
   Gold Glove, 53
   Manager of the Year, 53
   Most Valuable Player (MVP), 52, 411-413
   Rookie of the Year Award, 53, 414-415
   Silver Slugger, 53

B

Babe Ruth League, 321
backstop, 178
Bagwell, Jeff, 93
bailing out, 225
Baker, Dusty, 384
Baker, Frank "Home Run," 384
balk rule, 115-116
ball, 86-88
   baseball mud, 87
   construction, 86-87
   evolution of, 86
   weight/size restrictions, 87
ballparks, *see* stadiums
Ballparks Web site, 404
Banks, Ernie "Mr. Cub," 36, 268, 384

Barber, Red, 303, 384
Barlick, Al, 122
Barlow, Tom, 252
bases, dislodged bases, 118
base on balls, 112
   intentional walks, 171-172
base path, 74
base umpires, 126-127
Baseball America, 339, 403
   Web site, 404
Baseball Canada Web site, 404
Baseball Digest, 403
Baseball Encyclopedia, The, 399
Baseball Hall of Fame, 53-54
   members, 405-411
      family combinations, 32
      umpires, 122
   Web site, 404
baseball history, 13-29
   1900s, 15-16
   1910s, 17
   1920s, 18-19
   1930s, 19-21
   1940s, 22-23
   1950s, 23-24
   1960s, 24-25
   1970s, 25-27
   1980s, 27
   1990s, 28-29
   myth of Abner Doubleday, 13-14
   origins of the game, 13-15
baseball mud, 87
Baseball Uniforms of the 20th Century, 99
Baseball Writers Association of America (BBWAA), 52, 411
"Baseball's Sad Lexicon," 33
baseballs, *see* ball
baseline, 350
baserunning, 249-250
   best baserunners of all time, 277
   breaking up the double play, 253
   cardinal rule of baserunning, 249
   characteristics of good baserunning, 249
   pinch runners, 247-248
   sliding, 250

stolen bases, 251
  delayed steal, 252
  double-steal, 251-252
  stealing home, 252
  taking leads, 249-250
basestealers
  best of all time, 276-277
  throwing out, 210-211
bat
bats, 88-89
  aluminum bats, 315
  choking up, 221
  construction, 88-89
  corking, 89
  evolution of, 86
  gripping, 221
  metal bats, 89
  size restrictions, 88-89
  weight, 221
    restrictions, 88-89
batter's box, 74
  hitter's position in, 222
batting average, 337
batting gloves, 93
batting helmets, 92, 100-101
batting order, *see* lineup
batting, *see* hitting
Bauer, Hank, 244
BBWAA (Baseball Writers Association of America), 52, 411
beanballs, 172-173
beating out an infield hit, 113-114
Bechtel, Mark, 292
Beer and Whiskey League, 137
beisboru, 318
Bell, James "Cool Papa," 384
Belle, Albert, 384
Bench, Johnny, 384
  memorable moments from Bench's career, 68-70
  Vowels of Success, 350-351
bench coach, 261
bench players, managing, 262-263
Berg, Moe, 201
Berman, Chris, 384
Berra, Yogi, 187, 384
best of all time
  baserunners, 277
  basestealers, 276-277
  Bench's all-time offensive lineup, 268-272
  clutch hitters, 274-275
  games, 63-64
  memorable moments, 66-68
  pennant races, 62-63
  players, 45-48
    Bench's era, 48-50
  pure hitters, 272-273

teams, 50-51
  World Series, 65-66
Big Leaguers Web site, 404
big market vs. small market teams, 289-292, 348-349
  luxury tax system, 290-291
Big Red Machine (batting order), 237-239
Black Sox scandal, 17
Blackburne, Lena, 87
bleachers, 343
blocking the plate, 211-212
Blomberg, Ron, 384
blown saves, 338
Boake, J. L., 126
Bochy, Bruce, 263
Boggs, Wade, 384
Bonds, Barry, 172, 384
book, the, 256-257
books about baseball, 399-401
Boone, Bob, 187
Boras, Scott, 287, 384
Boston Red Sox, 42-43
Boston style caps, 100
bottom of the batting order, 236-237
Boudreau, Lou, 207
Bouton, Jim, 384
box scores
  common abbreviations for positions, 328
  common abbreviations for statistics, 330-332
  extended box scores, 328
  reading, 327-332
Branyan, Russell, 352
breaking in gloves, 90
breaking up the double play, 253
Brenly, Bob, 385
Bresnahan, Roger, 94, 385
Brett, George, 385
  pine tar incident, 95
bringing the infield in, 205-206
broadcasters, 307-310
  Bench's picks for best broadcasters, 308-310
  catch phrases, 304
  color commentator, 307-308
  malaprops, 306
  play-by-play man, 307-308
Brock, Lou, 211, 276, 385
Bronco League, 321
Brooklyn Dodgers, 100
Brooklyn style caps, 100
Brotherhood of Professional Base Ball Players, 137
Brown, Kevin, 385
Brown, Mordecai "Three Finger," 385
brushback pitches, 172-173

Buckner, Bill, 385
Budig, Dr. Gene, 385
Bull Durham, 165, 401-402
bullpen, 160, 175-176
  field layout, 80
  managing, 262-263
bullpen coach, 261
bunts, 114, 242-244
  defending, 208
  drag bunt, 243
  push bunt, 243
  rotation play, 208
  sacrifice bunt, 243-244
  safety squeeze, 114, 244
  squeeze bunt, 114
  suicide squeeze, 114, 208, 243-244
Burrell, Pat, 351
business of baseball, 282-294
  1998 team payrolls, 291
  amateur draft, 287-288
  corporate ownership, 282-283
  free agency, 285-287
    foreign players, 288
  front office, 283-284
  general manager (GM), 283-284
  luxury tax system, 290-291
  market size, 289-292, 348-349
  minor league affiliates, 288
  pension system, 293
  player agents, 287
  player salaries, justification of, 292-293
  post-season revenue, 294
  recent record-setting salaries, 286
  reserve clause, 25-26, 285-286
  salary arbitration, 293-294
  trades, 284-285
  work stoppages, 294

C

Cactus League, 143
calling games (catchers), 183-184
Campanella, Roy, 271, 385
Campaneris, Bert, 199
Canseco, Jose, 385
caps, 100-101
Caray, Chip, 385
Caray, Harry, 309-310, 385
Caray, Skip, 385
career batting leaders, 425-427
career pitching leaders, 427-429
Carew, Rod, 385
Caribbean World Series, 320
Carlton, Steve, 50, 157, 385
Carter, Joe, 274, 385
Cartwright, Alexander, 14, 386

"Casey at the Bat,"32-33
catchers
    as managers, 261
    blocking the plate, 211-212
    calling games, 183-184
    calming pitchers down, 185-186
    defense, 186
        best defensive catchers of
            Bench's era, 186-187
        best defensive catchers of
            today, 187-188
    equipment, 93-95
        chest protector, 94
        mask, 93-94
        mitt, 90
        safety measures, 180-181
        shin guards, 94-95
    injuries, 178-179, 181-182
    job description, 182
    left-handed catchers, 179
    one-handed style of catching,
        179-180
    recipe for the ideal catcher, 186
    signs, flashing, 165-166
    throwing out basestealers,
        210-211
catcher's interference, 118
catcher's mitt, 90
CBS Sportsline Web site, 404
center field backgrounds, 219
center fielder, 197-198
ceremonial first pitch, 40
Chadwick, Henry, 297-298, 386
Chance, Frank, 386
Chandler, A. B. "Happy,"386
change-up, 155
changing speeds (pitching), 168-169
Chapman, Ray, 86, 386
Charleston, Oscar, 386
Chavez, Eric, 351
check swing, 116, 224
Chen, Bruce, 352
Chesbro, Jack, 386
chest protector, 94
Chicago Cubs, 43
Chicago White Sox, 43
    Black Sox scandal, 17
choking up, 221
Cincinnati Red Stockings, 136
circle change-up, 155
cleanup hitter, 234
Clemens, Roger, 158, 386
Clemente, Roberto, 48-49, 386
clichés, 6-9
clocking pitch speeds, 168
closed stance (hitting), 222
closers, 161
clubhouse, 81
clutch hitters, 274-275

CNN/SI Web site, 339, 404
coaches, 261
    bench coach, 261
    bullpen coach, 261
    first base coach, 248
    hitting instructor, 261
    pitching coach, 261
    third base coach, 78, 248-249
coaches' boxes, 78-79
Cobb, Ty, 47, 218, 221, 386
Cochrane, Mickey, 386
Coleman, Leonard Jr., 386
college baseball, 315-316
Collins, Eddie, 386
color commentator, 307-308
Colorado Silver Bullets, 323-324
Colt League, 321
Combs, Earle, 386
Comeback Player of the Year
    Award, 53
Comiskey, Charles, 386
commissioner, 292
complete games, 160
Concepcion, Dave, 193, 386
Cone, David, 386
Conlan, Jocko, 122, 386
Connolly, Tom, 122, 126
contact hitters, 232
control (pitching), 151-152
cookie-cutter parks, 341
corked bats, 89
corporate ownership, 282-283
Costas, Bob, 386
count, the, 112
Creamer, Robert, 387
crew chief, 126
crews (umpires), 126-127
Cronin, Joe, 387
Croteau, Julie, 324
Cummings, Candy, 153
cups, 102
Curse of Babe Ruth, 43
curveball, 153
cutoff man, 196
cutoff plays, 202-205
Cy Young Award, 52, 413-414

D

Dalkowski, Steve, 169
dead-ball era, 86
Dean, Dizzy, 387
defense, 189-190
    catcher, 186
        best defensive catchers of
            Bench's era, 186-187
        best defensive catchers of
            today, 187-188

center field, 197-198
    double plays, 190, 192
    first base, 190-191
    Gold Glove Award, 53
    left field, 196-197
    pitchers, 174-175
    range, 190
    relays, 192
    right field, 198
    second base, 191-192
    shortstop, 193-194
    strategies
        blocking the plate, 211-212
        bringing the infield in,
            205-206
        bunts, defending, 208
        cutoff plays, 202-205
        getting into position, 201-202
        guarding the lines, 206
        infield shift, 207
        pickoff plays, 209
        relay plays, 202-205
        rotation play, 208
        throwing out basestealers,
            210-211
    third base, 194-195
    triple plays, 58-59, 190
        unassisted triple plays, 58-59
defensive interference, 118
defensive obstruction, 212
defensive specialists, 198-199
delayed steal, 252
Dent, Bucky, 387
designated hitter (DH), 108, 237
deuce, the, 153
diamond, 73
Dickey, Bill, 387
Dierker, Larry, 258, 264
DiMaggio, Joe, 47, 274, 387
division champions, 418-420
Division Series, 144
Doak, Bill, 86
Doby, Larry, 387
donuts, 95
double play combinations, 193
double plays, 190, 192
double switch, 206
double-steal, 251-252
Doubleday, Abner, 13-14, 387
doubleheaders, 140
drafting players, 287-288
drag bunts, 243
dropped third strike, 109
Drysdale, Don, 173, 387
dugout, 75, 80
Durocher, Leo, 266, 387

435

E

earned run average (ERA), 161-162, 337
Eckersley, Dennis, 387
Eckert, General William, 387
Einstein, Albert, 201
equipment, 85-96
    ball, 86-88
        baseball mud, 87
        construction, 86-87
        evolution of, 86
        weight/size restrictions, 87
    bat, 88-89
        aluminum bats, 315
        construction, 88-89
        corking, 89
        gripping, 221
        metal bats, 89
        size restrictions, 88-89
        weight, 88-89, 221
    batting gloves, 93
    batting helmet, 92, 100-101
    catcher's gear, 93-95
        chest protector, 94
        mask, 93-94
        mitt, 90
        safety measures, 180-181
        shin guards, 94-95
    cups, 102
    evolution of, 85-86
    eye black, 93
    glove, 90
        pocket, 86
    on-deck circle, 95
    pitcher's mound
        rosin bag, 95-96
        tongue depressor, 96
    plastic guards, 93
    sunglasses, 93
    uniforms, 97-106
        best and worst, 105-106
        caps, 100-101
        changing styles, 104-105
        evolution of, 97-99
        home uniforms, 100
        jerseys, 101-102
        nicknames, displaying of, 105
        numbers, 101
        pants, 102
        pinstripes, 98
        road uniforms, 100
        sanitary stockings, 102-103
        socks, 102-103
        spikes, 103-104
        stirrups, 102-103
ERA (earned run average), 161-162, 337

errors, 114
Escobar, Alex, 352
ESPN Magazine, 403
ESPN Web site, 339, 404
Evans, Billy, 122
Evers, Johnny, 387
expansion teams, 28, 139, 348
extended box scores, 328
extra innings, 111
eye black, 93

F

FANSonly Web site, 404
fastball, 152
Fastball Web site, 339, 404
Father of Baseball (Henry Chadwick), 297-298
father-son combinations, 32
Fehr, Donald, 387
Feller, Bob, 143, 169, 387
Fenway Park, 197
Fidrych, Mark, 387
field
    grounds crew, 82
    layout, 73-74
        bullpen, 80
        coaches' boxes, 78-79
        dugouts, 80
        fungo circles, 79
        home plate, 74
        on-deck circles, 79
        outfield, 77-78
        pitcher's mound, 76-77
    player positions, 75-76
Field of Dreams, 31-32, 402
field umpires, 126-127
fielding
    Gold Glove Award, 53
    triple plays, 58-59
    see also defense
fielding percentage, 338
fifth spot (lineups), 235
Fingers, Rollie, 157-158, 387
Finley, Charlie, 388
fireman, 176
first base coach, 248
first baseman, 190-191
first baseman's mitt, 90
Fisk, Carlton, 65, 388
five-tool player, 268-269
flashing signs (catcher), 165-166
Flood, Curt, 25-26, 388
Ford, Whitey, 388
foreign players, 288, 348
forkball, 154
Forster, Terry, 157
Foster, Rube, 388

foul lines, 74
foul pole, 74, 78
foul tip signal (umpires), 129
four-seam fastball, 152
Fox Sports Web site, 404
Foxx, Jimmie, 47, 388
free agency, 285-287
    foreign players, 288
Frick, Ford, 298, 388
Frisch, Frankie, 388
front office, 283-284
frozen rope, 112
full count, 112
full windup (pitching), 173-174
fungo, 79
fungo circles, 79
future of baseball, 345-354
    effects of the 1998 season, 345-347
    expansion, 348
    market disparity problem, 348-349
    player improvement, 350-351
    stars of today, 352-354
    stars of tomorrow, 351-352
    suggestions for improving the game, 349-350

G

Gaedel, Eddie, 388
Gaffney, John, 127
Game of the Week, 305
Gammons, Peter, 388
Garagiola, Joe, 388
Garciaparra, Nomar, 388
Gehrig, Lou, 46, 191, 388
Geisel, Harry, 87
general manager (GM), 283-284
Giamatti, A. Bartlett, 388
Gibson, Bob, 50, 157, 159, 388
Gibson, Josh, 388
Gilliam, Jim, 91
Glavine, Tom, 388
gloves, 90
    breaking in, 90
    catcher's mitt, 90
    evolution of, 85-86
    first baseman's mitt, 90
    pocket, 86
going the other way, 227
Gold Glove Award, 53
Gonzalez, Juan, 389
Gooden, Dwight "Doc," 389
Gorbous, Glen, 198
Gorman, Tom, 132
grand slam, 113

Grapefruit League, 143
Graves, Adam, 13-14
Green Monster (Fenway Park), 197
Greenberg, Hank, 389
Griffey, Ken Jr., 353, 389
Griffith, Clark, 389
Grimes, Burleigh, 389
Grote, Jerry, 186-187
ground-rule double, 77-78
grounds crew, 82
Grove, Lefty, 389
guarding the lines, 206
Guidry, Ron, 284
Gwynn, Tony, 273, 389

H

Hall of Fame, 53-54
    members, 405-411
        family combinations, 32
        umpires, 122
    Web site, 404
hand signals (umpires), 128
Hargrove, Mike, 178
Hartnett, Gabby, 389
Harwell, Ernie, 300
head groundskeeper, 82
Heath, Jeff, 317
helmets, 92, 100-101
Henderson, Rickey, 233, 250, 277, 389
Hernandez, Orlando "El Duque,"318
Hershiser, Orel, 389
Hirdt, Steve, 389
history of baseball, 13-29
    1900s, 15-16
    1910s, 17
    1920s, 18-19
    1930s, 19-21
    1940s, 22-23
    1950s, 23-24
    1960s, 24-25
    1970s, 25-27
    1980s, 27
    1990s, 28-29
    myth of Abner Doubleday, 13-14
    origins of the game, 13-15
hit-and-run, 208, 245-246
hitting
    bailing out, 225
    batting average, 337
    benchmarks of excellence, 230
    best hitters of all time, 272-275
    bunts, see bunts
    career batting leaders, 425-427

check swing, 116, 224
clutch hitters, 274-275
going the other way, 227
handling failure, 219
hit-and-run play, 245-246
hitting behind the runner, 245
home runs, 112-113
    players with 60 or more, 228
    quest for 70 home runs, 228
    World Series game-ending home runs, 274-275
mechanics of hitting, 221-226
    bat weight, 221
    choking up, 221
    focusing on the pitch, 223
    gripping the bat, 221
    positioning, 222
    stance, 222-223
    stride, 223
    swing, 224-225
mind-body connection, 219-220
on-base percentage, 338
opening up, 225
pinch hitters, 246-247
pressing, 218
protecting the plate, 202
pulling the ball, 226-227
quest for .400 average, 229-230
quest for 70 home runs, 228
run-and-hit play, 246
runs batted in (RBI's), 337
sacrifice fly, 245
seven ways to reach base, 242
Silver Slugger Award, 53
single-season batting leaders, 429-430
slugging percentage, 338
slumps, 217-219
switch-hitters, 113, 220
total bases, 338
toughest pitches to hit, 156-157
triple crown, 57
types of hitters, 220-221
why pitchers can't hit, 227
hitting instructor, 261
hitting the cutoff man, 194, 196, 202-205
hitting zone, 151
Hodges, Gil, 266
Holloman, Bobo, 9
home plate, 74
home plate umpire, 126-127
home runs, 112-113
    players with 60 or more, 228
    quest for 70 home runs, 228
    World Series game-ending home runs, 274-275

home uniforms, 100
hook, the, 153
Hornsby, Rogers, 47, 58, 258-259, 389
hot corner, 195
Hubbard, Cal, 122
Hubbell, Carl, 389
Hundley, Randy, 179-180, 186-187
Hunter, Jim "Catfish,"389

I

independent leagues, 316-317
independent teams, 317
infield fly rule, 117
infield shift, 207
infielders
    first baseman, 190-191
    second baseman, 191-192
    shortstop, 193-194
    third baseman, 194-195
inherited runners, 337
injuries, 178-179, 181-182
innings, 110-111
inside-the-park home run, 113
instant replays, 130
intentional walks, 171-172
interference, 118-119
interleague play, 141
International League, 318
Internet, *see* Web sites

J

Jackson, Bo, 50, 389
Jackson, Joe "Shoeless,"390
Jackson, Reggie, 275-276, 390
James, Bill, 390
Japanese baseball, 318-319
Jenkins, Ferguson, 150
jerseys, 101-102
Jeter, Derek, 390
John Skilton's Baseball Links Web site, 404
Johnson, Ban, 390
Johnson, Bancroft, 138
Johnson, Davey, 390
Johnson, Randy, 10, 158, 390
Johnson, Walter, 38, 48, 162, 390
Jordan, Michael, 50
Joss, Addie, 390
Jugs gun, 168
Justice, David, 103

K

Kaat, Jim, 174, 390
Kahn, Roger, 390
Kaline, Al, 390
Kapler, Gabe, 351
Keeler, Wee Willie, 390
Killebrew, Harmon, 390
Kiner, Ralph, 306, 390
Klein, Chuck, 390
Klem, Bill, 122
Knickerbocker Base Ball Club, 14, 97
knuckleball, 155-156
Koosman, Jerry, 157
Koufax, Sandy, 49, 157, 159, 390
Kuhn, Bowie, 390

L

La Russa, Tony, 236, 391
Lajoie, Napoleon "Nap," 99, 391
Landis, Judge Kenesaw Mountain,
    391
Lardner, Ring, 298, 391
Larsen, Don, 64, 391
Lasorda, Tommy, 132, 264, 391
Latin American World Series, 320
Latin players, 348
Lazzeri, Tony, 391
leadoff man, 233
leads (baserunning), 249-250
League Championship Series (LCS),
    144, 420-422
League of Their Own, A, 322-323, 402
leagues
    adult baseball leagues, 321-322
    forming, 323-325
    independent leagues, 316-317
    International League, 318
    Little League Baseball, 320-321
    minor leagues, 313-314
        comparing to college
            baseball, 316
    participating in, 319-320
    semipro leagues, 322
    women's baseball leagues,
        322-323
    youth baseball leagues, 320-321
        selecting the right level,
            319-320
left fielder, 196-197
left-handed catchers, 179
lefty vs. lefty matchups, 171
lefty vs. righty matchups, 171
Leib, Fred, 298
Leonard, Buck, 391

Leyland, Jim, 391
line drive, 112
line scores, 330
lineup, 231
    balanced lineups, 232
    Bench's all-time offensive
        lineup, 268-272
    Big Red Machine, 237-239
    bottom of the order, 236-237
    cleanup hitter, 234
    designated hitter (DH), 237
    fifth spot, 235
    leadoff man, 233
    meat of the order, 235
    protection, 235-236
    second spot, 233-234
    tailoring to ballparks, 232-233
    third spot, 234
Little League Baseball, 320-321
live ball era, 86
location (pitching), 169
lockouts, 294
Lombard, George, 351-352
Lombardi, Ernie, 391
long relievers, 160
Lopes, Davey, 276
Lopez, Al, 391
Lord Charles, 153
losses (pitching), 161
luxury tax system, 290-291
Lyons, Steve, 391

M

Mack, Connie, 265, 391
MacPhail, Larry, 300-301, 391
Maddux, Greg, 158, 174-175, 391
magic numbers, 336-337
Major League Baseball Web site,
    143, 339, 403
major leagues, 135-140
    American League, *see* American
        League
    history of, 136-140
    interleague play, 141
    National League, *see* National
        League
    Opening Day, 142-143
    playoffs, 144-145
    regular season schedule, 140-141
    spring training, 142-143
    World Series, 145-146
        game-ending home runs,
            274-275
        greatest of all time, 65-66
        Most Valuable Players
            (MVPs), 422-423
        yearly results, 422-424

Maloney, Jim, 56, 91, 177
Manager of the Year Award, 53
managers, 255-256
    all time best, 265-266
    bad players as managers, 258-260
    catchers as managers, 261
    confrontations with umpires,
        131-133
    decision-making, 257-258,
        262-263
    good players as managers,
        258-260
    managing styles, 258
    media, dealing with, 264
    non-Hall of Fame players as
        managers, 260
    players, dealing with, 263
    players' managers, 263
    strategies
        batting order, 231-237
        bench management, 262-263
        bringing the infield in,
            205-206
        bullpen management,
            262-263
        bunting, 242-244
        defending bunts, 208
        defensive replacements,
            198-199
        double switch, 206
        guarding the lines, 206
        hit-and-run, 208, 245-246
        hitting behind the runner,
            245
        infield shift, 207
        managing by the book,
            256-257
        pinch hitters, 246-247
        pinch runners, 247-248
        pitching changes, 175-176
        platooning, 171, 235, 247
        positioning players, 201-202
        rotation play, 208
        run-and-hit, 246
        sacrifice fly, 245
        scouting reports, 261-262
        statistical references, 257
        stolen bases, 251-252
    visits to the mound, 175
Mantle, Mickey, 46, 67, 269, 391
Marichal, Juan, 392
Maris, Roger, 67, 228, 392
market size, 289-292, 348-349
    luxury tax system, 290-291
Marshall, Mike, 392
Martin, Billy, 392
Martinez, Buck, 392
Martinez, Dennis, 392
Martinez, Pedro, 392

mask (catcher's gear), 93-94
Mateo, Ruben, 351
Mathews, Eddie, 392
Mathewson, Christy, 48, 392
Mauch, Gene, 266
Mays, Willie, 48, 269-270, 392
Mazeroski, Bill, 63, 192-193, 274, 392
McCarthy, Joe, 121, 392
McCarver, Tim, 392
McCovey, Willie, 48-49, 268, 392
McDonald, Arch, 301-302
McGowan, Bill, 122
McGraw, John, 265, 392
McGwire, Mark, 228, 271-272, 345-346, 393
McLain, Denny, 393
McLean, Billy, 126
McNamee, Graham, 299-300, 393
meat of the order, 235
mechanics of hitting, 221-226
    bat weight, 221
    choking up, 221
    focusing on the pitch, 223
    gripping the bat, 221
    positioning, 222
    stance, 222-223
    stride, 223
    swing, 224-225
media
    baseball writers, history of, 297-298
    dealing with (managers), 264
    radio broadcasting
        broadcasters, 307-310
        history of, 299-301
        re-creations, 301-302
    television broadcasting, 302-308
        broadcasters, 307-310
        Game of the Week, 305
        history of, 302-305
        improvements in coverage, 306-307
        This Week in Baseball, 306
Medwick, Joe, 393
Mendoza Line, 229
Merkle, Fred, 393
Merkle's Boner, 62
Merritt, Jim, 183
metal bats, 89, 315
middle relievers, 160
Miller, Jon, 393
Miller, Marvin, 393
Miller, Ray, 256
Mills Commission, 13-14
mind-body connection (hitting), 219-220

minor league affiliates, 288
Minor League Baseball Web site, 403
minor leagues, 313-314
    comparing to college baseball, 316
mitts, 90
Mize, Johnny, 393
Molitor, Paul, 273, 393
Monument Park (Yankee Stadium), 38
Morgan, Joe, 48, 238, 268, 393
Most Valuable Player (MVP) Award, 52, 411-413
Mota, Manny, 247, 393
mound, *see* pitcher's mound
movement (pitching), 151-152
movies about baseball, 401-403
MSNBC Web site, 404
mud (baseball mud), 87
Murdoch, Rupert, 393
Murphy, Dale, 393
Murray, Eddie, 393
Musial, Stan, 37, 47, 393

N

national anthem, 41
National Association of Base Ball Players, 136
National Association of Professional Baseball Leagues (NAPBL), 317
National Baseball Congress, 322
National League, 135
    Championship Series
        Most Valuable Players (MVPs), 420-421
        yearly results, 420-421
    Cy Young Award winners, 413
    division champions, 418-419
    history of, 137
    Most Valuable Player (MVP) Award winners, 411-412
    Rookie of the Year Award winners, 414-415
    triple crown winners, 57
    wildcard winners, 418
national pastime, 4
NCAA Baseball Web site, 404
Neat's foot oil, 90
Negro leagues, 18, 21
New York Yankees, 41-42
Newhouser, Hal, 393
Newsweek, 403
Nicholson, Bill "Swish," 172

nicknames
    displaying on uniforms, 105
    player nicknames, 35-36
    team nicknames, 33-34
        early 1900s, 16
Niekro, Phil, 393
no-hitters, 53, 56
numbers (uniforms), 101
    retired numbers, 39-40

O

object of the game, 108
obstruction, 119
obstruction signal (umpires), 129
O'Day, Hank, 126
off-speed pitch, 155
offensive interference, 118
offensive strategies
    breaking up the double play, 253
    bunting, 242-244
    hit-and-run, 208, 245-246
    hitting behind the runner, 245
    pinch hitters, 246-247
    pinch runners, 247-248
    platooning players, 171, 235, 247
    run-and-hit, 246
    sacrifice fly, 245
    stolen bases, 251-252
official scorer, 133-134
Oh, Sadaharu, 319
Okrent, Dan, 393
on-base percentage, 47, 338
on-deck circles, 79
    equipment, 95
one-handed style of catching, 179-180
open stance (hitting), 222
Opening Day, 142-143
opening up (hitting), 225
origins of baseball, 13-15
Ortiz, Junior, 185
Ott, Mel, 172, 394
out calls (umpires), 128
outfield
    field layout, 77-78
    outfield wall, 74
outfielders
    center fielder, 197-198
    hitting the cutoff man, 194, 196, 202-205
    left fielder, 196-197
    right fielder, 198
outs, 109-110

P

Paige, Satchel, 119, 394
palmball, 156
Palmer, Jim, 394
passed ball, 182
Patek, Freddie, 10
pennant races, 62-63
pennants, 38-39
pension system, 293
Perez, Tony, 239, 394
perfect games, 54-55
Perry, Gaylord, 394
Phillips, Richie, 394
physical attributes of players, 10
Piazza, Mike, 394
Pickering, Calvin, 352
pickoff plays, 209
pillbox-style caps, 100-101
pinch hitters, 246-247
pinch runners, 247-248
pine tar, 95
Piniella, Lou, 258
pinstripes (uniforms), 98
pitchers, 157-163
    ace, 160
    best of Bench's era, 163
    best of today, 163
    bullpens, 160
    starting rotations, 160
    throwing out basestealers,
        210-211
    toughest of Bench's era, 163
    types of pitchers, 157-161
    why pitchers can't hit, 227
pitcher's mound, 74, 76-77
    rosin bag, 95-96
    tongue depressors, 96
pitching, 149-157
    balk rule, 115-116
    blown saves, 338
    bullpen, 80, 175-176
    career pitching leaders, 427-429
    changing speeds, 151
    clocking pitch speeds, 168
    complete games, 160
    control, 151-152
    Cy Young Award, 52, 413-414
    earned run average (ERA),
        161-162, 337
    effects of good pitching, 149-150
    inherited runners, 337
    movement, 151-152
    no-hitters, 53, 56
    perfect games, 54-55
    pickoff plays, 209
    quick pitch, 117-118
    reading catcher signs, 165-166

saves, 161, 163, 338
shaking off catcher signs, 166
single-season pitching leaders,
    431-432
slide step, 210
statistics, 161-163
strategy, 165-176
    brushback pitches, 172-173
    changing speeds, 168-169
    defensive positioning,
        174-175
    full windup vs. the stretch,
        173-174
    intentional walks, 171-172
    lefty vs. lefty matchups, 171
    location, 169
    pitch selection, 165-166,
        169-170
    pitching around hitters, 183
    pitching changes, 175-176
    pitchout, 172
    righty vs. righty matchups,
        171
    setting up hitters, 167-168
stretch, 117, 173-174, 210
stuff, 151
types of pitches, 150-156
    change-up, 155
    curveball, 153
    forkball, 154
    four-seam fastball, 152
    knuckleball, 155-156
    palmball, 156
    screwball, 156
    sinker (two-seam fastball), 152
    slider, 154
    spitball (illegal pitch), 177
    split-fingered fastball, 154
    toughest pitches to hit,
        156-157
warmup pitches, 176
win-loss records, 161-163
windup, 117
pitching coach, 261
    visits to the mound, 175
pitching rubber, 76-77
pitchout, 172
plastic guards, 93
plate umpire, 126-127
platooning, 171, 235, 247
play-by-play man, 307-308
player agents, 287
player nicknames, 35-36
players
    greatest of all time, 45-48
        Bench's era, 48-50
    physical attributes, 10
Players League, 137
players' managers, 263
playoffs, 144-145

pocket (glove), 86
Pony League, 321
pop-up slide, 250
porch, 232-233
positioning players, 201-202
    bringing the infield in, 205-206
    bunts, defending, 208
    guarding the lines, 206
    infield shift, 207
    rotation play, 208
post-season revenue, 294
Povich, Shirley, 298
power hitters, 232
protecting the plate, 202
protection (lineups), 235-236
Puckett, Kirby, 394
pulling the ball, 226-227
purpose pitches, 172-173
push bunt, 243

Q-R

quick pitch, 117-118

radar guns, 168
radio broadcasting
    broadcasters, 307-310
        Bench's picks for best
            broadcasters, 308-310
        catch phrases, 304
        color commentator, 307-308
        malaprops, 306
        play-by-play man, 307-308
    history of, 299-301
        re-creations, 301-302
rain delays, 82-83
range, 190
Rawlings, 86-87
RBI's (runs batted in), 337
re-creations (radio), 301-302
Reagan, Ronald, 301-302
receiver, 178
records
    baseball's most unbreakable
        records, 59-61
    career batting leaders, 425-427
    career pitching leaders, 427-429
    single-season batting leaders,
        429-430
    single-season pitching leaders,
        431-432
Reese, Pee Wee, 394
Reinsdorf, Jerry, 394
relays, 192, 202-205
relief pitchers, 160-161
Rennert, Dutch, 125-126
reserve clause, 25-26, 137, 285-286
retired numbers, 39-40
Reuschel, Rick, 163

rhubarb, 132
ribbie, 337
Rice, Grantland, 298
Rickey, Branch, 100, 288-289, 314, 394
right fielder, 198
righty vs. lefty matchups, 171
righty vs. righty matchups, 171
Ripken, Cal Jr., 61, 352, 394
Ritter, Lawrence S., 394
Rizzuto, Phil, 394
road uniforms, 100
Robinson, Brooks, 195, 394
Robinson, Frank, 394
Robinson, Jackie, 22-23, 40, 394-395
Rodriguez, Alex, 395
Rodriguez, Ivan, 188, 395
Rookie of the Year Award, 53, 414-415
rope, 112
Rose, Pete, 27, 37, 48, 395
rosin bag, 95-96
rosters, 108
rotations, 160
rules, 108-119
    appeals, 116-117
    balk rule, 115-116
    defensive obstruction, 212
    dislodged bases, 118
    general instructions to umpires, 124-125
    infield fly rule, 117
    innings, 110-111
    interference, 118-119
    object of the game, 108
    outs, 109-110
    pitching deliveries, 117
    quick pitch, 117-118
    rosters, 108
    strike zone, 111-113
        umpires' interpretation of, 123, 130
    substitutions, 115
run scoring, 111-114
run-and-hit, 246
rundowns, 203
running the bases, 249-250
    breaking up the double play, 253
    cardinal rule of baserunning, 249
    characteristics of good baserunning, 249
    pinch runners, 247-248
    sliding, 250
    stolen bases, 251-252
    taking leads, 249-250
runs batted in (RBI's), 337
Rusie, Amos, 395
Ruth, Babe, 18-19, 45-46, 228, 395
    called shot, 66
Ryan, Nolan, 50, 56, 395

S

Sabino, David, 395
sacrifice bunt, 243-244
    defending, 208
sacrifice fly, 245
safe call (umpires), 128
safety squeeze, 114, 244
salary arbitration, 293-294
Sanders, Deion, 50, 395
sanitary stockings, 102-103
saves, 161, 163, 338
    blown saves, 338
Schmidt, Mike, 48, 268-269, 395
Schott, Marge, 395
scorecards, 332-336
    common scoring symbols, 334-335
    numbers assigned to positions, 334
scorekeepers, 133-134
scoring position, 112-113
scoring runs, 111-114
scouting reports, 261-262
screwball, 156
scroogie, 156
Scully, Vin, 308-309, 395
Seaver, Tom, 50, 157, 170, 395
second baseman, 191-192
second spot (lineups), 233-234
Selig, Bud, 292, 395
semipro leagues, 322
Senior Circuit, 135
setting up hitters, 167-168
setup men, 160
seven ways to reach base, 242
seventh-inning stretch, 41
shaking off signs (pitching), 166
shift, the, 207
shin guards (catcher's gear), 94-95
Shoeless Joe, 400
Shoeless Joe Jackson, 390
shoes, 103-104
shortstop, 193-194
Showalter, Buck, 172
Siebern, Norm, 254
signals (umpires), 128
signs, 166
    flashing signs (catcher), 165-166
    stealing, 166
    third base coach, 248-249
Silver Bullets, 323-324
Silver Slugger award, 53
Simmons, Al, 395
Singer, Bill, 163, 284
single-season batting leaders, 429-430

single-season pitching leaders, 431-432
Singleton, Ken, 395
sinker, 152
Sisler, George, 395
slide step (pitching), 210
slider, 154
sliding, 250
slugging percentage, 338
slumps, 217-219
small market vs. big market teams, 289-292, 348-349
    luxury tax system, 290-291
Small World Baseball Web site, 404
Smith, Lee, 396
Smith, Ozzie, 194, 396
Smoltz, John, 396
Snider, Duke, 396
Society for American Baseball Research Web site, 404
socks (uniforms), 102-103
Sosa, Sammy, 228, 345-347, 396
Spahn, Warren, 48, 270, 396
Spalding, 88
Spalding, Al, 100, 396
Spalding Official Baseball Guide, 298
Speaker, Tris, 396
spectator interference, 119
spikes, 103-104
spitball (illegal pitch), 177
split (doubleheaders), 140
split-fingered fastball, 154
Sport magazine, 403
Sporting Goods Business, 403
Sporting News, The, 339, 403
    Web site, 404
Sports Illustrated, 339, 403
Sports Illustrated for Kids, 403
Sportstyle, 403
spring training, 142-143
squeeze bunt, 114
stadiums
    artificial turf, 81-82, 341
    bleachers, 343
    center field backgrounds, 219
    cookie-cutter parks, 341
    grounds crew, 82
    history of, 340-342
    outdoor vs. indoor, 81
    porch, 232-233
    tailoring lineups to, 232-233
    watching games
        selecting the best seats, 342-343
        what to watch for, 343-344
stance (hitting), 222-223
standings, 336-337
"Star Spangled Banner, The," 41
Stargell, Willie, 396

starting pitchers, 160
starting rotations, 160
statistics, 337-338
    baseball's most unbreakable
        records, 59-61
    batting average, 337
    box scores
        common abbreviations for
            positions, 328
        common abbreviations for
            statistics, 330-332
        extended box scores, 328
        reading, 327-332
    common abbreviations, 330-332
    common abbreviations for
        positions, 328
    fielding percentage, 338
    magic numbers, 336-337
    managers' statistical references,
        257
    on-base percentage, 47, 338
    pitching, 161-163
        blown saves, 338
        earned run average (ERA),
            161-162, 337
        inherited runners, 337
        saves, 161, 163, 338
        win-loss records, 161-163
    runs batted in (RBI's), 337
    scoring games, 332-336
        common scoring symbols,
            334-335
        numbers assigned to
            positions, 334
    scouting reports, 261-262
    slugging percentage, 338
    standings, 336-337
    total bases, 338
    winning percentage, 337
stealing bases, 251
    best basestealers of all time,
        276-277
    delayed steal, 252
    double-steal, 251-252
    stealing home, 252
stealing signs, 166
Steinbrenner, George, 283, 396
Stengel, Casey, 259, 265, 396
stickball, 4
stirrups, 102-103
strategy
    batting order, *see* lineup
    bench management, 262-263
    bullpen management, 262-263
    defensive strategies
        blocking the plate, 211-212
        bringing the infield in,
            205-206

bunts, defending, 208
cutoff plays, 202-205
defensive replacements,
    198-199
guarding the lines, 206
infield shift, 207
lefty vs. lefty matchups, 171
pickoff plays, 209
pitching changes, 175-176
positioning players, 174-175,
    201-202
relay plays, 202-205
righty vs. lefty matchups, 171
righty vs. righty matchups,
    171
rotation play, 208
throwing out basestealers,
    210-211
double switch, 206
managers' statistical
    references, 257
managing by the book, 256-257
offensive strategies
    breaking up the double play,
        253
    bunting, 242-244
    hit-and-run, 208, 245-246
    hitting behind the runner,
        245
    pinch hitters, 246-247
    pinch runners, 247-248
    platooning players, 171, 235,
        247
    run-and-hit, 246
    sacrifice fly, 245
    stolen bases, 251-252
pitching strategy, 165-176
    brushback pitches, 172-173
    changing speeds, 168-169
    defensive positioning,
        174-175
    full windup vs. the stretch,
        173-174
    intentional walks, 171-172
    lefty vs. lefty matchups, 171
    location, 169
    pitch selection, 165-166,
        169-170
    pitching around hitters, 183
    pitching changes, 175-176
    pitchout, 172
    righty vs. lefty matchups, 171
    righty vs. righty matchups,
        171
    setting up hitters, 167-168
scouting reports, 261-262
stretch, 117, 173-174, 210
stride (hitting), 223
strike call (umpires), 128

strike zone, 111-113
    umpires' interpretation of,
        123, 130
strikeouts, dropped-third strike, 109
strikes, 294
stuff (pitching), 151
substitutions, 115
subtleties of the game, 11-12
suicide squeeze, 114, 208, 243-244
sunglasses, 93
superstition, 53
Sutter, Bruce, 157
Sutton, Don, 396
sweep (doubleheaders), 140
swing (hitting mechanics), 224-225
switch-hitters, 113, 220

T

tag up, 114
"Take Me Out to the Ballgame," 41
Team Licensing Business, 403
team nicknames, 33-34
    early 1900s, 16
teams, greatest of all time, 50-51
television broadcasting, 302-308
    broadcasters, 307-310
        Bench's picks for best
            broadcasters, 308-310
        catch phrases, 304
        color commentator, 307-308
        malaprops, 306
        play-by-play man, 307-308
    Game of the Week, 305
    history of, 302-305
    improvements in coverage,
        306-307
Texas League single, 236
Thigpen, Bobby, 396
third base coach, 78, 248-249
third baseman, 194-195
third spot (lineups), 234
This Week in Baseball, 306
Thomson, Bobby, 396
Thorpe, Jim, 64, 396
three-finger change-up, 155
throwing out basestealers, 210-211
Time magazine, 403
timeout signal (umpires), 129
Tinker, Joe, 396
tongue depressors, 96
tools of ignorance, 94
Torre, Joe, 266, 397
Total Baseball, 400, 403
    Web site, 339, 404
total bases, 338
Tovar, Cesar, 199
trades, 284-285

traditions, 31-34, 38-43
  "Casey at the Bat,"32-33
  ceremonial first pitch, 40
  hard-luck teams, 42-43
  national anthem, 41
  New York Yankees, 41-42
  pennants, 38-39
  player nicknames, 35-36
  retired numbers, 39-40
  seventh-inning stretch, 41
  team nicknames, 33-34
training umpires, 125-126
Traynor, Pie, 397
triple crown, 57
triple plays, 58-59, 190
  unassisted triple plays, 58-59
twin killing, 193
two-seam fastball, 152
two-sport stars, 50

U

Ueberroth, Peter, 397
Uecker, Bob, 397
umpires, 121-134
  accredited umpire schools,
    125-126
  base umpires, 126-127
  calling balls and strikes, 130
  confrontations with players/
    managers, 131-133
  controversial actions of, 122-124
  crew chief, 126
  crews, 126-127
  Hall of Fame umpires, 122
  home plate umpire, 126-127
  most difficult calls, 129-130
  post-season selection contro-
    versy, 131
  rulebook's general instructions,
    124-125
  signals, 128
  strike zone controversy, 123, 130
  temperaments, 123
  training, 125-126
umpire's box, 74
umpire's interference, 118
unassisted triple plays, 58-59
Uncle Charlie, 153
uniforms, 97-106
  best and worst, 105-106
  caps, 100-101
  changing styles, 104-105
  evolution of, 97-99
  home uniforms, 100
  jerseys, 101-102
  nicknames, displaying of, 105

  numbers, 101
    retired numbers, 38-40
  pants, 102
  pinstripes, 98
  road uniforms, 100
  sanitary stockings, 102-103
  socks, 102-103
  spikes, 103-104
  stirrups, 102-103
Union Association of Base Ball
  Clubs, 137
USA Today, 339, 403
  Web site, 404
USA Today Baseball Weekly, 339, 403
  Web site, 404
utility man, 199

V

Valenzuela, Fernando, 397
Van Slyke, Andy, 198
Vander Meer, Johnny, 66, 397
Vaughn, Mo, 397
Veeck, Bill, 397
Verducci, Tom, 397
Vincent, Francis "Fay,"397
Vowels of Success, 350-351

W

Waddell, Rube, 397
Wagner, Billy, 157
Wagner, Honus, 47, 397
Waitt, Charlie, 85-86
Walker, Fleet, 23
walks, 112
  intentional walks, 171-172
Walsh, Ed, 397
warmup pitches, 176
warning track, 78
Washington, Herb, 248
watching games at the park
  selecting the best seats, 342-343
  what to watch for, 343-344
Weaver, Earl, 256, 258, 266, 397
Web sites, 338-339, 404
  Ballparks, 404
  Baseball America, 404
  Baseball Canada, 404
  Baseball Hall of Fame, 404
  Big Leaguers, 404
  CBS Sportsline, 404
  CNN/SI, 339, 404
  ESPN, 339, 404
  FANSonly, 404
  Fastball, 339, 404

  Fox Sports, 404
  John Skilton's Baseball Links,
    404
  Major League Baseball,
    143, 339, 403
  Minor League Baseball, 403
  MSNBC, 404
  NCAA Baseball, 404
  Small World Baseball, 404
  Society for American Baseball
    Research, 404
  The Sporting News, 404
  Total Baseball, 339, 404
  USA Today, 404
  USA Today Baseball Weekly, 404
  Yahoo, 404
Wells, David, 397
Wheaton, William R., 126
whiffle ball, 4
wild card winners, 418-419
wild pitch, 182
wild-card teams, 144-145
Wilhelm, Hoyt, 91, 397
Williams, Bernie, 397
Williams, Ted, 47, 89, 207,
  270-271, 398
Wills, Maury, 276
Wilson, Hack, 398
win-loss records (pitchers), 161-163
windup (pitching), 117, 173-174
Winfield, Dave, 398
winning percentage, 337
wins (pitching), 161
women's baseball leagues, 322-323
work stoppages, 294
World Series, 145-146
  game-ending home runs,
    274-275
  greatest of all time, 65-66
  Most Valuable Players (MVPs),
    422-423
  yearly results, 422-424
Wrigley Field, 341-342
writers, history of baseball writers,
  297-298
Wynn, Early, 398

Y

Yahoo! Web site, 404
Yankee Stadium, 38
Yastrzemski, Carl, 398
Yeager, Steve, 181
Young, Cy, 47, 61, 167, 398
Youngblood, Joel, 285
Yount, Robin, 398
youth baseball leagues, 320-321
  selecting the right level, 319-320

About the Authors

Johnny Bench is almost certainly the greatest catcher to ever play the game of baseball. Born in Oklahoma City in 1947, Bench grew up in the nearby town of Binger, dreaming of becoming a major league baseball player. His father, Ted, a former semipro catcher, advised his son that catcher was the best position to realize that dream. Bench developed into a top-notch prospect and was selected by the Reds in the second round of the 1965 amateur draft. After less than three seasons in the minor leagues he was in the majors to stay—at the ripe old age of 19. He wouldn't be leaving any time soon.

No other catcher displayed Bench's all-around excellence. He revolutionized the position. He was uncommonly durable, catching 100 or more games for 13 straight seasons (1968–80). He won 10 consecutive Gold Gloves for his defensive excellence, and handled a Reds pitching staff that won six National League West titles, four National League pennants, and two World Series in the 1970s.

Oh, and he could hit a little, too. From 1968 to '77, Bench drove in an average of 103 runs a year, leading the National League three times. In 1970 he led the NL with 45 home runs and 148 runs batted in and was named the league's Most Valuable Player. Two years later, his 40 homers and 125 RBIs again lead the league, and he won his second MVP award. He finished his 17-year career in 1983 with 389 home runs, 327 of them as a catcher—more than any player at that position.

Besides his two MVP awards and 10 Gold Gloves, Bench was a 14-time All-Star and won the National League Rookie of the Year Award in 1968 and the World Series MVP award in 1976. In 1998 he was named the greatest catcher in history—and the 16th best player of all time—by *The Sporting News*. Bench was inducted into the Baseball Hall of Fame in Cooperstown, NY, on July 23, 1989. At the time of his election, only Ty Cobb (98.23) and Hank Aaron (97.83) had been named on a higher percentage of the Baseball Writers Association of America's ballots than Bench (96.4).

Bench's broadcasting background includes nine years with CBS Radio. He has also provided game analysis for ABC-TV and the Reds baseball network. Since the mid-1980s he has been a co-host of a daily in-season radio show on the Reds Radio Network. Bench also serves as a special consultant to the Reds.

Among the charitable organizations and worthy causes to which Johnny Bench lends his time are the American Cancer Society, the American Heart Association, the Cincinnati Symphony Orchestra, the Kidney Foundation, and the Muscular Dystrophy Association. He also founded and maintains the Johnny Bench Scholarship Fund, which has provided funds for 275 students to attend college in the Cincinnati area.

Larry Burke is a senior editor for *Sports Illustrated*, the author of *The Baseball Chronicles: A Decade-by-Decade History of the All-American Pastime*, and the co-author (with Cal Ripken, Sr.) of *The Ripken Way: A Manual for Baseball and Life*. Formerly the editor of *Inside Sports* magazine, he has covered major league baseball for the Associated Press, United Press International, and several major newspapers. A graduate of the University of Notre Dame, he lives in Darien, Connecticut, with his wife, Beth and three children.